TO THE GALATIANS:
A Translation and Commentary

TO THE GALATIANS:
A Translation and Commentary

Duane M. Johnson

OCABS PRESS
ST PAUL, MINNESOTA 55124
2018

TO THE GALATIANS:
A TRANSLATION AND COMMENTARY

Copyright © 2018 by
Duane M. Johnson

ISBN 1-60191-042-8

All rights reserved.

PRINTED IN THE UNITED STATES OF AMERICA

To the Galatians:
A Translation and Commentary

Copyright © 2018 by Duane M. Johnson
All rights reserved.

ISBN 1-60191-042-8

Published by OCABS Press, St. Paul, Minnesota.
Printed in the United States of America.

Books are available through OCABS Press at special discounts for bulk purchases in the United States by academic institutions, churches, and other organizations. For more information please email OCABS Press at press@ocabs.org.

To Paul Nadim Tarazi

Contents

Introduction	13
To the Galatians: A Translation	17
I. Paul, An Apostle (1:1-5)	27
II. The Gospel Revealed (1:6-12)	43
III. To What End Zeal? (1:13-24)	57
IV. Going Up to Jerusalem (2:1-10)	71
V. The Incident at Antioch (2:11-14): The Four Frameworks	81
VI. Our Being Declared Righteous (2:15-21)	97
VII. Why the Galatians are Foolish (3:1-5)	119
VIII. Why the Galatians are Sons of Abraham (3:6-22)	127
IX. Why the Galatians are One in the Christ (3:23-29)	163
X. Why the Galatians are Sons of God (4:1-7)	177
XI. The Current Danger (4:8-20)	199
XII. What Does Scripture Say? (4:21-5:6)	221
XIII. What Does the Gospel Say? (5:1-6)	255
XIV. A Matter of Persuasion (5:7-12)	275
XV. Walking Bodily In The Spirit (5:13-24)	291
XVI. Measuring Up to the Law of the Christ (5:25-6:10)	319
XVII. A New Creation (6:11-18)	343

Introduction

This commentary originated as part of a Bible Survey series that I taught at the Orthodox Church of St. Matthew in Columbia, Maryland. We covered Paul's letter to the Galatians in six sessions from late 2009 to early 2010, and each was devoted to a single chapter of the letter. An important influence on my presentation and interpretation of the material at the time was what I had learned from reading N.T. Wright's newly published study *Justification: God's Plan & Paul's Vision* (Inter-Varsity Press, 2009). The book provided what was for me a broadly focused perspective on the meaning of what I was reading in Paul's letters, and it did much to expand the traditional way in which I had hitherto understood this key New Testament work.

My approach was simple. I wanted to present two things: (1) what was Paul saying in his letter to the Galatian churches, and (2) why was he saying it. In order to communicate these two things it was necessary that I base whatever I said on a detailed examination of the Greek text. I had already parsed it and established a cursory working translation in my own hand, but my involvement with the text was such that I set out to offer a fresh translation based on my understanding of what the text contained and what it meant.

I wanted to produce an English translation designed above all *to be read aloud*. This was because so many of the currently available translations, while often tersely faithful to the original Greek, fall short in conveying what I suspect was a fuller personal impact that Paul's letters must have had upon his original listeners. Admittedly, my thought-world is that of a contemporary American Anglophone, and so I may be guilty of sensing a diminished expressive range and a reduced verbal impact where ancient Hellenophone listeners would have found none, but, all the same, I offer my translation as a direct elaboration of the way in which I have read and understood Paul's letter to the Galatians. I have arranged the printed version of my translation into lines, clauses and phrases as a way to indicate how I have broken down the text into basic sections of meaning. This arrangement was an important part of my study process, and hopefully it will help the reader to see some of the underlying connections and relationships which are, I think, an intrinsic part of Paul's communication with the Galatians. For all other scriptural passages I have relied primarily on the Revised Standard Version (RSV) translation along with occasional use of the Orthodox Study Bible's New King James Version (NKJV). At some points I do work from my own translations of certain Septuagint passages.

In drafting this commentary I have been guided along the way by the introductory works and commentaries written by Paul Nadim Tarazi. The only other critical work on Galatians of which I have made use has been the commentary by Hans Dieter Betz. I have not relied on any specifically patristic modes of interpretation, and I have consciously avoided relating what Paul writes in this letter to what he says in any of his other letters (there are, however, a few brief exceptions to this rule). My reading of Galatians is heavily dependent on a direct examination of the Greek text. I have included the latter when initially presenting each portion of my translated version. When exegetically required, I include some terminology and/or portions of the text in transliterated form. A working knowledge of New Testament Greek is not necessary in order to make use of this commentary, but, at the same time, there is no reason why any reader should not be able to pick up a few of the most important Greek terms and absorb them along the way. The reader will also see that, at many points, my commentary serves as a *de facto* explanation for the manner in which I chose to translate Paul's letter, but that is a not uncommon facet of biblical exegesis.

In so many ways the impetus for this translation-commentary project came from my reading of N. T. Wright's book on the Pauline theme of justification. His work alerted me to broader

A Translation

contexts for understanding what Paul is writing. Most immediately, his elaboration of the four overlapping frameworks for understanding the biblical scope and evangelical direction of Paul's gospel did much to season my own study of the Greek text and my reflections upon its meaning. In this commentary I do make comparative and referential use of the four canonical gospels, the Acts of the Apostles, and the letters of James and John. It goes without saying that any treatment of Paul's Galatian letter involves relating what he writes to what is contained in many books of the Old Testament, not least Genesis and Isaiah.

It was only after completing the six Bible Survey sessions devoted to Galatians that I arrived at my basic intuition about the overall meaning of the work. One day I sat down and wrote the following paragraph in one movement: it expresses what I think to be the essence of Paul's letter:

Paul's letter to the Galatian churches is first and foremost a statement about Christian *identity*, and it is only secondarily about *freedom*. And the freedom of which Paul does speak, which he so passionately advocates, is of a sort that has its true meaning not as an absolute principle of conscience or conduct, but as a condition derivative from the Christian believer's *new* sense of identity. All of what Paul says about freedom is rooted in what he has to say about identity: the reverse is never true.

Identity is a loaded concept. The modern word has associations and usages that could not be more distant from the world Paul inhabited, and, by the same token, the understanding of it that I am imputing to him is one that our time would have difficulty recognizing let alone accepting. One of the things that struck me when studying Galatians was the way in which the traditional "identity" language of Paul's time, for example, words or ideas having to do with being either Jewish or Greek, circumcised or uncircumcised, slave or free, pagan or non-pagan, etc. how these are transcended only by means of the gospel. Many Christian readers of the letter, perhaps without ever realizing it, would anachronistically include Christian and non-Christian among these paired opposites, but Paul's work is not about asserting a specifically Christian identity vis-à-vis a non-Christian one. To read Galatians with that idea in mind would be to miss the real purpose of the letter, namely, to hear again Paul's summons to his churches first about why they believe what they do, and second, on what basis they must continue to believe what Paul has declared to them. It is thus that the notion of identity in the Galatian letter only ever realizes itself by membership in the word-based messianic community as first proclaimed by Paul. He wants his hearers to know why the new identity attached to the believer is never reducible to the play of history, nationality, ethnicity, or sectarian zeal. Who the believer is, i.e. his identity, is entirely the result of the preached word about Jesus of Nazareth as the crucified Christ, and the degree to which he is obedient to what life-in-the-gospel calls him. This is the reason why, exclusively in the context of Paul's letter, I view his gospel-based identity as operating as kind of *anti-identity*, that is, as the word-based identity that now smashes all of the other possible contenders for our loyalty and forces us to evaluate them in the light of the new.

I have not said everything there is to say about Paul's letter, and no doubt there is much more that can be rightfully asserted about it and gleaned from it, but what I have heard by encountering this letter that we attribute to the man whom the Eastern Orthodox Church reckons as being THE APOSTLE, is some of the surest and most forceful music about *who* we are supposed to be. Paul writes to the Galatians in order to remind them of who they are by virtue of the gospel that he had first preached to them. He wants them to see once again—with a renewed clarity and a restored sense of purpose that only an adherence to the gospel itself can make possible—in whom they now have their identity and what that must continue to mean.

To the Galatians: A Translation

1 1 *Paul, an apostle not sent from men nor even by a man,
but by Jesus the Christ and God the Father,*
who raised him up from among the dead;
2 I, along with all of the brothers and sisters who are with me,
greet the churches of Galatia:
3 may grace and peace be with you
from God our Father and the Lord Jesus who is the Christ,
4 he who gave himself on account of our sins
in order that he might deliver us from this encompassing evil age,
it all being done in accordance with the will of our God and Father,
5 to whom be the glory unto the ages of ages. Amen.
6 I am astonished that
in this manner you are so quickly turning away from him who called you
in the grace of the Christ,
and that you are turning to a different gospel—
which is not another one—
7 but now there are some who are confusing you
and who even want to alter the gospel of the Christ.
8 But even if we or a messenger from heaven should preach to you a gospel
other than what we preached to you,
let him be accursed!
9 As we have said before, so now I am saying again:
if any one is preaching to you a gospel
other than that which you received from us,
let him be accursed!
10 For am I now winning over men or God?
Or am I seeking to please men?
If I were still pleasing men,
I would not be a slave of the Christ.
11 For I want you to know, brothers and sisters,
that the gospel preached by me,
it is not according to man;
12 for neither have I received it from a man
nor was I taught it,
rather it came by means of a revealing of Jesus the Christ himself.
13 For you have heard of my former life in Judaism,
how I was persecuting the church beyond measure
and that I was destroying her,
14 because I had advanced in Judaism beyond many of those among my own people
on account of the fact that I was so exceedingly zealous for the traditions of my fathers.

*15 But when it pleased God,
he who set me apart before I was born,
and who called me by means of his grace,
16 to reveal his Son through me
so that I might preach him among the nations,
I did not directly confer with flesh and blood,
17 nor did I go up to Jerusalem to the ones who were apostles before me,
rather I went away into Arabia
and again I returned to Damascus.
18 Then after three years I went up to Jerusalem to visit Kephas
and I stayed with him fifteen days,
19 but I saw no other apostles
except for James, the brother of the Lord.
20 As for the things of which I am writing to you,
behold, as God is my witness, I am not lying.
21 Then I went into the regions of Syria and Cilicia;
22 but as my face was unknown to the churches of Judea
that were in the Christ,
23 they only heard that, "He who persecuted us is now preaching the very faith
that he at one time was destroying,"
and so it was that through me they were giving glory to God.*

*2 1 Then after fourteen years I went up again to Jerusalem with Barnabas
and I took along Titus,
2 for I had gone up in accordance with the revelation;
and I laid before them the gospel that I am preaching among the nations,
but privately to those who were of reputation,
lest in any way I should be running or had run in vain.
3 Yet not even Titus who was with me,
who was a Greek,
was compelled to be circumcised.
4 I say this on account of those false brothers in the faith
who had come in secretly,
the ones who came in to spy out our freedom that we have in the Christ Jesus
so that they might bring us back into slavery;
5 but not for a moment did we submit to them in obedience
all in order that the truth of the gospel might be preserved for you.
6 And from the ones who were reputed to be something,
and what they were is of no consequence to me—
God does not go by appearances—
these men who were of repute added nothing to me;
7 but, to the contrary, when they saw that the gospel for the uncircumcised had fallen to me,
just as the gospel for the circumcised had fallen to Peter,
8 for he who was working through Peter for the mission to the circumcised*

was also working through me for the mission to the nations,
9 and when they came to know the grace given to me,
James and Kephas and John,
the ones who were reputed to be pillars,
they gave to me and Barnabas the right hand of fellowship,
in order that we might go to the nations
and they to the circumcised;
10 the only condition being that we might remember the poor,
and that very thing I was eager to do.
11 But when Kephas came to Antioch,
I opposed him to his face
because he was caught up in contradiction.
12 For before certain men came from James
he would eat together with the pagans,
but when they came,
he withdrew and separated himself
because he feared the advocates of circumcision.
13 And the other Jews were also hypocritical along with him,
so that even Barnabas was caught up in their hypocrisy.
14 But when I saw that they were not consistent about the truth of the gospel,
before them all I said to Kephas,
"If you who were born a Jew are now living like a pagan and not like a Jew,
how can you compel the pagans to live like Jews?"
15 But we, who by nature are Jews and not pagan sinners,
16 knowing that a man is not declared righteous on the basis of the works of the law
but by means of the faithfulness of Jesus as the Christ,
even we have believed in Jesus who is the Christ,
so that we might be declared righteous on the basis of the faithfulness of the Christ Jesus
and not on the basis of the works of the law,
because no man is declared righteous on the basis of the works of the law.
17 But if, when we are seeking to be declared righteous through our faith in the Christ,
we ourselves were found to be sinners,
is then the Christ a servant of sin?
Certainly not!
18 For if I am building up again these things that I have taken apart,
then I prove myself to be a transgressor
19 because by means of the law I have died to the law
in order that I might live to God.
I have been crucified along with the Christ;
20 and so it is no longer I who live,
but it is the Christ who is living through me,
and what I am now living in the flesh
I am living as a result of my believing in the Son of God,
who loved me and who gave himself on my behalf.

21 *I would not set aside the grace of God:*
for if righteousness did in fact come by means of the law,
then the Christ died for no reason at all.

3 1 *O foolish Galatians!*
Who has bewitched you that you should not obey the truth,
before whose eyes Jesus the Christ was clearly portrayed as crucified?
2 *Only this one thing do I wish to learn from you:*
Did you receive the Spirit on the basis of works of the law
or was it on the basis of a hearing with faith?
3 *Are you in this way so foolish, that, having begun with the Spirit,*
you are now completing yourselves in the flesh?
4 *Did you suffer so many things for no purpose*
—if it really was for no purpose?
5 *Therefore he who now graciously grants the Spirit to you*
and who works mighty acts among you,
does he do that on the basis of the works of the law
or on the basis of a hearing with faith?
6 *Just as Abraham believed God, and it was reckoned to him as righteousness,*
7 *therefore know that the ones who live on the basis of faith are the sons of Abraham.*
8 *And scripture,*
foreseeing that God would declare the nations righteous on the basis of faith,
proclaimed the gospel beforehand to Abraham, saying,
"through you shall all the nations be blessed,"
9 *so that the ones who live on the basis of faith will be blessed along with the faithful*
Abraham.
10 *For as many as there are who live on the basis of the works of the law,*
they are all living under a curse;
for it stands written,
"Cursed is every one who does not abide by all of the things written in the book of the law,
and do them."
11 *And as it is evident that by the law no one is declared righteous before God,*
because "he who is righteous shall live on the basis of faith,"
12 *for the law is not on the basis of faith,*
rather "he who does these things, by them shall he live."
13 *The Christ has bought us back from the curse of the law,*
having become himself a curse on our behalf,
because it stands written,
"Cursed is every one who hangs on a tree,"
14 *so that in the person of the Christ who is Jesus*
the blessing of Abraham might come upon all nations,
so that we might receive the promise of the Spirit by means of faith.
15 *Brothers and sisters, I am now speaking in human terms:*
no one nullifies or adds to a man's covenant once it has been ratified,

16 and the promises were made to Abraham and to his seed.
He does not say, "And to seeds,"
as if he meant many, but rather he meant one,
"and to your seed," who is the Christ.
17 And this I am saying:
the law that came four hundred and thirty years later
does not annul a covenant previously ratified by God
so as to remove the promise.
18 For if the inheritance is on the basis of the law,
it is no longer on the basis of a promise;
but God had given it to Abraham by means of a promise.
19 Why then the law?
It was added because of our transgressions
until such time as the seed would come to whom the promise had been made,
it having been ordained by angels at the hand of an intermediary.
20 Now the intermediary is not just one, but God is one.
21 Is the law then against the promises of God?
Certainly not!
For if a law capable of giving life had been given,
then in fact righteousness would be on the basis of the law;
22 rather, scripture has consigned all things under sin
in order that the promise that is based on the faith of Jesus the Christ
might be given to the ones who believe.
23 But before faith came,
we were being held under the law's watch,
bound together for the sake of the faith about to be revealed,
24 such that the law had become our tutor concerning the Christ
in order that we then might be declared righteous on the basis of faith.
25 But with the coming of faith
we are no longer under a tutor:
26 this is because all of you are sons of God
by means of the faith whose content is the Christ Jesus;
27 for as many of you as were baptized for the sake of the Christ
have clothed yourselves in the Christ:
28 there is no Jew and there is no Greek,
there is no slave and there is no free man,
there is no male and female,
because you are all one in the Christ Jesus.
29 And if you are the Christ's,
then you are the seed of Abraham;
you are heirs in accordance with the promise.

4 1 And I am saying that for however long the heir is a child, he is no better than a slave even though he is the lord of all things;
2 instead he is under guardians and stewards
until the time appointed by his father.
3 It is the same with us:
when we were children,
we were in servitude to the elemental things of this world;
4 but it was when the fullness of time had come
that God sent forth his Son,
who had been born of a woman,
who had been born under the law,
5 so that he might buy back those who are under the law,
so that we could receive the adopted status of sons.
6 And as proof that you are sons,
God has sent forth the Spirit of his Son into our hearts
where the Spirit cries out, "Abba, Father!"—
7 all so that you are no longer a slave,
but rather a son;
and if you are a son,
then it is through God that you also have been made an heir.
8 But when you did not know God,
you were enslaved to the things which were not by nature gods,
9 and now that you do know God,
or rather, now that you are known by God,
how is it that you are turning again to the weak and impoverished elements
to which you once more wish to enslave yourselves?
10 You go about observing days and
months and seasons and years—
11 I am afraid for you in the event that I have labored over you in vain.
12 Brothers and sisters, I am beseeching you, become as I am, for I too have become as you are.
13 You have done me no wrong;
and you know that it was on account of my bodily weakness
that I preached the gospel to you the first time;
14 and that trial which came upon you by way of my body
you neither despised nor rejected,
rather, you received me as a messenger of God
just as you had received the Christ Jesus.
15 So where is your blessing?
For I declare to you that, if possible,
you would have plucked out your own eyes and given them to me.
16 Have I then become your enemy by telling you the truth?
17 Their zealous concern for you is to no good purpose,
rather, they only want to exclude you

so that you might show zealous concern for them;
18 yet it is good to have zeal always for what is good
and not only when I am with you.
19 My children, you for whom I am once more laboring in birth
until the Christ himself might be formed among you,
20 I have wanted to be with you now
and to change my tone
because I been having doubts about you.
21 Tell me, you who wish to be under the law,
do you not hear what the law says?
22 For it stands written that Abraham had two sons,
one from a slave woman and
one from a free woman.
23 But the son from the slave woman was born according to the flesh,
and the son from the free woman by means of a promise.
24 These things have another meaning
because the women are two covenants:
one is from Mount Sinai and gives birth to slavery,
the one which is Hagar.
25 Now Hagar is Mount Sinai in Arabia;
and she corresponds to the current Jerusalem
because she along with her children serve as slaves.
26 But the Jerusalem above is free,
the one who is our mother;
27 for it stands written,
"Rejoice, o barren one, you who do not give birth!
Break forth and shout, you who are not in birth pains!
For the desolate one has many more children
than she who has a husband."
28 And we, brothers and sisters, are children of promise just as Isaac was.
29 But just as it was then when he who had been born according to the flesh
was persecuting him who was born according to the Spirit,
so too it is now.
30 But what does scripture say?
"Cast out the slave woman and her son;
for the son of the slave woman shall not inherit along with the son of the free woman."
31 Therefore, brothers and sisters, we are not children of the slave woman
but of the free woman.

5 *1 It is for freedom that the Christ has set us free;
therefore stand fast and*
do not place yourselves again in a yoke of slavery.
2 You see, I, Paul, am saying to you that
if you should let yourselves be circumcised,
then the Christ will be of no value to you.
3 For I am declaring to every man who lets himself be circumcised
that he is obligated to do the whole of the law.
4 You have been cut off from the Christ,
whoever you are who are being declared righteous by the law—
you have fallen away from grace.
5 For it is by the Spirit that we are eagerly hoping for the righteousness that is on the basis of faith.
6 because it is in the Christ Jesus that neither circumcision
nor uncircumcision amounts to anything,
but rather what does matter is faith activated by means of love.
7 You had been running so well.
Who hindered you then from being persuaded by the truth?
8 Your persuasion now does not come from him who calls you.
9 A little leaven leavens the whole lump.
10 I am persuaded that, being in the Lord, you will not think otherwise;
and he who is confusing you will bear his judgment, whoever he is.
11 And I, brothers and sisters,
if I am still preaching circumcision,
why am I still being persecuted?
If so, the scandal of the cross has been taken away.
12 I wish that the ones who are troubling you would cut themselves off!
13 For you have been called to freedom, brothers and sisters,
only do not use this freedom as an opportunity for the flesh,
rather, by means of love be servants of one another.
14 For the entire law is fulfilled in one word,
in this very scripture, "You shall love your neighbor as yourself."
15 But if you would rather bite and devour one another,
take care that you are not consumed by each other!
16 And I am saying to you, that if you are walking in the Spirit,
you shall not accomplish the wishes of the flesh.
17 For the flesh is arrayed against the Spirit,
and the Spirit likewise against the flesh;
and since these things are set against each other,
you will end up not doing the things you intended.
18 But if you are led by the Spirit,
then you are not under the law.
19 Now the doings of the flesh are evident ones,
they being adultery, fornication, uncleanness, lewdness,

20 idolatry, sorcery, hatred, contentions, jealousies,
outbursts of wrath, selfish ambitions, dissensions,
heresies,
21 envy, murders, drunkenness, revelries,
and the things that are like them;
concerning them I am warning you just as I warned you before—
that the ones who do practice such things will not inherit the kingdom of God.
22 But the fruit of the Spirit is love, joy, peace,
patience, kindness, goodness, faith,
23 gentleness, self-control;
and the law has nothing against them.
24 And those who belong to the Christ have crucified the flesh
along with its passions and desires.
25 If we are going to live by the Spirit,
let us also conform ourselves to the Spirit.
26 Let us not take up vain kinds of glory,
by challenging one another
or by envying each other.

6 1 Brothers and sisters,
if a man is caught up in a certain transgression,
let you who are walking in the Spirit restore such a man
in a spirit of gentleness
while keeping a close eye on yourselves lest you be tempted.
2 Bear one another's burdens
and in this manner you shall measure up to the law of the Christ.
3 For if anyone thinks himself to be something,
when he is nothing,
he is deluding himself;
4 but let each one test the mettle of his own work,
and only then will he have cause to boast in himself
and not in another.
5 For each man will have to bear his own load.
6 Let him who is instructed in the word
share in all good things with him who instructs.
7 Do not deceive yourselves—
for God is not mocked—
it being true that whatever a man sows,
this too he will reap.
8 For he who sows for the sake of his own flesh
will on the basis of the flesh reap what corrupts;
but he who sows for the sake of the Spirit,
he will on the basis of the Spirit reap what lives.
9 And let us not grow weary when doing good,

for in due season we shall reap if we do not lose heart.
10 So then, as we do have the opportunity,
let us do good to all men,
especially to those who are of the household of faith.
11 See with what large letters I have written to you with my own hand.
12 However many there are who want to put forward a good face in the flesh,
these are the same men who would compel you to be circumcised,
but only in order that they might not be persecuted for the cross of the Christ.
13 For even the ones who have been circumcised do not themselves keep the law,
yet they wish that you should be circumcised
in order that they might boast in your flesh.
14 But by no means let it be for me to boast in anything
except in the cross of our Lord Jesus the Christ,
through whom the world has been crucified to me
and I to the world.
15 For when we are in the Christ Jesus neither circumcision
nor uncircumcision is anything at all,
but rather what does matter is a new creation;
16 and for however many might conform themselves to this standard,
peace be upon them and
mercy be upon the Israel of God.
17 From this point forward let no one trouble me
because I bear the marks of Jesus on my own body.
18 May the grace of our Lord Jesus the Christ be with your spirit,
brothers and sisters. Amen.

I. Paul, An Apostle (1:1-5)

Aside from what Paul writes in his letter, the only chronological indication we have of when he was in Galatia is contained in the Acts of the Apostles.[1] Only twice does that work make explicit mention of Paul's travels near or through Galatia. The first time is in connection with the itinerary of his second missionary journey as recorded in Acts 16:6 (RSV): "And they went through the region of Phrygia and Galatia, having been forbidden by the Holy Spirit to speak the word in Asia." The second comes in Acts 18:22-23 (RSV) when Paul concludes the second and is beginning his third missionary journey: "When he landed at Caesarea, he went up and greeted the church, and then went down to Antioch. After spending some time there he departed and went from place to place through the region of Galatia and Phrygia, strengthening all the disciples." It is not possible to say with any precision when Paul wrote his letter to the Galatians because the only thing that the text indicates is that he had been there to preach the gospel at least once if not twice (4:13).

Though we may never be able to say exactly *when* Paul wrote the letter, we can say *why* he did. At issue are two closely interrelated points: (1) what was to be the basis for Paul's apostolic authority, and (2) what was the content of the gospel message that he preached. In Paul's mind, as we shall see, these two points are inseparable.

Comparatively speaking, the letter to the Galatians is Paul's most impassioned writing. It is a desperate yet measured statement about his own sense of identity in relation to the gospel he preaches. To ask the question, "Who is this man Paul?" is, in his own eyes, equivalent to asking, "What is the

---

[1] The only other New Testament references to Galatia occur in 1 Corinthians 16:1, 2 Timothy 4:10, and 1 Peter 1:1. None of these has any bearing on the general chronological consideration here.

gospel about?" The letter allows us to understand something about the seamless way in which Saul the Pharisee—through conversion, baptism, and the "new creation" of faith—was transformed into Paul the Apostle.

The issue of Paul's status as an apostle is apparent from the opening words of the letter (1:1-5) when he greets the Galatian churches in this manner: "Paul, an apostle not sent from men nor even by a man, but by Jesus the Christ and God the Father, who raised him up from among the dead; I, along with all of the brothers and sisters who are with me, greet the churches of Galatia: may grace and peace be with you from God our Father and the Lord Jesus who is the Christ, who gave himself on account of our sins in order that he might deliver us from this encompassing evil age, it all being done in accordance with the will of our God and Father, to whom be the glory unto the ages of ages. Amen."

Compared to the greetings found in his two earlier letters to the Thessalonian church, this salutation is loaded with rhetorical assertions. It is evident that Paul now wishes to make some points perfectly clear to those he has evangelized. From the outset he explicitly identifies himself *as an apostle*, and, though we cannot be completely certain about the circumstances of that initial evangelization, the content of the letter indicates that in the aftermath of Paul's first visit, other Christian missionaries of a Judaizing bent must have been active in these same communities. The entire letter represents his response to the inroads these latecomers must have made among the Galatian believers.

At the center of it all is the issue of the gospel: its content whether verbal or inscribed, its salvific purpose, and how both of these determine the way in which Paul would view his role as an apostle. As I said, these two things are inextricably related. Later in the letter Paul seeks to contextualize his apostolic status relative to "the ones who were apostles before me" (1:17), namely, James, Kephas (Peter), and John, the reputed "pillars"

I. Paul, An Apostle (1:1-5)

of the Jerusalem church. These men claimed a direct, personal connection to Jesus, who, because they were paschal participants, possessed an unimpeachable apostolic status, but Paul has only the remarkable circumstances of his own calling by the risen Christ and it is solely on these that he bases his appeal.

Paul knows that these so-called "Judaizers" (more on this term below) in the Galatian region must have questioned his legitimacy as an apostle. They most likely pointed out that he was an apostle of a seemingly lesser pedigree because he was not a personal acquaintance of Jesus and was not a direct witness to the resurrection events in Jerusalem and later in the Galilee. Thus they must have argued in favor of their apostolic directions as having more authority and therefore being more binding upon the new believers.

While there were probably multiple issues involved, Paul focuses in his letter on the issue of circumcision. It was no small matter in the early church. Witness the contention that arose among the Christians over this and related issues, a series of disputes that culminated in what can be described as the first apostolic council in Jerusalem. Acts 15 provides an account of the course and the content of the affair. It was specifically concerned with the question of what traditional Jewish practices were binding upon the non-Jewish believers. Was it necessary for them to be circumcised? Which portions of the law were they obliged to follow? How integral to the gospel were the requirements of the law? The initial Christian missionary efforts were comprised mainly of Jews, and so these kinds of questions naturally arose. It would be naïve to claim that from the outset of the Christian movement there was anything like a thoroughly universal agreement concerning them.

Acts 10 provides a scriptural telling of the way in which the general issue would emerge.[2] In the context of Peter's mission to

---

[2] I will not address the issue of the relative historicity of the Acts of the Apostles regarding these events except to say that the book furnishes a scriptural witness to

the centurion Cornelius we can read about that apostle's vision at Joppa, and how its inclusive meaning only becomes clear when the Holy Spirit falls upon Jew and Gentile alike in response to Peter's preaching. Here the point is only made implicitly when Peter himself poses the telling question: "Can any one forbid water for baptizing these people who have received the Holy Spirit just as we have?" (10:47, RSV)

It is already by the end of the narrative dealing with Paul's first missionary journey (Acts 13:1-14:28), a trek that took Paul and Barnabas as far inland as the cities of Pisidian Antioch, Iconium, Lystra, and Derbe, all points south of the Galatian region proper, that one reads about what happened when Paul and Barnabas had returned to their home base of Antioch: "But some men came down from Judea and were teaching the brethren, "Unless you are circumcised according to the custom of Moses, you cannot be saved." (Acts 15:1, RSV) The situation only worsened when the two went up to Jerusalem to report on their efforts: "But some believers who belonged to the party of the Pharisees rose up, and said, "It is necessary to circumcise them, and to charge them to keep the law of Moses." (15:5, RSV)

The resulting deliberations in Jerusalem over which "the apostles and the elders" presided (15:6) are interesting because, as recorded in Acts, Peter speaks entirely in favor of the Pauline line, namely, that God grants the Holy Spirit to Jew and non-Jew alike because "he made no distinction between us and them, but cleansed their hearts by faith. Now therefore why do you make a trial of God by putting a yoke upon the neck of the disciples which neither our fathers nor we have been able to bear? But we believe that we shall be saved through the grace of the Lord Jesus, just as they will" (15:9-11, RSV). James echoes this

---

what must have been a contentious and running issue in the early Christian decades. The fact that the author of the Acts depicts both Peter and James as advocating in a thoroughly Pauline manner should be kept in mind when considering what Paul describes in the second chapter of his Galatian letter.

I. Paul, An Apostle (1:1-5)

conclusion, and a statement containing the conclusions of this council in Jerusalem is drawn up and delivered by Paul and Barnabas to the church in Antioch. Its final words are telling and well worth remembering in connection with Paul's letter to the Galatians: "For it has seemed good to the Holy Spirit and to us to lay upon you no greater burden than these necessary things: that you abstain from what has been sacrificed to idols and from blood and from what is strangled, and from unchastity (*porneia*). If you keep from these, you will do well. Farewell." (15:28-29, RSV)

But it would be unrealistic to assume that the Jerusalem communication represented a definitive decision regarding the issue of what traditional Jewish customs, if any, pagan converts to the gospel were expected to observe, namely, that it had settled these questions conclusively from that point onward. The kind of centralized control and authoritative jurisdiction that we associate with later periods of church history simply were not in place at this time. The word from Jerusalem would remain just that, a word, for a long time to come—respected, considered, even cited on occasion—but all around it there still lingered the conviction that any new believer would only receive the fullness of salvation if he would but include some ritual Jewish observances. One of the most immediately obvious of these observations was the ritual act of circumcision, a practice that was in many ways the most emblematic sign of Jewish self-identity given that it was ancient, venerable, and outwardly unmistakable. From the Jewish perspective it was a seemingly non-negotiable requirement for belonging to God's people, and so it is easy to understand why so many early Christians, especially with the large numbers of Jews among them, would automatically assume that the mark of circumcision belonged as much as anything else to salvation's requirements.

Those who arrived on the scene in Galatia after Paul's preaching of the word were apparently insistent upon the need for circumcision, and for them to learn from the new converts that Paul had not insisted upon it was enough to set the stage for Paul's letter to the Galatians. Paul's opponents in Galatia (and elsewhere) are sometimes referred to as the "Judaizers," an expression that is unnecessarily misleading given that so much early Christian practice is patently Judaic in inspiration and content. I will not employ it here, in part because Paul himself never used the term as a direct designation for his opponents.[3] In order to keep matters properly focused, it would be better to use the apostle's own language. For example, in the Galatian letter (2:12) he simply refers to them as the "advocates of circumcision" (*hoi ek peritomēs*). As will become evident, this is a polemically precise designation on his part. An alternative rendering of the Greek phrase is the commonly used "circumcision party," and I will make occasional use of it.

But Paul knew that, if he was going to argue the issue of circumcision with the Galatians, he had to address the issue of his apostleship. He would have to provide them with a reminder of his credentials, and to present that account in a way that would once again establish his status as the most authoritative spokesman for the new salvation. Thus Paul begins his letter to them with an expanded salutation and greeting (1:1-5), words that will now carry his own particular appeal to validity:

¹ Παῦλος ἀπόστολος οὐκ ἀπ' ἀνθρώπων οὐδὲ δι' ἀνθρώπου
ἀλλὰ διὰ Ἰησοῦ Χριστοῦ καὶ θεοῦ πατρὸς
τοῦ ἐγείραντος αὐτὸν ἐκ νεκρῶν,
² καὶ οἱ σὺν ἐμοὶ πάντες ἀδελφοὶ
ταῖς ἐκκλησίαις τῆς Γαλατίας,
³ χάρις ὑμῖν καὶ εἰρήνη
ἀπὸ θεοῦ πατρὸς ἡμῶν καὶ κυρίου Ἰησοῦ Χριστοῦ
⁴ τοῦ δόντος ἑαυτὸν ὑπὲρ τῶν ἁμαρτιῶν ἡμῶν,
ὅπως ἐξέληται ἡμᾶς ἐκ τοῦ αἰῶνος τοῦ ἐνεστῶτος πονηροῦ

---

[3] The closest Paul comes to this in the letter is 2:14 when he confronts Peter at Antioch: "If you who were born a Jew are now living like a pagan and not like a Jew, how can you compel the pagans to live like Jews?" Paul's query "How can you compel the pagans to live like Jews?" (*pōs ta ethnē anangkazeis ioudaizein*) contains the infinitive form of the verb *ioudaizō*, which, in this context, only functions to highlight the implications of Peter's hypocrisy.

I. Paul, An Apostle (1:1-5)

κατὰ τὸ θέλημα τοῦ θεοῦ καὶ πατρὸς ἡμῶν,
⁵ ᾧ ἡ δόξα εἰς τοὺς αἰῶνας τῶν αἰώνων, ἀμήν.

¹ Paul, an apostle not sent from men nor even by a man,
but by Jesus the Christ and God the Father,
he who raised him up from among the dead;
² I, along with all of the brothers and sisters who are with me,
greet the churches of Galatia:
³ may grace and peace be with you
from God our Father and the Lord Jesus who is the Christ,
⁴ he who gave himself on account of our sins
in order that he might deliver us from this encompassing evil age,
it all being done in accordance with the will of our God and Father,
⁵ to whom be the glory unto the ages of ages. Amen.

Paul immediately identifies himself as an "apostle." This means that he is *apostolos*, one who has been sent somewhere in order to deliver a message, an emissary who is acting because he has been explicitly appointed to do so. The noun *apostolos* is derived from the Greek verb *apostellō*, which means "to send someone somewhere in order to do something." Thus, an *apostolos* is "he who has been sent somewhere in order to do something," and, in this case, it is to proclaim the good news concerning the salvation of all mankind through Jesus who is the Christ.

In 1:1 Paul is describing here the nature of his apostleship. He is asserting to the Galatians that he is an apostle who has been "not sent from men" (*ouk ap' anthrōpōn*), "nor even by a man" (*oude di' anthrōpou*), but that he has been sent specifically "by Jesus the Christ and God the Father" (*alla dia Iēsou Christou kai theou patros*). Later on Paul will give some information about the nature of his calling and the circumstances of his unfolding apostleship, but here the emphasis is simply on the directness of his calling. If the other missionaries have appealed to a Jerusalem "connection," that they operate on the basis of their either having known Jesus personally or else being entrusted with the gospel by those who did, then Paul once more asserts his own unique relationship with Jesus. Just as the risen Christ had commissioned Peter, James, John and the rest of the disciples to be his apostles, so too he has directly commissioned Paul.

He wants the Galatians to understand that he did not come by his gospel secondhand, that it was never just a matter of his having picked it up from other men, but rather it came to him directly from the Lord himself, who had been crucified and was now raised from the dead, just as Paul was to reiterate when he later confronts them in 3:1, "O foolish Galatians! Who has bewitched you that you should not obey the truth, before whose eyes Jesus the Christ was clearly portrayed as crucified?" In 1:1 he is linking Jesus with "God the Father, who raised him up from among the dead" (*theou patros tou egeirantos auton ek nekrōn*). Paul's contention here is that the origin of his apostleship is a direct commissioning from God and is not reducible to a human source. Paul will say many things to the Galatians, but this is the very first thing that comes from his mouth. This, along with the rest of 1:1-5, will be the content that underlies the whole of the letter.

In Paul's capacity as *apostolos*, it follows that his wish is that "grace and peace be with you from God our Father and the Lord Jesus who is the Christ" (1:3b). When he speaks of this "grace and peace" of the Lord, these are not figurative qualities, nor do they amount to a kind of spiritual afterglow or its lingering metaphoric atmosphere; rather they are the characteristic expressions of the positive, dynamic, and unilateral manifestation of God's own presence among the Galatians. But the true key to grasping both their possibility and their reality is to see them as what has been delivered to the "churches of Galatia" exclusively via Paul's uttered word.

The word "grace" is the Greek *charis*, a term that in its most basic meaning is used to denote the kind of self-evident benefit that one receives in connection with a genuine gift or a favor. Think of the transforming effect on our outlook that a completely unexpected and thoroughly undeserved gift has upon us, and then imagine what our frame of mind should be if that

I. Paul, An Apostle (1:1-5)

same gift should come directly and unmistakably from God himself. *This* is grace: the altering of whatever perceptions we might have of our situation in the light of a true gift—not an occasional present left on our doorstep, but a true gift—the kind that lies beyond any human calculus of giving and receiving. Divine grace is the communication of what makes for covenantal life, that is, what we are able to receive obediently as the word-based presence of God in our midst. As such, grace is never just a matter of warm and squishy feelings on our part because at its center is the gospel's relentless appeal to our hearts. There is nothing open-ended nor arbitrary about the grace of God: it points to the eschatological finality of peace.

The word "peace" should be understood in terms that go beyond a general sense of well-being or the loose presumption of a communal stability. The Greek word for peace is *eirēnē*, and, in Paul's characteristic usage, it signifies what becomes in effect the endpoint of all divine grace. If it is by grace that we abide in God's word and remain obedient to it, then peace is the culmination of the process—begun scripturally when God established the world as a created order—and it consists of the unconditional exhibition of those original, intended qualities. The Pauline peace, the *eirēnē*, is thus what corresponds to God's own *šalōm*, the Hebrew word for peace, a scriptural term that more fundamentally denotes the blessed sanity of creation when it is functioning obediently in accordance with the will of God.

Indeed, this regular association of the two terms and their (for now) two sources are shown as well in John 20:19-21 (RSV) when the resurrected Jesus comes into the midst of his assembled disciples (minus Thomas) and he bestows his "peace" upon them:

> On the evening of that day, the first day of the week, the doors being shut where the disciples were, for fear of the Jews, Jesus came and stood among them and said to them, "Peace (eirēnē) be with you." When he had said this, he showed them his hands and

his side. Then the disciples were glad (echarēsan) when they saw the Lord. Jesus said to them again, "Peace (eirēnē) be with you."

When John writes that the disciples "were glad," the text uses the verb *chairō*, a word etymologically associated with the noun *charis*, which is the word for "grace." The connection here is a simple one to trace: if by virtue of hearing and obeying the gospel you are unmistakably in God's presence, then, by virtue of the fact that you are the direct recipient of his grace (*charis*), such a presence will be the unmitigated cause for rejoicing (*chairein*), for the grace-mediated welling up in our hearts of that other etymological associate, the Greek word for "joy" (*chara*).

Even so, this juxtaposition of Jesus and God the Father in vv.1-3 is one that should not be too heavily invested theologically. It is sufficient for Paul's evangelistic purposes at this point that the Galatians understand the gospel's simple declaration of Jesus' sonship vis-à-vis the divine fatherhood. If it is "God the Father" who has raised Jesus from the dead, and if belief in Jesus as the Christ, the anointed one for God's purpose of salvation not just for the Jews but for all peoples of the world, establishes some kind of relationship between them that, while evangelistically proclaimed but not theologically detailed, then it is a relationship that the gospel itself will reveal in stages and by degrees, a process that in their own way the next two verses demonstrate.

Paul's blessing for the Galatians is that they will be full recipients of God's "grace and peace." This grace and peace have their source in "God our Father and the Lord Jesus who is the Christ," and in vv. 4-5 Paul further details the role Jesus plays in relation to the Father. He identifies Jesus as he "who gave himself on account of our sins in order that he might deliver us from this encompassing evil age, it all being done in accordance with the will of our God and Father, to whom be the glory unto the ages of ages. Amen." By now there are three christological elements to note in this relationship that Paul is presenting in vv. 1 and 4 concerning Jesus and God the Father.

I. Paul, An Apostle (1:1-5)

And these three elements form an interlocking triad that make up the fundamental Christian *kerygma* or proclamation. These are the three elements of power, sacrifice, and salvation.

First, back in v.1 it is God the Father "who raised him [Jesus] from among the dead." As Paul makes clear in Romans 1:1b-4 (RSV), he is an apostle:

> set apart for the gospel of God which he promised beforehand through his prophets in the holy scriptures, the gospel concerning his Son, who was descended from David according to the flesh and designated Son of God in power according to the Spirit of holiness by his resurrection from the dead, Jesus Christ our Lord.

God's raising of the crucified Jesus from the dead is the inaugural event of what is to be a new era, the dawning of an awareness that is as new as it is old, a knowledge first vouchsafed prophetically to the scriptural Israel and then one to be spread and shared among the nations of the world, namely, that in the Pascha this new and final era of salvation has begun.

Man is only able to comprehend the purposes of God by paying close attention to his actions, to what the Lord has done for the salvation of those who call upon his name and who obey his commandments, and how these things are the stuff of scripture, what the Hebrew would have understood as constituting, most broadly, "prophecy." The latter is the scriptural record of God's actions, the written account of his mighty acts and wonders done to make known his sovereign will and power vis-à-vis his people and ultimately as a witness to the whole world. The Christian proclamation that God has raised Jesus from the dead must be understood as belonging to this narrative of decisive action on God's part, that the resurrection of Jesus is the fulfillment of all earlier biblical prophecy precisely because it makes complete and brings to prophetic perfection all of what had stood written before.

Second, there is the declaration that this same Jesus, whom God the Father has raised from the dead, that he has given himself for our sins (*tou dontos heautou hyper tōn hamartiōn hēmōn*). Paul identifies the death from which Jesus has been raised in glory as a sacrificial one done for the sake of our sins. Later in the letter Paul will provide a framework for the understanding of this sacrifice: how it constituted the right kind of sacrifice given the nature of our predicament, and why it is that we can even begin to speak about there being a hope for salvation in the death of Jesus.

This latter point is related to the third christological element in Paul's introduction: "in order that he might deliver us from this encompassing evil age" (*hopōs exelētai hēmas ek tou aiōnos tou enestōtos ponērou*). This clause is an especially loaded one because it includes the eschatological element, that is, it explicitly mentions things that belong to the whole range of ancient Jewish ideas, beliefs, prophecies, and expectations related to the coming of the messiah. In order to have a fuller understanding of the earliest Christian preaching, it is vitally important to comprehend how the death and resurrection of Jesus were handled scripturally as being related to and fulfilling what was already a substantial amount of established messianic belief and expectation.

In those centuries before Jesus there emerged in all the groups that made up the Jewish tradition a body of anticipatory beliefs having to do with the culmination of history seen as the occasion for God's final intervention to save his people. This is the celebrated "day of the Lord" as contained in the Old Testament and textually developed in the writings of the prophets. It is a vision of wrath, judgment, and vindication in which God scripturally appears (*kata tas graphas*, i.e. "in accordance with the scriptures") in power and glory to punish the oppressor and to raise up the oppressed. There was no single biblical account of what was going to happen: therefore we find in the Jewish tradition multiple strands of belief having to do with God *rendering this judgment*, that is, visiting himself *as judge* not just upon the nations but also upon his own people in order that he might preside over them directly.

I. Paul, An Apostle (1:1-5)

Long before Jesus' time this growing body of beliefs included the ideas of the resurrection of the dead and a final judgment for all mankind who will have been raised from the dead (e.g. Daniel 12:1-3). Collectively these beliefs comprise the Jewish *eschatology*, which we should understand as being those teachings having to do with the end of a postulated current evil age in which the Jews are mired because they are disobedient to God's commandments. Their condition of bondage is a result of their sinful disobedience (a state of "cursedness" represented first and foremost by Roman rule), and they are still suffering defeat, humiliation, and exile before the beginning of a new time in which God's rule (i.e. literally his "ruling," or, more formally, his "kingdom") will manifest itself. The word "eschatology" is derived from the Greek adjective *eschatos*, which means "last." Therefore, eschatology is what we can say (the *logos*) about the things that will come about last of all (the *eschaton*).[4] These eschatological things will be the events that mark the transition from a present time of evil, violence, and suffering to an age in which God will do away with all of these things and establish his justice in the form of direct rule over his people once and for all. Thus eschatology is an extremely important concept, one that must be kept constantly in mind when reading not just Paul but the entire New Testament. As we shall see later in more detail, these "last things" are not an ancillary aspect of other more fundamental Christian doctrines; rather they are a central aspect of the basic Pauline message.

When viewed in this light, the first five verses of Paul's letter to the Galatians are a concise declaration of this core eschatology. First, Paul identifies himself as *apostolos*, and here the implication is that he is not just *an apostle* but rather *The Apostle*. Even though the word *apostolos* as it appears in 1:1 of the

---

[4] New Testament Greek is a declension-based language, and many parts of speech are rendered according to gender (masculine, feminine, or neuter). The Greek *eschatos* is the masculine nominative singular form of the word, its so-called "dictionary form." The *eschaton* is the neuter form of the same word, and it is this form that figures in the etymology of the term "eschatology."

Greek text contains no definite article, the rest of his letter bears out Paul's steadfast contention that, as far as the churches of Galatia are concerned, he is their only apostle. Second, that Paul is the Galatians' only apostle is due entirely to the fact that he is "not sent from men nor even by a man, but by Jesus the Christ and God the Father." Third, because God has commissioned Paul to be the bearer of his gospel to the world, it is precisely *as apostle* that he can write to the Galatian churches and greet them with the wish that they receive all the fullness of God's "grace and peace," that is, that they might continue abiding in the grace and living in the hope of the peace that comes only "from God our Father and the Lord Jesus who is the Christ." Fourth, with this double wish for the Galatians Paul expresses his fervent hope that the Galatian churches stay true to the beginning (grace) and the end (peace) that he has proclaimed to them in his gospel. Fifth, we see then the core eschatology at work in the Pauline gospel. When the listener abides in it, he will never lose sight of this new eschatological possibility because it is the Christ "who gave himself on account of our sins in order that he might deliver us from this encompassing evil age, it all being done in accordance with the will of our God and Father." The full force of this transition from a current time of evil and oppression to one of liberation and deliverance is expressed by the Greek verb rendered here as "deliver"*(exaireō)*, which literally means to pluck something out of something else, to remove it and to take it away. It is Jesus himself who is identified here as being the agent of this transition, taking us away "from this encompassing evil age," literally—and quite pointedly—this one in which we are standing.

And finally, recall that the Old Testament portrayed salvation in terms of divine victory, namely, that if God saves his people, then it is because he has won the victory for them, that he has established it over and against an enemy, and thus the Pauline gospel becomes an account of how this victory has been "done

I. Paul, An Apostle (1:1-5)

in accordance with the will of our God and Father."[5] If God is the author of that victory, if he has brought about all of what falls between what is demarcated here by the terms "grace" and "peace," then Paul justifiably affirms that it is only unto him that there shall be "the glory unto the ages of ages. Amen." Thus, in its own highly encapsulated way, 1:1-5 not only serves the purpose of the customary epistolary salutation, but, given what immediately follows it, the verses also function as a way for Paul to offer a prefatory laying of all his cards on the table.

---

[5] The Hebrew word *yeshū'ah* is translated, depending on context, as "salvation" or "victory." But in either rendering the consistent scriptural assumption behind its usage is that it is God who has won the victory for the sake of his obedient people.

II. The Gospel Revealed (1:6-12)

Paul does not waste any time in confronting the Galatians with what he has learned about them. After his introductory salutation he omits the customary thanksgiving section and in vv. 6-7 he straightaway writes:

⁶ θαυμάζω ὅτι
οὕτως ταχέως μετατίθεσθε ἀπὸ τοῦ καλέσαντος ὑμᾶς
ἐν χάριτι Χριστοῦ
εἰς ἕτερον εὐαγγέλιον.
⁷ ὃ οὐκ ἔστιν ἄλλο,
εἰ μὴ τινές εἰσιν οἱ ταράσσοντες ὑμᾶς
καὶ θέλοντες μεταστρέψαι τὸ εὐαγγέλιον τοῦ Χριστοῦ.

⁶ I am astonished that
in this manner you are so quickly turning away from him who called you
in the grace of the Christ,
and that you are turning to a different gospel—
⁷ which is not another one—
but now there are some who are confusing you
and who even want to alter the gospel of the Christ.

Paul has heard that other evangelists have come in his wake, that they have included in their preaching about Jesus of Nazareth admonitions aimed at convincing the new believers to adopt certain Jewish ritual requirements (most obviously here circumcision) because their adoption of these practices was presumably to have been in some way essential to their salvation.

He is writing to the Galatian converts in a spirit that is as direct as it is personal, as firm and deliberate as it is immediate and vulnerable. He is reacting to the news that those whom he had evangelized were now turning to embrace as primary the very things that his preaching had relegated to the status of secondary if not tertiary importance. Paul is beside himself in trying to understand why the content of his gospel should be modified in such a way, that the directness and the clarity with which he surely delivered it to the Galatians might have been so forthrightly forgotten.

He says that he is "astonished that in this manner you are so quickly turning away from him who called you in the grace of the Christ," and this passage contains an interesting grammatical ambiguity. To whom is Paul referring when he writes, "from him who called you in the grace of the Christ"—is it to himself or to God? On the one hand, in this context it is easy enough to understand if Paul intends the "him" mentioned here to refer to himself. After all, in the introduction he has already reasserted his divinely commissioned apostolic status to the Galatians. It is he who brought them the gospel, and, by virtue of his preaching, he has called them to be "in the grace of the Christ," that is, by responding faithfully to the message they will in turn conduct themselves in a manner that produces the spiritual fruit characteristic of life in the *aiōn* that is God's direct rule. But, on the other hand, it could just as well apply to God himself who has enlisted Paul to be his prophet and apostle, to reveal himself to the Galatians in the person of this most unlikely of messengers. We have already seen how closely Paul identified his gospel with the will of God (1:4), and this particular ambiguity in the text therefore helps Paul to bolster his appeal rhetorically. Not only is he confronting the Galatians with the fact that they are abandoning the apostolic messenger, but also—and more decisively—with the fact that it amounts to a rejection of him who sent the messenger in the first place.

But the crucial point here—indeed the whole reason in Paul's eyes for this crisis—is "that you are turning to a different gospel—which is not another one." Much of the rhetorical punch of v. 6 comes from the way in which Paul here employs two closely related Greek adjectives—"different" (*heteron*) and "another" (*allo*)—in order to begin making his case before the Galatians. In the first half of v. 6 he declares that they have turned away from the one who had called them "in the grace of the Christ" and gone over to "a different gospel." In Paul's eyes,

II. The Gospel Revealed (1:6-12)

the *only* gospel where the Galatians are concerned is the gospel they originally received through his preaching, and for Paul to learn that they are embracing the need to be circumcised means that this original gospel has been modified by subsequent preachers. It is in this sense that what the Galatians are currently obeying is a "different gospel" (*heteron euangelion*). Its "difference" lies in the ritual Jewish additions made to a message that was original and self-contained. Yet this "altered" form of the gospel is not however "another" gospel in the sense that it constitutes a competing version of it, a fully-fledged alternative that is internally consistent and therefore separately valid. To the contrary, Paul wants the Galatians to understand that what they are now embracing is an adulterated form of the original, true, and self-sufficient gospel—they have embraced an altogether *different* gospel and not simply *another* one!

Paul is asking the Galatians to make up their minds about *this question*: How many gospels are there? If Paul in his preaching had not included the ritual requirements which the Galatians are now pursuing at the prompting of the circumcision party, would there not be in effect two gospels of which they might speak— one explicitly based on faith and one implicitly based on obedience to the law? And if there are two discernible gospels, which one is true? For the ancient who had no reason to pay lip-service to diversity or who was not constrained to think in terms of a relativizing attitude as being its own virtue, this was a vital question, indeed, it would be the only question. Which gospel is the true one?

The key to understanding Paul's use of "different" and "another" in 1:6 is to keep in mind that, from start to finish, he insists on the primary and utter *singularity* of his original gospel. A circumcision-based gospel therefore would (a) never be anything more than *different* (*heteron*) in relation to his gospel-message, and (b) it would be accordingly false to presume that a circumcision-based gospel would have had any validity as *another* (*allo*) gospel.

In order to drive the point home about the reality of their situation, Paul declares to the Galatians "but now there are some who are confusing you and who even want to alter the gospel of the Christ." The verbs and their positioning here in the Greek text are instructive. The ones "who are confusing you" are *hoi tarrasontes hymas*, with the verb *tarassō* letting the Galatians know that those who came preaching after him were intent upon sowing misunderstanding by declaring a gospel that was, because of the novelties it contained, one that was *different* from what Paul had brought to them in the beginning. He tells them that these other evangelists are doing what they do because they are those "who even want to alter the gospel of the Christ": they are the ones who *thelontes metastrepsai to evangelion tou Christou*. It is this participial clause that provides the explanatory context for v. 7b, i.e. that these later evangelists are confusing the Galatians about the content and the meaning of the gospel *precisely because* they are intent upon altering its original content. The verb *metastrephō* means to turn something away from its original form or content and thus render it something different, it being the turn of phrase by means of which Paul seeks to indicate the fact that what he delivered to the Galatians is the gospel already full and complete and thus in no need of modification let alone addition.

And this finality of the gospel Paul underscores even further in vv. 8-9 when he makes it clear that what they have heard since he was among them and have come to follow in his absence is an unacceptable alteration of what was, for the purposes of their salvation, true and unalterable:

⁸ ἀλλὰ καὶ ἐὰν ἡμεῖς ἢ ἄγγελος ἐξ οὐρανοῦ εὐαγγελίζηται ὑμῖν
παρ' ὃ εὐηγγελισάμεθα ὑμῖν,
ἀνάθεμα ἔστω.
⁹ ὡς προειρήκαμεν καὶ ἄρτι πάλιν λέγω·
εἴ τις ὑμᾶς εὐαγγελίζεται
παρ' ὃ παρελάβετε,
ἀνάθεμα ἔστω.

⁸ *But even if we or a messenger from heaven should preach to you a gospel*

II. The Gospel Revealed (1:6-12)

> other than what we preached to you,
> let him be accursed!
> ⁹ As we have said before, so now I am saying again:
> if any one is preaching to you a gospel
> other than that which you received from us,
> let him be accursed!

Here the language is undeniably strident. Paul invokes a curse upon any one who would change what he in all faithfulness to God and his concomitant sense of apostolic duty has delivered to the Galatians. He declares that such a person should be *anathema*, a Greek word taken over into modern parlance in order to denote something which is "forbidden" or "unacceptable," but ancient Hebrew curses involved matters much more severe than the kind of relative verbal stigmatization that contemporary usage might suggest. In Paul's day for someone to utter the anathema-curse involved the *binding* wish that his name might never be mentioned again, that he would in effect cease to exist, which is of course an only slightly indirect way of calling for his extinction. We need to remind ourselves that in the more closely knit social structures of tribal societies, for a person's name never to be mentioned again was a *de facto* death sentence. It meant his consignment to the status of being a veritable non-person, who, because his name could not be uttered, was as good as dead. Oaths and curses were extremely serious matters among the ancients because the latter still operated on the principle that what a person said was really the same as what he is. This ultimately binding aspect of oaths and curses is something for which we as moderns have no corresponding sense let alone appreciation.

Part of Paul's determined insistence at this point is rooted in what could be called the tradition of *prophetic exasperation*. As we shall see, Paul did not take anything more seriously than his apostolic role, and in that capacity he saw it as his God-ordained responsibility to communicate the true message of salvation to the peoples of the world. This is consonant with what was a deeply rooted conviction in Israel's prophetic tradition, and, as an earlier example of it, we can consider Ezekiel 33:1-9 (RSV) where we find the prophet testifying to this same sense of a divinely mandated constraint[1]:

> The word of the LORD came to me: "Son of man, speak to your people and say to them, If I bring the sword upon a land, and the people of the land take a man from among them, and make him their watchman; and if he sees the sword coming upon the land and blows the trumpet and warns the people; then if any one who hears the sound of the trumpet does not take warning, and the sword comes and takes him away, his blood shall be upon his own head. He heard the sound of the trumpet, and did not take warning; his blood shall be upon himself. But if he had taken warning, he would have saved his life. But if the watchman sees the sword coming and does not blow the trumpet, so that the people are not warned, and the sword comes, and takes any one of them; that man is taken away in his iniquity, but his blood I will require at the watchman's hand. *So you, son of man, I have made a watchman for the house of Israel; whenever you hear a word from my mouth, you shall give them warning from me.* If I say to the wicked, O wicked man, you shall surely die, and you do not speak to warn the wicked man to turn from his way, *that wicked man shall die in his iniquity, but his blood I will require at your hand. But if you warn the wicked to turn from his way, and he does not turn from his way; he shall die in his iniquity, but you will have saved your life.*"

The pattern of prophetic responsibility here is a simple one: while actually delivering the message was one thing, the lasting reception of that message among the people was another but not totally unrelated matter. If the people received the message and kept it, then, in accordance with the traditional prophetic rationale, salvation (God's "victory") would run its proper and appointed course. But if the people did not keep the message, then the catastrophe of a deepening apostasy would result. Their continuing disobedience would be the undoing of God's will and lead to the eventual destruction of Israel.

---

[1] See also the earlier parallel passage in Ezekiel 3:16-27.

II. The Gospel Revealed (1:6-12)

Paul no doubt saw the situation in Galatia as potentially heading in the same direction. The seeming willingness on the part of the Galatian believers to adopt, when seen in the light of his own gospel proclamation, *nonessential* requirements for faith in the Christ and inclusion in the people of God, this must have struck Paul as a rejection of God himself (and certainly of the message entrusted to him by God). He would have shared in the lament of the prophet Jeremiah who in classic prophetic fashion derided the inhabitants of Judah and Jerusalem for their chronic refusal to heed the God of Israel because they "follow after vain and worthless things" (Jeremiah 2:5, OSB):

> "Therefore I will yet bring charges against you," says the Lord, "and I will bring charges against the sons of your sons. For pass by the islands of Chettim and see. Send to Kedar and consider diligently. See if such things happened, whether nations will change their gods; though they are not gods. "But my people changed their glory to a glory from which they will not profit. Heaven was amazed at this and was exceedingly horror-struck," says the Lord. For my people have committed two evils: They forsook Me, the fountain of living water, and hewed for themselves broken cisterns, unable to hold water. Is not Israel a slave or household servant?" (Jeremiah 2:9-14, OSB)

The above passage from Jeremiah is straightforwardly applicable on a number of points. The glory of which the prophet speaks is God's own glory, and, in Paul's case, this glory is what the gospel is intended to relay to the people—how the glory of God, namely, his steadfast love and enduring power for effecting what will be the salvation of mankind, has been made manifest in the person of Jesus who is the Christ. Paul may have come bearing this glory in his gospel, but now the Galatians have substituted a lesser, man-made glory for it: "a glory from which they will not profit." (Jeremiah 2:11) Just as the Lord himself declares that "heaven was amazed at this and was exceedingly horror-struck" (2:12) at this exchanging of the true gospel for a different one, so too Paul is "astonished' (*thaumazō*) that the Galatians are turning their back on the original gospel of glory as it has been presented to them by him in favor of a divergent one in which the crucified Christ is not foremost.

The rest of the Jeremiah passage in instructive. The prophet identifies two evils: (1) the people's forsaking of the living God, and (2) their making of "broken cisterns," containers "unable to hold water." It is hard to overestimate how important the image of water was for the inhabitants of the ancient Near East. It was the purest symbol of life itself, and its proximity and possession meant nothing less than survival. Cisterns were a necessary item for the preservation of water, and so the image employed here, that of the broken cistern, one intended to keep water (ostensibly derived from a source other than the "fountain of living water"), and failing to do that because it is broken or in some way defective, conveys the predicament of a rebellious Israel. If their cisterns are broken, then whatever water they do have ultimately will be lost, and with the loss of water comes death.

By now Paul wants his listeners to understand that they have made a terrible mistake, one that, given what is at stake, namely, salvation through their inclusion in the people of God, is neither a trifling matter nor a simple matter of ethnic preferences. To the contrary, all is now being wagered, and, in accordance with Paul's assurances, it is being won. He wants them to see that his gospel is God's own prophetic *living water*, that its content is nothing less than the Christ himself, and anything other than that is a false substitute, a defective vessel in the end unable to hold what is being offered to them in order that they might have eternal life.

The identification of Jesus with such "living water" as it is indirectly implied in this context is made explicit twice in John's gospel. The first time is when Jesus in his encounter with the Samaritan woman at Jacob's well declares (4:13-14, RSV): "Every one who drinks of this water will thirst again, but whoever drinks of the water that I shall give him will never thirst; the water that I give him will become in him a spring of water

II. The Gospel Revealed (1:6-12)

welling up to eternal life." The second comes later when Jesus at the height of the feast of Tabernacles declares to the Jews (7:37-39, RSV): "If any one thirst, let him come to me and drink. He who believes in me, as the scripture has said, 'Out of his heart shall flow rivers of living water.'" Now this he said about the Spirit, which those who believed in him were to receive; for as yet the Spirit had not been given, because Jesus was not yet glorified."

And John 7 is especially relevant comparative material for Paul's argument as it unfolds in his letter to the Galatians because the chapter's context is the contentious atmosphere prevailing in Jerusalem during this feast. It concerns the growing conflict between the possible status of Jesus as the Christ and the loyalties involved in the people's traditional observance of the Mosaic law. Prior to Jesus' "living water" declaration in 7:37-38, he had spoken to the Jews at the midpoint of the feast in terms that Paul in his own right will later come to echo (7:19-24, RSV):

> "Did not Moses give you the law? Yet none of you keeps the law. Why do you seek to kill me?" The people answered, "You have a demon! Who is seeking to kill you?" Jesus answered them, "I did one deed, and you all marvel at it. Moses gave you circumcision (not that it is from Moses, but from the fathers), and you circumcise a man upon the sabbath. If on the sabbath a man receives circumcision, so that the law of Moses may not be broken, are you angry with me because on the sabbath I made a man's whole body well? [cf. John 5:1-15] Do not judge by appearances, but judge with right judgment."

The Jews had questioned both Jesus' inexplicable knowledge of the law and his authority, and he responds to them by asking them to look beyond what they do know (the parameters of Mosaic practice) in order that they might see that God himself is at work in the very words he is teaching to them in the temple (the place of God's own presence) and in his healing works of salvation. Note the explicit contrast between the piously imperious need to make external marks on a man's body and the import of Jesus' simple assertion that "I made a man's whole body well." (7:23) Paul will return to this contrast especially in the closing portion of his letter (6:11-19). The point here is that the one is limited and temporal while the other is comprehensive and eternal, and later when Jesus does come to speak of the "living water," it is in connection with the telltale power and presence of the Holy Spirit. Paul will make very much the same kind of argument and appeal to the Galatians, and central to it is his contention that without the word, i.e. the true apostolic word, there is no Spirit.

And this brings us to what is a significant transitional verse in this early part of Paul's letter. Having pronounced *anathema* upon any man or angel who would proclaim a gospel other than what he had originally proclaimed to the Galatians, he continues in v. 10 with these words:

¹⁰ ἄρτι γὰρ ἀνθρώπους πείθω ἢ τὸν θεόν;
ἢ ζητῶ ἀνθρώποις ἀρέσκειν;
εἰ ἔτι ἀνθρώποις ἤρεσκον,
Χριστοῦ δοῦλος οὐκ ἂν ἤμην.

¹⁰ For am I now winning over men or God?
Or am I seeking to please men?
If I were still pleasing men,
I would not be a slave of the Christ.

The statement is a powerful one at this point because it pointedly raises the question about just what Paul has been doing and the incontrovertible circumstances of his having come to do it. On the one hand, to speak of "winning over men" implies a wholly worldly enterprise unworthy of God, indeed, one not rooted in him and therefore lacking divine authority. But, on the other hand, to speak of "winning over God" is an undertaking as foolish as it is impossible since there is no persuading God of anything (except in the formalist's fantasy world). And so what Paul wants the Galatians to ask themselves is that by his preaching of the gospel to them, whose bidding is

II. The Gospel Revealed (1:6-12)

Paul ultimately doing? Is he pursuing something devised by men, or do his actions derive from God's own direction? If Paul's gospel had included the need for circumcision, one could lazily argue that such a gospel with its ritual requirements would be enough to win over both men and God, that is, if such "persuasion" were just a matter of carrying out ritual requirements. But if God himself is the source of Paul's gospel, then there is no point in talking at all about "winning over" men or what even be meant by seeking to "please" them. Indeed, what Paul offers is something that has nothing at all to do with the kinds of things that are apt to please men.[2]

And that is precisely why this verse is so significant. It points in the direction that Paul will be taking for the remainder of his letter, namely, that with the events of the Pascha and his own apostolic commissioning by the risen Christ himself, Paul is ready to move beyond matters of traditional practice and cultic loyalty. All of what he writes to the Galatians is a reminder of this new eschatological situation in which they must all now obediently find their bearings. Paul insists that his gospel is the *only* means by which they will be able to position themselves in relation to the new age now dawning in their midst.

And he also wishes that there be no mistake in the mind of the Galatians about what is happening here. Paul's story is a remarkable one, necessarily bound up with the content of the gospel he preaches, and from this point on in his letter he will be emphasizing that it is above all a story of *obedience*. It is for this reason that he argues, "If I were still pleasing men, I would not be a slave of the Christ," that is, if his gospel had not come directly from God, then none of what the Galatians had seen and heard would have taken place, and there would have been *nothing new* about what would have been one more proclamation of God's power still kept within the ritual confines of the old. The point is precisely that something new has happened, that

---

[2] The language of "persuasion" is central to what Paul later contends in 5:7-12.

something anticipated in one way but yet wholly unexpected in another has taken place, and that the totally new is God's doing, the good news about a salvation that is through our faith in Jesus as the Christ. For this to be made into real salvation requires the unqualified obedience of the man previously known to the world as Saul the Pharisee, but who is now Paul the apostle, the "slave of the Christ."

Return for a moment to the passage quoted from Jeremiah 2, and recall v. 14 where the prophet says, "Is not Israel a slave or household servant?" In the Septuagint rendering of this verse, the word "slave" is the Greek *doulos*, the same word Paul employs in 1:10 when referring to himself. In ancient societies the slave's paramount virtue was selfless obedience to his master's will. Thus it is that what follows this rhetorical question in the Jeremiah text is a reminder that Israel's woes are the plain result of her disobedience, of her not being a true *doulos* where God's will is concerned. So when Paul identifies himself here as a "slave of the Christ" (*Christou doulos*), he is claiming that the substance of what he is obediently doing—the gospel that he proclaims and all of what it has required of him—is what is pleasing to God, and, by definition, not pleasing to men who by way of contrast will be filled (and therefore pleased) with their own preoccupations. If Israel *as slave* is to be obedient, then let her be obedient in the gospel as it has been delivered to her and to the world from Paul's own lips. In this way she will make for herself cisterns proper and secure, and, having done that, she will receive and keep the living water.

Paul is now ready to reassert the circumstances of his *doulos* status. In vv. 11-12 he again tells the Galatians:

¹¹ γνωρίζω γὰρ ὑμῖν, ἀδελφοί,
τὸ εὐαγγέλιον τὸ εὐαγγελισθὲν ὑπ' ἐμοῦ
ὅτι οὐκ ἔστιν κατὰ ἄνθρωπον·
¹² οὐδὲ γὰρ ἐγὼ παρὰ ἀνθρώπου παρέλαβον αὐτὸ
οὔτε ἐδιδάχθην,
ἀλλὰ δι' ἀποκαλύψεως Ἰησοῦ Χριστοῦ.

II. The Gospel Revealed (1:6-12)

> *¹¹ For I want you to know, brothers and sisters,*
> *that the gospel preached by me,*
> *it is not according to man;*
> *¹² for neither have I received it from a man*
> *nor was I taught it;*
> *rather it came by means of a revealing of Jesus the Christ himself.*

What Paul is claiming here about the origin of his gospel parallels what he has said about himself in 1:1. Just as he is an apostle "not sent from men nor even by a man, but through Jesus the Christ and God the Father," so too he declares that his gospel "is not according to man (*ouk estin kata anthrōpon*); for neither have I received it from a man (*oude gar egō para anthrōpou parelabon*), nor was I taught it (*oute edidachthēn*); rather it came by means of a revealing of Jesus the Christ himself (*alla di' apokalypseōs Iēsou Christou*)."

The key word in this passage is "revealing." It is the Greek word *apokalypsis*, from which we derive our modern English words "apocalypse" and "apocalyptic," terms routinely used in our now lurid and often unbiblical ways of describing short-term disastrous events as either constituting a lesser kind of "apocalypse" or being of a regrettably "apocalyptic" import. Things have been further clouded by the fact that in some overly casual Christian contexts the expression "apocalypse" is popularly understood as referring to a final cataclysmic confrontation between good and evil in which the greatest emphasis is placed on the physical destruction of things or even on the near annihilation of the human race. Scenarios like these often have more to do with pulp sensationalism or crude commercialism than they do with an accurate biblical understanding of such matters, but, all such misappropriation aside, the "apocalypse" category is of the highest importance in Paul's letter. The word *apokalypsis* is the substantive form of the verb *apokalyptō*, which means to reveal something that had been previously hidden and thus unknown. As such, the word *apokalypsis* denotes what is more properly understood as divine revelation, an event that, strictly speaking, never stands by itself as an objective occurrence, but rather it only ever "reveals itself" to us as a scripturally-mediated event.³

Paul is making it very clear to the Galatians that the very gospel he has preached to them is a matter of divine revelation. What he preaches is not of a mortal devising, nor did he receive it from someone else, and he rejects the idea that someone taught it to him. Paul eliminates all possibility of a human origin for what he preached to the Galatians in order that he might insist on the exclusively divine source for his proclamation. In 1:12 he writes without any hesitation: "for neither have I received it from a man nor was I taught it; rather it came by means of a revealing of Jesus the Christ himself." We can note here a grammatical ambiguity in the way we choose to read "rather it came by means of a revealing of Jesus the Christ himself." If we choose to read the noun-construct phrase "the revealing of Jesus the Christ himself" as a subjective genitive, it would indicate that Jesus directly revealed himself in what could be construed as a kind of revelatory one-on-one event. Or, if we choose to read it as an objective genitive, then it would denote a revealing of Jesus presumably done at God's direction. My translation leaves open either reading, but the objective-genitive reading is the one that the content of the letter most clearly supports.

---

[3] The Greek title of the last book of the New Testament is the ἀποκάλυψις Ἰωάννου (*Apokalypsis Iōannou*), which is suitably translated in the RSV as "The Revelation To John." Actual authorship of the book aside, the work is a compilation of apocalyptic visions and exhortations attributed to an authoritative figure in the early Christian centuries known as "John."

III. To What End Zeal? (1:13-24)

We see in Acts 9:1-19 (and twice more in 22:6-21 and 26:12-20) that the author of that book records how Paul encounters the risen Jesus on the road to Damascus, and those accounts, each one being forthrightly "apocalyptic" in content, correspond to a subjective genitive reading of 1:12. But in order for us to appreciate the proper sense of this "revealing" as intended by Paul in his letter, it will be necessary that we shift our attention away from a concern with *what has been revealed* to one that focuses on *who is revealing*.

Paul provides the relevant background for us in vv. 13-14 when he describes—consistent with what Acts recounts—how it was before he was transformed from being a determined persecutor of the faith to its most enterprising promoter:

*13 ἠκούσατε γὰρ τὴν ἐμὴν ἀναστροφήν ποτε ἐν τῷ Ἰουδαϊσμῷ,
ὅτι καθ' ὑπερβολὴν ἐδίωκον τὴν ἐκκλησίαν τοῦ θεοῦ
καὶ ἐπόρθουν αὐτήν.
14 καὶ προέκοπτον ἐν τῷ Ἰουδαϊσμῷ ὑπὲρ πολλοὺς συνηλικιώτας
ἐν τῷ γένει μου,
περισσοτέρως ζηλωτὴς ὑπάρχων τῶν πατρικῶν μου παραδόσεων.*

*13 For you have heard of my former life in Judaism,
how I was persecuting the church beyond measure
and that I was destroying her,
14 because I had advanced in Judaism beyond many of those among my own people
on account of the fact that I was so exceedingly zealous for the traditions of my fathers.*

Paul's determination to search out and to destroy the Jesus-cult was rooted in his Pharisee heritage. In the wake of the Babylonian exile in the sixth century B.C. the Jews had set about rebuilding Jerusalem. Jewish society experienced a great deal of conflict and upheaval as the Jews fought against invading enemies and then among themselves. Beginning in the fourth century B.C. Hellenistic culture made great inroads in those areas of the ancient Near East conquered by Alexander the Great. The re-established Jewish rump-state centered around Jerusalem was not immune to these influences, and the second-century B.C. Maccabean revolt (in effect a Jewish civil war over the issue of Hellenism) is linked to the emergence of a new social class among the Jews. This was the Pharisee class—those Jews who were concerned to preserve not only the Mosaic law as the authoritative foundation for Jewish life but also the oral tradition of interpretation and application that was growing up around it.

In the Greek text of the New Testament the Pharisees are called the *Pharisaioi*, a rendering of the original Hebrew designation *perūshīm*, a word derived in turn from the Semitic verbal root (ph-r-sh), which means "to separate" or "to divide" and which was never employed by the Pharisees themselves as a self-referential term. Other groups in Jewish society (Hellenized Jews, the Hasmoneans, and later the Herodian class, the Sadducees) used it as a label for those Jews who, because of their comparatively zealous dedication to the law, were the ones who had *set themselves apart* for the continuous study of the law and for ongoing meditation and discussion concerning its realization in daily life. Even though it was a legalistic tradition, it was at the same time a dynamically legalistic one that would eventually become the basis for what we know as rabbinic Judaism.

At the center of the Pharisee worldview was the most ardent belief that the entire content and purpose of Jewish life was contained in the Mosaic law. The first five books of the Old Testament (the so-called Pentateuch consisting of Genesis through Deuteronomy) contain the bulk of this "law" (known as the Torah in the Hebrew tradition), but we must keep in mind that what the first-century A.D. Jew understood as "law" went far beyond the lists of commandments and legal prescriptions contained as these are in some portions of the Pentateuch. The Jewish "law" also included the scriptural recounting of Israel's history from the creation of the world, through the Exodus, and

III. To What End Zeal? (1:13-24)

narratively going up to the point where the Israelites are poised to enter Canaan. Thomas L. Thompson summarizes the scriptural process at work in the emergence of the Old Testament in this fashion:

> Those who collected and wrote the Bible, wrote about being human. They wrote their philosophy in competing stories, in the form of divine laws, and in songs and moral poems sung by the old kings, priests, and prophets of history and legend. Like the knowledge condensed in old folk sayings, placed in the mouth of the wise king and teacher of the distant past, origin stories used the concept of the past on the principle that one is what one has been. To describe what one has been is to describe one's self-understanding. *The story told is instruction.*[1] (italics added)

The Hebrew word *tôrāh* is then, first etymologically and then quite literally, the instructional narrative concerning ancient Israel, the scripturally amalgamated story it told about itself: part cosmogony, part history, part codification, part idealization. Thus it would be wrong to view the Torah as a compendium of ancient Western Semitic hyper-legal minutiae: rather it is an affirmation of God's kingship over his creation.

The Pharisaic system was a rigorous mining of that story. It was an interpretive body of belief culminatng in the eschatological "day of the Lord," that time in the future when all men would be resurrected to face judgment before the throne of God. The only basis for the Jewish people's salvation—for their being declared *righteous* in the eyes of God—was through their obedience to the law. This is a vitally important point (to which we shall return later), but, for our present purpose, it is important to grasp that, for the Pharisee, salvation was seen as depending *entirely* on a personal obedience to the Mosaic law that must flourish and deepen without addition or dilution.

---

[1] Thomas L. Thompson, *The Mythic Past: Biblical Archaeology and the Myth of Israel* (London: Basic Books, 1999), 92-93.

Hence it was that the beliefs of the first Christians were *anathema* to Saul the Pharisee: the former were Jews who were no longer speaking of salvation in the unambiguous terms of obedience to the law; rather they were believing that it had to do with faith in the lordship of a crucified criminal, one Jesus of Nazareth, whom they proclaimed as having been resurrected from the dead. As we shall see, the Christian proclamation of Jesus' resurrection from the dead was in itself a highly objectionable one where the Pharisees' own eschatological views were concerned, and, just as Paul here claims that he was "so exceedingly zealous for the traditions of [his] fathers," he watched in dismay as the aberrant sect started to grow and he at once set about to eradicate this new and inexcusable error that had come upon the scene. Thus he set about "persecuting the church beyond measure [and] destroying her."

But everything changed with the "revelation" to the Pharisee Saul. And, whether we understand what Paul writes in vv. 15-17 in the light of the account given in Acts 9 or not, it is not directly material to the apostolic claims he continues making:

¹⁵ ὅτε δὲ εὐδόκησεν ὁ θεὸς
ὁ ἀφορίσας με ἐκ κοιλίας μητρός μου
καὶ καλέσας διὰ τῆς χάριτος αὐτοῦ
¹⁶ ἀποκαλύψαι τὸν υἱὸν αὐτοῦ ἐν ἐμοί,
ἵνα εὐαγγελίζωμαι αὐτὸν ἐν τοῖς ἔθνεσιν,
εὐθέως οὐ προσανεθέμην σαρκὶ καὶ αἵματι
¹⁷ οὐδὲ ἀνῆλθον εἰς Ἱεροσόλυμα πρὸς τοὺς πρὸ ἐμοῦ ἀποστόλους,
ἀλλ᾽ ἀπῆλθον εἰς Ἀραβίαν
καὶ πάλιν ὑπέστρεψα εἰς Δαμασκόν.

¹⁵ But when it pleased God,
he who set me apart before I was born,
and who called me by means of his grace,
¹⁶ to reveal his Son through me,
so that I might preach him among the nations,
I did not directly confer with flesh and blood,
¹⁷ nor did I go up to Jerusalem to the ones who were apostles before me,
rather I went away into Arabia,

III. To What End Zeal? (1:13-24)

and again I returned to Damascus.

Here Paul interprets. He assigns meaning to an event whose reality he was in no position to deny because the central feature of what had happened to him—the content of the "revelation to him"—he has no choice but to move it to the foreground of his appeal to the Galatians. No one was more aware of the stupendous ironies involved in his situation than Paul himself. As a trained Pharisee, a man raised in the ways of the "strictest party of our religion" (Acts 26:5, RSV), he knew what it meant for God to act and to act often in ways completely at odds with human understanding: even when it was a matter of seeming reversal, the point would always be one of continuity.

It would be superficial at this point to approach the circumstances of Paul's "conversion" as being a matter of Paul simply moving beyond the seemingly limited perspective of his Pharisaic adherence to the law and his prioritizing of obedience to it in order that he might come to embrace the greater relative "freedom" of an unadorned faith in Jesus as the redeemer of mankind: that would be a case of placing the cart before the horse. We should focus instead on what Paul is actually saying here. Immediately before this he has briefly described his determined efforts to stamp out the Jesus-cult, an undertaking he viewed as reflecting the highest order of obedience to the will of God. But now God has *directly intervened* in Paul's life, and, when he says in vv. 15-16b, "when it pleased God, he who set me apart before I was born, and who called me by means of his grace, to reveal his Son through me, so that I might preach him among the nations," he is drawing his listeners' attention to the profoundest of things. I would suggest that there is more to be gained in our understanding of Paul's intentions in this passage if we keep our focus on *revelation* rather than on *conversion*.

Now, when we think in terms of the latter, there is a tendency for us to stress the element of discontinuity. Once again, rather than it being just a matter of movement from a backward-looking Pharisaism to the opening up of a wholly new and unencumbered relationship with God through faith in his Son, Paul is concerned to show us that the one thing constant in his life both and after his experience on the road to Damascus is God himself. We are apt to approach the narrative drama in Acts 9 in conversion-psychology terms, as a simple before/after dichotomy that, in Paul's own thoroughly remarkable case, only suffices to illuminate half of what is taking place. When Paul speaks of God setting him apart before he was born, he wants the Galatians to see that there is a perfect continuity at work in what has happened to him, that it was not simply a matter of him "seeing the light" (both literally and figuratively) and therefore embarking upon an entirely new course of action, but rather his is a narrative that emphasizes how God's righteous will is always in motion. If God had set him apart from birth for the preaching he now undertakes "among the nations," it was a path that also would have had to include his preparation by the law and the zealousness of mind he displayed as a Pharisee. God had called him "by means of his grace, to reveal his Son through me," and the circumstance of that calling was the Lord's own direct revelation to Paul. It is not for nothing that Paul is here writing about God having called him "by means of his grace" (*dia tēs charitos autou*), a phrase that clues us in on this aspect of direct revelation. There was ample scriptural precedent for such an account as Paul is offering here. Much as God had commissioned Moses to be his instrument for leading the Israelites out of Egypt by revealing himself in the form of a burning bush (Exodus 3), so too Paul becomes a man who must now live in the aftermath of such a literally "apocalyptic" encounter and seek to do justice both to what it was and what it is going to mean.

Something of the immensity of this is suggested by the phrase "to reveal his Son through me." There is the enduring purpose of God's will in the fact that this unrelenting Pharisee, so seemingly dedicated to exterior matters of obedience and ritual observance, should now in his interior self come face to face with the Lord in a blaze of blinding light and be called upon by

III. To What End Zeal? (1:13-24)

name. All of this took place in the way that it did so that God might "reveal his Son through me," and it is the prepositional phrase "through me" that underscores the ultimate meaning of this revelational encounter and Paul's purpose in relating it again to the Galatians. The phrase is sometimes translated "to me" or even "in me" (the latter being the most literal way of translating the Greek prepositional phrase *en emoi*). But the latter are renderings that, while acceptable in some ways, do not fully communicate the singularity of the encounter that Paul is seeking to emphasize: namely, that if God truly has revealed his Son "through me," then, with no diminishment of its unmistakable reality and with a full accounting of the fact that *it shall proceed via Paul's own person*, it has all taken place "so that I might preach him among the nations." There is a directly causative linkage at work in the way that Paul has constructed this passage. He declares this circuitous working of God's will as being for the purpose of turning a zealous persecutor of the Church into the *apostolos* who has delivered the gospel to the Galatians for their salvation. Thus, all of what took place before Paul arrived among the Galatians was expressly *so that* he might preach the Christ among the nations. The directness of Paul's apostolic commissioning is elaborated in Acts 9:3-9 (RSV) when the author of that work recounts:

> Now as he [Paul] journeyed he approached Damascus, and suddenly a light from heaven flashed about him. And he fell to the ground and heard a voice saying to him, "Saul, Saul, why do you persecute me?" And he said, "Who are you, Lord?" And he said, "I am Jesus, whom you are persecuting; but rise and enter the city, *and you will be told what you are to do*." The men who were traveling with him stood speechless, hearing the voice but seeing no one. Saul arose from the ground; and when his eyes were opened, he could see nothing; so they led him by the hand and brought him into Damascus. And for three days he was without sight, and neither ate nor drank. (italics added)

Verse 6b contains the directive "and you will be told what you are to do" (*kai lalēthēsetai soi ho ti se dei poiein*), an indication of

God's purposefulness where Paul is concerned. The account of his assignment continues in 9:13-19a (RSV) when God sends the initially reluctant Damascene disciple Ananias to complete his commissioning of the blinded Saul the Pharisee:

> But Ananias answered, "Lord, I have heard from many about this man, how much evil he has done to thy saints at Jerusalem; and here he has authority from the chief priests to bind all who call upon thy name." *But the Lord said to him, "Go, for he is a chosen instrument of mine to carry my name before the Gentiles and kings and the sons of Israel; for I will show him how much he must suffer for the sake of my name."* So Ananias departed and entered the house. And laying his hands on him he said, "Brother Saul, the Lord Jesus who appeared to you on the road by which you came, has sent me that you may regain your sight and be filled with the Holy Spirit." And immediately something like scales fell from his eyes and he regained his sight. Then he rose and was baptized, and he took food and was strengthened.

Acts 9:15-16 (the italicized portion above) provides a threefold description of this commissioning. First, there is the scriptural declaration that God considers Paul to be "a chosen vessel of mine" (*skeuos eklogēs estin moi houtos*). Second, there is the stipulation that Paul's apostleship will be for the express purpose of "carrying my name before the Gentiles and kings and sons of Israel." The designation "my name" (*to onoma mou*) is a standard scriptural trope for referring to the will of God, the content of his commandments, and the obedience he requires of those who hear them. Paul's preaching of Jesus as the Christ both in this context and in the whole of his Galatian letter belongs to his making known the name of God "before the Gentiles and kings and sons of Israel." The sequence of Gentiles-kings-sons of Israel is intentional on the part of the author of the book of Acts in that it constitutes a summary of the Pauline mission as the apostle himself more comprehensively treats it in his letter to the Romans. And third, God declares that "for I will show him much he must suffer for the sake of my name" (*egō gar hypodeixō autō hosa dei auton hyper tou onomatos mou pathein*), a passage that

III. To What End Zeal? (1:13-24)

poignantly relates to the closing of Paul's letter to the Galatians when he writes of how he "bears the marks of Jesus on my own body." (6:17)

In order to make the singularity of his revelatory experience even more apparent, Paul continues his account in vv. 16c-17 by writing that in the wake of this revelation to him: "I did not confer with flesh and blood, nor did I go up to Jerusalem to the ones who were apostles before me; rather I went away into Arabia and again I returned to Damascus." This sequence of events corresponds to his earlier claim in vv. 11-12: "For I want you to know, brothers and sisters, that the gospel preached by me, it is not according to man; for neither have I received it from man nor was I taught it; rather it came by means of a revealing of Jesus the Christ himself." There has been much speculation about just what Paul did when he "went away into Arabia," but the most probable answer is that when he slipped away into those territories anywhere to the east of Damascus (the term "Arabia" applies to them), he did what God had commissioned him to do, namely, to preach the gospel of the crucified Christ.

Now just when this Arabian "mission" took place in relation to the narrative provided in Acts 9 or even how long it lasted is not completely certain. It could have happened after Paul had regained his strength and was able to move about on his own (Acts 9:19ff.), or else it could have taken place after his escape from Damascus when he became the target of an assassination plot (9:25ff.). But, given the account that Paul is shaping for the Galatians, the more likely time of occurrence is right after Paul has recovered and before he begins appearing in the local synagogues as recounted in 9:20. Another textual indication in support of the latter reading is Paul's use in v. 16c of the conjunctive adverb *eutheōs*. It is a part of speech usually translated as "immediately" or "right away," but here it is translated as "directly." It is a regularly used feature in New Testament narratives and denotes one thing that happens in close succession to another. Its appearance in this passage only highlights the fact that Paul did not linger in the city after his recovery and that he made his way into the regions east of Damascus. In addition, the fact that Paul writes in 1:17c that "again I returned to Damascus" after his being in Arabia makes it unlikely that he would have returned very soon to a city from which he previously had been forced to flee for his life.[2]

Alternatively, he very well would have done what a Pharisee does best, namely, he would have re-read scripture and done that with reference to what had happened to him. This must be balanced with the frequency (beginning with Acts 9:20) with which the author of the Acts of the Apostles refers to Paul as going to the synagogues and proclaiming Jesus as the Christ. It is not critical that Acts does not explicitly mention any Arabian missionary phase, but, assuming that Paul did just that, in still dutiful Pharisaic fashion he would have taken with him his scrolls and scrutinized once more their accounts of creation, salvation, and prophecy. Thus he "read" Jesus in the light of scripture and saw him as God's own *Christos*, his anointed and suffering servant.

Thus the unit 1:15-17 may not be about a physical itinerary *per se*. The emphasis is on how the Christ was revealed to Paul, how that constituted his commissioning to preach the gospel, and how that had nothing at all to do with the mother church in Jerusalem. Acts 9:1-30 is the principal scriptural detailing of that direct revelation and its circumstances, and the geographic focus throughout the passage is entirely on the city of Damascus.[3] Paul

---

[2] It is not ultimately imperative that the two scriptural accounts (Galatians and Acts) be reconciled with regard to their respective details. At this point in Paul's letter he is emphasizing both the direct origins and the immediacy of his apostolic activity, while the purpose of Acts is to place his activities in a perhaps broader but by no means *different* context. What Acts 9:23-25 details about the Jewish-led plot to kill him in Damascus, though it dovetails in part with what Paul writes in 2 Corinthians 11:30-33, should not vex any person who hears scripture given that Paul encountered and survived many dangers during his apostolic career.

[3] Likewise in the two parallel accounts in Acts 22 and 26. The "visions and revelations of the Lord" (*optasias kai apokalypseis kyriou*) that Paul recounts in 2 Corinthians 12:1-4

III. To What End Zeal? (1:13-24)

writes that he consulted with no other person, that he did not "go up to Jerusalem to the ones who were apostles before me," and instead "I went away into Arabia." Given the way that later in chapter four he will identify Arabia as the locale of Mount Sinai (4:24-25), as the place where the enslaving covenant that he "allegorically" links with the figure of Hagar originated, we can read Arabia, not as a geographic reference, but as a symbol for Torah-based Judaism. If so, when Paul "went away into Arabia," it was to re-examine the Torah in the light of God's revelation in the Christ. Look at the way 1:17 ends after Paul tells of having gone into Arabia: "and again I returned to Damascus." In other words, Paul looked once more at the scriptural world of the Torah (represented by going off to Arabia), and *only then* did he return to Damascus, to the site of God's initial revelation and command to preach the gospel.

Although Paul wishes to highlight the unique circumstances of his own particular history and his calling to apostleship, he is at the same time concerned to show that he is no renegade and that he stands in a firm and quite certain relationship with those who had personal acquaintance with Jesus. His account is crafted to communicate the fact of his first meeting with the Jerusalem apostles, and it contains no detail beyond what Paul wants to reassert to the now possibly doubtful Galatians, namely, that from this point on in his apostolic service he will be intimately and forcefully connected with the very source of apostolic authority itself. In vv. 18-20 he writes:

^{18} ἔπειτα μετὰ ἔτη τρία ἀνῆλθον εἰς Ἱεροσόλυμα ἱστορῆσαι Κηφᾶν
καὶ ἐπέμεινα πρὸς αὐτὸν ἡμέρας δεκαπέντε,
^{19} ἕτερον δὲ τῶν ἀποστόλων οὐκ εἶδον
εἰ μὴ Ἰάκωβον τὸν ἀδελφὸν τοῦ κυρίου.
^{20} ἃ δὲ γράφω ὑμῖν,
ἰδοὺ ἐνώπιον τοῦ θεοῦ ὅτι οὐ ψεύδομαι.

---

immediately follow in that text what he says in passing of the King Aretas-connected plot to assassinate him in Damascus. The sequence of events found in 2 Corinthians 10-12 represents a reverse-order telling when compared with what Acts relates.

> *18 Then after three years I went up to Jerusalem to visit Kephas
> and I stayed with him fifteen days,
> 19 but I saw no other apostles
> except for James, the brother of the Lord.
> 20 As for the things of which I am writing to you,
> behold, as God is my witness, I am not lying.*

Kephas is a Greek rendering of Simon Peter's Aramaic name. The Aramaic word *kīpha'* means "rock." In Matthew 16:18 (RSV) Jesus declares to the confessing disciple Simon, "And I tell you, you are Peter (*Petros*), and on this rock (*petra*) I will build my church, and the powers of death shall not prevail against it." The Greek word for "rock" is *petra*, and, while the Hellenized form "Kephas" retains the phonological flavor of the original Aramaic name, it is of no use when the Greek text of Matthew 16:18 makes its punning point. James is "the brother of the Lord," a male relative of undetermined order (possibly a cousin) who according to tradition became the first bishop of Jerusalem. Paul names these two men and here declares his having had this contact with them in order to make it clear that he was not on his own and working in a potentially renegade fashion outside the orbit of legitimate Christian missionary work.

His appeal for credibility here is a bold one. He establishes a few basic facts: that he encountered the risen Christ, that no man taught him the gospel (a claim that does not preclude his clarifying and perfecting through fellowship with other believers what was an original instance of revelation), that he went to Jerusalem, and that he met with Peter and James, but now he assures the Galatians that "the things of which I am writing to you, behold, as God is my witness, I am not lying." This means that, very much like the gospel itself, no other person can (or need!) vouch either for the meaning or for the validity of what Paul is claiming. The only reliable "witness" is God himself, and Paul is swearing an oath of truthfulness "in the presence of God," which is what the phrase translated here "as God is my witness" (*enōpion tou theou*) means when it is rendered literally. It

III. To What End Zeal? (1:13-24)

is thus a declarative act far more serious and personally binding than what we often manage today.

Paul continues his account in vv. 21-24, relating what must have been an accurate description of what would have happened to him in the Judean region given that the majority of those living in Palestine at that time would have remembered him only as the indefatigable persecutor of the believers in Jesus as the Christ.

> ^{21} ἔπειτα ἦλθον εἰς τὰ κλίματα τῆς Συρίας καὶ Κιλικίας·
> ^{22} ἤμην δὲ ἀγνοούμενος τῷ προσώπῳ ταῖς ἐκκλησίαις τῆς Ἰουδαίας ταῖς ἐν Χριστῷ.
> ^{23} μόνον δὲ ἀκούοντες ἦσαν ὅτι ὁ διώκων ἡμᾶς ποτε νῦν εὐαγγελίζεται τὴν πίστιν
> ἥν ποτε ἐπόρθει,
> ^{24} καὶ ἐδόξαζον ἐν ἐμοὶ τὸν θεόν.

> ^{21} *Then I went into the regions of Syria and Cilicia;*
> ^{22} *but as my face was unknown to the churches of Judea that were in the Christ,*
> ^{23} *they only heard that, "He who persecuted us is now preaching the very faith that he at one time was destroying,"*
> ^{24} *and so it was that through me they were giving glory to God.*

The passage helps to reiterate that Paul undoubtedly regarded (as far as the Galatians are concerned) his own story as *the* most noteworthy and continuously unfolding example of God's power, purpose, and mercy. It is also rhetorically linked to what Paul said in vv. 15-16b, "But when it pleased God, he who had set me apart before I was born, and who called me by means of his grace, to reveal his Son *though me*," because the final phrase of that passage "through me" is repeated in v. 24 in connection with first the fear but then the astonished thanksgiving that overtakes those who made up "the churches of Judea that were in the Christ" because the persecutor had become the preacher: "so it was that *through me* they were giving God the glory." In both cases the phrase is the Greek *en emoi*, and each passage serves to illustrate how God's majestic power is able to make use of sometimes the most unlikely persons and more often completely contradictory circumstances in order to make his ways manifest.

IV. Going Up to Jerusalem (2:1-10)

Although v. 24 marks the end of the first chapter according to the traditional Western division of the text, there is no real break in the narrative as Paul is building it. In fact there is a certain parallelism at work in what follows at the beginning of the second chapter. As we shall see, the portion of Paul's letter consisting of 1:11-2:10 forms a distinctive narrative unit of two parts that is a necessary transition from what preceded it in 1:1-10 (when Paul confronts the Galatians with their defection from the gospel they had received from him), and which sets the stage for the pivotal material that follows it in 2:11ff. This parallelism does not become apparent until Paul continues the account of his dealings with the apostolic leadership in Jerusalem in 2:1-2:

*¹ ἔπειτα διὰ δεκατεσσάρων ἐτῶν πάλιν ἀνέβην εἰς Ἱεροσόλυμα
μετὰ Βαρναβᾶ
συμπαραλαβὼν καὶ Τίτον·
² ἀνέβην δὲ κατὰ ἀποκάλυψιν·
καὶ ἀνεθέμην αὐτοῖς τὸ εὐαγγέλιον ὃ κηρύσσω ἐν τοῖς ἔθνεσιν,
κατ' ἰδίαν δὲ τοῖς δοκοῦσιν,
μή πως εἰς κενὸν τρέχω ἢ ἔδραμον.*

*¹ Then after fourteen years I went up again to Jerusalem with Barnabas
and I took along Titus,
² for I had gone up in accordance with the revelation;
and I laid before them the gospel that I am preaching among the nations,
but privately to those who were of reputation,
lest in any way I should be running or had run in vain.*

The key portion occurs in 2:2a, "for I had gone up in accordance with the revelation." Paul is now referring to a second visit he made to Jerusalem, one that takes place ostensibly so that Paul could cement his ties with the Jerusalem authorities and thus establish beyond any doubt his own apostolic credentials, but what Paul will describe in 2:1-10 is directly connected with the preceding material in 1:11-24. The clue to this connection comes with the phrase "in accordance with the revelation."

Paul writes about going up to Jerusalem again, only this time he explicitly mentions that he did not go unaccompanied (as 1:18-19 would indicate). He takes with him the Jewish co-evangelist Barnabas and his "Greek" colleague Titus. Their inclusion here is not without significance, and the pairing of Barnabas and Titus must be seen in relation to the gospel that Paul himself is proclaiming. Barnabas is a Hellenized Jew from Cyprus and of Levite lineage. He makes his first scriptural appearance in Acts 4:36-37 (RSV) when the early Christian community in Jerusalem was attracting converts and contributions: "Thus Joseph who was surnamed by the apostles Barnabas (which means, Son of encouragement), a Levite, a native of Cyprus, sold a field which belonged to him, and brought the money and laid it at the apostles' feet." In this context the figure of Barnabas represents the Jewish potentiality of Paul's gospel—that it is a message intended "first and foremost" for the Jews but which at the same time is not one intended exclusively for them. Titus is an uncircumcised Greek and a pagan convert to the faith, the kind of believer who naturally represents the gospel's possibilities "among the nations."

Paul is going up to Jerusalem a second time and in the company of these two men who represent the gospel's living potentiality both among the Jews and the non-Jews, but the direct reason for Paul's visit is given in the phrase "in accordance with the revelation." It is this phrase that allows us to see how 1:11-2:10 forms a unit with two parts. Within this unit the word "revelation" (*apokalypsis*) first occurs in 1:12 when Paul uses it in connection with, what is by his own reckoning, the simultaneous origin of his gospel and his becoming an apostle: "for neither have I received it [the gospel] from man nor was I taught it; rather it came by means of a revealing of Jesus the Christ himself." There Paul used the prepositional phrase "by means of a revealing" (*di' apokalypseōs*) in order to indicate the distinctively divine origin of his gospel/apostleship, and now in the second part Paul again resorts to the word "revealing" in 2:2a (*apokalypsis*

III. To What End Zeal? (1:13-24)

in both instances) because he is telling the Galatians that his decision to go to Jerusalem a second time was completely in line with the original "revealing" of 1:12.

Here the telling detail is the prepositional phrase "in accordance with the revelation" (*kata apokalypsin*). Paul is informing the Galatians that his making of this trip to Jerusalem and its results are in accordance with God's own will and prompting, and the indication that this dynamic is at work is the sentence structure in 2:1-2. When Paul writes "...I went up again to Jerusalem with Barnabas and I took along Titus, and I went up in accordance with the revelation," he is not necessarily drawing attention to any specific occurrence of some vision or noetic communication in which God specifically directs him to go to Jerusalem at that time. Acts contains plenty of such episodes in which Paul experiences just this kind of thing, and so a similar event in this instance cannot be ruled out completely. It is necessary for Paul that the Galatians see this second trip to Jerusalem completely in the light of the original "revealing," namely, that this second journey is in the most complete accord with Acts 9 and that it represents in its own way a development perfectly consistent with what Paul experienced on the road to Damascus. The Galatians needed to see that, as far as divine direction is concerned, this trip to Jerusalem was on the same footing as the risen Christ's visionary revealing of himself to Paul.

Paul's use of *apokalypsis* in 2:2a is what ties the section comprising 2:1-10 to the preceding portion of his letter, and it also provides us with some clue, I think, into Paul's own religious psychology. Far from representing the kind of self-seeking, idiosyncratic, or even autocratic outlook that is sometimes attributed to him, Paul's insistence that God is directly involved in every step of his apostolic activity would have been a typical assumption for a first-century A.D. Jew to have and especially for one of Pharisee persuasion. While the immediacy and assuredness of Paul's convictions in this regard are on display in all of his letters, he was as practically minded as the next fellow. Thus he knew that he could not avoid contact with the apostolic authorities in Jerusalem and that there had to be an official sanctioning of what he was preaching "among the nations, but privately to those who were of reputation, lest in any way I should be running or had run in vain."

Paul must have been under no illusions about what awaited him in Jerusalem, that there he would come face to face with fellow believers who were as interested (if not more so) in Jewish ritual purity as they were in the cross, and that such attitudes constituted in his eyes a fundamental misunderstanding of the gospel message. But even when seen in this light, his second trip to Jerusalem was not a strictly confrontational venture on Paul's part because more deeply he wanted its outcome to serve as a legitimation of those more essential features of the gospel which he felt were being threatened by what he considered to be the superficial concerns of his opponents. It would seem that Paul held his ground simply by keeping to gospel basics, a position that did not force any of the issues that were now very much on Paul's mind when writing his letter to the Galatians. He must have known that he would be closely watched, that there were those who would have liked to draw him out publicly about matters having to do with Jewish ritual observance and possibly even to engage him in disputes about just what was expected of any believer in the resurrected Jesus. But Paul, on his guard and knowing what he was potentially facing, knew that his appearance in Jerusalem was neither the time nor the place for such a contest, and that, for the time being, there were bigger fish to fry. His own astute but straightforward account of things in 2:3-5 lets us know that, relatively speaking, things must have turned out well enough for him:

^{3} ἀλλ᾽ οὐδὲ Τίτος ὁ σὺν ἐμοί,
Ἕλλην ὤν, ἠναγκάσθη περιτμηθῆναι·
^{4} διὰ δὲ τοὺς παρεισάκτους ψευδαδέλφους,
οἵτινες παρεισῆλθον κατασκοπῆσαι τὴν ἐλευθερίαν ἡμῶν ἣν ἔχομεν ἐν Χριστῷ Ἰησοῦ,

III. To What End Zeal? (1:13-24)

ἵνα ἡμᾶς καταδουλώσουσιν,
⁵ οἷς οὐδὲ πρὸς ὥραν εἴξαμεν τῇ ὑποταγῇ,
ἵνα ἡ ἀλήθεια τοῦ εὐαγγελίου διαμείνῃ πρὸς ὑμᾶς.

³ Yet not even Titus who was with me,
who was a Greek,
was compelled to be circumcised.
⁴ I say this on account of those false brothers in the faith
who had come in secretly,
the ones who came in to spy out our freedom that we have in the Christ Jesus
so that they might bring us back into slavery;
⁵ but not for a moment did we submit to them in obedience
all in order that the truth of the gospel might be preserved for you.

I think that what Paul says here is some indication of the relatively fluid situation that must have prevailed in those early decades of the faith, that the whole question of whether Jewish ritual practices were incumbent on believers was something that witnessed a good deal of variation. In short, matters were by no means firmly established in either direction, but, as Paul testifies here, exerting pressure in one way or another must have been common enough.

Rhetorically, the passage is fascinating because of the language Paul uses here. Those who were interested in the prospect of an uncircumcised ex-pagan like Titus receiving the Mosaic mark on his body are described as "false brothers in the faith" (*pseudadelphoi*, literally "lying brothers"). Paul makes it clear that, if these fellows who are so insistent on complying with ritual prescription had had their way, Titus would have been duly circumcised, but such was not the case. A stronger and more compelling sense of Christian fellowship must have prevailed during the visit, and so in what was its own kind of mixed company it would have been uncomfortably divisive for any person to insist upon the immediate necessity of such a thing. Paul baldly states the agenda of these "false brothers," namely, that they circulated in the fraternal ranks as "spies" in relation to the relative freedom (*eleutheria*) that Paul and his colleagues (and perhaps even others in Jerusalem as well) enjoyed by virtue of their being faithful followers of the Christ. The setting of the Christian community masked in part the deception in which these "false brothers" were engaged because their ultimate (and thus true) goal was to take away that "freedom" of which Paul speaks—to undo it—and to do this by bringing them back into a state of slavery (expressed here by the Greek verb *katadouloō*), by making men in effect *even more* superficially obligated to the law than ever before.

Paul apparently stood his ground. We do not know exactly how he managed to do this or even how delicately (we cannot rule out the possibility that Paul made his case cogently enough in the presence of the circumcisers such that Titus remained uncircumcised), but he never the less writes to the Galatians that in this instance there was no submission on his part to the wishes of those who preferred that these matters having to do with traditional Jewish law should be observed. He is stating that if there was any kind of purity to be guarded here, it was the purity of the gospel itself. The passage fully implies that it was through his own unstinting dedication to "the truth of the gospel" in the face of pressure to adulterate it with ritualizing observances that the Galatians were later able to receive it from him pure and undefiled. Paul is supremely confident about the purity of the gospel he preaches, that, because of what it contains, his message of salvation through belief in Jesus as the Christ stands in no need of addition, interpolation, or, as he most boldly makes clear in 2:6-10, any form of personal connection in order to make it legitimate:

⁶ἀπὸ δὲ τῶν δοκούντων εἶναί τι,
- ὁποῖοί ἐστε ἦσαν οὐδέν μοι διαφέρει·
πρόσωπον ὁ θεὸς ἀνθρώπου οὐ λαμβάνει -
ἐμοὶ γὰρ οἱ δοκοῦντες οὐδὲν προσανέθεντο,
⁷ἀλλὰ τοὐναντίον ἰδόντες ὅτι πεπίστευμαι τὸ εὐαγγέλιον τῆς ἀκροβυστίας
καθὼς Πέτρος τῆς περιτομῆς,
⁸ὁ γὰρ ἐνεργήσας Πέτρῳ εἰς ἀποστολὴν τῆς περιτομῆς
ἐνήργησεν καὶ ἐμοὶ εἰς τὰ ἔθνη,

III. To What End Zeal? (1:13-24)

*⁹καὶ γνόντες τὴν χάριν τὴν δοθεῖσάν μοι,
Ἰάκωβος καὶ Κηφᾶς καὶ Ἰωάννης,
οἱ δοκοῦντες στῦλοι εἶναι,
δεξιὰς ἔδωκαν ἐμοὶ καὶ Βαρναβᾷ κοινωνίας,
ἵνα ἡμεῖς εἰς τὰ ἔθνη,
αὐτοὶ δὲ εἰς τὴν περιτομήν·
¹⁰μόνον τῶν πτωχῶν ἵνα μνημονεύωμεν,
ὃ καὶ ἐσπούδασα αὐτὸ τοῦτο ποιῆσαι.*

*⁶And from the ones who were reputed to be something,
and what they were is of no consequence to me—
God does not go by appearances—
these men who were of repute added nothing to me;
⁷ but, to the contrary, when they saw that the gospel for the uncircumcised had fallen to me,
just as the gospel for the circumcised had fallen to Peter,
⁸ for he who was working through Peter for the mission to the circumcised
was also working through me for the mission to the nations,
⁹ and when they came to know the grace given to me,
James and Kephas and John,
the ones who were reputed to be pillars,
they gave to me and Barnabas the right hand of fellowship,
in order that we might go to the nations
and they to the circumcised;
¹⁰ the only condition being that we might remember the poor,
and that very thing I was eager to do.*

The thing to notice about this passage is not that "the right hand of friendship" given by James, Peter, and John to Paul and Barnabas is the official legitimation Paul was seeking and ultimately needed: that would be to miss the entire point of what Paul is saying. He makes it clear in 2:6 that, once more, what ultimately counts is not human approbation but the acceptance that comes from God when he is properly obeyed. On the one hand, Paul is in no position to question the automatic status attributable to "the ones who were apostles before me"; but, on the other hand, he makes it clear that "these men who were of repute added nothing to me." This means that Paul's gospel was in his eyes the true and essential one, complete in all respects and in need of nothing that would potentially make it more complete (and again the implication for the Galatians here is that it is precisely *this* gospel they have received). This implication on Paul's part is corroborated in the text by the re-appearance here of the verb *prosanatithēmi* in 2:6. It occurred earlier in 1:16 when he was detailing the fullness of the gospel message entrusted to him:

> *15 But when it pleased God,*
> *he who set me apart before I was born,*
> *and who called me by means of his grace,*
> *16 to reveal his Son through me,*
> *so that I might preach him among the nations,*
> *I did not confer* (prosanethemēn) *with flesh and blood,*
> *17 nor did I go up to Jerusalem to the ones who were apostles before me,*
> *rather I went away into Arabia*
> *and again I returned to Damascus.*

In 2:6 we hear a parallel assertion about this same fullness of the Pauline gospel when he writes, "these men who were of repute added nothing (*ouden prosanethento*) to me." The "me" language in 2:6 should be read as an indirect reference to the gospel that Paul preached to the Galatians, a turn of phrase on his part that once more allows us to see the coincidence of Paul's person with the message that he proclaimed. Thus, what the Galatians heard from Paul was *the* gospel message, divinely commissioned and choate in every respect.

While the first Christians had some leeway when it came to the adoption of Jewish customs, as we shall see, to push such considerations to the foreground and in effect make them essential to salvation was to play a potentially dangerous game of distortion where the truth and integrity of the gospel were concerned. Paul is making his claim that there is one basic gospel, the essential message of salvation on which these men in their Jerusalem meetings could agree and in relation to which all other considerations would be of a strictly secondary nature.

When Paul speaks of there being two "missions"—one to the circumcised and one to the uncircumcised "nations"—it would

III. To What End Zeal? (1:13-24)

be wrong to infer from this passage that there were in effect two "versions" of the gospel: one tailored to appeal to Jewish audiences by making acceptance of the gospel directly dependent on the formal and quite deliberate inclusion of traditional Jewish practices, and another in which this approach was consciously avoided. There is some evangelistic practicality involved in what Paul says, but, as he makes it clear, it is one that has resulted as much from God's own direction as it has from consideration of what might constitute the most beneficial kinds of respective missionary "turf." Precisely because Paul is a *diaspora* Jew, this means that he is ideally suited for making his way among the nations, that he would be able to make his own proper appeal for the gospel. He would achieve this, not by sanitizing it of its inherently Jewish elements for the sake of greater acceptance among pagan audiences, but by his being able to transpose the gospel's own undeniable rootedness in Jewish scripture (cf. Romans 1:1-2) into modes that would resonate with societies accustomed as they now were to hearing things in accordance with the rhetorical practices of the day. The Palestinian Christians who made up the original apostolic band were, comparatively speaking, less cosmopolitan either in rhetorical skill or outlook, and thus they would be better suited, if only for the time being, for directing their efforts at Jewish communities or in those segments of society where they were present.

What Paul says in 2:10, "the only condition being that we might remember the poor, and that very thing I was eager to do," is a consistent element in Paul's missionary work. Both his letters and the relevant portions of the Acts of the Apostles contain references to his ongoing efforts to collect money for the relief of the poor in Jerusalem. Paul was not entirely self-sufficient and he was anything but the rogue Pharisee some suspect him even to this day of having been. There are few ideas more enduringly Hebrew than caring for the poor: God mandated it first through his law and he vehemently reiterated it through the mouths of the prophets who called Israel to repentance and obedience in his name. It was of course an ancient idea, but it was now given even more impetus through the early Christian testimony concerning Jesus and his abiding and fully eschatological concern for the poor among us. If Paul was singularly devoted to the preaching of the gospel among the nations, one practical sign of his dedication and sincerity to the cause of making God known among the nations came in the form of his determination to collect and to deliver funds intended to relieve the plight of the poor in the city of his new faith's origin, Jerusalem.

V. The Incident at Antioch (2:11-14): The Four Frameworks

A digression at this point would be useful because so far a great deal of textual ground has been traversed without offering any overall summary of Paul's position. The expectation is that something identifiable as Paul's "theology" might be coming into view, but employing that word in this context would be an unjustifiably anachronistic step. We are unfortunately hampered by our own tradition-bound understanding of the word "theology": how the task of elucidating scripture has been gradually usurped by the requirements of a Platonically oriented approach to the text. In general this consists of imposing an extrinsic philosophical framework upon the text and thus treating it as a source book for transcendental concepts and ideas. Modern exegetes have attempted to correct some of these long-standing tendencies by advocating a "biblical theology" approach to the canonical texts, but these efforts—no less competitive among themselves but helpful in some identifiable ways—still vary in philosophical and/or ideological intensity. The basic problem with the modern theologically-tinged approach is that it has few rigorously applied ways to control the imposition of its philosophical presuppositions *a posteriori* upon the text. It is thus methodologically constrained to conduct one eisegetical exercise after another ostensibly in the name of letting the text "speak for itself."

It thus does no good to introduce the notion of a Pauline theology. Paul was not a theologian; he was an apostle. This means that—despite much very determined effort to paint him in theological colors—*Paul did not think theologically; he was only capable of thinking scripturally*. This means that the range of his understanding of who God is and what he has done is framed almost exclusively by the Hebrew scriptural tradition: how the latter is an inscribed interpretation of the cumulative experience of the Jewish people and the way in which they were to understood their own history in relation to God. It was a way of thinking about the world and the self in it that is framed by what the sacred texts contain. Imagine a way of life in which all of what one thinks—either practically or speculatively—is done largely if not wholly in terms of the categories and illustrative episodes found in a collection of holy books. As a Pharisee Paul inherited and inhabited such a world, a cognitive environment in which matters were never addressed in terms of the neutral conceptuality we freely presume to wield. We do not hesitate to think of things or to approach a situation in ways that have nothing at all to do with scripture, but for Paul the single most important and therefore the most determinative frame of reference was the one that he or any of his co-religionists encountered in scripture. It is thus more accurate to say that Paul thought in accordance with scriptural meanings, symbols, and images rather than with any of the abstractions that make up our modern consciousness—reason, objectivity, free will, history, freedom, individuality, personal psychology, materialist causality, etc. It is not that these ideas were wholly absent; rather it is simply that they were clothed and presented in accordance with the ideational world of ancient Hebrew scripture. What this means is that for a person like Paul what he thought was, comparatively speaking, a much more circumscribed way of dealing with the world than anything to which we are accustomed. His point of departure for all things was the self-sufficient content of the written word of God.

It is necessary to stress this situation because, when Paul was faced with making sense of his own experience of Jesus, he did so in terms of the only fundamental truth he knew, namely, that of scripture. His encounter with the resurrected Christ was—scripturally speaking—an indubitably real one, and, *for that reason alone*, it was all the more necessary that it be reconciled with the rest of his world whose very contours had been shaped by scripture. The way in which we interpret, for example, the events of Acts 9 and what Paul says throughout his Galatian letter will depend in part on whether we wish to emphasize what we read

V. The Incident at Antioch (2:11-14): The Four Frameworks

in terms either of continuity or of it being a radical break. Both of these aspects are true and relevant, but the key to seeing how they fit together will only be found in Paul's scriptural outlook and the way in which it continuously integrates what so many of our modern theological methods and interpretive habits often seek to separate.

There are four overlapping perspectives that will help us to make a more integrated sense of the Galatian letter. I have borrowed them from N. T. Wright's book *Justification: God's Plan & Paul's Vision*.[1] Each perspective constitutes an integral aspect of the Hebrew religious tradition, and, as needed, each can be considered thematically in order to distinguish it from the others, but they necessarily belong together by virtue of their organic connection with each other. They are the building blocks of the Hebrew religious experience and its corresponding psychology.

The first perspective is that of covenant (Hebrew *berīth*, Greek *diathēkē*). It is the most consistent theme of the Old Testament. It is the binding bilateral agreement made between two parties—in this case, God and the individuals and/or groups with whom God wishes to be bound by covenantal agreement—and the agreement is predicated on certain promises being made by either party with the expectation that each party will act in accordance with those promises of commitment and loyalty. There were covenants with several figures—Noah, Abraham, Moses, David—but Paul will treat the one with Abraham as the paradigmatic covenant.

Genesis 12:1-3 (OSB) is the first and most fundamental expression of God's intentions for his covenant relationship with Abraham:

> "Get out of your country, from your kindred and from your father's house, to a land I will show you. I will make you a great

---

[1] N.T. Wright, *Justification: God's Plan & Paul's Vision* (Downers Grove, Illinois: InterVarsity Press, 2009), 97-108.

nation; I will bless you and make your name great; and you shall be a blessing. I will bless those who bless you, and curse those who curse you; *and in you all the tribes of the earth shall be blessed."* (italics added)

The essence of the covenant is God's enduring plan to save the world through Abraham/Israel/the faithful Israelite (these three "persons" coalesce into one during the scriptural course of Israel's covenantal history). Our tendency is to think of covenant in the more restrictive Mosaic sense as involving a chauvinistic obedience to the cultic requirements of the law, but basic to all biblical talk about covenant is the principle that God needs Israel to be faithful (*pistos*) in order for the covenant's content to be obeyed and for it to serve as the vehicle for the world's salvation. Covenant refers then to (a) God's promise to Abraham, that in him "all the nations of the world shall be blessed," and (b) all that will be required of Israel so that she might fulfill her part against the Old Testament backdrop of creation, fall, redemption, and the eschatological consummation of history.

The second perspective—that of the lawcourt—is closely related to the first, and it concerns the most important inner workings of the covenant relationship. Even though God is Israel's partner in the covenant, he is also the Judge, and he judges in accordance with the language of blessing and cursing (Deuteronomy 27-30). God is faithful (*pistos*) according to his covenant promises (his own chosen means to put things right by bringing covenantal blessing to Israel and through Israel to the world), but he also punishes according to the curse. Central to the biblical tradition is the conviction that God—as the righteous judge—will only ever judge in ways that reflect his righteousness, his undeterrable commitment to the covenant he has made with Israel. Psalm 51:3-4 (RSV) is emblematic of this scriptural understanding:

For I know my transgressions, and my sin is ever before me. Against thee, thee only, have I sinned, and done that which is

V. The Incident at Antioch (2:11-14): The Four Frameworks

evil in thy sight, so that thou art justified in thy sentence and blameless in thy judgment.

God is forever "just" (*dikaios*) vis-à-vis the covenant he has made with Israel, and this justice is indistinguishable from what Paul also means when he is talking about the "righteousness of God" (*dikaiosynē tou theou*). While it certainly also includes the extent of God's "steadfast love" and his "abundant mercy" (Psalm 51:1), Paul uses it in his letter to the Galatians as a reference to God's unswerving faithfulness to his covenant, which is his plan to bless the world through the way he orders salvation.

The basic meaning of such language in the Galatian letter is that, when Paul speaks of a man being "just/justified/righteous" (*dikaios*), it primarily concerns a person's *status* with regard to the content and purpose of the covenant and only secondarily does it ever refer to his personal moral *character*. It must be understood in terms of the judgment call that establishes either the innocence or the guilt of someone in relation to a legal charge, in this case, the inquiry concerning whether he is being faithful to the covenant agreement. But, scripturally speaking, Israel was chronically unfaithful, and, even with the law, she was forever falling short of the righteousness (i.e. the reciprocal covenant faithfulness) God was demanding of her. Idolatry/apostasy, sin, and mortal dereliction continued to be the result.

In order for Israel to be reestablished as the "righteous/just" partner in the covenant, for God to find in Israel's favor once and for all concerning the charge made against her, for God's plan of salvation (which includes dealing with sin and its deleterious effects, and creating a remedied worldwide family), God needs a faithful Israelite, one who will be supremely *dikaios* (definitively fulfilling and thus declared not guilty with regard to the charge). That person, according to the gospel preached by Paul, is Jesus of Nazareth, whose crucifixion and resurrection from the dead are the inaugural signs of the *eschaton* (literally, the "last thing"), the now-and-not-yet of Israel's hope in the promise of salvation.

Paul claims that, by being raised from among the dead, Jesus has been "vindicated" by God, literally, that Jesus has been "declared righteous" (*dikaiōthēnai*), that the lawcourt verdict has been rendered in his favor and he is therefore the eschatological *dikaios*, the truly "righteous" or "justified" one, and that all those who belong to him, who confess their faith in him as the Messiah (*ho Christos*) and as the Son of God, they shall belong to him as well through their sharing in his vindicated status by means of faith and baptism.

The third perspective concerns eschatology and it follows closely upon the preceding points. If the covenant was God's chosen means for putting things right, if it was all along his plan to save the world through Israel, then the resurrected Jesus is the sign of our transition into the new age, the "last" (*eschaton*) or culminating age of God's righteous judgment. Post-exilic Jewish belief concerning the resurrection reserved it for all people on the Day of the Lord, but now, in the case of Jesus, what had been a future promise for all is a current and wholly unexpected reality for one. If Jesus is preached as having been "raised up from among the dead" (1:1), then the *only* basis for this seeming vindication of him must be his supreme righteousness.

The Pharisaic Jews of the first century A.D. believed that the ones to be vindicated in the age to come would be those who were faithfully keeping the precepts of the Torah. This was the principal source for the zealotry of the Pharisee Saul of Tarsus whose understanding of "salvation" flowed from this belief, but now the apostle Paul is declaring that this verdict which was to have characterized a new and future age has been moved up into the present—in the person of Jesus of Nazareth whose resurrection from the dead Paul openly proclaims—and thus his gospel is the proclamation of the eschatological here and now! It should be stressed, however, that the real emphasis of eschatological thinking—regardless of the way in which it is

V. The Incident at Antioch (2:11-14): The Four Frameworks

framed in either the Old or the New Testament—is on decision-making, on whether or not the hearer of scripture will accept its message as the authoritative word of God and obey what he hears.[2]

The fourth perspective—that of christology—ultimately serves as the convergence point for the preceding three perspectives. Christology is the way in which we understand *who* Jesus is: what kind of person he is, the nature of his relationship to God, and what that all means when you take into account the scriptural vision of Israel's history, what we know about him from the gospel accounts, and how those who knew him and/or heard the gospel proclamation about him understood his person. Thus it is that the basic Old Testament idea of a person who is anointed for God's purpose (Hebrew *mashīah*/Greek *christos*) is developed from every direction in the books of the New Testament with reference to Jesus and the emerging Christian faith concerning him. Even though both testaments do not contain a single, comprehensive statement regarding christology (with the possible exceptions of the foundational John 1:1-18 or the even more concisely expressive John 3:16), christological thinking was an inherent component of the way in which the nascent Christian movement began and the directions in which it developed. It is crucial, however, to keep in mind that Pauline christology is only ever a matter of interpreting the messiahship of Jesus, i.e. how he is preached as the *christos* of God and how salvation flows from that declaration. It is not the anachronistic locating of the Orthodox Church's later christological formulations in the letters that Paul has written to his churches.

Central to this development is the scriptural contention that through his death and resurrection Jesus is the simultaneous culmination and perfection of faithfulness to the covenant. It is by virtue of his sacrificial death and resurrection from among the dead—his resurrection being the way that God has declared him

---

[2] Paul Nadim Tarazi, *The New Testament: Introduction, Volume 2: Luke And Acts* (Crestwood, New York: St. Vladimir's Seminary Press, 2001), 20.

to be "righteous"—that he has been revealed as Israel's most faithful (*pistos*) and therefore the most righteous (*dikaios*) servant before God's lawcourt. In the Old Testament to be a "son of God" meant, in effect, to be an exemplary covenant-partner (ideally in the person of the king), an association that adds depth to those other key christological terms (*kyrios*, "lord," and *basileus*, "king"). In accordance with the teaching that Jesus is the perfect sacrifice, that is, that he functions as Israel's blameless and thus final offering of herself, Jesus in his resurrected glory (who is not just *christos* but who is now, as Paul's gospel makes explicit, *ho Christos*, "*the* Christ") becomes righteousness *in excelsis*. He presents the self-sacrificial love of Jesus dead on the cross—rooted as it is in his obedient faithfulness—as the consummate expression of God's own *dikaiosynē*.

Christology begins in Paul's scriptural presentation of Jesus as the literal embodiment of membership in God's family. This is the foundation of a Christian identity, of our belonging to the Christ and thus in possession of a wholly new status vis-à-vis God, his creation, and its history. It will be through a Christian faith (*pistis*) in this faithfulness (*pistis*) of Jesus, and by means of our baptism into his death and the new life we will share with him that we are admitted (i.e. reckoned as belonging) to God's new *eschatological* family, the one God began building long ago from Abraham's house.

These four perspectives will form the general framework for the way in which the Galatian letter can be understood and, I think, appreciated for the bold and uncompromising appeal concerning the kind of Christian identity that Paul makes in the defense of the gospel he had delivered to the Galatian churches. The letter's content through 2:10 was in many ways a setting of the stage for what follows in the rest of the letter, and it is at this point that Paul makes the transition from general considerations and applies himself to more specific ones of substance that will begin to reveal the essential nature of the gospel that God himself had commissioned him to proclaim.

V. The Incident at Antioch (2:11-14): The Four Frameworks

It bears repeating once more that the paramount issue behind Paul's gospel is what revolves around *our new covenant-identity in the Christ*: to whom does the believer belong and what establishes the foundations for his belonging. In other words, given that identity *per se* is not a scriptural term, I contend that in Paul's letter to the Galatians it is at least a thoroughly implicit idea, present indirectly in his recurrent language about our belonging to the Christ (*tou Christou*). Paul Nadim Tarazi has reminded me that—on one unmistakable level, that of explicit cultural, ethnic or religious identification-making—identity serves as the very opposite of the kind of belonging entailed by the Pauline gospel. That particular level is immediately obvious when, for example, Paul writes in 1:13-14:

13 For you have heard of my former life in Judaism,
how I was persecuting the church beyond measure
and that I was destroying her
14 because I had advanced in Judaism beyond many of those among my own people
on account of the fact that I was so exceedingly zealous for the traditions of my fathers.

Here Paul is speaking of Judaism (*Ioudaismos*) as a religious and cultural framework for personal identity, a view that accorded with what was certainly the customary religious-ethnic model in the ancient world, but it was one that Paul's gospel was going to confront and shatter. His new point of departure contained what was, even when compared to our still prevailing habits, not so much one more regular form of identity as a thoroughgoing *anti-identity* based not on ethnicity but on the slave's relationship to his master.

In the Roman imperial empire of Paul's day only a free Roman citizen had an identity by virtue of his legally recognized status, and that, in relation to him, any slave that he owned had no identity. That is formally true, but it also stands to reason that whatever identity the slave does have functions as a kind of anti-identity in the sense that it exists only in relation to his master.

On the one hand, even though the slave belongs to his master and thus has no formal or legal identity of his own, it is still the case that, on the other hand, it is in his selfless obedience to his master's will that the slave receives what amounts to the anti-identity entailed by unconditionally belonging to his master. I would argue that the kind of identity in which the Pauline gospel does deal—not to be construed in ontological terms or understood as a culturally-based framework of collectivizing identification—is precisely this kind of anti-identity, and that it is intimately bound up with (and precedes) the gospel-based freedom about which Paul writes in his letter. Indeed, the latter consists of the scripture-based and grace-guided free fall that occurs when we engage the word of God, when we hear it, accept it, and obey it. In short, the Pauline anti-identity, because it is scripturally mediated, is our only actual identity before God.

Once again, if we take the Acts of the Apostles as our one scriptural indication of how the faith began in Jerusalem, we read about how the people reacted to Peter's Pentecost speech in 2:37-42 (RSV), a passage that directly bears on what comes next in Paul's letter:

> Now when they heard this they were cut to the heart, and said to Peter and the rest of the apostles, "Brethren, what shall we do?" And Peter said to them, "Repent, and be baptized every one of you in the name of Jesus Christ for the forgiveness of your sins; and you shall receive the gift of the Holy Spirit. For the promise is to you and to your children and to all that are far off, every one whom the Lord our God calls to him." And he testified with many other words and exhorted them, saying, "Save yourselves from this crooked generation." So those who received his word were baptized, and there were added that day about three thousand souls. And they devoted themselves to the apostles' teaching and fellowship (*koinōnia*), to the breaking of bread and prayers.

If the earliest Christian sense of identity manifested itself as "fellowship" (*koinōnia*), on what was such fellowship ultimately

V. The Incident at Antioch (2:11-14): The Four Frameworks

based? The rest of his letter to the Galatians contains Paul's answer to this question.

The most general point contained in Paul's narrative of how he had gone up to Jerusalem, conferred with "the ones who were reputed to be something," and received from them "the right hand of fellowship" was that the gospel in which they were all sharing would have had at its core a basic premise concerning the nature of the fellowship that is only possible in the Christ. His account so far has not indicated on what that fellowship is based, but now in what follows, Paul brings this issue dramatically to the forefront and uses it as the link to the entirety of his gospel message. The developing picture of fraternal apostolic agreement as indicated in 1:18-2:10 is disrupted when Paul resumes his letter in 2:11-13:

*¹¹ ὅτε δὲ ἦλθεν Κηφᾶς εἰς Ἀντιόχειαν,
κατὰ πρόσωπον αὐτῷ ἀντέστην,
ὅτι κατεγνωσμένος ἦν.
¹² πρὸ τοῦ γὰρ ἐλθεῖν τινας ἀπὸ Ἰακώβου
μετὰ τῶν ἐθνῶν συνήσθιεν·
ὅτε δὲ ἦλθον,
ὑπέστελλεν καὶ ἀφώριζεν ἑαυτὸν
φοβούμενος τοὺς ἐκ περιτομῆς.
¹³ καὶ συνυπεκρίθησαν αὐτῷ καὶ οἱ λοιποὶ Ἰουδαῖοι,
ὥστε καὶ Βαρναβᾶς συναπήχθη αὐτῶν τῇ ὑποκρίσει.*

*¹¹ But when Kephas came to Antioch,
I opposed him to his face
because he was caught up in contradiction.
¹² For before certain men came from James
he would eat together with the pagans,
but when they came,
he withdrew and separated himself
because he feared the advocates of circumcision.
¹³ And the other Jews were also hypocritical along with him,
so that even Barnabas was caught up in their hypocrisy.*

The scene has now shifted from Jerusalem to Antioch, a cosmopolitan center along the seaboard of the eastern Roman

Empire and an early home base for Paul's missionary activity, a city that was a far cry from the Jewish parochialism that must have characterized the place of the new faith's origins in Judea. It was here that Paul found something amiss in the behavior of Peter and the other apostles with more direct ties to Jerusalem. In his eyes it involved a discrepancy where the very spirit and the meaning of the gospel were concerned, and what precipitated the incident was the practice of table fellowship.

Briefly, it had been standard Jewish practice especially among the Pharisees to regard table fellowship with anyone who was openly disobedient to the law as not permissible, and, in the case of eating meals with the non-Jewish pagans, strictly forbidden. The situation in Antioch with regard to Peter's behavior on this point is one that, while it is not flattering to him as it is reported here, must be seen as providing a springboard from which Paul wished to make what he saw as being a far more salient point concerning the gospel. It was a simple enough situation. It was Paul's initial observation that Peter's behavior had been consistent given what the gospel demanded, namely, that table fellowship—that all-hallowed Jewish symbol of commonality and fellowship predicated first on obedience to the law and only secondarily on ethnic identity—be extended to all with whom a faith in Jesus as the crucified and risen Christ was shared. In Antioch Peter could be seen at table with the pagan converts to the faith, a practice that would have been in complete accord with what Acts 10 relates about the meaning of Peter's vision. What he says in vv. 34-43 (RSV) before the centurion Cornelius and those gathered at the latter's house in Caesarea is worth quoting in full:

> *"Truly I perceive that God shows no partiality, but in every nation any one who fears him and does what is right is acceptable to him.* You know the word which he sent to Israel, preaching good news of peace by Jesus Christ (he is Lord of all), the word which was proclaimed throughout all Judea, beginning from Galilee after the baptism which John preached: how God anointed Jesus of Nazareth with the Holy Spirit and

V. The Incident at Antioch (2:11-14): The Four Frameworks

with power; how he went about doing good and healing all that were oppressed by the devil, for God was with him. And we are witnesses to all that he did both in the country of the Jews and in Jerusalem. *They put him to death by hanging him on a tree; but God raised him on the third day and made him manifest; not to all the people but to us who were chosen by God as witnesses, who ate and drank with him after he rose from the dead.* And he commanded us to preach to the people, and to testify that he is the one ordained by God to be judge of the living and the dead. To him all the prophets bear witness that every one who believes in him receives forgiveness of sins through his name." (italics added)

It was "before certain men came from James" that Peter, presumably because of the way he understood the gospel on this point, had not hesitated to commune with the non-Jewish members of the Christian groups in Antioch, but his conduct and that of some of his Jewish brothers in the new faith changed with the arrival of these "advocates of circumcision," some men from Jerusalem whose physical presence must have created a ticklish situation for some of the Jewish Christians in that city who might very well have sensed with the arrival of such men upon the scene a pressure to behave in older, more traditional ways where table fellowship was concerned. Their lapsing into that older pattern of a division dictated solely by a formalistic observance of the law and a correspondingly formalized holiness based on separation created for Paul an intolerable contradiction with regard to the unity that must accompany the gospel's flowering in the hearts of men. By his own account, he did not hesitate to bring it to the attention of Peter and the others. In itself the issue of table fellowship was not a peripheral one because the apparent *volte face* that Paul witnessed at Antioch— this reintroduction of division in a setting where the gospel had abolished division—had everything to do with the question of how identity was going to be reckoned in gospel terms. It had to do with how the believer's sense of identity—formed by his reaction to the gospel—was now going to be the basis for the way in which he would view human relationships.

There is no downplaying the importance of what Paul now writes. The situation as he describes it and his response to his Jewish-Christian brothers in the faith introduces a fundamental statement of what is going to make for a presentation of what—in accordance with his gospel—will be the rules for the new table fellowship. It will stand in opposition to the traditional Jewish one because it is rooted in and reflective of the new understanding of how the biblical God *acts* to produce the eschatological reality proclaimed by the Pauline gospel. It is a transformation only made possible by the source of that new faith, who, as Paul shortly makes clear, is the crucified Jesus of Nazareth. In v. 14 Paul confronts Peter with this contradiction:

¹⁴ ἀλλ᾽ ὅτε εἶδον ὅτι οὐκ ὀρθοποδοῦσιν πρὸς τὴν ἀλήθειαν τοῦ εὐαγγελίου,
εἶπον τῷ Κηφᾷ ἔμπροσθεν πάντων,
εἰ σὺ Ἰουδαῖος ὑπάρχων ἐθνικῶς καὶ οὐχὶ Ἰουδαϊκῶς ζῇς,
πῶς τὰ ἔθνη ἀναγκάζεις ἰουδαΐζειν;

¹⁴ *But when I saw that they were not consistent about the truth of the gospel, before them all I said to Kephas,*
"If you who were born a Jew are now living like a pagan and not like a Jew, how can you compel the pagans to live like Jews?"

While the issue of table fellowship might have been the proximate cause for Paul's public challenging of their behavior, it was not limited to the plain inconsistency of Peter and the others doing one thing then and another thing now depending on whether or not the members of the circumcision party were on hand. It was also and—as we shall see later in the letter—more decisively connected with the newfound urgency to impose circumcision upon non-Jewish converts to the faith, in Paul's eyes an unjustifiable imposition when the gospel clearly calls for none at all. Thus, when Paul confronts Peter and the others with their not being "consistent about the truth of the gospel," he is raising the issue of how those who have heard the gospel and profess to believe in it are going to be declared righteous, not in

V. The Incident at Antioch (2:11-14): The Four Frameworks

men's estimation, but in God's discerning eyes. Paul is throwing down the gauntlet over the integrity of his gospel.

VI. Our Being Declared Righteous (2:15-21)

The remainder of the second chapter (2:15-21) is the pivotal foundation for what follows in the rest of the letter. The passage consists of two closely related parts in which (1) the primacy of faith in the faithfulness of Jesus as the Christ vis-à-vis the law is asserted when it comes to being declared righteous, and (2) that this faith is the sole precondition for the possibility of the grace of God in our lives.

In vv. 15-16 Paul begins his bold challenge to those who would have our being declared righteous based on anything else but Jesus himself:

¹⁵ ἡμεῖς φύσει Ἰουδαῖοι καὶ οὐκ ἐξ ἐθνῶν ἁμαρτωλοί·
¹⁶ εἰδότες δὲ ὅτι οὐ δικαιοῦται ἄνθρωπος ἐξ ἔργων νόμου
ἐὰν μὴ διὰ πίστεως Ἰησοῦ Χριστοῦ,
καὶ ἡμεῖς εἰς Χριστὸν Ἰησοῦν ἐπιστεύσαμεν,
ἵνα δικαιωθῶμεν ἐκ πίστεως Χριστοῦ
καὶ οὐκ ἐξ ἔργων νόμου,
ὅτι ἐξ ἔργων νόμου οὐ δικαιωθήσεται πᾶσα σάρξ.

¹⁵ But we, who by nature are Jews and not pagan sinners,
¹⁶ knowing that a man is not declared righteous on the basis of the works of the law
but by means of the faithfulness of Jesus as the Christ,
even we believed in Jesus who is the Christ,
so that we might be declared righteous on the basis of the faithfulness of the Christ Jesus
and not on the basis of the works of the law,
because no man is declared righteous on the basis of the works of the law.

Bringing out the true import of these two verses (plus much of what follows) will require a detailed analysis of the Greek text, with particular attention being paid to certain grammatical aspects of the Greek language and how these function to convey the remarkable message of the gospel which Paul here seeks to reaffirm for the Galatians. Of equal significance is the framework introduced in the previous section and consisting of the four overlapping perspectives—covenant, lawcourt, eschatology and christology—which, when allowed to sound together, make for a more integrated and coherent way to understand the text.

The first thing to notice is the sheer rhetorical cleverness of Paul's appeal. At this point his words are still directed at Peter, Barnabas, and the others who had been "caught up in their hypocrisy" of having been born Jews and in the name of the gospel "living like a pagan and not like a Jew" in the Christian circles of Antioch but then abruptly changing their behavior. When those "certain men came from James," it was as if the earlier truth of the gospel by which they were living had evaporated and now had been replaced with requirements of no essential or binding consequence. Paul simply wishes to know what had happened in the interim for such a contradiction to manifest itself so openly. He underscores the depth of the contradiction at hand by asserting in 2:15-16a that "we, who by nature are Jews and not pagan sinners" know "that a man is not declared righteous on the basis of the works of the law, but by means of the faithfulness of Jesus as the Christ." He is telling Peter and company that they should have known better, that their renewed zeal for the implementing of exclusionary Jewish custom was a mistake better suited to the less instructed and more superstitious sensibilities of the pagans who, by Paul's reckoning, would have been more prone to thinking in terms of a perfunctory obedience to the law's formal requirements as being acceptable in the eyes of their god.

The point is not a new one. Recall that it was precisely this kind of mechanistic ritualism that the prophets of Israel had condemned because its prevalence among the people meant that the Israelites were not enjoying the directness of communion to which the law testified but which an overly formalized behavior did not automatically equal. If as Jews they had first begun to

VI. Our Being Declared Righteous (2:15-21)

appreciate this important point, then as believers in the gospel they are without excuse if they are now behaving as if such behavior was commendable before God. Indeed it is on this point that Paul continues his defense of basic Christian faith in the remainder of v. 16: "even we [who are Jews] believed in Jesus who is the Christ, so that we might be declared righteous on the basis of the faithfulness of the Christ Jesus and not on the basis of the works of the law, because no man is declared righteous on the basis of the works of the law."

It has become traditional to interpret this passage in light of the faith vs. works dichotomy so central to the Protestant Christian tradition, namely, that what ultimately leads to a man being "justified" (i.e. declared righteous) is the steadfast purity of his faith in the gospel message, and that this primacy of faith is what must be maintained and defended against any suggestion that our being justified and ultimately "saved" is at all dependent upon and/or related to "works." The problem here is not that the Protestant contention is wholly invalid, but that, in terms of what the Greek text is actually saying, there is something of a greater priority being expressed, and, in order to grasp the implications of what it does say, it is imperative that we take a closer look at the way Paul uses two prepositions in this passage.

Greek prepositions are notorious in the history of Christian thought for the chronically complicating role they have played in just about every exegetical debate down through the millennia. But there is no escaping either their textual importance or the task of nailing down their approximate semantic meaning when we do encounter them. The two prepositions in question here are *ek* and *dia*. We will be looking very closely at their occurrence in v. 16 where *ek* is used a total of four times and *dia* appears once. There is a general principle of translation which ideally states that, whenever a particular word appears in a text, it should be translated each time with the same corresponding English word or words. After examining the way in which Paul employs these two prepositions in v. 16, I decided to follow this principle and render each occurrence of the preposition in exactly the same way, and, when I did this, I discovered that the passage gained much in clarity and import. It did nothing to change the fundamental significance of its content (aside from a slight shift in emphasis, to be explained below), but it helped make for a fuller picture of what Paul was saying. I found that by rendering the passage in this manner the four perspectives presented earlier—covenant, lawcourt, eschatology, and christology—were each given their due, and, if anything, what Paul writes takes on an even more fundamentally Christian urgency. Nothing is lost, but so much more is gained.

The traditional post-Reformation reading of this passage goes very much like this: Paul is saying that man's justification is not accomplished by works of the law, i.e. that there is nothing we can do to earn a justified status in God's eyes and thus escape condemnation. Rather it only happens if the individual has faith and believes that Jesus is the Son of God and therefore his savior. Here allowance must be made for the use of the "justification" language that has been so central to the Protestant understanding of the meaning of this passage, and much of this usage hinges on the way the Greek verb *dikaioō* is approached.

The active voice form of the verb means "to declare someone righteous (*dikaios*) and thus innocent of the charge against him." If in this context one keeps to the strictly lawcourt sense of the word already discussed, things would be clear enough, but in the development of the Protestant concept of "justification by faith," being "justified" took on a distinctively moral connotation and came to be associated more with the inward disposition of the believer—his inner pious stature (his "righteousness") as reflected in the degree of faith he possesses—than it did with God actually accomplishing something here. This Protestant shift of emphasis is not an inherently wrong one since our "justified" status is certainly something intimately connected with our salvation in the Christ, but, given what Paul is actually saying in this passage, it becomes

VI. Our Being Declared Righteous (2:15-21)

something of an interpretive gloss and does not necessarily correspond to what Paul is explicitly declaring here.

So what is Paul really saying? Three things must be emphasized here: (1) that the occurrences of the verb *dikaioō* in 2:16 (and in practically all other instances where Paul uses it in his letters) are in the passive voice. This means that we *are being* declared righteous, that God is doing something here, hence Paul's rightful insistence that what is going on here does in fact have nothing at all to do with works of the law; (2) that the ordering and the respective meanings of the two prepositions *ek* and *dia* let us know just what God has accomplished and how all else stands in relation to it; and (3) that the phrase "by means of the faithfulness of Jesus as the Christ" (*dia pisteōs Iēsou Christou*) in 2:16a is rendered as a subjective genitive construction (more on this below). It is now time to look at the meaning of these two prepositions and the way Paul uses them in v. 16.

The basic meaning of the preposition *ek* is "out of" or "from," while that of *dia* is "through" or "on account of something." In the Greek New Testament there is plenty of semantic overlap between these two prepositions because each is often used to denote the idea of *instrumentality*. Very frequently both *ek* and *dia* are used to indicate the means or mechanism(s) by which something is done, so differentiating between the two usages in a single verse involves some careful consideration. Let there be no mistake about this point: the way in which these two prepositions function in this verse is, in our English language-navigating eyes, almost identical. Each is used in connection with the way in which something is being effected, but, as will be shown below, there is a "hierarchy of instrumentality" at work in what Paul says, and the real thrust of the passage is contained in what I think is the quite deliberate way in which he employs these prepositions. In this passage I have chosen to render *ek* as "on the basis of (something)" and *dia* as "by means of (something)," and the justification for the regularity of this rendering lies in the un-haphazard way each is used.

In our customary English parlance, if you do something *on the basis of* another thing, it means that this "other thing" has made it possible for the something under consideration to be accomplished. The "basis" in question here connotes (a) a preexisting possibility of achievement, and (b) that there is both a predetermined *and* a pre-determinative connection between the two things. If we claim that X takes place *on the basis of* Y, we are acknowledging that Y directly set the stage for, but was not necessarily the proximal cause of, X happening. By translating the Greek preposition *ek* as "on the basis of," I wish to highlight what is a broader context of causality, one that is presupposed by the scriptural vision contained in Paul's gospel.

But if you do something *by means of* another thing, then that "other thing" is the more directly instrumental factor in its accomplishment: it is what causes it to happen and it does not happen without it. There is thus a temporal difference in what Paul's employment of these two prepositions tells us. Whatever happens *on the basis of* (*ek*) something is a more remotely positioned causality; while whatever happens *by means of* (*dia*) something occurs in a more direct or contemporaneous fashion.

The first part of v. 16 is key because it contains the initial occurrence of *ek* and the only occurrence of *dia*. If we add v.15 to make for a more complete context, look at the text with the respective prepositions added to the English rendering:

15 But we, who by nature are Jews and not pagan sinners,
16 knowing that a man is not declared righteous on the basis of (ek) the works of the law
*but by means of (*dia*) the faithfulness of Jesus as the Christ,*
even we believed in Jesus who is the Christ,

Remember that Paul is confronting Peter with his inconsistent behavior and he wants his apostolic brother to remind himself that, because they are both Jews who have embraced the Christian faith, there should be no question about their understanding of what righteousness (i.e. the state of being

VI. Our Being Declared Righteous (2:15-21)

declared righteous) now consists. It was since the Pentecost that men were being declared righteous (*dikaios*), not on the basis of the works of the law (the path prescribed by the Pharisaic ideology), but by virtue of what the crucified and resurrected Jesus has now made possible—this new Christian confession of faith in the very faithfulness of Jesus as the Christ. It is this nuanced difference between these two modes—as reflected in the text by the prepositions *ek* and *dia*—that introduces the above-mentioned "hierarchy of instrumentality."

Think of it this way: for the Jews righteousness had been a simple proposition—it was by Jewish reckoning a function of their individual obedience to the law. For the sake of fairness and completeness here, we should add that it was not merely the formal observance of the law *per se* and its regulatory shaping of one's life that *caused* a man to be declared righteous, but the actual obedience involved in each individual response to the demands of the law, an obedience that had to be based ideally on a personal faith that the law was God's consummate gift to his people, that it had been received at Sinai in the wake of the exodus, that it was the means by which God could know his people and the Israelites could know God, etc. It was in this simultaneously comprehensive yet limiting way that righteousness was viewed as law-based, but behind all this reckoning was the even more basic understanding that it was still God who makes his people righteous, and, in accordance with the reigning Pharisaic understanding of the law, the obedient Jew did this "on the basis of" (*ek*) the law, i.e. whether or not a person obeyed and kept it. By extending the same framework I am proposing here, the obedient Jew would reason that it was "by means of" (*dia*) God having given the law to Israel in the first place that this was even possible.

Thus, even in the old scheme we can see how *dia* plays a more determinative role than *ek*, and keep this in mind when we look again at Paul's declaration. The old covenant and obedience to it were based on God's giving of the law, but now with the coming of Jesus, his crucifixion and resurrection, and the eschatological conviction that he is the Christ, *this* is the new foundational event founded on God acting to raise the crucified Jesus from the dead and thus inaugurating the new eschatological age. We can certainly say that God accomplished this through his power, but we can also assert in an equally adamant way that it was accomplished "by means of (*dia*) the faithfulness of Jesus as the Christ," that Jesus embodied and fulfilled all of what scripture stipulated about the salvation of Israel ultimately being a matter of obedience. It is at this point that Paul brings together the four perspectives of covenant, lawcourt, eschatology, and christology. Jesus is proclaimed as the "foundational event" of the new covenant because by his sacrificial death and resurrection he showed himself to be the "righteous one"—the truest Israelite of all. He is proclaimed as the Christ of Israel's salvation—and thus, in the lawcourt language of God's justice, he is worthy of being declared supremely *dikaios* for the sake of all, an accomplishment tied to and being the start of the eschaton itself.

Paul is telling Peter, his confused Jewish-Christian brothers in the faith, and the Galatians that the new righteousness is rooted in the faithfulness (*pistis*) of Jesus who—"by means of" that faithfulness—fulfilled all of what had been prophesied concerning the Christ of God. It is in this vein that he continues in v. 16, and, once again backing up some:

> [15] *But we, who by nature are Jews and not pagan sinners,*
> [16] *knowing that a man is not declared righteous on the basis of* (ek) *the works of the law*
> *but by means of* (dia) *the faithfulness of Jesus as the Christ,*
> *even we [Jews] believed in Jesus who is the Christ,*
> *so that we might be declared righteous on the basis of* (ek) *the faithfulness of the Christ Jesus*
> *and not on the basis of* (ek) *the works of the law,*
> *because no man is declared righteous on the basis of* (ek) *the works of the law.*

The "we" here refers firstly to any Jewish believer in the gospel during Paul's day, and secondly to any person who becomes a

VI. Our Being Declared Righteous (2:15-21)

Christian believer. What is incumbent upon any believer is a sustained knowledge of just what God has done through the man Jesus, namely, that it is "by means of" him that the promise of salvation made to Abraham would be fulfilled not just for Israel but for all the nations of the world. This "economy" of salvation—the whole dramatic narrative of the Pauline gospel—hinges on the faithfulness of the Christ, who in the scriptural telling of him fulfilled all the requirements of a true and righteous Israel, and was thus able to make supremely manifest what the law could only teach and what the idea of obedience to it could only suggest.

If any of us is going to reckon now in terms of what constitutes "righteousness" (literally, in more biblical terms, *how* we will be declared to be righteous), then it will only be first by means of (*dia*) the faithfulness of Christ to this divine plan of salvation so that, second, we "might be declared righteous on the basis of *(ek)* the faithfulness of the Christ Jesus." It will not happen on the basis of (*ek*) the works of the law because—from God's point of view—the law was never the final and conclusive means by which men could be declared righteous. Jesus does what the law by itself could not do, and responding in faith to this message about what Jesus does is the essence of Paul's gospel.

It is at this point that I must say a few things about the phrases "the faithfulness of Jesus as the Christ" and "the faithfulness of the Christ Jesus" as these appear in 2:16. This is still a controversial issue because the grammatical construction used in both cases is an ambiguous one: it is a genitive-case phrase ("the faith/faithfulness of ...."), but New Testament Greek allows for the genitive case to be used with either an objective or a subjective meaning. An objective reading of it could be translated as "a faith(fulness) *in* Jesus Christ," while a subjective reading of it can be translated as "the faith(fulness) *of* Jesus Christ." I have opted for a subjective reading of the phrase in 2:16 because, as I will seek to show, it accords better with what

Paul argues in the rest of his letter. He wants his listeners to realize that anything we choose to call faith must have as its foundation an understanding of *what God has accomplished by means of Jesus*. This awareness, together with the scriptural dynamic involved in the four overlapping perspectives, is what, in my opinion, makes the case for accepting the subjective genitive reading of the phrase.

Since the Reformation, however, there has been an entirely conscious decision to interpret this passage in the light of the Protestant faith vs. works dichotomy, and it is this prevailing emphasis which has caused people to read this particular phrase as an objective-genitive construction and therefore to see it as direct scriptural evidence for the privileging of a conscious faith in Christ as the key to our salvation as opposed to an alleged approach hinging on salvation by works. I would argue that in this passage Paul is describing something much more foundational than either the personal or the collective stuff of our faith *per se* and thus more formative where the latter is concerned, something that, because it is antecedent to the individual orientation which we understand as faith, possesses a significance that precedes any of the dichotomizing formulae pursued by our Western Christian brothers in the faith.

So where does personal faith fit into any of this? Interestingly enough, Paul actually allows it to appear in this verse when he writes, "even we have believed in Jesus who is the Christ, so that we might be declared righteous *on the basis* of the faithfulness of the Christ Jesus." Here he uses the more customary Greek verbal rendering of "believing in (someone)" (*kai hēmeis eis Christon Iēsoun episteusamen*). This is a more explicit indication compared to the genitive-faith phrases since it uses the verbal phrase "to believe in (someone)" (*pisteuō eis tina*) in the way that requires a direct object. But even in this context, what might be construed as being a matter of personal faith is still entirely dependent upon what Paul is more fundamentally asserting, namely, that we who do believe in Jesus believe in him only to

VI. Our Being Declared Righteous (2:15-21)

the extent that his declared status as the Christ is a function—most directly and economically—of his supremely righteous (*dikaios*) embodiment of covenant faithfulness. I have already said that 2:15-21 is the foundation for what is contained in the rest of the letter, but, in its own entirely justifiable fashion, one could also claim that the remainder of Paul's letter to the Galatians represents a sustained exposition of what he is asserting right here in this one verse.

Paul makes use of the episode in Antioch with its attendant inconsistencies in order to draw our attention to more fundamental and telling matters, to what he feels lies at the very heart of his own gospel, a message to the world that, for the most compelling internal reasons, must focus on the Christ and the significance of the cross. His gospel will not negate anything preceding it, but at the same time it will not be second to any of those other things. Our being declared righteous depends first and foremost upon our trusting conviction that Jesus fulfills all the requirements of righteousness, upon his being the most true and faithful Israelite, upon his most perfect realization of the law through an obedience that was unto his own death. Let there be no mistake about the *radical* implications of this fundamental Christian vision. On the one hand, one could assume, following Paul's own argument, that just as Jesus had become obedient and fulfilled the law, so too we can now aspire to the same level of obedience in his name, an assumption that we at no time should peremptorily dismiss as impossible; but, on the other hand, we who have heard about this same obedience as it is recounted in the gospel can be inspired by the Holy Spirit to attain it to the degree that grace makes it possible, that is, that we will strive with all of our heart, soul, mind, being, and strength to follow in the footsteps of Jesus and to live as his committed disciples, but we will live that life not bound by the codified requirements of the old age but by the *inspiration* of the new. We are called to exemplify covenant faithfulness in our lives, to be persons steered by grace into the obedience of faith, into the new realm of our work as Paul will shortly show in what remains of chapter 2. To endure in the Christ is the work of faith, and for faith to work we must obediently endure in the Christ. The gospel of Paul declares the Christ's presence to be the foundational reality for the Christian life: without it, we run the risk of substituting an empty Christian formalism for the vitality of a life rooted in and guided by the Holy Spirit. This is the charismatic potentiality that Paul connects with the hearing of the "truth of the gospel" (2:5).

When these two visions of our being declared righteous—that of obedience to the law and of faith in Jesus as the Christ—are laid side by side, there is a seeming disparity between the two that might strike us. The law aims at a formal completeness of behavior, an attitude based on the assumption that, if we but faithfully and fully abide by its precepts, then there will be no gaps, no shortcomings, no backsliding or occasionality in our behavior—and inconsistency will not mar the latter because in itself the law is consistent, and thus obedience becomes its only requirement. Faith, however, when compared to the comprehensive behavioral framework of the law, will seem more like a sieve, like a situation in which whatever is supposed to be consistent about Christian behavior will be seen as depending entirely upon the thinnest and most unregulative of foundations, namely, a person's own faith in Jesus as the Christ, something that in its seemingly less substantial way could be viewed as providing fewer objective guarantees about the continuing appearance of sinful behavior. It is just this perception that prompts Paul to declare in verse 17:

*17 εἰ δὲ ζητοῦντες δικαιωθῆναι ἐν Χριστῷ
εὑρέθημεν καὶ αὐτοὶ ἁμαρτωλοί,
ἆρα Χριστὸς ἁμαρτίας διάκονος;
μὴ γένοιτο.*

*17 But if, when we are seeking to be declared righteous through our faith in the Christ,
we ourselves were found to be sinners,
is then the Christ a servant of sin?*

VI. Our Being Declared Righteous (2:15-21)

Certainly not!

Just as failure to obey the law does not negate the formal validity of the law, so too allowance can be made for the believer's not being impervious to sin. By virtue of the gospel, the formal, external guarantees of the law and the brand of righteousness that it entailed must now give way to a newer and, in Paul's eyes, more compelling order of righteousness, one based on belief and a personal turning toward this Jesus of Nazareth whom God has revealed to be his Christ, his own agent (*diakonos*) of salvation. The reason why I rendered the first part of v. 17 as "But if, when we are seeking to be declared righteous through our faith in the Christ..." (*ei de zētountes dikaiōthēnai en Christō*), was that, by interpolating the phrase "through our faith," I wanted to highlight the wider faith-dynamic presupposed by Paul's biblical vision of salvation: (1) there is the foundational faithfulness of the Christ (prefigured by Abraham), followed by (2) our own faithful trust in the faithfulness of the Christ, and (3) what shall be the inspired state of our life in him.

The basis for this shift in Israel's reckoning of what constitutes our being declared righteous in the eyes of God, and thus what forms the stuff of salvation, cannot be understood in any terms other than what is contained in the gospel declaration of Jesus as the Christ. The point here is not one of a mechanical supersession, of the Christian gospel simply coming along to displace the Jewish law as a fundamentally new and final revelation of God's grace among his people; rather, all emphasis should be placed upon fulfillment and transition, on the crucial role of the law in preparing and indeed, making possible, the revelation that is Jesus the Christ. It is this very process of which Paul writes in vv. 18-19a:

^{18} εἰ γὰρ ἃ κατέλυσα ταῦτα πάλιν οἰκοδομῶ,
παραβάτην ἐμαυτὸν συνιστάνω.
^{19} ἐγὼ γὰρ διὰ νόμου νόμῳ ἀπέθανον,
ἵνα θεῷ ζήσω.

*¹⁸ For if I am building up again these things that I have taken apart,
then I prove myself to be a transgressor
¹⁹ because by means of the law I have died to the law
in order that I might live to God.*

These words are often interpreted as offering plain scriptural evidence for the kind of simple and crudely thorough supersessionism mentioned above, namely, that among the gospel's functions is the across-the-board replacement of the law by the gospel, the former being thoroughly negated and cast aside as irrelevant and no longer necessary let alone in any way binding. Paul's language here, though suggestive of a straightforward substitution, is actually more nuanced than some might suppose, and the clue to that can be found in what he says here and in the following verses.

First, he speaks of "taking things apart" and the verb he uses is *katalyō*, a word that means "destroy," "take apart," or even "abolish" and "invalidate," so the general meaning of *katalyō* is "to undo something." Paul had come to the Galatians preaching a gospel of salvation through a Christ crucified and raised from the dead, and he thought he had made it abundantly clear to them that it would ultimately be *on the basis of (ek)* our trusting in the righteous faithfulness of Jesus that we ourselves are declared righteous in the eyes of God. So it was not simply the case of Paul proclaiming that a new mode of being declared righteous was now categorically displacing another and making the latter forever null and void. Instead the gospel declaration can only stand on its own, that is, in direct relation to the scriptural images of righteousness that had preceded it, but at the same time stretching forward beyond them in order to complete and realize fully what the earlier witness contained and anticipated. If Paul now writes with alarm about the apparent backsliding of the Galatians, about their now inexplicable willingness to take up once again as primary (i.e. circumcision) what the original terms of the gospel had not so much supplanted as they had revealed as secondary, it is because there was henceforth supposed to have been—in accordance with his preaching—a unifying

VI. Our Being Declared Righteous (2:15-21)

identity bestowed on those who heard his message and received it in obedient love.

Second, he reminds the Galatians of what a return to circumcision would mean under such circumstances: "if I am building up again these things that I have taken apart, then I prove myself to be a transgressor." The word rendered here as "transgressor" is *parabatēs*, a word regularly used in the Hebrew tradition to designate a person who disobeys the law (literally, passing it by) and thus fails to "do" even a single commandment. It is used, for example, in the letter of James (2:8-11, RSV) when the author is admonishing his listeners about the sin of partiality, i.e. of inconsistently obeying the law:

> If you really fulfill the royal law, according to the scripture, "You shall love your neighbor as yourself," you do well. But if you show partiality, you commit sin, and are convicted by the law as transgressors (*parabatai*). For whoever keeps the whole law but fails in one point has become guilty of all of it. For he who said, "Do not commit adultery,' said also, "Do not kill." If you do not commit adultery but do kill, you have become a transgressor (*parabatēs*) of the law.

James' purpose is to make sure that his listeners would not be neglectful of the general social and moral imperatives enshrined in the law (and curiously, his letter makes no explicit mention of circumcision), and Paul will later make his own distinctive use of this principle of how disobeying even a single point law amounts to disobeying the whole law, but for now take notice of how he employs a traditional designation for something having been "taken apart" but not disavowed or even cast aside.

And third, this brings us to the real point of how Paul chooses to view the law in the light of Jesus being the Christ. By proclaiming the good news of Jesus' death and resurrection, he declares that the law must now take a relative second place to *whom*—according to his gospel—occupies first place. This is the gospel-based primacy of the crucified Christ. But if we have heard this gospel and now choose to act openly as if what is secondary has become primary, then we are "building up again these things that we have taken apart, and we prove ourselves to be transgressors" of the law. In this context we are "transgressors" not only of the law to the extent that we have failed to keep a focused view of the formative and in every way preparatory role of the law, but also "transgressors" of the gospel to the extent that we are willing to substitute peripheral matters for the primary ones demanded by the gospel.

Paul makes the connection in this way when in 2:18b-19a he writes, "...I prove myself to be a transgressor because by means of *(dia)* the law I have died to the law in order that I might live to God." When Paul speaks here of his having "died to the law," he is referring to the *relative* supremacy of the law as once having been the most decisive factor in our being declared righteous in the eyes of God. It is only by virtue of the gospel that the law can no more be that foremost factor because our being declared righteous is henceforth a direct function of the faith that we hold concerning Jesus as the Christ. It is in this way that our "living to God" is the concomitant flipside to our "dying to the law." Paul wants the Galatians to grasp that the two elements—dying to the law/living to God—necessarily belong together because of what only God can do and has done in the person of his Christ. It is no accident that at this point Paul writes in the first person.

It is his dying to the law—what, in gospel terms, becomes paradoxically his ultimate "obedience" to it—that Paul wishes to stress now as belonging to what will make possible his being alive to God. His argument is that, if he is "living to God," it is only because he has first "died to the law" by virtue of what his own gospel demands. It is thus that Paul's "dying to the law" is the scriptural reality now made possible—as he contends — because the equally scriptural law is the former's own necessary setting. But in what sense can the law itself be the means of Paul's dying to the law? The law and obedience to it had stood as the centerpiece of Jewish covenant-salvation, but now—in the light of Paul's gospel—that same law and obedience to it would

VI. Our Being Declared Righteous (2:15-21)

be brought to its ultimately exemplary expression in the proclamation of the crucified Christ. On the one hand, there is the gospel declaration of the crucifixion of Jesus, but, on the other hand, whether or not that makes even one lick of difference is how that message is received. If Paul dies to the law "by means of the law" (*dia nomou*), how does this counter-intuitive transformation that he immediately stipulates as belonging to what allows him to "live in God" occur? The sole basis for this paradoxical alchemy is the trusting stance he calls faith, and, more specifically, faith in the crucified Christ and what that thereafter requires of us (5:1-14).

This context also helps us to see the meaning of the controversial passage in Matthew 5:17-20 (RSV) where, in v. 17, Jesus initially employs the same verb *katalyō* in connection with the law: "Think not that I have come to abolish (*katalysai*) the law and the prophets; I have come not to abolish (*katalysai*) them but to fulfill them." The following two verses are puzzling to many because on the surface it appears that Jesus is endorsing the idea of a rigidly Pharisaic adherence to the law's prescriptions: "For truly, I say to you, till heaven and earth pass away, not an iota, not a dot, will pass from the law until all is accomplished. Whoever then relaxes one of the least of these commandments and teaches men so, shall be called least in the kingdom of heaven; but he who does them and teaches them shall be called great in the kingdom of heaven." In the light of Paul's gospel, however, we should not be surprised to hear the decisive consideration as it comes from Jesus' lips in v. 20: "For I tell you, unless your righteousness (*dikaiosynē*) exceeds that of the scribes and the Pharisees, you will never enter the kingdom of heaven." Paul's preaching to the Galatians was all about how our being declared righteous in God's lawcourt was a function of our obedience to that message. Thus, if our righteousness is going to "exceed that of the scribes and the Pharisees," it will have to be a righteousness rooted in the degree to which we are obedient to the Pauline gospel and live in a fashion reflective of it.

Paul's dying to the law was an instrumental part of what he presents here as a two-step process. He had to die to the law in order that the "faithfulness of Jesus as the Christ" (2:16) might reign supreme, not displacing the law but allowing Paul to see it as secondary to the more immediate gospel imperative of faith in Jesus as the Christ. It is only in this way that the believer will now be able to live to God. Paul expands on the implications of this line of thinking when he writes in vv. 19b-20:

Χριστῷ συνεσταύρωμαι·
²⁰ ζῶ δὲ οὐκέτι ἐγώ,
ζῇ δὲ ἐν ἐμοὶ Χριστός·
ὃ δὲ νῦν ζῶ ἐν σαρκί,
ἐν πίστει ζῶ τῇ τοῦ υἱοῦ τοῦ θεοῦ
τοῦ ἀγαπήσαντός με καὶ παραδόντος ἑαυτὸν ὑπὲρ ἐμοῦ.

I have been crucified along with the Christ;
²⁰ and so it is no longer I who live,
but it is the Christ who is living through me,
and what I am now living in the flesh
I am living as a result of my believing in the Son of God,
who loved me and who gave himself on my behalf.

Paul makes it clear that from this point forward covenant-salvation will explicitly consist of faith (*pistis*) rather than any formal obedience to the law (*nomos*). He describes the shift from the latter to the former as a dying to the law in order to live to God, and, as part of this process, he writes that he has been "crucified along with the Christ" (*Christō synestaurōmai*). What kind of sharing does he intend with a description like this? Is it a figurative mysticism on his part? What exactly does Paul mean when he writes about his having been co-crucified with the Christ? Paul contends that our being able to "live to God" will involve more than just a mental reorientation where what had been the absolute status of the law is concerned. Indeed, it will go beyond a merely factual understanding of our no longer having the law as an immediate master because the gospel is telling us as much. It requires an obedient restructuring of the self in accordance with the refocused commandment of the Old

VI. Our Being Declared Righteous (2:15-21)

Testament given to us first in the Pauline gospel and then mirrored by Jesus himself in John's gospel and the first epistle attributed to that author:

> A new commandment I give to you, that you love one another; even as I have loved you, that you also love one another. By this all men will know that you are my disciples, if you have love for one another...If you love me, you will keep my commandments...If a man loves me, he will keep my word, and my Father will love him, and we will come to him and make our home in him...As the Father has loved me, so I have loved you; abide in my love. If you keep my commandments, you will abide in my love, just as I have kept my Father's commandments and abide in his love. (John 13:34-35;14:15, 23; 15:9-10, RSV).

> Beloved, I am writing you no new commandment, but an old commandment which you had from the beginning; the old commandment is the word which you have heard...Beloved, let us love one another; for love is of God, and he who loves is born of God and knows God...We love, because he first loved us. If any one says, "I love God," and hates his brother, he is a liar; for he who does not love his brother whom he has seen, cannot love God whom he has not seen. And this commandment we have from him, that he who loves God should love his brother also...For this is the love of God, that we keep his commandments. And his commandments are not burdensome. (1 John 2:7; 4:7-8, 19-21; 5:3, RSV)

The gospel summons us to a new way of life resting on nothing more than the mortal trusting that is faith. The believer only ever grasps the meaning of this new life when he views it strictly in terms of the one death that does count, that is, the paradigmatic death of Jesus on the cross, a death that in Paul's gospel serves didactically as love's most perfect expression. The kind of love to which we are called originates in the love that the Christ himself personified—unfeigned, unflinching, wholly sacrificial, and thus perfect—and for any man to wager such a love in faithful obedience and to bear all that it entails means that he will face the prospect of his own crucifixion in the sense that if he wishes to love like the Christ then he too will have to be crucified like the Christ. The believer cannot realistically expect to duplicate the conditions of Jesus' sacrificial death, but, by means of his own faith in the gospel message concerning the faithfulness of the Christ Jesus, the believer joins his savior by means of his own self-crucifying act of belief.

Implicit in 2:19-20 is the question of what most fully realizes the law: obedience to it or the Christ's crucifixion. If Paul will soon write in 3:1 about his having clearly preached Jesus the Christ as crucified, the context there will be based on what he detailed in verse 20:

> [20] *and so it is no longer I who live,*
> *but it is the Christ who is living through me,*
> *and what I am now living in the flesh*
> *I am living as a result of my believing in the Son of God*
> *who loved me and gave himself on my behalf.*

In other words, Jesus' crucifixion functions scripturally as the fullest possible realization of the law, an obliterating response to every demand and problem raised by the mere formalism of the Mosaic law. It is only in this sense that Paul writes of his parallel "dying to the law by means of the law" in 2:19. For that to happen, for that kind of love to be the new reality and not just one more form of pretense, it will be necessary for the Christ himself to be our animating spirit disclosed to us at every moment by our heeding the gospel and living in obedience to it. When Paul writes that he has been "crucified along with the Christ," he is acknowledging that he is in the end not his own man, that he now stands totally subject to a new dynamic framed by faith in Jesus as the Christ. Whatever he now accomplishes "in the flesh" (*en sarki*), he does so only because Jesus has been his commanding spirit: "it is no longer I who live, but it is the Christ who lives through me." Paul describes the substance of this new life in terms of its only possible origin and sustaining power: "what I am living in the flesh I am living as a result of my believing in the Son of God, who loved me and who gave

VI. Our Being Declared Righteous (2:15-21)

himself on my behalf." Paul is thus telling the Galatians that, if it is true that "it is no longer I who live," this is a self-extinguishing reality predicated on the fact that the Christ now lives in him through his "believing in the Son of God." His point here is not to indicate an inner mystical condition, but rather to underline the fact that his is a perpetual commission to preach the same gospel that the Galatians first heard from him. 2:20b ("but it is the Christ who is living through me") contains the same prepositional phrase *en emoi* (literally, "in me") that we saw earlier in 1:16 and 1:24, two contexts that clearly dealt with the divine source of Paul's apostolic role and his efficacy in the preaching of the crucified Christ. It is thus that 2:20c ("and what I am now living in the flesh") is a reference to his continuing apostolic work and the revelatory faith on which it is founded. The point here is that—contrary to much mystical theologizing—the Christ *only lives* to the extent that Paul preaches him and those who hear him respond in faithful obedience.

Paul's compact description of this new life in vv. 15-21 weaves together the four frameworks: (1) the Christ's sacrifice of love upon the cross is the new basis for the *covenant* because (2) our being declared righteous in the divine *lawcourt* henceforth turns on our obedient reception of (3) the *eschatological* proclamation of his aeon-shifting gospel, the saving message that shares the (4) *christological* truth about Jesus as the Son of God and why he is our one true hope for the judgment to come. Paul makes the christological declaration that his faith in Jesus as the Christ and now as the "Son of God" is rooted in the fact that Jesus "loved me and…gave himself on my behalf." Here he is taking the Galatians back to the cross, to a reality only ever communicated to them via his preaching. It is thus that Paul continues in v. 21 in a way that directly connects the grace of faith with the gospel's proclamation of the cross:

²¹ οὐκ ἀθετῶ τὴν χάριν τοῦ θεοῦ·
εἰ γὰρ διὰ νόμου δικαιοσύνη,
ἄρα Χριστὸς δωρεὰν ἀπέθανεν.

²¹ I would not set aside the grace of God:
for if righteousness did in fact come by means of the law,
then the Christ died for no reason at all.

The righteousness of which Paul here speaks is the righteousness that is established when one is declared to be righteous (i.e. fully faithful to the covenant) in the eyes of God. Paul argues that such righteousness, when it is understood in the light of his gospel, is not at all derivative from the law and its many divisive prescriptions, but flows directly and solely from belief in the unifying death of Jesus on the cross. The fullness of God's grace thus precedes and is only then linked with a trusting response to the gospel, and, as Paul will make more clear in chapter 3, it is strictly on the basis of faithfulness (*ek pisteōs*) to his scriptural promises that God will declare the believer to be righteous. For the time being, the Pauline logic stands only in outline form in order that the righteousness of God might come to all men. It will come to them as a one-way gift announced by the faith-dependent gospel that he preaches. This is because, as Paul here maintains, any presumption that it still comes in a comparable fullness by means of the law (*dia nomou*) is to render the gospel's contents insignificant and to relegate the cross to the status of a distant and ultimately unnecessary tragedy.

VII. Why the Galatians are Foolish (3:1-5)

Having brought the Galatians to this point, Paul has them where, rhetorically speaking, he now needs them to be: at a veritable crossroads where they can survey the two possible directions in which they might proceed in their understanding of the gospel's power. In 2:21 Paul sets out these two possibilities: "for if righteousness did in fact come by means of the law, then the Christ died for no reason at all." On what then does the gospel's power depend? What is the only true and effective basis of our salvation? Of what will our righteousness before God consist? This is Paul's maneuver: he wishes to learn from the Galatians if those things will hinge on whether or not they are circumcised, and, by implication, just how the working of God's Spirit is linked with that or any of the other observations of the law. In 3:1-5 he delivers to the Galatians a high-flying rhetorical rebuke:

¹ Ὦ ἀνόητοι Γαλάται,
τίς ὑμᾶς βάσκανεν τῇ ἀληθείᾳ μὴ πείθεσθαι,
οἷς κατ' ὀφθαλμοὺς Ἰησοῦς Χριστὸς προεγράφη ἐσταυρωμένος
2 τοῦτο μόνον θέλω μαθεῖν ἀφ' ὑμῶν·
ἐξ ἔργων νόμου τὸ πνεῦμα ἐλάβετε
ἢ ἐξ ἀκοῆς πίστεως;
3 οὕτως ἀνόητοί ἐστε, ἐναρξάμενοι πνεύματι
νῦν σαρκὶ ἐπιτελεῖσθαι;
4 τοσαῦτα ἐπάθετε εἰκῇ
εἴ γε καὶ εἰκῇ.
5 ὁ οὖν ἐπιχορηγῶν ὑμῖν τὸ πνεῦμα
καὶ ἐνεργῶν δυνάμεις ἐν ὑμῖν,
ἐξ ἔργων νόμου
ἢ ἐξ ἀκοῆς πίστεως;

¹ *O foolish Galatians!*
Who has bewitched you that you should not obey the truth,
before whose eyes Jesus the Christ was clearly portrayed as crucified?
² *Only this one thing do I wish to learn from you:*

> *Did you receive the Spirit on the basis of works of the law
> or was it on the basis of a hearing with faith?
> ³ Are you in this way so foolish, that, having begun with the Spirit,
> you are now completing yourselves in the flesh?
> ⁴ Did you suffer so many things for no purpose
> —if it really was for no purpose?
> ⁵ Therefore he who now graciously grants the Spirit to you
> and who works mighty acts among you,
> does he do that on the basis of the works of the law
> or on the basis of a hearing with faith?*

Did Paul come to the Galatians preaching a gospel in which the very grace of God and the law were inseparable? Was their reception of the gospel the occasion for a following of the law's requirements, or was it characterized by their reception of and continuing obedience to his proclamation of the gospel? And if the Galatians are now concerned about the urgent necessity of things like circumcision, Paul is demanding to know from them on what basis does any of that have to do with the power made manifest among them. As Paul asks in 3:2, "Did you receive the Spirit *on the basis of (ek)* the works of the law, or was it *on the basis of (ek)* a hearing with faith?"—a rhetorical query that serves as a direct reminder that his preaching was not a message about salvation by means of circumcision, but one in which salvation only comes about by means of faith in Jesus as the Christ.

The first five verses of chapter 3 are scripturally resonant without directly relying on Old Testament quotation: they form a splendid rhetorical prelude to the rest of the third chapter where scriptural quotation is a key feature. A closer look at 3:1 reveals preparatory things for what will be Paul's main contention in the letter. First, there is his memorable characterization of the Galatians as "foolish" (*anoētoi*), a word whose function in this context goes far beyond mere insult. What this means is that, if Paul deliberately addresses the Galatians in this way, then he must have more in mind than judging them for their lack of intelligence. Recall that the wisdom literature of the Old Testament consistently contrasts the wise man's way with that of

VII. Why the Galatians are Foolish (3:1-5)

the fool. It is the former's acceptance of divinely established wisdom that establishes his status, while what characterizes the fool is his rejection of that same wisdom. The customary Septuagint rendering of "fool" is *aphrōn* (literally, he who is without the thinking discernment that the noun *phronēsis* entails), and the adjectival noun *anoētos* (singular of *anoētoi*) is a virtual synonym. Thus, whoever ranks as *anoētos* is by definition he who with "foolish" intention rejects the will of God as it is expressed in scriptural decrees, ordinances, and commandments. What helps us to see this term's scriptural valence is that the word *anoētos* also occurs in the Emmaus narrative in Luke 24.[1] In 24:25 Jesus confronts Cleopas and his unnamed companion with their refusal to believe what had already been proclaimed to them by the women:

> And he said to them, "O foolish men (*anoētoi*), and slow of heart to believe all that the prophets had spoken! Was it not necessary that the Christ should suffer these things and enter into his glory?" And beginning with Moses and all the prophets, he interpreted to them in all the scriptures the things concerning himself. (24:25-27, RSV)

By having the resurrected Jesus address the unbelieving pair in this way, the author of Luke's gospel is making the same connection between not believing the gospel's already proclaimed message and being *anoētos*. In parallel fashion both the Galatians and the men outside Emmaus had already heard the gospel message and each was experiencing a willful reluctance (what Paul construes as bewitchment in the Galatians' case) to "obey the truth."

---

[1] *Anoētos* also appears in 1 Timothy 6:9 and Titus 3:3 in contexts where the term is applied to a pre-gospel state of "foolishness." Paul also uses the term in Romans 1:14-15 (RSV): "I am under obligation both to Greeks and to barbarians, both to the wise and the foolish (*anoētoi*); so I am eager to preach the gospel to you who are also in Rome." In that context he clearly implies both those who have never heard the gospel and those who, having heard the message, understand it incompletely. The only point here is Paul's apostolic obligation and not how he would rate the inhabitants of Rome on anything like a sliding scale.

The truth in question here is the gospel's content, and this brings us to the second preparatory element contained in 3:1. When Paul asks, "Who has bewitched you that you should not obey the truth, before whose eyes Jesus the Christ was clearly portrayed as crucified?", he is yanking the delinquent Galatians back to the point where all things began for them. It was "before their eyes" (directly present and not through hearsay or second-hand acquaintance) that "Jesus the Christ was clearly portrayed as crucified." I find the phraseology in the second half of 3:1 to be inherently fascinating because of the way Paul uses it to remove himself temporarily from the equation while keeping the argument rolling. First, there is no mistake that the Galatians heard the gospel directly in the sense that it was initially received "by them [literally] in accordance with what their eyes saw" (*hois kat' ophthalmous*). Second, the gospel they heard ("saw") was about Jesus the Christ (once again, literally) "pre-sented (to them) as crucified". The aorist passive verb *proegraphē*, translated here as "clearly portrayed," literally means to "depict initially" (with the full implication that the initial depiction is the only viable one). Unlike the modern English language where representational media are readily distinguished, New Testament Greek collectively lumps all representation together by means of the verb *graphō*. Thus, when writing something down or producing a piece of sculpture or even rendering what we would term a painted image, the same verb would be used for all of these "representational" activities seen by the eye. As Paul was the first to preach the gospel to the Galatians, he was the first (*pro-*) to "represent" (*-graphō*) Jesus the Christ to them as crucified (*estaurōmenos*), i.e. he was the sole agent of the *prographē* (the single clear portrayal) referenced in 3:1. Thus what makes the Galatians "foolish" is their falling away from the foundational image of the Christ that Paul had preached to them.

The position established here is that Paul's gospel message was not couched in any terms other than that of "Jesus the Christ....clearly portrayed as crucified." If this is the case, then Paul demands in 3:2 to learn but "this one thing" (*touto monon*)

VII. Why the Galatians are Foolish (3:1-5)

from the Galatians: "Did you receive the Spirit on the basis of the works of the law or was it on the basis of a hearing with faith?" In 3:1-5 Paul is laying out the direct and necessary connection among the following three elements: (1) the gospel as he had preached it to them; (2) the Galatians' reception of that content on the basis of "a hearing with faith"; and (3) the Spirit-graced continuity of their obedience to that message. Given all of these things, Paul wants to know why there is now any need to carry out the requirements of the law, a point that is nowhere better summarized than in v. 3: "Are you in this way so foolish (*anoētoi*) that, having begun with the Spirit, you are now completing yourselves in the flesh?" If their initial reception of the gospel was on the basis of a hearing with faith, and, by implication, *that alone* resulted in their reception of the Spirit, then, "having begun with the Spirit" in this fashion, they should be concerned to continue in that mode. Instead they have opted for carrying out the requirements of the law as indicated here by Paul's reference to "completing yourselves in the flesh (*nyn sarki epiteleisthe*)."

Paul wants the Galatians to recall the sequence of God's own powerful outpourings here and understand that these things are not unconnected: that he came preaching the gospel of the crucified Christ, that they heard it with faith, and, as a result, they received the Spirit in their midst and were witnesses to its thus conditional manifestation. In addition, what they experienced must not have been without its own unique cost: "Did you really suffer so many things for no purpose—if it really was for no purpose?" We do not know for certain what kind of price the first Galatian believers had to pay for their acceptance of the gospel, but, if Paul's other letters are any indication in this regard, then it must have been some mixture of ridicule, ostracization, or outright persecution endured for the sake of the new faith. But, given all of what this must have involved and what the Galatians saw of the Spirit's power in those early days, for them to act now as if their initial hearing of the gospel and their faithful acceptance of it could be brushed aside in order that they might graduate to the seemingly higher requirement of circumcision was the trigger for Paul's determined intervention.

3:5 supplies the reality on which Paul insists in contrast to the mistaken apostasy he indicates two verses earlier: "Therefore he who now graciously grants the Spirit to you and who works mighty acts among you, does he do that on the basis of the works of the law or on the basis of a hearing with faith?" The thing to notice here is the contrast indicated in the translated text by what I view as the two now's. Although only 3:3 contains the adverb of time *nyn* ("now"), I have translated 3:5 to include it because of the pointed contrast on which Paul is relying. Their paired occurrence here serves to underscore these two mutually exclusive responses to the Pauline gospel. This is evident when the two verses are placed side by side:

> *Are you in this way so foolish, that, having begun with the Spirit, you are now completing yourselves in the flesh? (3:3)*
>
> *Therefore he who now graciously grants the Spirit to you and who works mighty acts among you, does he do that on the basis of the works of the law or on the basis of a hearing with faith? (3:5)*[2]

The point is that each verse indicates a separate and, as Paul rhetorically presents it here, concurrent response to his gospel which is the *only* point of departure available to the Galatians. If the Galatians are guilty of indulgently treating both responses (3:1-2 and 3:3) as being simultaneously possible, Paul is simply telling them that they cannot have their cake and eat it too. In other words, the foundation contained in 3:1-2 necessarily has 3:5 as its attendant corollary.

---

[2] This can be related to a third "now" that appeared in 2:19c-20: "I have been crucified along with the Christ; and so it is no longer I who live, but it is the Christ who is living through me, and what I am *now* (*nyn*) living in the flesh I am living as a result of my believing in the Son of God, who loved me and who gave himself on my behalf." This underscores how both Paul and the Galatians are equally bound by the same gospel.

VII. Why the Galatians are Foolish (3:1-5)

Paul does not wish for the Galatians to sell short what can only ever be the foundational gift of their faith, and that they might now be willing to see it as something incidental rather than as central and decisive to what they themselves have witnessed has earned them the apostle's rebuke. Paul's gospel to the nations was never in any sense about salvation through the adoption of Jewish ways. Neither was it about the necessity of even a lesser, qualified obedience to the law. It was instead about the God "who graciously grants the Spirit to you and who works mighty acts among you." And it is this aspect of things—the gift of the Spirit and the gospel-communicated power of him who "graciously grants" that living gift to the believer who hears the word—of which Paul seeks to remind the Galatian churches.

VIII. Why the Galatians are Sons of Abraham (3:6-22)

In 3:1 Paul declares that the gospel is about the crucified Christ, and it is by means of the *prographē* of his original preaching to them that the Galatians first "saw" and understood the crucifixion *as God's mightiest act*. Paul proclaimed that salvation comes through the death of a Jewish nobody, a man born in history and anointed by God to perform mighty acts of his own—healing the sick and the diseased, preaching the kingdom of God, casting out demons, and raising men from the dead in anticipation of his own glorification by God—and to become a message too improbable and contrary to the world's ways to be compelling in any customary fashion. What Paul writes in 3:1-5 recapitulates the course of his original evangelization of the Galatians, and at the core of it is one Jesus of Nazareth, communicated to the world as crucified, raised from the dead, and now glorified at the right hand of God.

It is for this reason that we must be mindful of the standing need to see all of Paul's talk about "righteousness" in the twin lights of the covenant and of faithfulness to it. There are other points in the letter (chapters 5 and 6) where Paul is prepared to speak about righteousness in its practical terms of personal piety and moral exertion, but the overall context for his continuing discussion of righteousness remains very much what was introduced earlier. The only righteousness in question here, indeed the only determining righteousness, is God's own righteousness as this has been indicated scripturally. In a word, it is understood as his faithfulness to his own covenant purpose and the correspondingly perfect righteousness demonstrated by Jesus by his self-sacrificial "obedience unto death, even death on a cross." (Philippians 2:8, RSV)

Paul will now elucidate the scriptural basis for this understanding of righteousness. If the Galatians are to grasp his epistolary appeal to them, what is in effect a re-*presentation* of the gospel in letter form, then he must offer a concise and scripturally-based unpacking of this righteousness and, specifically, of the nature of its source in the story of God's relationship with Israel. As we shall see, Paul will argue that what God initiated with Abraham has been consummated now in the Christ. Beginning in 3:6 and continuing to the end of chapter 4 Paul offers a retrospective interpretation of God's covenantal relationship with his people, and the scriptural focus throughout is on the figure of Abraham. 3:6-9 is the introduction of Abraham to the argument:

> ⁶ καθὼς Ἀβραὰμ ἐπίστευσεν τῷ θεῷ, καὶ ἐλογίσθη αὐτῷ εἰς δικαιοσύνην·
> ⁷ γινώσκετε ἄρα ὅτι οἱ ἐκ πίστεως, οὗτοι υἱοί εἰσιν Ἀβραάμ.
> ⁸ προϊδοῦσα δὲ ἡ γραφὴ ὅτι ἐκ πίστεως δικαιοῖ τὰ ἔθνη ὁ θεός, προευηγγελίσατο τῷ Ἀβραὰμ ὅτι ἐνευλογηθήσονται ἐν σοὶ πάντα τὰ ἔθνη·
> ⁹ ὥστε οἱ ἐκ πίστεως εὐλογοῦνται σὺν τῷ πιστῷ Ἀβραάμ.

> ⁶ *Just as Abraham believed God, and it was reckoned to him as righteousness,*
> ⁷ *therefore know that the ones who live on the basis of faith are the sons of Abraham.*
> ⁸ *And scripture,*
> *foreseeing that God would declare the nations righteous on the basis of faith,*
> *proclaimed the gospel beforehand to Abraham, saying,*
> *"through you shall all the nations be blessed,"*
> ⁹ *so that the ones who live on the basis of faith will be blessed along with the faithful Abraham.*

But this section of the text is so closely linked with what precedes it that many often miss the closeness upon which Paul is counting. Focus on the way in which v. 6 reads: "Just as Abraham believed God, and it was reckoned to him as righteousness" and notice the following elements:

(1) The line begins with the connective "just as" (*kathōs*), a conjunction that Paul intends to use as a rhetorical bridge between what 3:1-5 presents as having been the Galatians' original experience with Paul's preaching and what in Paul's argument will

VIII. Why the Galatians are Sons of Abraham (3:6-22)

be the prototypical figure of Abraham. It points to a direct connection between what the Galatians have experienced and what scripture tells us about Abraham. In other words, Paul wants them to see that their own experience (what he is now in effect challenging them to deny) stands parallel with the faith-rooted experience of Abraham. If Abraham believed God (*episteusen tō theō*) and that scriptural fact was, quite literally, "spoken of" (*elogisthē*) as having made him righteous in the lawcourt of God, then, as Paul presses the Galatians, if they received his preaching "on the basis of a hearing with faith (*ex akoēs pisteōs*)," then what does that say about their kinship with Abraham?

(2) Paul is quoting Genesis 15:6, a passage that deserves review in its entirety. The Abraham narrative in Genesis comprises 14 chapters of material (11:27-25:18) that chronicle the story of God's unique relationship with a man who stands as the scripturally-pedigreed ancestor of Israel. There are five "promise episodes" in which God declares that through Abraham all the nations will be blessed because it will be through his own son that a great nation will be founded, and it will inhabit a land that the Lord has promised to grant this nation to possess.

We have encountered the first promise episode in Genesis 12:1-3, and much has taken place scripturally before the second one occurs in chapter 15: Abraham's departure from Haran and his journey to Canaan, the sojourn in Egypt, dividing the land with his nephew Lot, the war with the eastern alliance of kings, the rescue of Lot's household, and the encounter with the mysterious figure of Melchizedek, the king of Salem. By the beginning of chapter 15 Abram (not yet renamed Abraham) has complained to God about the lack of a son and a true heir for what has been promised to him. The passage 15:3-6 in the RSV translation is worth quoting in full:

> And Abram said, "Behold, thou hast given me no offspring (*sperma*); and a slave born in my house will be my heir." And behold, the word of the LORD came to him, "This man shall not be your heir; your own son shall be your heir." And he brought him outside and said, "Look toward heaven, and number the stars,

if you are able to number them." Then he said to him, "So shall your descendants (*sperma*) be." And he believed the LORD; and he reckoned it to him as righteousness.

Paul quotes Genesis 15:6 because it makes the fundamental point about the nature of the promise made by God, namely, that the promise is now being made for the second time under no less "promising" circumstances, yet "he [Abraham] believed the LORD; and he reckoned it to him as righteousness." In a situation that clearly pointed in the opposite direction, i.e. Abraham's continuing lack of a male heir, this wandering Aramaean reaches the point where he believes what God has told him, and it is this act of *believing* despite all indications to the contrary that "[God] reckoned to him as righteousness." Even though Paul quotes 15:6 in its Septuagint Greek rendering which casts the verb used for reckoning in the passive voice ("and it was reckoned to him as righteousness"), the original Hebrew employs an active voice verb, in which it is God himself who does the reckoning, but the difference is not a critical one because it is obvious that God's reckoning of such is all that matters. The emphasis of the passage surely remains the fact of Abraham's believing under such conditions, and that his intentional belief in the face of them is what constitutes his righteousness.

In the remaining text of chapter 15 there is the Lord's promise to Abraham that he shall inherit the land in which he now sojourns, followed by his command for Abraham to render an eerily atmospheric animal sacrifice, an act that culminates in 15:18-20 (RSV):

> On that day the LORD made a covenant (*diathēkē*) with Abram, saying, "To your descendants (*sperma*) I give this land, from the river of Egypt to the great river, the river Euphrates, the land of the Kenites, the Kenizzites, the Kadmonites, the Hittites, the Perizzites, the Rephaim, the Amorites, the Canaanites, the Girgashites and the Jebusites."

VIII. Why the Galatians are Sons of Abraham (3:6-22)

The points to note here are that Genesis 15 includes: (1) Abraham's believing in God's promise, and that this belief was "reckoned to him as righteousness"; (2) the first mention of the word "covenant" (*diathēkē*) in connection with Abraham is associated with this event; and (3) the word "covenant" is not used again until chapter 17 when Abram is renamed as Abraham, and it is only then that circumcision is imposed in connection with the third promise episode.

By quoting Genesis 15:6 at this point, Paul wants the Galatians to see belief as preliminary and, by implication, of more basic importance than any subsequent cultic requirement like circumcision. When circumcision is at last introduced in Genesis 17, it is presented as being a physical sign or an emblem of a covenant already announced and, scripturally speaking, in place. The implication here is clear: belief is antecedent to circumcision, and that the latter was an important though secondary consideration in the history of God's covenant relationship with Israel. What precedes the language about circumcision in Genesis 17 is the story of Abraham fathering a son Ishmael through his wife Sarah's Egyptian maid, Hagar, in chapter 16, a chronicle that would seemingly detract from the belief previously credited to Abraham in chapter 15. But the fathering of a son through Hagar comes at the invitation of Sarah, a fact that expresses if anything her own human desperation over her state of barrenness. It does nothing either to negate the promise made by God or even to cancel the significance of Abraham's clearly stated response to it.

And it is after the birth of Ishmael that the next promise episode comes in chapter 17. In Genesis 17:5-11 (RSV) God speaks to his servant:

> "No longer shall your name be Abram, but your name shall be Abraham; for I have made you the father of a multitude of nations. I will make you exceedingly fruitful; and I will make nations of you. And I will establish my covenant (*diathēkē*) with you and your descendants (*sperma*) after you throughout their

generations for an everlasting covenant (*diathēkē*), to be God to you and to your descendants (*sperma*) after you. And I will give to you, and to your descendants (*sperma*) after you, the land of your sojourning, all the land of Canaan, for an everlasting possession; and I will be their God." And God said to Abraham, "As for you, you shall keep my covenant (*diathēkē*), you and your descendants (*sperma*) after you throughout their generations. This is my covenant (*diathēkē*), which you shall keep between me and you and your descendants (*sperma*) after you: Every male among you shall be circumcised. You shall be circumcised in the flesh of your foreskins, and it will be a sign (*sēmeion*) of the covenant (*diathēkē*) between you and me."

Given the emphasis that Paul wishes to place on belief over circumcision, this text would appear to be just as problematic as the chapter 16 account of Ishmael's birth, but the introduction of circumcision here as a "sign of the covenant" only comes after the content of the covenant is given once again in the most direct possible language: that Abraham will be the "father of a multitude of nations" and that "an everlasting covenant" will be established so that the Lord might be "God to you and to your descendants after you." Circumcision is thus a sign *subsequent* to the covenant and is not in any credible sense the substance of it: it is at best an emblem of something more fundamental, more necessary, and ultimately more decisive, namely, an abiding human faith in the purposes of God.

It should be no wonder that the remaining half of Genesis chapter 17 is taken up with a reiteration of God's promise to Abraham that he will bring forth from Sarah's womb a son whose name he now declares will be Isaac. While God acknowledges the fruitfulness of Ishmael and his descendants in Genesis 17:19-21 (RSV), he makes his own covenantal intentions clear with regard to the son to be born of Sarah:

> God said, "No, but Sarah your wife shall bear you a son, and you shall call his name Isaac. I will establish my covenant (*diathēkē*) with him as an everlasting covenant (*diathēkē*) for his descendants (*sperma*) after him. As for Ishmael, I have heard you; behold, I will

VIII. Why the Galatians are Sons of Abraham (3:6-22)

bless him and make him fruitful and multiply him exceedingly; he shall be the father of twelve princes, and I will make him a great nation. But I will establish my covenant (*diathēkē*) with Isaac, whom Sarah shall bear to you at this season next year."

It is worth noting in this passage that the language about "covenant" and "descendants" is used only in connection with Isaac. The promises made by God concerning Ishmael and the fate of his offspring have to do with multiplying him so that he becomes the father of a "great nation." Paul will take up again the differences between what scripture has to say about Isaac and Ishmael later in the letter.

Please recall the earlier discussion concerning the four frameworks for understanding the Galatian letter—covenant, the court-of-law language, eschatology, and christology—and especially in connection with the way in which the concept of covenant was to be understood: that God's plan for the salvation of the world involved what he would accomplish by means of Israel. God's own adherence to this plan is what constitutes his righteousness (*dikaiosynē*), what makes him *dikaios*, and his chosen medium for the accomplishment of this salvation was the people of Israel. The latter's origin was in Abraham, and scripture testifies to the fact that Israel (understood as being the descendants of Abraham) was, humanly speaking and at this point in the Genesis narrative, born from Abraham's own adherence to the covenant and, above all, to the unfulfilled promise of it. Thus it is that when Paul quotes Genesis 15:6 in 3:6, "Just as Abraham believed God, and it was reckoned to him as righteousness," he is stating that Abraham's faith in the promise made by God stands as his own inimitable righteousness or steadfast adherence to the salvific purposes contained in the covenant relationship. Genesis of 15:6 makes the connection as succinctly as possible: Abraham believed in what God had promised to him, and the actuality of this faith (*pistis*) is what allows him to share in God's own "righteous" adherence to the world-saving covenant.

Having established this link and all of its attendant scriptural associations in 3:6, Paul then declares in the following verse what it should mean for the Galatians:

> [6] *Just as Abraham believed God, and it was reckoned to him as righteousness* (dikaiosynē),
> [7] *therefore know that the ones who live on the basis of faith* (pistis) *are the sons of Abraham.*

The phrase translated as "the ones who live on the basis of faith" is one of those uniquely compact expressions often found in the New Testament. In Greek it is *hoi ek pisteōs*, and it literally means "the ones who are on the basis of faith." But how one *is* depends on how one lives, or, more exactly, on what makes him live, that is, what is the true basis for his existence, not just in mere biological terms, but what constitutes the basis for the way in which he stands in relation to God. In short, on what must a person's relationship with God depend? Paul is making the argument that the basis for this relationship with God must be one of faith, that it must be all about the Galatians believing—"just as Abraham believed"—in the promise made long ago and its continuity with the promise now fully realized in their midst. Now if this kind of faith was reckoned to Abraham as righteousness (his faith in what God had promised and not yet realized), then their faithful (*pistos*) hearing of Paul's gospel, which resulted in the gift of the Spirit, would place them in the same league as Israel's ancestor and it would be solely on this basis that they in turn could be counted as "sons of Abraham."[1]

That Paul is seeking to establish this connection—that it is *on the basis of faith* that people become the true descendants of Abraham—is confirmed in 3:8-9:

---

[1] There is a prepositional parallelism at work in the phrases *hoi ek pisteōs* ("the ones who live on the basis of faith") and *hoi ek peritomēs* ("the advocates of circumcision") introduced in 2:12. In each case we see what defines its fundamental mode of standing in righteous relation to the covenant.

VIII. Why the Galatians are Sons of Abraham (3:6-22)

⁸ *And scripture,*
foreseeing that God would declare the nations righteous on the basis of faith,
proclaimed the gospel beforehand to Abraham, saying,
"Through you shall all the nations be blessed,"
⁹ *so that the ones who live on the basis of faith will be blessed along with the faithful (*pistos*) Abraham.*

Verse 9 contains the same phrase "the ones who live on the basis of faith" as was found in v. 7, and this second occurrence serves to bring out the fullness of the original covenantal promise. In v. 7 "the ones who live on the basis of faith" are straightforwardly identified as sons of Abraham, but in v. 9 this same group is also declared to be sharers in the blessing that will come to the members of all nations who exhibit the same kind of faith as "the faithful Abraham." This latter phrase, "the faithful Abraham," is literally "the believing (*pistos*) Abraham," a designation that underscores Paul's basic contention, namely, that one is reckoned as a descendant of Abraham primarily on the basis of faith and not by any of the cultic observations required by the law.

Paul is in the process of establishing a basic contrast, a dichotomous pairing of things which will stand, not in absolute opposition, but in a mutually illuminating relationship with each other. In what follows, he will provide the outlines of a covenantal anthropology that illustrates his view of the mechanics behind human salvation, i.e. the things on which it depends and what will make it possible. In verse 10 he supplies the other half of this contrasting pair for which he is arguing:

¹⁰ ὅσοι γὰρ ἐξ ἔργων νόμου εἰσίν,
ὑπὸ κατάραν εἰσίν·
γέγραπται γὰρ ὅτι
ἐπικατάρατος πᾶς ὃς οὐκ ἐμμένει πᾶσιν τοῖς γεγραμμένοις ἐν τῷ βιβλίῳ τοῦ νόμου
τοῦ ποιῆσαι αὐτά.

¹⁰ *For as many as there are who live on the basis of the works of the law,*
they are all living under a curse;

for it stands written,
"Cursed is every one who does not abide by all the things written in the book of the law,
and do them."

Just as the category "the ones who live on the basis of faith" occurred in vv. 7 and 9, there is now a *de facto* contrasting category in v. 10. The initial clause "For as many as there are who live on the basis of the works of the law" (*hosoi gar ex ergōn nomou eisin*) is a reference to the Jewish cultic focus on salvation as entirely dependent on obedience to the Mosaic law. However, here the category refers not so much to a historical group as it does to a mode, one that Paul must distinguish from what he has already described in 3:7-9. Either category is a designation for a specific mode of life, and here "life" must be understood strictly in terms of how one stands in relation to God and his covenant. What then will be the basis for the fullness of that life, and what, concretely speaking, will constitute the terms for its realization? In short, under what conditions will man be able to participate in the fullness of the covenantal life to which God is calling him?

Paul's appreciation of covenantal life in terms of a starkly simple choice is nothing new. It is a brand of scriptural admonition seen throughout the Old Testament, and it is no accident that in v. 10 Paul quotes from its most relevant example, namely, Moses' culminating appeal to the Israelites in chapters 27-30 of Deuteronomy. Those chapters are a presentation of the Two Ways, a pair of choices that will decide the covenantal fate of Israel: one way being a path of blessing predicated on obedience to the commandments which make up the covenant, and the other way consisting of Israel being cursed as the result of her disobedience. The choice is summarized by Moses in the concluding lines of chapter 30 (RSV):

"I call heaven and earth to witness against you this day, that I have set before you life and death, blessing (*eulogia*) and curse (*katara*); therefore choose life, that you and your descendants may live, loving the LORD your God, obeying his voice, and cleaving to

VIII. Why the Galatians are Sons of Abraham (3:6-22)

him; for that means life to you and length of days, that you may dwell in the land which the LORD swore to your fathers, to Abraham, to Isaac, and to Jacob, to give them."

Note that Paul is doing very much the same thing here, retaining the same language about a relative blessing (3:9 and 3:14) or a curse (3:10) but this time with a disturbingly novel twist.

Just as the Jewish Torah climaxes with the Deuteronomic vision of the Two Ways—a scenario whose outcome is based on whether the people will accept the law or reject it, whether they will be blessed or cursed—so too does Paul's dichotomous vision of things present what would appear to be a case of accepting the law or rejecting it. But now the very blessing of which Paul speaks is dependent on what—as his opponents would charge—amounts to a conscious rejection of the law's primacy in favor of the stance of faith he has been advocating. Was it possible that Paul's opponents were right? Were they correct when they charged him with arguing against the law and preaching a gospel based on things not at all connected with Israel's history? And why is Paul now identifying the observation of the law with being accursed?

In vv. 6-9 he has already identified the blessing of God as being what is due to the ones who believe (*hoi ek pisteōs*), that this is what qualifies them to be "sons of Abraham." And now, having stipulated that God's ultimate blessing and the true life that results from it depend upon an Abraham-ic attitude of faith, in contrast to this he declares in v. 10 that the ones "who live on the basis of the works of the law" are under a curse. He quotes Deuteronomy 27:26 in order to back up this claim: "Cursed is every one who does not abide by all of the things written in the book of the law, and do them." But how can the law, what is seen as God-given and thus the traditional center of Jewish religious life, in any way constitute a curse? What does it mean in this context to declare the doers of the law to be "living under a curse"? Recall that the biblical understanding of being "accursed" amounted to a kind of death sentence, the realization that you and your household were doomed to die and to be forgotten. The Greek word for "cursed" in Deuteronomy 27:26 is *epikataratos*, which literally means to have had the curse pronounced upon you.

The Deuteronomy quote makes it clear that the law, though inherently good by virtue of its divine origin and the way in which it had structured the daily life of the people of Israel, is not so much defective as it was unable to guarantee that "as many as there are who live on the basis of the works of the law" will be declared righteous before God. Any man might embrace the law and seek to live in accordance with its statutes with what is an exemplary dedication, but like any other man he is still fated to die and to remain dead until the hoped-for day of resurrection. Now the Pharisee Paul understood that the resurrection of the "justified" ones (i.e. the ones who would be declared righteous (*dikaios*) in the eyes of God upon resurrection) was to have been on the basis of their adherence to the law in accordance with Pharisaic insistence in this regard, but that was a wholly future expectation: observing the law = being declared righteous (*dikaios*) = resurrection from the dead unto salvation. The resurrection of Jesus changed his thinking on this subject because Jesus, the crucified Nazarene, God himself had raised from the dead, and he resurrected Jesus in the here and now rather than on the day of the Lord, and so the standard Pharisaic line of reasoning in this matter could no longer stand: if Jesus had been raised from the dead here and now, it was because he was not only *dikaios*, but supremely *dikaios*.

Paul knew that it did not matter how many loving souls dedicated to the pious observance of the law had gone to the grave because not a single one of them had ever been resurrected. Thus he continues in vv. 11-12:

^{11} ὅτι δὲ ἐν νόμῳ οὐδεὶς δικαιοῦται παρὰ τῷ θεῷ δῆλον,
ὅτι ὁ δίκαιος ἐκ πίστεως ζήσεται·
^{12} ὁ δὲ νόμος οὐκ ἔστιν ἐκ πίστεως,
ἀλλ᾽ ὁ ποιήσας αὐτά ζήσεται ἐν αὐτοῖς.

VIII. Why the Galatians are Sons of Abraham (3:6-22)

*11 And as it is evident that by the law no one is declared righteous before God, because "he who is righteous shall live on the basis of faith,"
12 for the law is not on the basis of faith, rather "he who does these things, by them shall he live."*

Verse 11 is one of the most compact ever written by Paul by virtue of the multiple elements found in it. First, it builds on the revision of Pharisaic thinking concerning the relationship between observance of the law and resurrection as experienced by Paul in the wake of his encounter with the resurrected Christ, a fact which led him to conclude that being declared righteous (*dikaios*) was not a strict result of executing the works of the law. Second, if he has preached Jesus as resurrected from among the dead, it was because the latter was truly *dikaios*, and his declared righteousness (*dikaiosynē*) was linked to his faithful adherence to the totality of the law, and, as we shall see, his submission to God's plan of salvation for the whole world. And third, as the quotation from Habakkuk 2:4 makes clear, faith in God's ultimate and saving purpose for the entire world is what creates the possibility of true and everlasting life for those who hear the gospel.

It is worth taking a closer look at Habakkuk's prophecy in order to understand why Paul chose it at this juncture in his argument. What concerns us is the initial part of the three chapters that comprise the book of Habakkuk, specifically the section 1:1-2:5. The text represents a four-part dialogue between the prophet and God. The first part (1:1-4) opens with the prophet complaining to God about the continuing violence and injustice he sees all around him and the fact that the Lord has done nothing to alleviate it. God replies in the second part (1:5-11) with a pregnant admonition for the prophet (1:5, RSV): "Look among the nations, and see; wonder and be astounded. For I am doing a work in your days that you would not believe if told." In this passage God declares the rampaging Chaldeans (Babylonians) to be the instrument of his impending judgment upon a disobedient people, but in the third part (1:12-2:1) the prophet responds by appealing to God's merciful greatness and declaring his own faithful patience concerning it. It is in connection with both the prophetic promise and Paul's own evangelistic purpose that in 1:12 he delivers the key declaration: "Art thou not from everlasting, O LORD my God, My Holy One? We shall not die." The third part concludes with the prophet uttering, "I will take my stand to watch, and station myself on the tower, and look forth to see what he will say to me, and what I will answer concerning my complaint." God provides an answer in the fourth part (2:2-5), and the text of 2:2-4 (RSV) is worth quoting in full:

> *² And the LORD answered me:*
> *"Write the vision;*
> *make it plain upon tablets,*
> *so he may run who reads it.*
> *³ For still the vision awaits its time;*
> *it hastens to the end--it will not lie.*
> *If it seems slow, wait for it;*
> *it will surely come, it will not delay.*
> *⁴ Behold, he whose soul is not*
> *upright in him shall fail,*
> *but the righteous (dikaios) shall live by his faith."*

Paul was interested in the Habakkuk prophecy because of the connection between the exclamation found in 1:12 ("We shall not die."), which the Greek Septuagint renders in a way that is perhaps more translatable as "And let us not die!", and the portion of 2:4 which he quotes in his letter. When Paul quotes Habakkuk 2:4b, "because he who is righteous (*dikaios*) shall live on the basis of faith," he does so because in his eyes the passage is an answer to the prophet's statement in 1:12. If the eternal God has promised life to us, that is, if we are going to live according to the life he has promised to us, then that life will be realized on the basis of faith. He has already asserted that righteousness does not come in any ultimate or definitive sense by adhering to the dictates of the law, rather it only truly and finally comes through the believer's acceptance of Jesus as the Christ, of Jesus being God's most rationally incomprehensible

VIII. Why the Galatians are Sons of Abraham (3:6-22)

and therefore most mighty act of salvation which is, to quote Habakkuk once more, "a work in your days that you would not believe if told." (1:5)[2]

The importance of Habakkuk 2:4b at this point is that the text establishes a link between being declared righteous (*dikaios*) and faith (*pistis*). Paul has been making the case for Abraham's example, and he has even gone so far as to assert that the gospel's content was there all along in those patriarchal days when he asserts in 3:8, "And scripture, foreseeing that God would declare the nations righteous (*dikaios*) on the basis of faith (*pistis*), proclaimed the gospel beforehand to Abraham, saying, "Through you shall the nations be blessed." If the prophet Habakkuk speaks about God's goodness and the triumph of his justice in the face of so much suffering and oppression experienced by those "who live on the basis of the works of the law," then the prophet's words point us in the direction of faith in God's purpose and the substance of his actions, and, as Paul consistently argues, these latter things have been consummately realized in the crucified Christ.

It is Paul's contention that one should not approach the crucified Christ solely in terms of the law and the formal obedience presupposed by it. As we will see shortly in 3:13-14, the more immediate issue is not the blessing of obedience but the curse of disobedience. It is thus done instead on the basis of a faith in who he is and what God has accomplished through him. In v. 12 Paul asserts "for the law is not on the basis of faith, rather "he who does these things, by them shall he live," and the quotation provided here is from Leviticus 18:5, a text that would seemingly support the opposite of what Paul is arguing, namely, that by obeying and doing what the law commands, then one shall live as a result of it. But here, once again, a closer look at

---

[2] The author of Acts depicts Paul quoting this same verse at the end of his synagogue speech at Pisidian Antioch during his first missionary journey (13:41). The passage in which it occurs, Acts 13:36-47, stands as a summary of much that Paul argues in chapter 3 of Galatians.

the Greek text is warranted because, in my opinion, the prepositional phrases at work there are telling.

The Greek Septuagint rendering of Leviticus 18:5, when translated literally into English, reads: "he who does these things, he shall live in them," and the phrase "these things" refers to what the first half of 18:5 (RSV) mentions: "You shall therefore keep my statutes and my ordinances." For the sake of a fuller context, Leviticus 18:1-5 (RSV) states that God, having brought the Israelites out of Egypt where they were surrounded by Egyptian pagan practices and now led them to Canaan where they would once again encounter Canaanite paganism, announces to the people of Israel that "You shall do my ordinances and keep my statutes and walk in them (*poreuesthe en autois*). You shall therefore keep my statutes and my ordinances, by doing them a man shall live: I am the LORD." (18:4-5) It is in such a context that "doing the statutes and ordinances" amounts as much to a strategy for collective preservation as it does being obedient to God. In a word, when scripture speaks here of "by doing them a man shall live," the implication is that, if he does not do them, then he will be swallowed up (i.e. die) in a syncretizing sea of pagan practices that are already by the law's own reckoning the domain of the accursed. This is corroborated by the prepositional phrase contained in the way Paul renders the text as "he shall live in them (*zēsetai en autois*)." What was said earlier in connection with the instrumentality of the prepositions *ek* ("on the basis of") and *dia* ("by means of") does not apply so matter of factly here because phrases employing the preposition *en* ("in") more often connote actual and durable arrangements which make it possible for things to be realized practically. Think of the latter as an instrumentally locative mode, i.e. how being located *within* something, i.e. under its aegis and responding to its authority, functions to determine the arrangement.

Paul quotes Habakkuk 2:4b in order to establish an instrumental connection between faithful trust and not dying in relation to God and his wishes. After invoking this scriptural

VIII. Why the Galatians are Sons of Abraham (3:6-22)

association in this way, his citing of Leviticus 18:5 is meant to point out a crucial difference between (a) believing in God's purpose and the kind of life that will result from it, and (b) a day-to-day obedience to the law and its works so that the nation might survive as a cohesive group until such time as God would reveal the fullness of his purpose and move to execute it. In its own way each of the above two positions is about life, each is about our human living and the circumstances that affect it, but life conducted decisively *on the basis of* faith is here (3:11) made out to be the more urgent proposition, and it is central to Paul's vision of salvation.

It is for this reason that Paul moves to make the telling contrast in 3:12 when he says "for the law is not on the basis of faith, rather "he who does these things, by them (*en autois*) shall he live." Thus, when the Israelites, in the face of so much surrounding pagan influence, remain "in" the statutes and the ordinances of the law, they will indeed "live," i.e. they will survive as a group by remaining obedient to God in this fashion, but what they will have achieved "by them" will be no more than just that, surviving over time and not being dissolved among the pagan nations. In this way living "in" the law amounts to a preservation strategy, the only way in which the ethnic and religious integrity of the Hebrew people could be safeguarded over time. Keep in mind too the implicit point that in this same context the law is serving a short-term didactic purpose, an aspect of which Paul himself will soon enough make mention in his letter.

This quick succession of quotations from the Torah is intended by Paul to drive home the following points: (1) that the law, though inherently good and instructive, does not in itself guarantee any man being righteous before God, (2) that the law is an incomplete remedy for sin, and (3) that the law is not an end-point, in a word, that it is not God's final and saving gift to us. These three points constitute the law's "cursedness"—the fact that, as helpful as the law is, by itself it is not enough to defeat the devil, sin and death. *Something more* was needed, something final, decisive, and, as Paul himself would so expressly contend, *eschatological* in the sense of it marking a definite historical climax and the discernible transition to a new age.

Paul declares this "something more" in vv. 13-14, a passage that stands in the closest possible relationship to what preceded it in vv. 6-12, and in which Paul now begins to outline how what went before is intimately related to what has only now become apparent to the Galatians in their own time:

¹³ Χριστὸς ἡμᾶς ἐξηγόρασεν ἐκ τῆς κατάρας τοῦ νόμου γενόμενος ὑπὲρ ἡμῶν κατάρα,
ὅτι γέγραπται,
ἐπικατάρατος πᾶς ὁ κρεμάμενος ἐπὶ ξύλου.
¹⁴ ἵνα εἰς τὰ ἔθνη ἡ εὐλογία τοῦ Ἀβραὰμ γένηται ἐν Χριστῷ Ἰησοῦ,
ἵνα τὴν ἐπαγγελίαν τοῦ πνεύματος λάβωμεν διὰ τῆς πίστεως.

¹³ The Christ has bought us back from the curse of the law,
having become himself a curse on our behalf,
because it stands written,
"Cursed is every one who hangs on a tree,"
¹⁴ so that in the person of the Christ who is Jesus,
the blessing of Abraham might come upon all the nations
so that we might receive the promise of the Spirit by means of faith.

Even in the Greek text the ordering of these words must be closely examined. We are accustomed to thinking and speaking in a more or less linear fashion. We string statements and clauses together in a sequential order of relative causality--we declare first A, then B, followed by C, an ordering which entails that A causes B, which in turn results in C, etc. We would read v. 13a in just this way, registering the seemingly primary fact that Jesus "has bought us back from the curse of the law" and seeing that it is followed by what would appear to be a secondary detail in the clause "having become himself a curse on our behalf." But in order to appreciate the causal thinking at work here and the full (and therefore *christological*) significance of what Paul is asserting,

VIII. Why the Galatians are Sons of Abraham (3:6-22)

it would be more instructive to read v. 13a in the following way: "*because* the Christ himself has become a curse on our behalf, he has bought us back from the curse of the law." When read in this fashion, the emphasis has been shifted away (albeit temporarily) from the not insignificant fact of Jesus having "bought us back from the curse of the law," and it is placed instead on the means which made it possible for him to have accomplished this redemptive purchasing of our selves.

The Greek word used here for "buying back" is the verb *exagorazō*, a term etymologically related to *agora*, the word that referred to the large open space usually located near a city's gate and which served as its marketplace area. It was in the agora, in that common public space where things were bought and sold, that the daily trade constituting the lifeblood of the polity was conducted. The verb *exagorazō* is often and justifiably translated as "to redeem," and any "redemption" that results from our having redeemed something is, as this word literally indicates, a "buying back from something" (*ek* 'back" + *agorazō* "to buy" = *exagorazō*). In v. 13a the buying back in question is Jesus buying us back "from the curse of the law" (*ek tēs kataras tou nomou*), and this act, the very foundation of the way in which Paul understood our salvation, must be approached in terms of the answer we shall give to the question, "What does it mean when we say that Jesus became a curse on our behalf?"

We have already taken note of the scriptural language concerning the curse. First, that it is associated with Israel's failure to acknowledge the God who led them out of Egypt and to obey his commandments. If the Israelites obeyed, then God would "bless" them with continuing existence as his people. But if they did not obey his commandments, then he would "curse" his people with disintegration and exile. Secondly, we should remind ourselves at this point that the scriptural background for this "cursedness" was established in the Genesis 3 narrative of man's accursed fall into disobedience. God had already ordained to Adam and Eve that "you shall not eat of the fruit of the tree which is in the midst of the garden, neither shall you touch it, lest you die." (3:3, RSV) In the wake of the serpent's temptation and Adam and Eve's succumbing to its suggestion, God pronounces a curse upon each of them in 3:14-19 (RSV), a key text which should be quoted in full because it contains as much language about promise-through-obedience as it does about being accursed-through-disobedience:

> *The LORD God said to the serpent,*
> *"Because you have done this,*
> *cursed (*epikataratos*) are you above all cattle,*
> *and above all wild animals;*
> *upon your belly you shall go,*
> *and dust you shall eat*
> *all the days of your life.*
> *I will put enmity between you and the woman,*
> *and between your seed (*sperma*) and her seed (*sperma*);*
> *he shall bruise your head,*
> *and you shall bruise his heel."*
> *To the woman he said,*
> *"I will greatly multiply your pain in childbearing;*
> *in pain you shall bring forth children,*
> *yet your desire shall be for your husband,*
> *and he shall rule over you."*
> *And to Adam he said,*
> *"Because you have listened to the voice of your wife,*
> *and have eaten of the tree of which I commanded you,*
> *'You shall not eat of it,'*
> *cursed (*epikataratos*) is the ground because of you;*
> *in toil you shall eat of it all the days of your life;*
> *thorns and thistles it shall bring forth to you;*
> *and you shall eat the plants of the field.*
> *In the sweat of your face you shall eat bread*
> *till you return to the ground,*
> *for out of it you were taken;*
> *you are dust,*
> *and to dust you shall return."*

Genesis 3 details what happened when Adam and Eve chose to disobey the single thing that God had told them not to do. The

VIII. Why the Galatians are Sons of Abraham (3:6-22)

simplicity of the narrative is sufficient to make a single scriptural point, namely, that disobedience of God's express commandment entails the termination of his blessing. God's cursing verdict on Adam and Eve for their disobedience is not the imposition of mortal death—as classical Christian theology strays into supposing—but rather the introduction of the scriptural principle that whatever is not of God's blessing is automatically the stuff of his curse. The latter can be summarized schematically in this way: disobedience/sin = curse = exile = death. God's garden had been the setting for the fullness of his blessing, but now it has become the scene of man's punishment for his disobedience. Death was henceforth to be understood in terms of man spending the length of his days without the "fullness" implied from his having been able to eat from the tree of life (only the tree of the knowledge of good and evil had been forbidden). In Genesis 3:23-24a (RSV) God exiles Adam and his wife from the garden in accordance with the punishment he has pronounced:

> therefore the LORD GOD sent him forth from the garden of Eden, *to till the ground from which he was taken*. He drove out the man; and at the east of the garden of Eden he placed the cherubim, and a flaming sword which turned every way, to guard the way to the tree of life.

Man's existence outside of the garden would now be marked by the fact that the ground was cursed "because of him" and thus the toil and discomfort of cultivating that ground for the same food that God had freely offered to him in the garden would constitute his punishment: "In the sweat of your face you shall eat bread *till you return to the ground*, for out of it were you taken; you are dust, and to dust you shall return." (3:19)

Genesis 3 sets the stage for the scriptural history of mankind's plight as it unfolds in Genesis 3-11. It is the story of mankind's progressive alienation from God, of the human race's retreat into disobedient rebellion and self-assertion vis-à-vis the express will of God. The result was an entire human race plagued by fragmentation, conflict, and sinful arrogance. Prior to the appearance of Abraham and the covenant of trust that God would make with him even before the giving of the law, the story of the tower of Babel (11:1-9) functions as the epitome of men's wish to "make a name for ourselves, lest we be scattered abroad upon the face of the whole earth." (11:4) The point of the given account is that mankind has reached the apogee of its desire to assert itself unilaterally *without the blessing of God*, and—in a way that parallels the end of Genesis 3—it results in God dispersing the assembled tower-builders and scattering them in what amounts to exile from the site of what has been their consummate disobedience.

What now changes the direction of the scriptural narrative is the introduction of Abraham, the theme of a covenant based on faithful obedience, and the express declaration of God that his was a salvation intended for all the peoples of the earth, that they might be declared righteous in his eyes. Toward that end God sent the law, but, as Paul indicated in 3:11-12, even the law did not suffice to guarantee a man being declared righteous before God because "the law is not of the basis of faith." Paul cites Habakkuk 2:4b to support his argument for faith's necessity, and his quotation of Deuteronomy 27:26 serves to bring into focus the "cursed" condition of those who wager to live—albeit never perfectly—in accordance with "all the things written in the book of the law." (3:10)

When Paul proclaims in 3:13a that Jesus has bought us back from the "curse of the law," that he has redeemed us from the law's inability to procure a verdict of righteousness before God (due more to human disobedience than the law's impossibility), and that he has done this by becoming a "curse on our behalf," he is referring once again to the clear connection between accursedness and the Christ's own dying, because in v. 13b he continues his line of argument:

VIII. Why the Galatians are Sons of Abraham (3:6-22)

because it stands written,
"*Cursed* (epikataratos) *is every one who hangs on a tree,*"

This quotation from Deuteronomy 21:23 serves as a grim scriptural reminder about some of the penal dynamics involved in crucifixion and similar forms of execution. Paul extracted it from Deuteronomy 21:22-23, a passage which has a direct relevance to the crucifixion narratives found in the gospel accounts, namely, that the body of someone put to death in this fashion could not remain "hanging on a tree" past the sunset which marked the ending of that same day (Matthew 27:57-60; Mark 15:42-46; Luke 23:50-56; John 19:31-42):

And if a man has committed a crime punishable by death and he is put to death, and you hang him on a tree, his body shall not remain all night upon the tree, but you shall bury him the same day, for a hanged man is accursed (*kekatēramenos*) by God; you shall not defile your land which the LORD your God gives you for an inheritance.

The Greek Septuagint rendering of "accursed" in Deuteronomy 21:23 is *kekatēramenos*, and, even though Paul renders it as *epikataratos*, the two terms are of sufficient semantic likeness so as to produce no interpretive difficulties. *Kekatēramenos* is arguably a more explicit rendering of "accursed" than *epikataratos* since the former is the perfect participle of the verb *kataraomai*, and thus literally means "he who has been cursed." To be cursed is a death sentence: it is to be marked for death in a way that involves extinction apart from God's blessing. The serpent had tempted Adam and Eve in the garden, luring them into disobedience, the hard fact of sin, an absolute either/or condition relative to the will of God. Genesis 3 is the aetiology (foundational myth) of mankind's descent into a state of disobedient alienation from God, from him who is the very source of blessed life rather than cursed existence.

If disobedience results in the "curse of the law," then the only antidote for man's chronic condition of disobedience and willful self-assertion would be an act of ultimate obedience, of the Christ offering himself up for the sake of all who would believe in him and the significance of his sacrifice (1:4, 2:20). In this context it is not just by the fact of Jesus having died, but above all by his submissively dying an *accursed* death (à la Deuteronomy) that the Christ could become the curse. By submitting to death on the cross, itself that most savage symbol of the curse, Jesus became "himself a curse on our behalf" (*genomenos hyper hēmōn katara*). This helps us to understand the parallelism at work in the language of 2:19-20 where Paul asserts that "by means of the law I have died to the law in order that I might live to God." Living to God will only be possible if there is new life after our having been "crucified along with the Christ."

It is now that we are in a position to appreciate the way in which the four framework ideas are combined in vv. 13-14, and N.T. Wright sums up the significance of their interplay in this fashion:

> The Messiah became a curse for us by hanging on the tree, coming himself to the place of the curse as indicated by Deuteronomy—and thereby making a way *through the curse and out the other side*, into the time of renewal when the Gentiles would at last come into Abraham's family, while Jews could have the possibility of covenant renewal, of receiving the promised Spirit through faith (as in Galatians 3:2, 5).[3]

Taking the four elements in reverse order, we should see that Jesus' death on the cross was the pivotal eschatological event because it is the clear inauguration of our deliverance from "this encompassing evil age" (1:4). It shows us that the christological valence of Jesus' self-sacrificial death is communicated to us by the gospel's insistence that God is henceforth operating explicitly in these terms when it comes to effecting the salvation not just of the Jews but of all the nations. The lawcourt vindication of Jesus (why he is most truly righteous and thus the

---

[3] Wright, *Justification*, 125.

VIII. Why the Galatians are Sons of Abraham (3:6-22)

Christ) is linked to the believer's trusting faith in the gospel message concerning him, and how this is now the basis for covenant relationship, for the believer's membership in God's family.

Paul's entire focus in vv. 13-14 is on the Jesus who submitted to death on a cross, and how that forms the core of the saving message he preached to the Galatians. It is worth repeating the passage at this point:

> [13] *The Christ has bought us back from the curse of the law,*
> *having become himself a curse on our behalf,*
> *because it stands written,*
> *"Cursed is every one who hangs on a tree,"*
> [14] *so that, in the person of the Christ who is Jesus,*
> *the blessing* (eulogia) *of Abraham might come upon all the nations,*
> *so that we might receive the promise of the Spirit by means of faith.*

This blessing (*eulogia*), initially vouchsafed to Abraham in Genesis 12:1-3 and never impossible even when men were busy disobeying the Mosaic law, can now "come upon all the nations" because it is the gift of God freely given to all men and now to be received "by means of faith." The Jewish law was there all along, as that standing witness to God and recorded blueprint for being declared righteous. It was there as an instructor, as a safeguard, as a bulwark against the many temptations of paganism, but what had always contained the formal means of belonging to the covenant-family was subjected to parochializing misconstrual. In other words, what always had to do with repentant obedience was being subsumed by a spirit of particularist zeal (hence what Paul writes in 1:13-14 and 2:14-16).

The Pauline gospel is based on a faithful surrender to God's purposes as these have been revealed to us "in the person of the Christ who is Jesus." It is thus a message open to all men. Here there was no discrimination, no particularizing, no specificity rooted in anything other than a gospel proclamation offered to all the peoples of the earth about who Jesus is and why it is all about faith. The sign of its immediacy as well as of its potency was to be found in the manifestation of the Spirit. What Paul means by the Spirit I will seek to explain below. In the meantime Paul is outlining the true flowering of God's promise, and his language here is revealing. He argues that, if the Christ has bought us back from that curse by himself becoming a curse (his accursed death paradoxically but perfectly realizes the obedience demanded by the law and thus releases its blessing), then this makes two things possible, each one conveyed in v. 14 by its own separate yet closely connected subjunctive clause. First, it will be "*so that*, in the person of the Christ who is Jesus, the blessing of Abraham might come upon all the nations", and second, "*so that* we might receive the promise of the Spirit by means of faith."

The first result is that "in the person of the Christ who is Jesus" the blessing that God had ordained for the nations as coming through Abraham will have become a reality. The phrase which I translated here as "in the person of the Christ who is Jesus" is much longer than the corresponding phrase in the Greek text, and my rendering amounts to a christological elaboration of those mere three words in the Greek: *en Christō Iēsou*. This phrase could be translated literally (and often is) as "in Christ Jesus," but the justification for rendering it as "in the person of the Christ who is Jesus" derives from the inner logic of vv. 13-14. Paul has already stated that it is the Christ who "has bought us back from the curse of the law" and there is no question about the identity of this Christ: Jesus of Nazareth is the crucified Christ, and now *in him*, in the gospel-mediated person of Jesus crucified and raised from the dead, the Christ has been revealed, and *to what end?* It is Paul's contention that the children of Israel, the descendants of the same Abraham to whom God had spoken of a blessing to come, that they are now witness to this blessing in their midst "in the person of the Christ who is Jesus." Just as the earlier citation of Leviticus 18:5 was an assurance to the Israelites that their doing the law would be the guarantee of their survival "in the law," so too Israel

VIII. Why the Galatians are Sons of Abraham (3:6-22)

would henceforth not just survive but attain to very fullness of life by believing in the Christ preached by Paul. The basic gospel claim contained in the first subjunctive clause about the universal availability of Abraham's blessing is then given its grounding in the second subjunctive clause "so that we might receive the promise of the Spirit by means of faith."

What has happened here? Paul is making a most radical claim, one often not fully understood or appreciated even by Christians, namely, that the culmination of the salvific process contained in his gospel—the proof of the blessing promised by God to Abraham and its substance—is the reception and the manifestation of the Holy Spirit among the ones who believe. This is a situation only made possible "by means of faith," by a steadfast acceptance and affirmation of Jesus as the "Christ crucified." Christian existence, in order to conform to the gospel as presented by Paul, will have to be a *scripturally-bound life of obedience*. Paul's language about the Spirit at this point should not be understood as denoting a self-standing reality apart from the scriptural word. In other words, without the gospel and a hearing of it with faith, there is no Spirit! If this is true, then Paul would like to know why the Galatians are now so eagerly running off to be circumcised, why they are "building up again these things that I have taken apart." (2:18)

The nature of this charismatic mode must not be misunderstood because otherwise we risk completely missing the point of Paul's letter. Recall that in 3:2-5 Paul asks the Galatians about receiving the Spirit. He is presupposing the Spirit's initial presence among them in the form of their obedience to his gospel word when, in the face of their newfound concern for circumcision, he is brought to ask, "Only this one thing do I wish to learn from you: *Did you receive the Spirit* on the basis of the works of the law or was it on the basis of a hearing with faith? Are you in this way so foolish, that, *having begun with the Spirit*, you are now completing yourselves in the flesh?" In other words, the Spirit's presence among the Galatians is not a matter of their experiencing (inter)subjective, ethereal realities, but rather of their remaining steadfastly obedient to the word as Paul has preached it to them, about the self-sufficient basis of a "hearing with faith."

At this point in the text Paul does not relent in his focus upon Abraham. Having now identified God's covenantal promise to Abraham as being in fact a "promise of the Spirit" (*epangelia tou pneumatos*), he continues in his linking of the Christ with the covenant, the latter now framed entirely in the language of promise (*epangelia*):

¹⁵ ἀδελφοί, κατὰ ἄνθρωπον λέγω·
ὅμως ἀνθρώπου κεκυρωμένην διαθήκην οὐδεὶς ἀθετεῖ ἢ ἐπιδιατάσσεται.
¹⁶ τῷ δὲ Ἀβραὰμ ἐρρέθησαν αἱ ἐπαγγελίαι καὶ τῷ σπέρματι αὐτοῦ.
οὐ λέγει· καὶ τοῖς σπέρμασιν,
ὡς ἐπὶ πολλῶν ἀλλ' ὡς ἐφ' ἑνός·
καὶ τῷ σπέρματί σου, ὅς ἐστιν Χριστός.
¹⁷ τοῦτο δὲ λέγω·
διαθήκην προκεκυρωμένην ὑπὸ τοῦ θεοῦ ὁ μετὰ τετρακόσια καὶ τριάκοντα ἔτη γεγονὼς νόμος
οὐκ ἀκυροῖ εἰς τὸ καταργῆσαι τὴν ἐπαγγελίαν.
¹⁸ εἰ γὰρ ἐκ νόμου ἡ κληρονομία,
οὐκέτι ἐξ ἐπαγγελίας·
τῷ δὲ Ἀβραὰμ δι' ἐπαγγελίας κεχάρισται ὁ θεός.

¹⁵ *Brothers and sisters, I am now speaking in human terms:*
*no one nullifies or adds to a man's covenant (*diathēkē*) once it has been ratified,*
¹⁶ *and the promises (*epangeliai*) were made to Abraham and to his seed*
*(*sperma*).*
He does not say, "And to seeds,"
as if he meant many, but rather he meant one,
*"and to your seed (*sperma*)," who is the Christ.*
¹⁷ *And this I am saying:*
the law that came four hundred and thirty years later
*does not annul a covenant (*diathēkē*) previously ratified by God*
so as to remove the promise.
¹⁸ *For if the inheritance is on the basis of the law,*
*it is no longer on the basis of a promise (*epangelia*);*

VIII. Why the Galatians are Sons of Abraham (3:6-22)

*but God had given it to Abraham by means of a promise (*epangelia*).*

In vv. 15-18 Paul is making a calculated reference to some of the inviolable attitudes associated with the treatment of a human will. The Greek word *diathēkē* ordinarily refers to a human "last will and testament," but it is also the word used to translate "covenant" in the Greek Septuagint. Paul will avail himself of the meaning of the word *diathēkē* "in human terms" (*kata anthrōpon*) in order to make a few points about God's covenantal relationship first with Abraham and later with all of Israel. The single point to remember here is that in either instance *diathēkē* denotes what is supposed to be the unqualifiable expression of the author's ratified intentions, i.e. the unambiguous statement of his personal will and wishes. Paul's invocation of *diathēkē* is designed to help make the point that God's promise to Abraham and the resulting ratification of the covenant intended to contain it (expressed not so much by the institution of circumcision in Genesis 17 as it is by the birth of Isaac in chapter 21) means that its promissory content has been set and it shall not be amended in any way.

Once more Paul will refer back to the accounts in Genesis of God's promises (*epangeliai*) to Abraham. Having first made the point that no human will can be annulled or modified after it has been ratified (established and authenticated), he applies the same line of reasoning to the divine will, referring to the initial mention of the promise in chapter 12, and specifically to God's addressing Abraham when the latter has paused outside of Shechem. Genesis 12:7 (RSV) reads: "Then the LORD appeared to Abram, and said, "To your descendants (*sperma*) I will give this land. So he built there an altar to the LORD, who had appeared to him." In 3:16 Paul explicitly interprets the singular "seed" (*sperma*) in this passage as a prophetic reference to the Christ, and the language in Genesis 12:7 about "this land" is an extrapolative reference to the blessing of all the nations through Abraham and his descendants. The "land" in Canaan becomes a concrete symbol for the whole of Abraham's inheritance/blessing: the latter will not materialize and mature unless Abraham remains *in the land* and brings forth a male heir by his wife Sarah. In this connection it should be noted as well that the singular *sperma* also refers to Isaac, who stands as the first figure in the line of descent stretching from Abraham to Jesus of Nazareth (cf. the two genealogies of Jesus contained in Matthew 1:1-17 and Luke 3:23-34).

Paul points out that the law, stipulated by him as having come 430 years later, cannot be regarded as having in any way altered what the initial promise contained. It is in v. 18 that Paul tightens up this interpretive line of thinking when he introduces the word "inheritance" (*klēronomia*), a term which will have the greatest scriptural significance for the presentation of his gospel because it serves as a summarizing designation for the very specific way in which Paul understands the history of human salvation. Briefly stated, it comes down to this: it is God's will (*diathēkē*, "in human terms") to save the world (i.e. to bless all the nations) through Abraham and his seed (*sperma*), and God establishes his will (*diathēkē*, but now as scriptural covenant) by means of his promise (*epangelia*) to Abraham. This seed will germinate and become the nation of Israel that will one day include in its line of descent one Jesus of Nazareth who is the Christ. It is the Christ who will accomplish for Israel, bound as she is under the law (*nomos*) because of sin's hegemony, what she could not do for herself—to be fully and completely faithful (*pistos*) and thus "fulfill all righteousness" (cf. Matthew 3:15)—by being supremely righteous (*dikaios*) through death on the cross. The unquestionable sign of that righteousness is his resurrection from the dead. Thus what the Christ has accomplished by means of his faith (*pistis*) is that in which the believer will come to share on the basis of his own faith. Just as Christ was crucified in accordance with the promise made to Abraham and the faith with which the latter responded to it, so too shall the believer simultaneously *on the basis of* faith and *by means of* it participate in God's plan of salvation. It is this end-point, namely, the faith-based prospect of our being "in the Christ" (what Paul outlines

VIII. Why the Galatians are Sons of Abraham (3:6-22)

in 2:15-21), that will derive from our own faithful response to the gospel. It will only be realizable to the extent that we come to believe that Jesus is this Christ as Paul is summoning us to do, that Jesus crucified and raised from the dead is the culmination of God's wish to save humanity from the threefold tyranny of the devil, sin, and death.

This is the inheritance (*klēronomia*) of which Paul speaks, which he states cannot be "on the basis of the law" (*ek nomou*) because the law only divides, distinguishing Jew from non-Jew, and it has no universalizing power to unite. Rather, the inheritance (our participation in the salvation of Israel and, by extension, of the entire world) can only be "on the basis of a promise" (*ek epangelias*), the one originally given by God to Abraham, and which is supposed to result in the blessing of all the nations when that which Paul proclaims comes full circle, when "on the basis of faith" (*ek pisteōs*) we shall be numbered as "sons of Abraham" (cf. 3:6-7, "the ones who live on the basis of faith are sons of Abraham").

The sequencing of the prepositions in 3:18 is crucial. Paul contends that if the gospel of Christ had been ultimately about the salvific power of the law (and, by implication, what would render the Galatians righteous in their newfound attention to its statutes), then the saving inheritance offered by God—man's ability to participate in the fullness of salvation—would have been predicated on the law all along because the law is what will have made it possible ("For if the inheritance is on the basis of the law…"). But it is this privileging of the law, the assumption addressed in 3:15 that the law in some way "nullifies or adds to a man's covenant once it has been ratified" ("the inheritance…is no longer on the basis of the promise") that Paul rejects. What is subsequent to the promise ("four hundred and thirty years later") cannot be seen as having altered in any way the dynamic content of that original promise.

Paul wants the Galatians to see the historical sequencing of scripture as mirroring the actual working out of God's purposes here: "but God had given it [the inheritance] to Abraham by means of a promise." The two preceding occurrences of the preposition *ek* ("on the basis of") present us with a contrasting pair (think of them as the two possible sources of salvation), with each element—the promise and the law—presented as a distinctive but yet not wholly separate, equitable, or even self-sufficient possibility. When left in just such an opposition as this, neither the promise nor the law element is explicitly privileged. What breaks this scriptural tie is the preposition *dia* ("by means of"), which serves to highlight God's *direct action* in the coming of blessing/salvation to mankind. If man is to be blessed/saved, and the promise and the law are the two scenarios of that blessing/salvation, then it will be strictly a matter of God's own initiative and action allowing us to see how he accomplishes it. At a more theoretical level we can ask ourselves, "By means of *what* will God do it?" As Paul proceeds in his argument, it will become more apparent that he only thinks of salvation as being by means of a *Whom*.

It is critical to grasp Paul's line of thinking at this point in his letter. It would be easy for us to approach his argument in terms of what is the standard Protestant faith vs. works dichotomy, and to argue for the primacy of faith in just such a manner (good faith vs. bad works), but to do so prevents us from seeing Paul's consistently *scriptural vision* of the working out of our salvation. This is a vision that will take into account a primary promise and a secondary law, but which will see these two things as being in a fruitful tension with each other, and then accedes to God his own direct action in the resolution of this tension. Centuries of Protestant either/or interpretation have unfortunately impaired our ability to see and to appreciate the fundamental fullness of Paul's view of the law in relation to faith, namely, that where the Christ is concerned, neither faith nor the law is sufficient *by itself* because each must be seen in relation to the gospel-mediated Christ: by the law he is prophesied, but by faith he is received and by obedience he becomes truth.

VIII. Why the Galatians are Sons of Abraham (3:6-22)

But, as much as we by now might be willing to acknowledge the necessity of faith and its primacy in connection with what has been proclaimed to us by Paul, at the same time we might remain yet a little bit puzzled over just how we are to regard the law. Given the overall thrust of Paul's argument so far, it would be quite easy to assume at this point that the status of the law vis-à-vis the faith now required of us was simply a matter of supersession, namely, that the law could be ignored if not even entirely discounted because it was to have been replaced in every respect by an attitude characterized above all by a personal faith. How Paul deals with this question is contained in the remainder of chapter 3 and the whole of chapter 4. But now he continues, directly addressing the question of the law in vv. 19-22:

¹⁹ τί οὖν ὁ νόμος;
τῶν παραβάσεων χάριν προσετέθη,
ἄχρις οὗ ἔλθῃ τὸ σπέρμα ᾧ ἐπήγγελται,
διαταγεὶς δι᾽ ἀγγέλων ἐν χειρὶ μεσίτου.
²⁰ ὁ δὲ μεσίτης ἑνὸς οὐκ ἔστιν, ὁ δὲ θεὸς εἷς ἐστιν.
²¹ ὁ οὖν νόμος κατὰ τῶν ἐπαγγελιῶν τοῦ θεοῦ;
μὴ γένοιτο·
εἰ γὰρ ἐδόθη νόμος ὁ δυνάμενος ζῳοποιῆσαι,
ὄντως ἐκ νόμου ἂν ἦν ἡ δικαιοσύνη·
²² ἀλλὰ συνέκλεισεν ἡ γραφὴ τὰ πάντα ὑπὸ ἁμαρτίαν,
ἵνα ἡ ἐπαγγελία ἐκ πίστεως Ἰησοῦ Χριστοῦ
δοθῇ τοῖς πιστεύουσιν.

¹⁹ Why then the law?
It was added because of our transgressions
until such time as the seed would come to whom the promise had been made,
it having been ordained by angels at the hand of an intermediary.
²⁰ Now the intermediary is not just one, but God is one.
²¹ Is the law then against the promises of God?
Certainly not!
For if a law capable of giving life had been given,
then in fact righteousness would have been on the basis of the law;
²² rather, scripture has consigned all things under sin
in order that the promise that is based on the faith of Jesus the Christ
might be given to the ones who believe.

This passage must be understood in terms of the scriptural chronology that always characterized Paul's thinking. Recall the three elements that constitute man's mortal predicament: (1) tempted by the serpent, man falls into the (2) chronic condition of sinful disobedience, and the latter places him in (3) perpetual danger of living life in cursed separation from the deity. God promises blessing/salvation to Abraham when in Genesis 22:18 (RSV) he declares, "by your descendants (*sperma*) shall all the nations of the earth bless themselves because you have obeyed my voice." The law is an integral part of the covenant, a divine instruction in the most practical sense of the word. Recall that the Hebrew word Torah means "instruction," and without the content of its moral and ethical teaching, the specifications of its cultic rules, and the didactic chronicle of God's relationship with his people Israel, there would have been no survival of Abraham's seed. Central to Paul's scriptural understanding was the idea that, even though the salvation of mankind depended on a promise, we must for the time being (prior to its "fullness," 4:4) submit to the law's guidance and instruction.

Paul is at his most matter of fact here when he writes that the law "was added because of our transgressions." If disobedience was the daily blot in man's existence, then God ordained that a law should be given to his people in order that they would have a basis for distinguishing obedience to God's will from disobedience, for aiming at blessing and life rather than incurring the curse of exile and death apart from God. The law was thus God's indisputable gift to his people, a guide "ordained by angels at the hand of an intermediary [Moses]," but behind the biblical narrative of Israel's history with its sometimes complex cast of characters there was always the singular purpose of God and the promise containing it ("but God is one"). Why else does Paul reply so vehemently, "Certainly not!" when he rhetorically asks, "Is the law then against the promises of God?" in v. 21a? It is because, as he then indicates in v. 21b, that "if a law capable of giving life had been given, then in fact righteousness would have been on the basis of the law." The key point here is the life-

VIII. Why the Galatians are Sons of Abraham (3:6-22)

giving *insufficiency* of the law, that if the latter had been fully and directly "capable of giving life," then it would have served as the unqualified fulfillment of the promise. As a Pharisee Paul was content to regard the strictest obedience to the law as the only guarantee that any man who lived in that fashion would be resurrected on the day of the Lord, but the resurrection of Jesus and Paul's own encounter with him irrevocably altered the entire equation. The raising of Jesus from the dead could not, in any one-for-one mechanical sense, be construed as the result of a hyper-exact obedience of the law's minutiae; rather it was based on his crucifixion having been the most obediently self-sacrificial act and therefore the ultimate fulfillment of the law. It was in this sense that Jesus, when he was hanging dead on the cross, was the perfect embodiment of the righteous obedience that God sought from Israel, and the proof, indeed, the most indubitable sign of that righteousness, was his resurrection from the dead.

So the law was not an end in itself, and the only way it could be such an end would be if it were in itself "life-giving" (*zōopoiein*), that is, apart from whether it was obeyed or not. Now the Pharisees viewed the law as being the one life-giving thing to which they could cling, but the law's capacity to give life for them was a highly specific one. The law was the focus of Hebrew existence, the organizing principle for the national life of the people as well as for individual behavior, and, as we have already noted, adherence to it was a prerequisite for being raised in righteousness on the day of the Lord. Pharisaic piety was wholly a matter of the adherent's scrupulous observance of the law.

This was the scriptural logic which Paul followed (reflected in his citation of Leviticus 18:5 in 3:12 above)—one that had made perfect Pharisaic sense to him before his encounter with the risen Christ, but, once that had taken place, it was one that was no longer plausible when seen in the light of that encounter. The law was not "against the promises of God" firstly because, as

Paul observes, "scripture has consigned all things under sin." This simply means that the scriptural history of Israel's relationship to the law was one of repeated rejection and rebellion. It was not possible for any man—let alone the people—to obey the law comprehensively. Secondly, it was because the law formed—by virtue of the scriptural story—the preparatory context for the very reception of those promises and the only way to guarantee Israel's survival until such time as the promises would be fulfilled. Paul's contention that our being declared righteous can no longer be automatically *and exclusively* predicated on our adherence to the law must be seen in connection with the apostle's declaration of Jesus as the risen Christ. It is in this connection that Paul outlines the new eschatological covenant-reality in v. 22 (with 21b prefixed here):

For if a law capable of giving life had been given,
then in fact righteousness would have been on the basis of the law;
²² rather, scripture has consigned all things under sin
in order that the promise that is based on the faithfulness of Jesus the Christ
might be given to the ones who believe.

This is the great transitional passage. This is the point in Paul's argument where he announces not the law's cancellation but rather the *fulfillment* of all things in his day. He is speaking to the Galatians again—this time in writing—as the apostle of the crucified and risen Christ, the true seed of Abraham (3:16), and the gospel which he has proclaimed to them was not so much about a new reality as it was about a *truer* reality rooted in the revelation of Jesus as messiah, as the anointed one, as the *Christos* of prophecy, and how he is now the expectant hope of the nations.

IX. Why the Galatians are One in the Christ (3:23-29)

Paul steadfastly refuses to regard the law as being in any way evil or defective and thus deserving of rejection. He only wishes to stress—where our being declared righteous is concerned—why it does not have an *absolutely determinative* status. In 3:21-22 he declares the law to be incapable of giving life, but this is not because the law was flatly ineffective. Indeed, if man could obey it wholly and indisputably, all righteousness would have been on the basis of the law, but sin sabotaged human obedience to the law. It is Paul's understanding that the law was not impervious to sin: it only "worked" when men obeyed it. The law was such that it could only ever be pursued and realized *among men*, but, given that "scripture has consigned all things under sin" (scripture tells the story of Israel's failure to obey the law), and, because any human effort to realize the law's demands could not rise above the uneven level of our mortal captivity to sin, the law could not be a genuine avenue to life.

It is the scriptural story of Israel's sinful disobedience and subsequent standing under the curse (3:10) that allows Paul to position the law in relation to his gospel. In 3:23-24 Paul sketches the law's preparatory role in relation to it:

²³ πρὸ τοῦ δὲ ἐλθεῖν τὴν πίστιν
ὑπὸ νόμον ἐφρουρούμεθα
συγκλειόμενοι εἰς τὴν μέλλουσαν πίστιν ἀποκαλυφθῆναι,
²⁴ ὥστε ὁ νόμος παιδαγωγὸς ἡμῶν γέγονεν εἰς Χριστόν,
ἵνα ἐκ πίστεως δικαιωθῶμεν.

²³*But before faith came,*
we were being held under the law's watch,
bound together for the sake of the faith about to be revealed,
²⁴ *such that the law had become our tutor concerning the Christ*
in order that we then might be declared righteous on the basis of faith;

This was no ruse or deception on God's part. He did not intend the law to fool men but rather to instruct them, that even though it functioned to "produce" sin among them, it also served as the means by which the lives of men could be focused and productive "before faith came": "we were being held under the law's watch, bound together for the sake of the faith about to be revealed." When Paul writes concerning this "faith about to be revealed" (*tēn mellousan pistin apokalyphthēnai*), he is referring to what can be seen as the inherently *apocalyptic* content of his gospel, to the fact that it is a revelatory declaration about revelation itself (a proclaimed *apokalypsis* concerning God's *apokalypsis*, a revealing of what God has revealed, what he is doing by means of his crucified messiah). It is thus that his proclamation of the gospel to the Galatians can be the only true eschatological moment for them in that it was foundationally necessary "in order that the promise that is based on the faithfulness of Jesus the Christ might be given to the ones who believe." (3:22) This means that the faith (*pistis*) of which he writes in v. 23 is not strictly a reference to the individual's act of believing, but rather a statement about how *pistis* can only ever be seen in relation to what requires *pistis*.

In this connection Paul states quite clearly the law's preparatory function in v. 24: "such that the law had become our tutor concerning the Christ in order that we might be declared righteous on the basis of faith." He is asserting that in the interval between the giving of the law and the coming of the Christ, the most commendable way in which we might one day receive him, for us to understand the meaning of his faithfulness, and thus to learn what is required for our faith, is to submit to the law's tutoring. Here the Greek text tells us that the law functioned as man's "tutor" (*paidagōgos*), and that this tutoring had always been a matter "concerning the Christ" (*gegonen eis Christon*).[1] But what is the proper tutorial for receiving the

---

[1] The preposition *eis* (εἰς) also means "toward something," "in view of something," or "for the sake of something." In this context I have distilled these other possible meanings into the rendering "concerning the Christ."

IX. Why the Galatians are One in the Christ (3:23-29)

Christ? Does one receive him simply by virtue of his own birthright, by his being born and raised in a community steeped in the law and thus prepared for the day when the Christ would be proclaimed? Does one receive the Christ by submitting to a set of cultic requirements and the ethnic identification that goes with them? No, because if the instruction was "concerning the Christ," then the pedagogical goal is the Christ himself and not the law *per se*! As noted earlier, the law (*nomos*) in Paul's hands includes more than the regulatory prescriptions contained in the Pentateuch (what we might assume to be the "law" proper). For much of chapter 3 Paul is in familiar Pentateuchal territory: he invokes Abraham and Moses, but in 3:22 he writes that "scripture (*hē graphē*) has consigned all things under sin." What he means is that the whole body of the Old Testament (the Pentateuch, the prophets, and the wisdom literature) testifies to the reality of Israel's failure to obey the law and how that resulted in her accursed condition of an "exilic return," i.e. even though the Jews had physically returned to the land, they were still living in disobedience to the law. But even if, scripturally speaking, all things are compromised by sin, what counts is the promise contained in the way that scripture foresaw that "God would declare the nations righteous on the basis of faith." (3:8) Thus for Paul there was not going to be a strictly law-based way out of Israel's predicament: rather the only possible avenue of escape from it would be by means of (a) a trusting faith in what God had promised to do, and (b) a corresponding trust (*pistis*) that "in the person of the Christ who is Jesus the blessing of Abraham might come upon all nations." (3:14) The law therefore functioned in Paul's eyes as the only possible tutor for us where the Christ was concerned, the one proper *paidagōgos* for the promised day when "we then might be declared righteous on the basis of faith."

In this passage the image of the *paidagōgos* is an important one. In the ancient world no man was self-sufficient. In the organized social life of men any person who wished to mature and to become a man had to submit to instruction whether it was personally or professionally oriented. There was really no such thing as a self-made man because in order to become *anything* a person had to be taught, and, in theory, he should be taught by a reputable teacher: if his teacher was qualified and capable, then not only he but all others could rely upon the results. Paul is banking on this set of associations when he describes the relationship of the law's pedagogical role to his gospel declaration of the Christ and our reception of it "on the basis of faith." Here the law's divine pedigree serves as the assurance that the instruction is as good as it is reliable, and, since any instruction is a preparation, when the true purpose of that instruction does arrive, then the student will have been well served.

But there is the moment when the instruction ends and the tutor's job is finished. If the law was neither the whole of God's promise nor its exhaustive content, and if it was there to prepare men for the fulfillment of that promise, then—in Paul's eyes—the law's appointed purpose will have been to instruct men "concerning the Christ" (*eis Christon*), and that moment when we are no longer being guided by the tutor's instruction is the eschatological day of faith (3:1-5). In vv. 25-26 Paul continues this thought (here with v. 24 prefixed):

²⁴ ὥστε ὁ νόμος παιδαγωγὸς ἡμῶν γέγονεν εἰς Χριστον,
ἵνα ἐκ πίστεως δικαιωθῶμεν.
²⁵ ἐλθούσης δὲ τῆς πίστεως
οὐκέτι ὑπὸ παιδαγωγόν ἐσμεν.
²⁶ πάντες γὰρ υἱοὶ θεοῦ ἐστε
διὰ τῆς πίστεως ἐν Χριστῷ Ἰησοῦ·

²⁴ *such that the law had become our tutor concerning the Christ*
in order that we then might be declared righteous on the basis of faith.
²⁵ *But with the coming of faith*
we are no longer under a tutor:
²⁶ *this is because all of you are sons of God*
by means of the faith whose content is the Christ Jesus;

IX. Why the Galatians are One in the Christ (3:23-29)

There is once more a telling progression of the Greek prepositions in vv. 24b-26. It begins with the assertion of being "declared righteous on the basis of *(ek)* faith" in v. 24b, and recall that the use of the Greek preposition *ek* has been used throughout Paul's letter to indicate what makes things ultimately possible in the sense of providing the underlying conditions for their realization. Whatever happens "on the basis of *(ek)* something" takes place because its scriptural possibility has been established already precisely *on that basis and on no other basis*, that is, it is only in this way and under these terms that we can approach it as a standing possibility. But v. 25 marks the transition from faith as a possibility to faith as a reality. Paul speaks of the "coming of faith" and how that means the end of the tutor's charge "because all of you are sons of God." What made the difference? The relative beginning of our maturity, the end of our apprenticeship to the law, is accomplished 'by means of *(dia)* the faith whose content is the Christ Jesus." The Greek preposition *dia* has the same basic instrumental meaning as the preposition *ek*, but it denotes the more immediate and dynamic operation of that instrumentality: what had been openly possible "on the basis of *(ek)* faith" is now fully realized "by means of *(dia)* faith." The progression of these two prepositions again serves to express the difference between scriptural promise and apostolic fulfillment, between an open-ended possibility and an accepted reality.

The faith of which Paul speaks here is "the faith whose content is the Christ Jesus." I have chosen to render v. 26 as "because all of you are sons of God by means of *(dia)* the faith whose content is the Christ Jesus." The first clause "this is because all of you are sons of God" is the plainest consequence of the immediately preceding "But with the coming of faith we are no longer under a tutor." Faith's arrival puts an end to the tutor's didactic task because it has transformed our status, elevating us to the dignity of being faith-born "sons of God." What caused that transformation to occur was our faithful response to the hearing of the gospel, and Paul renders the second clause of v. 26 as *dia tēs pisteōs en Christō Iēsou*, literally "through the faith that is in the Christ Jesus." What are we to make of the Greek phrase *en Christō Iēsou*, and specifically the semantic functioning of the Greek preposition *en* in relation to the preceding and following elements? My rendering of this second clause as "by means of the faith whose content is the Christ Jesus" I would justify for the following reasons:

- It is our faith in the gospel message concerning Jesus of Nazareth, the declaration that he is God's anointed servant, crucified for our sakes and raised from the dead as the surest sign of his messiahship, that causes us to be sons of God.

- Since this faith results from what the gospel contains and communicates, it can only ever have a specific kerygmatic content and that content is the proclamation of Jesus as the Christ.

- When the Greek text tells us that this faith (*pistis*) is "in the Christ Jesus," I would refer the reader back to the way in which the same preposition functioned in Paul's citation of Leviticus 18:5 in 3:12. There the preposition indicated that "he who does these things [the law's precepts], by them (*en autois*) shall he live," a simple statement that the Old Testament viewed obedience to the law as what secures the blessing of God. The preposition *en* in 3:26 functions in a grammatically parallel fashion to the way it appears in the Leviticus citation: each serves to indicate what will be the parameters of life lived under God's blessing. The believer's new life as a "son of God" is rooted "in the Christ Jesus," in what Paul's gospel tells us about him and how the fullness of God's blessings for him who

IX. Why the Galatians are One in the Christ (3:23-29)

believes will henceforth occur only in relation to and *by means of* this highly specific content.

In 3:27-29 Paul elaborates this saving faith, this belief by which men are now to be declared righteous. In these concluding verses of chapter 3 Paul is prepared to say something about the implications of our new status in his gospel, about what the advent of our new identity that is *in the Christ Jesus* is going to mean:

²⁷ ὅσοι γὰρ εἰς Χριστὸν ἐβαπτίσθητε,
Χριστὸν ἐνεδύσασθε.
²⁸ οὐκ ἔνι Ἰουδαῖος οὐδὲ Ἕλλην,
οὐκ ἔνι δοῦλος οὐδὲ ἐλεύθερος,
οὐκ ἔνι ἄρσεν καὶ θῆλυ·
πάντες γὰρ ὑμεῖς εἷς ἐστε ἐν Χριστῷ Ἰησοῦ.
²⁹ εἰ δὲ ὑμεῖς Χριστοῦ,
ἄρα τοῦ Ἀβραὰμ σπέρμα ἐστε,
κατ' ἐπαγγελίαν κληρονόμοι.

*²⁷ for as many of you as were baptized for the sake of the Christ
have clothed yourselves in the Christ:
²⁸ there is no Jew and there is no Greek,
there is no slave and there is no free man,
there is no male and female,
because you are all one in the Christ Jesus.
²⁹ And if you are the Christ's,
then you are the seed of Abraham;
you are heirs in accordance with the promise.*

There is no indication, scripturally speaking, that baptism was ever regarded as a Christian option. If you heard the gospel and accepted its message in faith, then baptism was the next step in accordance with the logic of Christian initiation. It was a ritual step—a public act—that amounted to more than a mental assent or even a private conviction on the part of the believer.

Paul is speaking now to the Galatians about something they do know: he reminds them that they were all baptized "for the sake of the Christ" (*eis Christon*), that is, for the sake of what they have heard about him through the gospel that Paul had preached to them ("before whose eyes Jesus the Christ was clearly portrayed as crucified", 3:1). The Greek verb for "clothing oneself" is *endyomai*, and the idea of putting on a distinctive kind of apparel in order to declare one's allegiance is an act that is as strong and meaningful today as it was in ancient times. If a person belonged to someone (a king, general, chieftain, even a teacher, etc.), then he displayed his allegiance and its corresponding component of identity by the specific kind of clothing he wore. It is therefore no passing metaphor for Paul when he speaks here of "clothing yourselves in the Christ," and the language is fully intentional on his part. It is meant to underscore the fact that if the Galatians have been baptized *eis Christon* ("for the sake of the Christ"), it will have been as a result of their having heard his gospel with faith. The more customary rendering of *eis Christon* simply as "into Christ" can be seen as underlining the identity-related dimension just as explicitly. In either case it is about belonging.

Paul builds on this theme of what is the only viable basis for the believer's identity by continuing with a series of paired contrasts. The many ways in which the world has divided itself—Jew/Greek, slave/free man, male/female—are not what should any longer impinge on or directly determine the believer's status before God given that he has been baptized as an outward sign of his belonging to the Christ. The point here is not that baptism definitively clinches the matter for the believer in the sense of permanently fixing the believer's new identity in the Christ, but only that it serves as a ritual expression for what a preaching of the gospel and a "hearing with faith" has already secured. Paul makes his most lapidary declaration about what counts as the parameters of this gospel-based mode of identity when he writes, "there is no Jew and there is no Greek, there is no slave and there is no free man, there is no male and female, because you are all one in the Christ Jesus."

This particular verse is widely misunderstood because, when it is taken from its immediate context, it has led many to assume

IX. Why the Galatians are One in the Christ (3:23-29)

that Paul is declaring these distinctions (and their corresponding social relationships) to be no longer valid or even justifiable in a Christian setting. The only thing that Paul is doing here is making a crystal-clear statement about the nature of this new "anti-identity" and how it stands in relation to the older, more parochially ordered one. The controversy that prompted his letter to the Galatians was one that ultimately turned on the issue of identity, or, more exactly, on the question of what was identity to be based in the Pauline churches. Was it to be one still tinged with elements of traditional Jewish practice such that the male Christian would have to look at something like circumcision as being essential to his identity in the Christ? Or was it an identity wholly rooted in his faithful acceptance of the gospel and the way in which his subsequent baptism symbolized it?

Paul was adamant that the issue of circumcision could never simply be a matter of personal choice let alone a mandatory requirement. To approach the issue in either manner went too deeply against what in his mind was truly and absolutely essential, namely, the hearing of faith, our baptismal clothing in the Christ, and the daily pursuit of a life lived in accordance with the gospel's requirements. It is this—and not things like circumcision—that is incumbent upon all Christian believers and what unites them. It is what constitutes the sole basis for Paul's declaration that the Galatians are "one in the Christ Jesus" (*heis en Christō Iēsou*). But what does "one" mean here? The Greek word for "one" is fully declinable, and, depending on context, it appears in corresponding masculine, feminine, or neuter forms. Here Paul uses the masculine nominative singular form *heis*, and, assuming his usage to be fully deliberate, to what does *heis* refer in this context? The most obvious explanation is that *heis* refers to the Christ.[2] It is only "in the Christ Jesus" that the Galatians

---

[2] One could also interpret *heis* as an oblique reference to Paul and his apostolic preaching given that the Galatians owe their original knowledge and experience of the Christ to him.

are constituted as "sons of God" (3:26)[3]. Notice once more the occurrence of the Greek preposition *en* in the phrase "in the Christ Jesus". If we are indeed "one in the Christ Jesus", then it is because the gospel-mediated Christ sustains us in that status from one moment to the next, and the Christ is only ever "there" by virtue of the "faith whose content is the Christ." It is because the believer does belong to him *on that basis* that he can partake of this oneness despite the everyday divisions and the more obvious physical facts of our created being.

And it is this assertion—that we belong to the Christ, that is, as a slave belongs to his master and vicariously partakes of *his* identity—that allows Paul to declare in v. 29, "And if you are the Christ's, then you are the seed of Abraham; you are heirs in accordance with the promise." Here the Greek genitive construction makes Paul's basic point even more explicit: the phrase *(tou) Christou* literally means that we belong to the Christ, that we are his possession, and, if we belong to him, then his possession of us is what defines our identity. The crucial point is that we only ever belong to the Christ "on the basis of a hearing with faith." It is what makes us "one in the Christ Jesus." But now Paul is able to bring things full circle and complete what he had begun in the earlier part of chapter 3 in connection with Abraham: if we belong to the Christ by means of faith and baptism, then we can be counted as being of Abraham's true seed by virtue of our adherence to the promise and our choosing to live in its realization, a prospect made possible only by proclamation of the Christ Jesus.

---

[3] The neuter nominative singular form *(hen)* occurs in John's gospel in passages where Jesus declares that, "I and the Father are one (*egō kai ho patēr hen esmen*) (10:30; also 17:11, 21-23). The difference in declension (masculine *heis* vs. neuter *hen*) is at a minimum attributable to the fact that the unity in question is of a qualitatively different sort from what Paul is addressing in 3:25-29. His emphasis is on what forms the unity of the messianic community, namely, what incorporates all of mankind's disparate identities into the one identity formed by the proclamation of the crucified Christ. The language in John 15:1-17 about Jesus as the true vine and God as the vinedresser is, I think, an articulation of these differences in perspective.

IX. Why the Galatians are One in the Christ (3:23-29)

And there is simply no downplaying the provocative nature of Paul's argument at this point in his letter. The traditional Jewish understanding of being a "son of Abraham" was predicated on things like circumcision, communal participation in the law, and of course physical descent; but now Paul is brushing those things away in favor of what is to be a truer form of sonship, one based on a promise and one ultimately defined in terms of faithfulness to that promise. The apostle has declared that it does not matter if you are a Jew or a Greek. Do you believe? He says that it is of no consequence if you are a slave or a free man. Have you been baptized "into the Christ Jesus"? He announces that it makes no difference to your status before God if you are a man or a woman. Do you cultivate a life of obedience to his will? It is by virtue of the latter that all who belong to the Christ are one in him.

The progression of terminology in the briefness of v. 29 is important. First, there is the propositional statement, "And if you are the Christ's," which functions something like a rhetorical invitation. It is almost as if Paul is saying, "And if you really do believe, if you have been baptized in the name of the Christ, then you will belong to him to the extent that you execute what he is now demanding of you." It is only by a faith fully mindful of its origin in the proclaimed word of God and put into practice on that basis that we can only ever truly belong to the Christ, and the most relentless requirement we face in that regard is the conscious replenishment of that faith in the word that gave birth to it.

Second, given this preamble and presuming a positive response to it, Paul is able to assert, "then you are the seed of Abraham," and what makes these words so powerful is that Paul is positing a *necessary* connection between (a) the believer's trusting faith in God's purpose as revealed in the Pauline gospel, and (b) the scriptural record concerning the "faithful" Abraham as Paul has presented it. Recall that in 3:6-7 Paul began by appealing to the "righteous" trust that Abraham exhibited in response to God's promise (this the explicit context of Genesis 15 from which he quotes). It is on the basis of the believer's trust in what God has promised to him who believes that he will be numbered among Abraham's seed (*sperma*).

Third, Paul has offered his own distinctive reading of the sections of Genesis which deal with Abraham, and all of what it said about God's promise (*epangelia*) to Abraham he now directly links to the Galatians' reception of Paul's own gospel when he writes, "and [you are] heirs according to the promise." To believe in the Christ is the one thing which will allow them to be counted as belonging to Abraham's seed and thus to rank as his true descendants. Thus far the emphasis has been on the necessity of a trusting faith in the Pauline gospel as it was originally preached to them, but, as Paul will make clearer in chapters 5 and 6, the Galatians will only ever be the true descendants of Abraham when they walk as he did. The terminology of inheritance beginning in chapter 3 (and continuing to the end of the letter) is not a matter of certainties or foregone conclusions, but rather of conditional parameters. What it means to be the inheritors (*klēronomoi*) of what God had promised (*kat' epangelian*) as his lasting blessing is presented as what Paul announces and God brings to completion.

It is in this way, by virtue of a common faith rooted in the gospel message that Paul preached to the Galatians, that they "are all one in the Christ Jesus." Paul now blends together the instrumental meanings of the two prepositions *ek* and *dia* in a way that allows us to see how the unity of Christian faith is formed. Faith's foundation is rooted in the scriptural promise of God to Abraham. It is *on the basis of* (*ek*) the faithfulness initially attributed to Abraham and then demonstrated by Jesus (rising to the level of *dia* by his own faithfulness) that we stand any chance of being declared righteous in the sight of God, and we, as believers, cooperate with this *by means of* (*dia*) our faithful response and willingness to live according to God's statutes. But a trusting belief in the gospel amounts to more than mere

IX. Why the Galatians are One in the Christ (3:23-29)

consent. What ultimately matters is obedience to what it commands, that men might actually live in a way that reflects what the gospel demands of us. It is only by believing in the Christ as preached to us by Paul and by living obediently to that proclamation that we can ever hope to belong to him and stand in his line of inheritance. If we belong to the Christ, if we are going to participate in this identity that smashes all of the other rival identities that characterize "this encompassing evil age" (1:4), then, as Paul tells the Galatians, not only must we believe in his gospel, we must also never waver in our returning to what we heard.

X. Why the Galatians are Sons of God (4:1-7)

In the last half of chapter 3 (3:15ff.) Paul employs the Old Testament theme of the inheritance, relating it to the notions of covenant and promise. In 3:16 he points out that "the promises were made to Abraham and to his seed," while 3:17 makes it clear that God's promises to Abraham were wholly covenantal in nature and must be seen as constituting the original and thus more binding covenant between this man and his god. Paul contrasts the law "that came four hundred and thirty years later" with what preceded it, and insists that it "does not annul a covenant previously ratified by God." There is a widespread tendency to think of the Mosaic law as being what most fully defines God's covenant relationship with the biblical Israel, but Paul has kept his interpretive focus on Abraham as what most fundamentally defines that relationship. If the covenant relationship is ultimately a matter of what is contained in God's promise to Abraham, then what has been promised is what Paul understands as the substance of the inheritance. He makes it clear in 3:18 that "if the inheritance is on the basis of the law, it is no longer on the basis of a promise," but this inheritance is precisely what God has given to Abraham "by means of a promise." Of what is this inheritance going to consist in Paul's hands? Will it simply be a matter of hearing the apostolic message with faith, being baptized in the messianic community centered around the belief that Jesus is the Christ, and then reckoning oneself as belonging to it? The rest of chapter 3 is an explication of how a faithful response to the gospel is a precondition for our being "one in the Christ Jesus," and the chapter culminates in 3:29 where Paul writes, "And if you are the Christ's, then you are the seed of Abraham: you are heirs in accordance with the promise." This verse combines the three thematic concerns—covenant, promise, and inheritance—and what binds them together is the centrality of the gospel message itself, how Paul's preaching to the Galatians communicated to them the way in which ancient scripture and prophecy were now being realized in their midst.

The beginning of chapter 4 is about the meaning of inheritance, and the consistent focus throughout is in on how God's will is being achieved through the person of Jesus the Christ. In vv. 1-2 Paul continues his account of the idea of inheritance by describing it with the help of another analogy (with 3:29 added to keep the focus on our identity in the Christ):

²⁹ εἰ δὲ ὑμεῖς Χριστοῦ,
ἄρα τοῦ Ἀβραὰμ σπέρμα ἐστε,
κατ' ἐπαγγελίαν κληρονόμοι.
¹ λέγω δέ, ἐφ' ὅσον ὁ κληρονόμος νήπιός ἐστιν,
οὐδὲν διαφέρει δούλου κύριος πάντων ὤν,
² ἀλλ' ὑπὸ ἐπιτρόπους καὶ οἰκονόμους
ἄχρι τῆς προθεσμίας τοῦ πατρός.

²⁹ *And if you are the Christ's,*
then you are the seed of Abraham:
you are heirs in accordance with the promise.
¹ *And I am saying that for however long the heir is a child,*
he is no better than a slave even though he is lord of all things;
² *instead he is under guardians and stewards*
until the time appointed by his father.

The Greek word for "heir" is *klēronomos*, meaning the one who receives the inheritance (*klēronomia*) of his father's wealth and estate, and here Paul builds upon our ordinary human experience of inheritance in this world—how, even though he will one day preside over all the things in his estate, the child remains a child "until the time appointed by his father." The basic idea is one already presented in 3:21-26, namely, that from the time of God's promise to Abraham and the subsequent giving of the law, Israel was under the law's tutelage until "the coming of faith" (3:25), and this would be a time when "we are no longer under a tutor." But with the death and resurrection of Jesus, God's eschatological timetable is made apparent: those who hear the gospel of Jesus as the Christ and who receive it with faith are

X. Why the Galatians are Sons of God (4:1-7)

now ready to constitute the new people of God because he will now have revealed them as belonging—by means of said faith—to the true "seed of Abraham." In the same way that we were once children with regard to the faith, so now, having heard the gospel, we are prepared to claim our rightful inheritance, one not dictated by descent or an ethnically-organized set of obligations, but the one that God in accordance with his will revealed for the sake of the world's salvation.

What we said earlier about the elements that make up the fourfold framework for understanding the Galatian letter—covenant, lawcourt language, eschatology, and christology—all of these come together in the verses that make up the first part of chapter 4. The biblical covenant was always supposed to be about the deliverance of all men from the plight of Genesis 3-11: man's fall into death-dealing sin and the fracturing of the human community (with Babel as its culminating symbol). Thus covenant equals the whole of God's plan for the salvation of the human race. The Old Testament is the account of that covenant's progress, its scriptural history. It needed a vehicle, a human group to carry it and which would live in accordance with it: the Israelites were that group and it was the law that ordered their existence and sustained them through the centuries. To the extent that the Israelites thought of themselves as sons of Abraham, as being his seed, his direct physical descendants, they were correct. Their preoccupation with the necessity of circumcision as a sign of obedience to the law became its own kind of metaphor for an inheritance received and nurtured but only superficially understood: one that was literally only skin-deep. Up until the coming of Jesus as the Christ, being a member of Abraham's family could be reckoned in terms of circumcision and the practices for which it stood, but, in the light of the faith that is the fruit of the gospel, there could now only be *one basis* for membership in the family of God and its source was the faithfulness of Jesus to the divine covenant plan.

The gospel is the declaration that Jesus is the righteous one, that God has declared him to be *dikaios*. In light of the charges pending against any man by virtue of the disobedience that is sin (why we must see ourselves continuously in relation to the divine lawcourt), Jesus was sin-less and therefore legally innocent. But what made Jesus legally innocent, what constituted the basis for God declaring him to be righteous (*dikaios*) was his faithfulness (*pistis*) to the divine will. It is by sharing in this faith that the believer is reckoned as a member of God's family, a status wholly conditional on his living in accordance with the *pistis* now expected of him. It is a membership intended for all men, so the conditions for that membership were such that any person might be able to meet them—whether we are Jew or Greek, whether we are a free man or a slave, both male and female—and none of those things mattered because our identity in the Christ is no longer a question of division but one of inclusion: what the law divided, the gospel now unites. If we are one, then our oneness is a function of our common faith in the Christ. If we believe in the gospel, then we are by virtue of that belief members of God's family because our identity will henceforth be a matter of *our belonging to the Christ*, and, if we belong to him, then our sins are forgiven because in him we will have been declared *dikaios*, the status of a provisional innocence that corresponds to an equally provisional absolution of our sin.[1]

It is only in this sense that the *eschaton* has begun. The Pauline gospel is inherently eschatological. It is the declaration that God the Father has won for the world a newness of life (recall that salvation is always a matter of God's victory) when he raised the man Jesus from among the dead (1:1). Paul *as apostle* announces

---

[1] The broader implications of this provisional righteousness are concisely presented by Marc Philip Boulos in the concluding section "Teaching How to Love" of his *Torah to the Gentiles: St. Paul's Letter to the Galatians* (St. Paul, Minnesota: OCABS Press, 2014), p. 126. He quotes 1 Corinthians 4:1 and writes: "This does not mean that Paul is acquitted. On the contrary, both Paul and his disciples are *assumed guilty* until acquitted by God in the judgment. "Do not pass judgment before the time," Paul warns, "but wait until the Lord comes" (1 Corinthians 4:5). In anticipation of that day, Paul is responsible to teach *only* what is written."

X. Why the Galatians are Sons of God (4:1-7)

the sacrificial death of Jesus (1:4, 2:20) as being what makes possible our deliverance "from this encompassing evil age." Christology here only amounts to the understanding that God's purposes, that is, his designs for the salvation of the world, are to be understood in relation to what Paul's preaching communicates to us about Jesus *as the Christ*. This is the extent of the christological reasoning contained in Paul's letter to the Galatians, and its content is entirely based on the faithful obedience Jesus exhibited on the cross. It is in this sense that the letter's eschatology and christology are inextricable concerns. Each is impossible to understand without the other, and the same can be said about the question of covenant and the lawcourt disposition of things it inherently entails.

What marked the old aeon was the oppressive rule of sin and the corresponding inescapability of a death encumbered by it. Sin caused man to be condemned to death *without God*. This was because—in what was the consistent biblical pattern—sin manifested itself as the revolt against the covenantal relationship God seeks with man, and what it bred in man was a state of hopeless death, that is, death apart from God and the inherent blessings of the covenant. At sin's root is rebellion, our individual and collective tendency to want life apart from God, the overpowering wish to have it on our own terms, and thus to walk away from God. Sin is thus the comprehensive label for our having become "sons of disobedience" who choose to live in a willful, intentional, and thus tragic condition of rebellious self-sufficiency. The entirety of Hebrew scripture testified to these broad outlines, and the ways in which all these elements related to each other were often complex, overlapping, and repetitive, but the basic pattern—that of man's corrupting fall into sin and God's continuous effort to deliver him from bondage to it—was consistently apparent throughout the Old Testament.

It is thus that 4:1-2 epitomizes the whole range and content of the Hebrew scriptures. Paul speaks of how it is for the "heir" when he is yet a child: on the one hand, he is "no better than a slave (*ouden diapherei doulou*)," but, on the other hand, he is at the same time "the lord of all things (*kyrios pantōn ōn*)."[2] The heir is "under guardians and stewards"—the law, the judges, the righteous kings, and the prophets—but he is not yet of age: Israel is not mature because Israel's "time appointed by his father" has not yet come. It is at this point that Paul continues in vv. 3-5 with a passage that underscores this eschatological transition from one time to that of another:

³ οὕτως καὶ ἡμεῖς,
ὅτε ἦμεν νήπιοι,
ὑπὸ τὰ στοιχεῖα τοῦ κόσμου ἤμεθα δεδουλωμένοι·
⁴ ὅτε δὲ ἦλθεν τὸ πλήρωμα τοῦ χρόνου,
ἐξαπέστειλεν ὁ θεὸς τὸν υἱὸν αὐτοῦ,
γενόμενον ἐκ γυναικός,
γενόμενον ὑπὸ νόμον,
⁵ ἵνα τοὺς ὑπὸ νόμον ἐξαγοράσῃ,
ἵνα τὴν υἱοθεσίαν ἀπολάβωμεν.

³ It is the same with us:
when we were children,
we were in servitude to the elemental things of this world;
⁴ but it was when the fullness of time had come
that God sent forth his Son,
who had been born of a woman,
who had been born under the law,
⁵ so that he might buy back those who are under the law,
so that we could receive the adopted status of sons.

The first thing to notice here is what I would call the "eschatological pivot" that begins to take place in vv. 1-4. It consists of a progression of temporal indicators used by Paul to

---

[2] Paul has already used the verb *diapherō* in 2:6 when he remarks concerning the Jerusalem "pillars" that "what they were is of no consequence to me" (*hopoioi pote ēsan ouden moi diapherei*). The clear implication in both 2:6 and 4:1 is that without the fullness of the Pauline gospel neither the Jerusalem authorities nor the metaphorical "heir" is anything at all.

X. Why the Galatians are Sons of God (4:1-7)

frame the ending of one era and the dawning of the new. We have already seen how what characterized the old era was the relative immaturity of the heir in v. 1: "that for however long the heir is a child...." The Greek phrase "for however long" is *eph' hoson chronon* (literally, "for however long the time is..."). It contains the Greek word *chronos*, which is the term used for chronological time, i.e. time that is calendrical in nature and consists of increments in a strict relative order to each other, in short, what we would know as "clock time." *Chronos* stands in contrast to the other Greek word for "time," *kairos*, which denotes the moment when all that is truly proper to a specific event occurs and its meaning is fully expressed: time understood as the most direct and proper expression of an event's intended meaning. Even though Paul uses language in v. 2 about "the time appointed by his father," he does not specifically employ the word *kairos* in this instance, but instead uses *prothesmia*, a term which, in accordance with the social analogy upon which he is relying here, was used to denote any preset point of legal heirship.[3] The focus remains entirely on the father's intentional action, one of the motifs that dominate the entirety of chapters 3 and 4. Another passage that displays the scriptural interplay at work among *chronos*, *kairos*, and *prothesmia* is Acts 1:1-8, and in particular vv. 6-8 (RSV) where the disciples are interrogating the risen Jesus about when the kingdom shall be restored to Israel:

> So *when* they had come together, they asked him, "Lord, will you at this time (*chronos*) restore the kingdom to Israel?" He said to them, "It is not for you to know times (*chronos*) or seasons (*kairos*) which the Father has fixed by his own authority. But you shall receive power *when* the Holy Spirit has come upon you; and you shall be my witnesses in Jerusalem and in all Judea and Samaria and to the end of the earth."

---

[3] The Greek substantive *prothesmia* is a compound noun derived from the pronoun *pro-* ("before") and the verb *tithēmi* ("to set in place"), viz. "the time pre-appointed by the father."

Note how the two occurrences of "when" help to organize the passage according to God's temporality. In v. 6 "when" is expressed through a participial clause that sets the scene of the disciples gathering together with Jesus and encloses what will be the mundane nature of their questioning. In v. 7 Jesus announces that such is not a matter of "times or seasons" (*chronous ē kairous*) because the timetable for the kingdom's restoration is entirely the Father's prerogative (i.e. his *prothesmia*).[4] What does matter here in this short narrative is "*when* the Holy Spirit has come upon you." It is the latter scriptural moment (what Paul has announced in 3:1-5 and 3:14) that combines *chronos*, *kairos*, and *prothesmia* into a single reality. While it is the case that in 4:10 Paul shortly makes use of *kairos* in a context having to do with the seasons set for pagan cultic observance, he later returns to *kairos* in a passage (6:9-10) that deals with the open-ended opportunity that characterizes life in the Spirit.

But now in v. 3 Paul continues with the analogical line of thinking he introduced in vv.1-2: "It is the same with us: when we were children, we were in servitude to the elemental things of this world." Just as in vv. 1-2, the phrase "when we were children" (*hote ēmen nēpioi*) not only continues this same idea of an earlier stage of relative immaturity, but now it is made to correspond to being "in servitude to the elemental things of this world." What does Paul mean here by "the elemental things of this world"? The Greek word *stoicheia* is hard to translate because its ancient connotations had to do with those things that were constituent of the material world, what we as moderns might construe as being the plain physical elements. I think that a good enough sense of what Paul is saying here can be had without trying to read too much into the passage about the exact identity or composition of the *stoicheia* simply by seeing the latter as being the stuff of created matter and nothing *more than* that. In other words, the *stoicheia* is creation seen in isolation from God, that is,

---

[4] The contrast between vv. 6 and 7 is further underscored by means of the μὲν...δέ particles.

X. Why the Galatians are Sons of God (4:1-7)

without it being a mediating reflection of the divine. This is what corresponds to the classic description that Paul offers in Romans 1:18-23 (RSV), what happens when man chooses to see creation apart from God:

> For the wrath of God is revealed from heaven against all ungodliness (*asebeia*) and wickedness (*adikia*) of men who by their wickedness suppress the truth. For what can be known about God is plain to them, because God has shown it to them. Ever since the creation of the world his invisible nature, namely, his eternal power and deity, has been clearly perceived in the things that have been made. So they are without excuse; for although they knew God they did not honor him as God or give thanks to him, but they became futile in their thinking and their senseless minds were darkened. Claiming to be wise, they became fools, and exchanged the glory of the immortal God for images resembling mortal man or birds or animals or reptiles.

Key to this passage are the two terms "ungodliness" (*asebeia*) and "wickedness" (*adikia*). The first alpha-privative term in Greek means "impiety," the lack of any proper regard for God. The second term summarizes what becomes of human behavior when it rejects God as the basis for anything and proceeds in a merrily self-sufficient fashion by forsaking what makes a man *dikaios* in God's eyes. Together they express what is the primary human failure to worship God: "for although they knew God they did not honor him as God or give thanks to him."

It is, I think, the potentially distracting dominion of the immediate world that Paul is isolating here and making characteristic of our time spent as "children" who, even though we may have possessed the law and the prophets in our pre-gospel days, never quite managed to break free from the countless forms of servitude we devise and derive from the workings of the world. When Paul writes in v. 3, "It is the same with us" (*houtōs kai hēmeis*), he has in mind how the youthful heir is subject to older, greater forces ("guardians and stewards") as long he remains underage. Paul emphasizes the unrelieved calamity of our sinful condition through the parallel use of servitude terminology in vv. 1 and 3: when the heir is still a child, he is "no better than a slave (*doulos*)"; and in our pre-gospel condition we are "in servitude (*dedoulōmenoi*) to the elemental things of this world."

But vv. 4-5 tell us that this exilic state of affairs has changed. The *prothesmia tou patros* of v. 2 has occurred. God the Father has acted, and what time had framed is now the setting for time itself being shattered, reconstructed, and redirected. Indeed, time (*chronos*), what we only ever sense as relative bits of duration, is the setting for divine action. What Paul identifies in v. 4 as the "fullness of time" (*plērōma tou chronou*) is the arrival of the *prothesmia*: "but it was when the fullness of time had come that God sent forth his Son, who was born of a woman, who had been born under the law." The "fullness of time" is only ever a reflection of the divine initiative and the unexpected way in which it is manifested. It involves the transformation of *chronos* (regular clock time) into *kairos* (divinely appointed time), or, more exactly, it is the narrative of how *kairos* invades *chronos* in order to announce the victory of God.

The backdrop for v. 4 is man's sinful condition, his state of servitude to *what lies below*, his captivity to the enslaving forces of sin and death. What really colors the first eleven verses of chapter 4 is the Exodus narrative, and, in his own distinctively scriptural way, Paul is here retelling the story of Israel's delivery from bondage in Egypt. The Old Testament book of Exodus recounts how the God of Abraham's covenant came to make his power known in the most unanticipated way. God had already established his covenant with the patriarchal forebears of the Israelites, but now they were enslaved by the Egyptians in a land that was not their own. "Egypt" thus became a scriptural symbol for the enslavement that is sin and the mortal calamity that is death, and to be delivered from that oppressive state, to have one's shackles removed, and to be granted the freedom to move to the land that is their appointed inheritance, that is the stuff of

X. Why the Galatians are Sons of God (4:1-7)

the exodus, of God delivering his people from bondage and establishing them in covenantal freedom.

This is why v. 4 marks an eschatological shift, the transition from the "Egypt" of the present era to the new eschatological age inaugurated by the coming of the Christ and consisting of the righteousness (*dikaiosynē*) that corresponds to God's kingdom. The period leading up to this posited "fullness of time" is one in which the covenant promise has been stuck in the Deuteronomic curse, in the fact that, even though the law exhorts us to choose the way it represents and thus to live, the law itself was never any more than a practical wisdom because it was incapable of neutralizing sin's power and thus eradicating death. The scriptural Exodus had culminated in Israel's acquisition of Canaan, of that "land of milk and honey," the biblical symbol of delivery from Egyptian oppression and of a renewed covenant living with the Lord, but the grim persistence of sin and death was the spiritual reminder of things left undone, of God's power and rule not yet realized among men. This persistence of sin and death (what amounted, scripturally speaking, to an abiding Egyptian bondage, and, by extension, a Babylonian exile and captivity) is what characterized the "unfulfilled" time of man's lingering exilic condition. But now Paul declares that, with the coming of the Christ, time has been "fulfilled" because the announcement of God's victory by means of the Christ Jesus is what is on his apostolic lips, and from his lips—as he reminds the Galatians—it goes out to those who hear it with faith (3:1-5).

There is a tendency for us to approach the meaning of 4:4 in light of the Christian doctrine of the Incarnation. This is due in no small measure to the fact that we Orthodox Christians regularly hear the 4:4-7 pericope in connection with the Feast of the Nativity, but that is not the automatic scriptural functioning of what Paul writes in 4:4. How else would the Galatians have known about any potential "fullness of time" if Paul had not first preached to them that "God sent forth his Son" (*exapesteilen ho theos ton huion autou*)? Indeed, the last time Paul had referred to Jesus as the "Son of God" was in 2:20: "I have been crucified along with the Christ; and so it is no longer I who live but it is the Christ who lives in me, and what I am now living in the flesh I am living as a result of my believing in the Son of God, who loved me and who gave himself on my behalf," a passage that must be seen in connection with the comparatively terse declaration Paul is making here. Jesus is identified in 4:4 as the "Son," and the sole purpose of his being "sent forth" is the redemption of men (more on its specific content below), and it is this context of redemption that links the two passages. There is a set of associations at work here: if Jesus is the Christ, then he must be the one who is designated/anointed by God to be the agent of salvation for his people, and this setting aside, this declaration of a person by whom the Exodus-event will again be realized, this man is God's messianic "Son," who is not just a "christ" but "the Christ" *par excellence*. In 2:20 Paul writes that what Jesus does has been done "on my behalf" (*hyper emou*), but beginning in 4:5 he gives further indication of what this "loving action" mentioned in 2:20 consists. But in the meantime he qualifies his announcement with two brief clauses that are christologically significant, i.e. they clue us in on how Paul proclaimed Jesus as the Messiah, as God's Christ. Thus what he writes should not be approached in terms of it being the raw materials for the classic Christian theological concerns and their formulations in later centuries because his level of treatment is more properly kerygmatic in nature. It is precisely this kerygmatic thrust of 4:4-7 that governs how the terms, propositions, and conclusions made in that passage interrelate with each other.

First, the Son is declared to be "born of a woman" (*genomenon ek gynaikos*) in order to make it clear that the man Jesus was born in a fully mortal fashion. In other words, the original gospel proclamation did not view Jesus either as a demigod figure or as a mythological being whose miraculous birth was the guarantee of his status as "Son of God." 3:13-14 encapsulates how this

X. Why the Galatians are Sons of God (4:1-7)

was, kerygmatically speaking, entirely a matter of his sacrificial death on the cross. In addition, while the resurrection is not an explicit theme of the letter, Paul most certainly assumes the centrality of it to his message (1:1-5). The point to keep in mind here is that the salvation preached by Paul is not at all a direct function of the relative mixture of human and divine elements within the person of Jesus. To the contrary, it is entirely a matter of *this man* Jesus having been crucified and then God raising him from the dead.

Second, the Son is "born under the law" (*genomenon hypo nomon*), a statement that has two implications: (1) that Jesus was fully human in the sense that he was as subject to temptation ("the elemental things of this world") as any mortal soul is, and (2) that the law applied as much to him as it did to any other Jew born at the time. When it comes to Jesus and temptation, the Christian does not confess that Jesus was above temptation and in some way impervious to it; on the contrary, we know from scripture that temptation was as real and as terrible to him as it is to any of us, but what distinguished Jesus was his response to temptation. He was able to confront it and not to let it master him. The second implication is closely connected to the first one, namely, that because Jesus was as much "under the law" as any other Jew, what must be stressed is Jesus' obedient realization of the law. It is true that he was able to defeat temptation, but, more importantly, Jesus became himself the eschatological fulfillment of the law by becoming the perfect Israelite and thus fulfilling all *righteousness* (cf. Matthew 3:15). It is a path that led from the River Jordan to Golgotha, but, in every sense of the word, it is a course framed by the law and the requirement that it—this indispensable indication of God's will—be realized faithfully. By hanging on a tree and thus becoming the *curse of the law* (3:13), Jesus simultaneously became the *blessing*, the fulfillment of the law by means of his faithfulness (*pistis Christou*) to it. In this way the new covenant blessings could be made to flow out into the world when this same faith is preached and followed.

The gospel's own unity of content and purpose is reflected when Paul continues in v. 5: "so that he [Jesus] might buy back those who are under the law, so that we could receive the adopted status of sons." God's sending forth of his Son is an act of redemption, but redemption understood here in the original and most practical sense of the word. The Greek verb used in this passage for "to buy back" is *exagorazō*, and Paul has already employed it in 3:13 ("The Christ has *bought us back* from the curse of the law, having become himself a curse on our behalf"), and I would only add here that the verb's original meaning of "buying something back from its availability in the agora-space" is even more relevant in this context when we recall that one of the most common commodities found in ancient marketplaces was slaves. The coming of this Christ, this Son of God—the crucified Jesus of Nazareth—had culminated in a redemptive death, one that would "buy back those who are under the law," but, since it is only in the previous verse that Jesus is himself is declared to be "under the law," how can someone who is under the law redeem those who are likewise under the law? In short, how are we to understand the mechanics of a redemption presented in these terms?

Some clue can be found in the Old Testament. The specific Greek verb *exagorazō* is never used in the Septuagint in the contexts dealing with Israel's redemption by the hands of God. The verb most often used in those texts is *lytroumai*, but this is a word that even more directly denotes the paying of a ransom in order to set a person free. The purchase of a slave in the ancient world involved the payment of a ransom-price, the sum sufficient to set the slave free if only long enough for him to become the prompt possession of another master. In the Old Testament explicit reference is made to the Exodus as being the redemption (*lytrōsis*) of the Israelite slaves (*douloi*) from the "house of bondage" (*oikos douleia*) they knew in Egypt. The idea here is that of the transition from a state of slavery (*douleia*) to the bonded state of covenant (*diathēkē*). Deuteronomy 7:6-9 (RSV) illustrates all these elements:

X. Why the Galatians are Sons of God (4:1-7)

> For you are a people holy to the LORD your God; the LORD your God has chosen you to be a people for his possession out of all the peoples that are on the face of the earth. It was not because you were more in number than any other people that the LORD set his love upon you and chose you, for you were the fewest of all peoples; but it is because the LORD loves you, and is keeping the oath which he swore to your fathers, that the LORD has brought you out with a mighty hand, and *redeemed* (*elytrōsato*) you from the house of bondage (*ex oikou douleias*), from the hand of Pharoah, king of Egypt. Know therefore that the LORD your God is God, the faithful (*pistos*) God who keeps covenant (*diathēkē*) and steadfast love (*eleos*) with those who love him and keep his commandments, to a thousand generations.

The basic Hebrew idea is that of the *go'el*, the "redeemer," he who buys back (Hebrew verb *ga'al*) the relative who has been forced into a condition of servitude (cf. Leviticus 25:25-54), thus paying the debt which the relative was unable to pay himself so that the redeemed Israelite might once again participate as a free man in the joy of covenant belonging. The practice was also incorporated into the jubilee-year observances done every seven years, a cyclical time in which there was to have been a general remission of debts and a freeing of slaves. This "sabbatical year" aspect of the jubilee celebration was linked to the time Israel spent in Egyptian bondage (Leviticus 25:54-55, RSV): "And if he is not redeemed by these means, then he shall be released in the year of the jubilee, he and his children with him. For to me the people of Israel are servants, they are my servants brought forth out of the land of Egypt: I am the LORD your God."

The jubilee celebration is expanded even further by being compounded into a "seven times seven" super-jubilee event, that is, every forty-nine years there is a great "jubilee of jubilees" in which ancestral properties were to have been restored as well. The fundamental idea here is that the jubilee symbolized the restoration of God's justice (Hebrew *mishpat*/Greek *dikaiosynē*) here on earth. Making it real among men was the truly eschatological event: both God's people and his creation would be restored and thus *redeemed*. It is an idea that is given one of its grandest expressions in Isaiah 61:1-3 (RSV), the same portion of text read *and interpreted* by Jesus in the synagogue at Nazareth (Luke 4:16-21), a passage that the author of Luke not incidentally positions as marking the beginning of the Lord's public mission:

> *The Spirit of the Lord GOD is upon me,*
> *because the LORD has anointed me*
> *to bring good tidings to the afflicted;*
> *he has sent me to bind up the brokenhearted,*
> *to proclaim liberty to the captives,*
> *and the opening of the prison*
> *to those who are bound;*
> *to proclaim the year of the LORD's favor,*
> *and the day of vengeance of our God;*
> *to comfort all who mourn;*
> *to grant to those who mourn in Zion—*
> *to give them a garland instead of ashes,*
> *the oil of gladness instead of mourning,*
> *the mantle of praise instead of a faint spirit;*
> *that they may be called oaks of righteousness* (dikaiosynē),
> *the planting of the LORD, that he may be glorified.*

This is the prophet Isaiah's vision of the unfolding of God's redemptive purposes, of the Lord's steadfast wish to restore creation to its manifestly just workings and to its originally glorious potential. This will be the point when earthly time (*chronos*) is converted into a sacred time (in effect, a perpetual state of *kairos*), and then God's creatures will share directly in redemption's arrival in their midst. In short, it is the scriptural promise of the eschatological moment when, as scripture points out again and again, we come to see that it is a matter of God granting his gifts to us.

Paul's language here about our "adopted status of sons" (*huiothesia*) is an idea rich in significance. First, he has announced the Son of God's coming in the person of Jesus of Nazareth, born as a man and subject to (but not giving in to) all mortal constraints. Second, he has declared this to be "so that he might

X. Why the Galatians are Sons of God (4:1-7)

buy back those who are under the law," which means that the Christian believer is redeemed from being a slave to sin. The problem is not that the law *per se* is what must be remedied, but the broader issue of man's sinful condition framed by and ultimately revealed by his being "under the law." This deliverance, this liberating purchase from our slave condition is accomplished so that we might be transferred from our old master of sinful bondage and meaningless death to our new master who is life, light, and love. It was the case in the ancient world that slaves were sometimes bought/redeemed so that they might then be made the adopted children of their master. The idea here was that the redeemer became the slave's familial protector, and he cemented this relationship in the form of legal adoption and the former slave's full incorporation into his household as one of his own children. Keep in mind the possibility that a freed slave might very well be left to his own devices and he would remain vulnerable, unprotected, and unguided under those circumstances. But the slave who had been freed so that he might then be incorporated into the household of a gracious benefactor will receive all the benefits and protections such an arrangement would entail. We tend to imagine that social relations in the ancient world were more rigid and exclusionary in comparison to our own, but there is ample evidence to show that these societies were at times capable of an astonishing degree of elasticity when it came to kinship, and often allowed for a flexibility in practice which modern patterns and habits would neither permit nor conceive. I think that in this context Paul has in mind the relative importance of the former (the protected and now privileged status of the believer) over that of the latter (the mystically communal sense of inclusion inherent in such language) in order to make what follows even more clear.

Paul had already made it clear to the Galatians in 3:26 how this adoption has taken place: "because all of you are sons of God by means of the faith whose content is the Christ Jesus." It is this assertion, namely, that our sonship is predicated on the faith we have concerning Jesus as the Christ, which makes possible the dynamic recasting and reorientation of our persons that is central to what it means here to be adopted by God as his own sons. And if we are now the adopted sons of God by means of the faith that is the most immediate fruit of the gospel's proclamation, this means that we too shall possess what the original Son possesses, and Paul describes the nature of this remarkable privilege in vv. 6-7:

⁶ ὅτι δέ ἐστε υἱοί,
ἐξαπέστειλεν ὁ θεὸς τὸ πνεῦμα τοῦ υἱοῦ αὐτοῦ εἰς τὰς καρδίας
ἡμῶν
κρᾶζον· αββα ὁ πατήρ.
⁷ ὥστε οὐκέτι εἶ δοῦλος
ἀλλὰ υἱός·
εἰ δὲ υἱός, καὶ κληρονόμος διὰ θεοῦ.

⁶*And as proof that you are sons,*
God has sent forth the Spirit of his Son into our hearts
where the Spirit cries out, "Abba, Father!"—
⁷ *all so that you are no longer a slave,*
but rather a son;
and if you are a son,
then it is through God that you also have made an heir.

What was stipulated in the string of subjunctive possibilities listed in v. 5—"so that he might buy back those who are under the law, so that we could receive the adopted status of sons"— Paul now links in v. 6 to what the Galatians had experienced themselves: "And as proof that you are sons..." Having made clear the necessary relationship between faith and sonship, Paul now points out what must accompany faith's dynamic habitation in us and in that way what will reveal itself as the surest sign of God having made us his sons: we will have "the Spirit of his Son in our hearts where the Spirit cries out, "Abba, Father!" because it is God himself who will have put it there.

Paul identifies the Spirit as being the God-sent "Spirit of his Son," but how shall we understand what is meant by this

X. Why the Galatians are Sons of God (4:1-7)

reference to the "Spirit"? We find the most direct clues in 3:1-5 and 3:14. What ties these two passages together is the way Paul makes each entirely a matter of hearing the gospel with faith and how that faith is both manifested and confirmed by reception of the Spirit. If faithful obedience is what made Jesus the Christ, who was just as much "born of a woman" as any of us, then should not the faithful reception of the Spirit stand as the "proof" that we too are "sons"? It is only in this sense that God's Spirit can be conceivable as the "Spirit of his Son." In other words, instead of declaring that we are abstractly witness here to some inscrutable pneumatological mystery, Paul is continuing to challenge the Galatians about just what God is doing in their midst. It is as if he is saying to them, "If you have heard the gospel and believe, do you not have the Christ's own Spirit in you, and is not the only possible proof of that presence that you are bearing what should be the most distinctive kind of fruit?" Precisely this will be Paul's focus in chapter 5, but for now this concentrated, supremely focused zeal for what is righteously faithful is epitomized by Paul when he describes the Spirit as crying out in our hearts, "Abba, Father!"

The phrase "Abba, Father!" has been the subject of much nonsensical commentary. It is true that the first term "Abba" is the Aramaic word for "father," and even though the precise origins of what would appear to be its formulaic pairing with the Greek "father" (*ho patēr*) are lost to us, the suggestion that it originally represented (and continued to represent) a more childlike or intimately familiar way of addressing God *as father* ("Daddy!") is one that cannot be reliably substantiated, and, even if it could, it would not add anything more profound or even significant to what Paul is already indicating in this passage. Recall for a moment the adoption scenario upon which Paul has been relying. Recall that it involves the redemption of a formerly desperate slave who will now be incorporated into his new beneficent master's household, a place where he will henceforth enjoy privilege, comfort, and power. The conferring of this kind of social blessing, if it is understood for what it truly is—as a supremely merciful act rooted in compassionate love and exquisite majesty—would that not result in the slave-who-is-now-a-son exclaiming with the most deeply grateful conviction, "Father!"? And would not a newly adopted son under those circumstances wish to be perfectly obedient to his new father's wishes? Would he not be inwardly moved and inspired in every way to live in exemplary obedience and commitment to the furtherance of such a father's will? This is a description of things that does not ignore the role of personal closeness or how love, affection, and familiarity enter into the believer's relationship with the living God. Indeed, all those things are presupposed by Paul's more basic assertion about the nature of our redemption through this man Jesus who is the Christ. It allows for the necessary play of emotions like love's quiet ecstasy, but what makes them possible in the first place is the simple continuation of God's own merciful love for us in the way that the manifestation of that power in the Pauline gospel has changed our status.

Paul confirms this arrangement of things when he states that the gift of this Spirit in our hearts and his crying out to God for us is "'all so that you are no longer a slave, but rather a son; and if you are a son, then it is through God that you also have been made an heir." He is contending that the reception of the Spirit must serve as the most indisputable sign of our gospel-mediated transition from slavery to sonship, and, more fundamentally, that this transition has occurred at all is due to God's power to help us, to heal us, and to save us. This is the reason for Paul's invocation of *inheritance* (*klēronomia*) at this point because it is crucial to his line of argumentation. What had traditionally formed the basis of Israel's inheritance—obedience to the law—is now a matter of faith in the gospel concerning Jesus as the Christ, and here Paul is making the most unequivocal declaration about how possession of the Spirit is the one and only marker of that status as son and thus heir (*klēronomos*) to the promise of salvation made by God to Abraham (cf. 3:18). The proof of our sonship in the Lord will be the advent of the Spirit's energy among us, a stipulation that does not cancel the law, but rather one that moves the issue of our salvation-as-identity-in-the-Lord to a higher, more revolutionary set of requirements.

The phrase that really must be emphasized in v. 7 is "through God" (*dia theou*). Ever since 2:15-16 Paul has used the Greek preposition *ek* ("on the basis of") to indicate the possible mode by which God will declare man righteous. So far his argumentation has revolved around how being declared righteous in God's eyes is not "on the basis of the works of the law" (*ex ergōn nomou*), but rather "on the basis of a faithfulness" (*ek pisteōs*). Whether the faithfulness in question is that exhibited by Jesus himself or how he who hears the gospel responds to it in faithful obedience does not entirely matter because the focus in either case is on the response to what God is doing. If the preposition *ek* is Paul's way to indicate the circumstances under which the redemption proclaimed in his gospel is possible, then his use of the preposition *dia* ("by means of") is how he indicates what makes it real. 2:15-3:29 is his exposition of how God's promise/inheritance/salvation are received (and thus, humanly speaking, actualized) by means of faith (*dia pisteōs*). However, 4:1-7 is the passage that marks the point in Paul's exposition where what could have been formally distinguished in terms of the way the prepositions *ek* and *dia* had functioned hitherto now coalesces into the more focused view of the whole gospel: what God had made possible, God is now making real in the vivid eschatological immediacy of the Holy Spirit. It is thus that I have chosen to render this detail of the Greek text in 4:7 as "through God" since the overall context is one in which there should be no question of God's identification as the sole effecting agent of the salvation proclaimed in Paul's gospel. It is only *through God* (*dia theou*) that salvation as a divinely intended inheritance comes to us: "through [him] you also have been made an heir."

XI. The Current Danger (4:8-20)

It is the recognition of God as being the dynamic author of our salvation that is the key to what follows in vv. 8-11, a passage in which Paul returns to the forceful mode of addressing the Galatians that we saw in 3:1-5. When reading it, keep in mind the issue of *initiative*, that sole prerogative of the redeemer who purchases the slave for the purpose of a new identity that will be constituted by the ex-slave's relationship to him:

*⁸ ἀλλὰ τότε μὲν οὐκ εἰδότες θεὸν
ἐδουλεύσατε τοῖς φύσει μὴ οὖσιν θεοῖς·
⁹ νῦν δὲ γνόντες θεόν,
μᾶλλον δὲ γνωσθέντες ὑπὸ θεοῦ,
πῶς ἐπιστρέφετε πάλιν ἐπὶ τὰ ἀσθενῆ καὶ πτωχὰ στοιχεῖα
οἷς πάλιν ἄνωθεν δουλεύειν θέλετε;
¹⁰ ἡμέρας παρατηρεῖσθε καὶ
μῆνας καὶ καιροὺς καὶ ἐνιαυτούς,
¹¹ φοβοῦμαι ὑμᾶς μή πως εἰκῇ κεκοπίακα εἰς ὑμᾶς.*

*⁸ But when you did not know God,
you were enslaved to the things which were not by nature gods,
⁹ and now that you do know God,
or rather, now that you are known by God,
how is it that you are turning again to the weak and impoverished elements
to which you once more wish to enslave yourselves?
¹⁰ You go about observing days and
months and season and years—
¹¹ I am afraid for you in the event that I have labored over you in vain.*

There is a remarkable wealth of elements in this text because Paul is operating on multiple levels and moving in different directions all at once. It might seem at first glance that there is some question as to whether Paul is talking specifically about the Galatians' pre-gospel pagan practices, the traditional observances of *diaspora* Jews living in that region, or the practices to which the advocates of circumcision were enjoining the new Christian believers. The answer is that Paul is addressing them all at once, lumping traditional Jewish practice with pagan custom, a highly provocative move on his part but one intended to make a fundamental point about the nature of the gospel he had preached among the Galatians and to which he was now recalling them.

Keep this mixed audience in mind especially in v. 8 when Paul writes, "But when you did not know God, you were enslaved to the things which were not by nature gods." The general thrust of the statement would have been obvious enough for any pagan convert to understand: their previous pagan beliefs and practices had no real god corresponding to them. But to place that same idea in the ears of those who had been traditional Jewish believers was a most inflammatory thing to say because they at least would have been under the impression that their possession of the law meant that in a completely meaningful way they already "knew God," that even though the law by itself was an insufficient vehicle for the salvation of Israel, its possession and observance would have counted for something vis-à-vis a full-blown pagan ignorance.

And yet it is on this point—that the Jew already knew God, though perhaps in an incomplete fashion—that Paul is quietly but purposely insistent. In v. 9a he brings them up to date where the gospel's power among them is concerned: "and now that you do know God, or rather, now that you are known by God..." It is precisely this phrase "and now that you do know God" (*nyn de gnontes theon*) that introduces Paul's double-whammy declaration about how God works through the gospel. He is asserting here that it is only in that adverbial interval called "now" (*nyn*) that the Galatians can say that they know God, indeed, it is only in the wake of Paul's original mission among them when they first heard the gospel message from him. Thus it is not primarily a matter of them now possessing a definitive body of knowledge concerning God which accounts for their new status, but rather it is entirely due to the fact that *only now*, by virtue of their having heard the gospel from him *before* the arrival of the circumcision advocates, that God knows them. In other words, it is only

XI. The Current Danger (4:8-20)

through their hearing of the gospel and their reception of it in faith that they can now see and say that they are standing in the right kind of covenantal relationship with God. As Paul will make clearer in chapters 5 and 6 of his letter, the most immediate basis for God's "knowing" the Galatian believers will be the extent to which they are obedient to the commands contained in his gospel. A father knows his son when the latter is obedient. If God has indeed "sent forth the Spirit of his Son into [their] hearts" (4:6b) in conjunction with the trust they have placed in what they have heard from Paul, then the only genuine proof of their reception of the Spirit will be entirely a matter, not of exclamations, but of faithful conduct.

Having once more in this fashion asserted the primacy of faith in the gospel that summons its hearers to obedience, Paul can continue his interrogation of the Galatians in vv. 9b-11 (with v. 9a prefixed), when, with not a little anxious concern, he asks:

⁹ and now that you do know God,
or rather, now that you are known by God,
how is it that you are turning again to the weak and impoverished elements
to which you wish to enslave yourselves once more?
¹⁰ You go about observing days and
months and seasons and years—
¹¹ I am afraid for you in the event that I have labored over you in vain.

Paul only wants the Galatians to comprehend the gravity of what he sees as their current dereliction. First, by indicating the terms of covenantal election contained in the gospel based as these are on faith, baptism, and the reception of the Holy Spirit, and second, by confronting them about the apparent changes wrought in their priorities and practices by the advocates of circumcision. It is as if vv. 9-11 pungently summarize all of what Paul has been arguing in his letter up to this point. As the man who has brought the gospel to the Galatians, as the man who has shared the message of the crucified Jesus as a life-saving and life-giving proclamation about God's love for man, as the man who has presided over the irruption of the Holy Spirit in their midst, and as the man who has forged the Galatians into a Spirit-ruled body united in faith and conduct, Paul now wishes to know why they have turned away from what he has established. As the man who has accomplished all of this he now asks, "how is it that you are turning again to the weak and impoverished elements to which you wish to enslave yourselves once more?"

The terminology in v. 9b is especially interesting. That the Galatians "are turning again" is *epistrephete palin*, a verbal construction whose etymology communicates the very orientational sense in which the ancients conceived of religious belief in general, that is, as a basic orientation of the person, as a turning in the direction of something, or, more exactly, *as a loyalty*. If you are loyal to something or someone, then your loyalty is a matter of *strephein* to that object, literally, your turning toward it. Prior to the arrival of the circumcision party, the basic orientation of the Galatians was toward the gospel as Paul had preached it to them (and the God it presupposes), but now, under the influence of these newcomers, they have switched their loyalty back (*epistrephein*) to the things of which Paul has already spoken in 4:3.

In that verse Paul had written in analogical terms of the believer's minority status during the pre-gospel time, of how, even though the latter is the heir, he was still a child where the faith is concerned: "when we were children, we were in servitude to the elemental things of this world." It is in v. 9b that Paul returns to this idea of being subject to these "elemental things" (*stoicheia*) in connection with the Galatians' decision to embrace the gospel according to what the advocates of circumcision had taught them. He wishes to know why these same Galatians, those who through his gospel have been blessed by the grace-full power of the Holy Spirit, why they should now consciously be turning back to what he now describes here as "the weak and impoverished elemental things." Just as in 4:3, he once more uses the Greek word *stoicheia* for the "elemental things," yet now he has sharpened his language and labels them not just the

XI. The Current Danger (4:8-20)

"elements," but the "weak and impoverished elements" (*asthenē kai ptōcha stoicheia*). The "elemental things" are modified by a pair of adjectives which derive their significance from the explicit contrast being made at this point: if the Holy Spirit is strong, then these elemental things are weak (*asthenēs*); if the Holy Spirit is rich, then by comparison the elemental things are by their very nature "poor" or "impoverished" (*ptōchos*). If the Galatians themselves have experienced both the power and the richness of the Holy Spirit in their lives, how can they exchange their unmistakable experience of that for something that is of a lesser, inferior nature? Why would they want to "enslave themselves" (*douleuein*) once again to something they had formerly abandoned?[1] Would they not want what their own experience had taught them to be true, powerful, and life-changing?

And to what were they turning? In v. 10 Paul furnishes us with a most curious description because it does not mention circumcision explicitly and focuses instead on other matters: "You go about observing days and months and seasons and years—" It would be easy enough to construe Paul's listing here of the days, months, seasons, and years as being the stuff of the annual Hebrew religious calendar with its appointed assemblies and feast-day occasions, but his phrasing here is, I think, quite deliberate given the overall emphasis in 4:1-11 on the *passage of time* from the old to the new, and specifically, on what is the eschatological dimension of the Galatians' new life in the gospel.

And it is this new eschatological consciousness and experience that mark the advent of the new age (*aiōn*). The first eleven verses of chapter 4 comprise an extremely tightly-knit section of the letter, and they roughly break down into three sub-sections (vv. 1-3, 4-7, and 8-11), but these form part of a larger thematic unit that runs from 3:23 to 4:11. What links them together is the progression from the older pre-gospel era (1:4b, "this

---

[1] The participial construction based on the verb *douloomai* in 4:3 ("we were in servitude to the elemental things of this world") reflects this same idea of being *doulos* to the wrong master.

encompassing evil age") dominated by the law and the curse it brings to those who disobey it, to the new status of salvation to be had in the gospel of the Christ. I have already mentioned the "eschatological pivot" that Paul signals in vv. 1-3, while vv. 4-7 are the declaration of this new life offered to us by God through the gospel and its manifestation by means of the "Spirit of his Son," and finally, given all of this, vv. 8-11 are Paul's remonstrance with the Galatians for what appears to be their forsaking of what they themselves have received and experienced.

The way in which this larger unit is structured brings together not only all of the frameworks on which we have relied so far—covenant, lawcourt language, eschatology, and christology—but also the relevant Exodus imagery and the overriding theme of inheritance. What ultimately binds it together is the role played by the divine initiative in Pauline gospel. This is expressed most clearly in 4:2, "instead he is under guardians and stewards *until the time appointed by his father*," a verse that functions as the structural center of the unit because the "time appointed by his father" (*prothesmia hypo tou patros*) is the pivotal assertion around which all the surrounding sections and what they describe revolve. The structural parallelism at work in 3:23-4:11 is as follows:

```
3:23-24
        3:25-29
                4:1
                        4:2[2]
                4:3
        4:4-7
4:8-11
```

---

[2] The "time appointed by the father" (*prothesmia tou patros*) is the direct expression of the father's will, and Paul's analogy should be seen in relation to what he writes in the introduction to his letter: "May grace and peace be with you from God our Father and the Lord Jesus who is the Christ, he who gave himself on account of our sins in order that he might deliver us from this encompassing evil age, *it all being done in accordance with the will (thelēma) of our God and Father*, to whom be the glory unto the ages of ages. Amen." (1:3-5)

XI. The Current Danger (4:8-20)

The key to understanding this structuring is time. The blocs of text listed above are loaded with temporal indicators, and these help to orient each one in relation to the structural center. If the gospel's entry into human history is wholly a matter of the Father's prerogative (1:4c), then the indication of that is found abruptly stated in 4:2. This is flanked by the two verses (4:1, 4:3) that tell of how we were we yet "children" in relation to the coming of the gospel. The next two parallel sections (3:25-29, 4:4-7) detail the reality of the life that is to be found in the gospel. The two outer sections (3:23-24, 4:8-11) are related but in antithetical ways: the first tells of a righteousness to be had by trusting in the gospel to come, while the second is about that same gospel initially received but now reportedly abandoned.

But abandoned for what? There was nothing inherently wrong with the Jewish observance of sabbath and the annual festivals, but, even in their law-ordained function (3:23, "But before faith came, we were being held under the law's watch, bound together for the sake of the faith about to be revealed"), such observations had little more than a prophetic utility. While they may have proclaimed the Christ only tangentially, Paul is arguing that in their details the "days and months and seasons and years" were not the occasion for the reception and display of the Holy Spirit. In other words, Paul is asking why, given the eschatological realities of their own indubitable gospel-experience, the Galatians are now turning their attention from spiritual truth to material practices, away from what they have directly experienced and in the direction of what others are now urging. It should be emphasized here that Paul's contrast is a *relational* one and not a strictly qualitative one: given what the Galatians have experienced (3:1-5, 4:6), why revert to something that is less than this fullness? It is basic Christian eschatology: the days, months, seasons, and years (the old *aiōn*) have been surpassed, not as illusions, but as belonging to the more "elemental things" (*stoicheia*) which cannot compare to the fullness of Christian life in the gospel that inaugurates the new *aiōn*.

But alas, it would appear from Paul's letter that his fears must have been real enough, that at least to some degree the Galatians have been distracted by the circumcision party and are embracing what the apostle views as that group's retrograde concerns. Given that the Galatians "go about observing days and months and seasons and years," in v. 11 he continues with this expression of his concern, "I am afraid for you in the event that I have labored over you in vain." If the Galatians have been coaxed into making lesser matters into central ones, if the Galatians are emptying the gospel of its life-giving content by substituting for it ritual concerns and obligations, then, in the light of Paul's own undeniable role as the agent of that original gospel's irruption into their lives, the apostle can only view the advent of this alleged behavior as being the sign that his labors on behalf of the gospel have been in vain, that his efforts do not appear to be bearing the kind of fruit consistent with their quite specific seed.

Recall in this connection the idea of "prophetic exasperation," that biblical singularity of purpose, the reason why the prophet-apostle is guided by an uncompromising, imperturbable conviction that there is nothing arbitrary or open-ended about his mission and that he is following the greatest imperative to accomplish it. Indeed, the relative success of the apostolic mission can be measured in terms of two considerations: (1) was the message proclaimed in accordance with God's commissioning of it, and (2) was it received and to what extent. We can presume that Paul did not arrive among the Galatians with any reservations about the precise meaning of the gospel he was prepared to preach in their midst. But much had preceded his arrival, and in vv. 12-20, Paul alludes to some of these circumstances, and while some of his language at certain points is imprecise if not cryptic, we can sketch out a complete enough picture of what must have been a highly personal situation that developed when Paul first made his way to the Galatian region.

XI. The Current Danger (4:8-20)

It is precisely at this point—when he has confronted the Galatians about what he sees as their dereliction where the gospel is concerned—that Paul makes his most emotional appeal to them. His words require some explanation given that they can be misunderstood easily. Having voiced his anxious concern over their situation in v. 11, he then continues in v. 12a by pleading,

¹² γίνεσθε ὡς ἐγώ, ὅτι κἀγὼ ὡς ὑμεῖς, ἀδελφοί, δέομαι ὑμῶν.

¹² Brothers and sisters, I am beseeching you, become as I am, for I too have become as you are.

This plea is the beginning of Paul's more personalized wish for the Galatians to reconsider just what it has been that he and they have shared together. Despite Paul's addressing them once more as "brothers and sisters" (the Greek vocative *adelphoi*, though a masculine plural, is, just like it was in 3:15, a semantically inclusive usage), his language is strange to modern ears. The imperative "become as I am" (*ginesthe hōs egō*) might strike us as a piece of presumptive pleading on Paul's part, but the following clause "for I too have become as you are" (*hoti kagō hōs hymeis*) allows us to see the point of his appeal.

On the one hand, Paul can and does speak with the evangelist's authority. It was he who brought the gospel to the Galatians, proclaiming it among them and witnessing himself the Spirit-based founding of the Christian community in the region. Thus there was the indisputable fact of his own personal example among them: obviously the Galatians were in a position to recall what was the nature of Paul's leadership and conduct during his previous visit(s). As the bearer of the original message, such speech as he exhibits here was Paul's prerogative, but, on the other hand, the point is not the assertion of a hierarchical authority *per se*, but rather the strict solidarity that Paul shares with them *given that both he and the Galatians are subject to the same gospel*. Therefore, let the Galatians become as Paul is, that is, obedient to the same gospel message, because all along in his own obedience to the gospel Paul has become like the Galatians, that is, hearing the gospel, believing in it, and, *as a result*, receiving the Holy Spirit (with the by now clear implication that none of this was ever conditional on anything like a formal observation of the Jewish law).

It is as if Paul is asking the Galatians to remember how things were in the beginning, if they could remind themselves for just a moment of the exact circumstances of that beginning, and how things had come about when he first appeared among them saying what he did. But, at the same time, he wants them to understand that, though he is writing to them with the deepest possible concern about their situation, he does not regard them as having done him any wrong. In vv. 12b-14 he writes:

¹² οὐδέν με ἠδικήσατε·
¹³ οἴδατε δὲ ὅτι δι᾽ ἀσθένειαν τῆς σαρκὸς
εὐηγγελισάμην ὑμῖν τὸ πρότερον,
¹⁴ καὶ τὸν πειρασμὸν ὑμῶν ἐν τῇ σαρκί μου
οὐκ ἐξουθενήσατε οὐδὲ ἐξεπτύσατε,
ἀλλὰ ὡς ἄγγελον θεοῦ ἐδέξασθέ με,
ὡς Χριστὸν Ἰησοῦν.

¹² You have done me no wrong;
¹³ and you know that it was on account of my bodily weakness
that I preached the gospel to you the first time;
¹⁴ and that trial which came upon you by way of my body
you neither despised nor rejected,
rather, you received me as a messenger of God
just as you had received the Christ Jesus.

If by this point the Galatians have recalled with any detail what it was like when Paul first delivered the gospel to them, then they might have a growing sense about why he is now so concerned, but even so, Paul assures them in v. 12b that "you have done me no wrong," a statement of gentle reassurance given the direct way he has been confronting them about their behavior. There is no reason to suspect that this change in tone is part of a rhetorical strategy on Paul's part; to the contrary, the way in

XI. The Current Danger (4:8-20)

which he reminisces about the shared circumstances of his arrival in the region is genuine and sincere enough, but it also helps him to make a point. That point concerns what he and the Galatians actually did *share*, namely, his bringing of the gospel and their reception of it *according to the original terms in which he preached it to them.*

The passage that follows has been the subject of much speculation about just what those first circumstances included. In v. 13 he writes, "and you know that it was on account of my bodily weakness that I preached the gospel to you the first time," and the phrase "on account of my bodily weakness" (*di' astheneian tēs sarkos*) has been interpreted variously as a reference to some kind of physical illness or possibly even a chronic medical condition. If any kind of malady was involved, it is at least clear that his illness/condition was a direct factor in Paul's preaching of the gospel to the Galatians, presumably causing him to preach it there as opposed to somewhere else. When understood this way, his language does suggest—but does not confirm—that if he had not become ill, then he might not have preached it to them at all.

But is that what Paul is saying? I am not convinced that he is referring to any kind of way-laying sickness here. There are plenty of New Testament contexts where the Greek word *astheneia* is read to mean illness or bodily ailment, but even in those passages its occurrence is never just a plain instance of an isolated medical pathology because human disease appears scripturally as the occasion either for the manifestation of God's power or for the lesson found in the latter's absence. Paul uses it in contexts where there is an explicit dualism between human *astheneia* ("weakness") and the divine *dynamis* ("power"). The point in such passages is to highlight the simple fact that, when it comes to our salvation at the hands of God, our relative condition of mortal weakness (*astheneia*) stands in complete contrast to God's effecting power (*dynamis tou theou*). The former is forever incomplete, while the latter is what sovereignly completes. In 2 Corinthians 10-13 Paul writes what is a sustained scriptural paean to this duality. It expresses how Paul understands human weakness vis-à-vis not only the divine initiative but also the manifestation of that power. 12:8-10 (RSV) encapsulates all of what Paul wishes to emphasize in this connection:

Three times I besought the Lord about this, that it should leave me; but he said to me, "My grace is sufficient for you, for my power (*dynamis*) is made perfect in weakness (*astheneia*)." I will all the more gladly boast of my weaknesses (*astheneiais*), that the power of Christ (*dynamis tou Christou*) may rest upon me. For the sake of Christ, then, I am content with weaknesses (*astheneiais*), insults, hardships, persecutions, and calamities; for when I am weak (*astheno*), then I am strong (*dynatos*).

When Paul writes in 4:13 that "it was on account of my bodily weakness that I preached the gospel to you the first time," he is more likely referring to the unwavering obedience required of him by his own apostolic vocation. In other words, he first preached the gospel in the Galatian regions because that was in strict accordance with the evangelistic imperative he had followed from the beginning: "But when it pleased God, he who had set me apart before I was born, and who called me by means of his grace, to reveal his Son through me so that I might preach him among the nations…" (1:15-16).

The adverbial phrase "the first time" (*to proteron*) in v. 13 is ambiguous with regard to chronology. By itself *to proteron* can be used either to refer to a single past instance or to more than one occasion. But the overall context at this point in the letter demands that the focus be on the initial time of Paul's preaching to the Galatians because all of what Paul is arguing here depends on the circumstances of that visit, what happened during his stay, and certainly what happened after it.

It might seem too that the language of v. 14a continues hinting at some possible medical condition as the reason for Paul's

XI. The Current Danger (4:8-20)

apostolic appearance among the Galatians "and that trial which came upon you by way of my body you neither despised nor rejected." The Greek word rendered here as "trial" is *peirasmos*, which is also the same word used to denote "temptation" or any kind of challenging test. We cannot be entirely sure about just what kind of trial was involved for the Galatians when Paul first arrived, but there is reason to surmise here that the apostle's reference to a trial at this point is his own intentionally ironic description of the Galatians' initial reception of him when he came bearing his gospel. If Paul had first preached among the Galatians because his gospel demanded it, then what he preached was indeed most likely something of a trial for them. The clause "which came upon you by way of my body" (*en tē sarki mou*) is another way for Paul to indicate no more than his direct physical presence among the Galatians proclaiming a message that probably "tried" not a few of them. Regardless of whatever *peirasmos* Paul's preaching inflicted upon the Galatians, it was such that it did not interfere with the joyous outcome contained in the rest of v.14: "you neither despised nor rejected [it], rather, you received me as a messenger of God just as you then received the Christ Jesus." In other words, Paul preached and then the Galatians had to do something about what they heard. Did they respond in faith (3:2)? Or did they dismiss this annoying chatterbox and his discomfiting message? Did they realize that, having heard this message, they now had to do something one way or another about it? This then was the potential nature of the Galatians' *peirasmos*: their being put to the test and challenged by the Pauline gospel to say, whether they cared to do it or not, yeah or nay to its message.

Paul reminds them that they "neither despised nor rejected" (*ouk exouthenēsate oude exeptysate*) this text[3] because "you received me as a messenger of God just as you had received the Christ Jesus." This means that they came to accept the gospel because

---

[3] The verb used here for "to reject" is *ekptyō*, which literally means "to spit something out."

they both (a) accepted Paul as the first and therefore the legitimate bearer of the message, and (b) they received the word about Jesus and his life-giving death and resurrection. While it is true that the verb meaning "to receive" (*dechomai*) only appears in the first clause ("you *received me* as a messenger of God") and it does not appear in the second clause ("just as [you had received] the Christ Jesus"), the strict verbal correlation between the two clauses is signaled in the Greek text by a single connective "just as" (*hōs*). This is crucial to Paul's argument because it links the Galatians' initial recognition of Paul as a "messenger of God" with their willingness to accept the gospel in the terms he preached it to them, that is, in his capacity as the legitimate messenger of God.

And if Paul had been such a trustworthy soul in the eyes of the Galatians, so much so that they freely received the gospel from him and became believers, then what has happened to all of what Paul and the Galatians shared together in the beginning? This is what Paul wishes to know when he writes in vv. 15-20:

¹⁵ ποῦ οὖν ὁ μακαρισμὸς ὑμῶν;
μαρτυρῶ γὰρ ὑμῖν ὅτι εἰ δυνατὸν
τοὺς ὀφθαλμοὺς ὑμῶν ἐξορύξαντες ἐδώκατέ μοι.
¹⁶ ὥστε ἐχθρὸς ὑμῶν γέγονα ἀληθεύων ὑμῖν·
¹⁷ ζηλοῦσιν ὑμᾶς οὐ καλῶς,
ἀλλὰ ἐκκλεῖσαι ὑμᾶς θέλουσιν,
ἵνα αὐτοὺς ζηλοῦτε·
¹⁸ καλὸν δὲ ζηλοῦσθαι ἐν καλῷ πάντοτε
καὶ μὴ μόνον ἐν τῷ παρεῖναί με πρὸς ὑμᾶς.
¹⁹ τέκνα μου, οὓς πάλιν ὠδίνω
μέχρις οὗ μορφωθῇ Χριστὸς ἐν ὑμῖν·
²⁰ ἤθελον δὲ παρεῖναι πρὸς ὑμᾶς ἄρτι
καὶ ἀλλάξαι τὴν φωνήν μου,
ὅτι ἀποροῦμαι ἐν ὑμῖν.
15 So where is your blessing?

For I declare to you that, if possible,
you would have plucked out your own eyes and given them to me.
¹⁶ Have I then become your enemy by telling you the truth?

XI. The Current Danger (4:8-20)

*17 Their zealous concern for you is to no good purpose,
rather they only want to exclude you
so that you might show zealous concern for them;
18 yet it is a good thing to have zeal always for what is good
and not only when I am with you.
19 My children, you for whom I am once more laboring in birth
until the Christ himself might be formed among you,
20 I have wanted to be with you now
and to change my tone
because I have been having doubts about you.*

Paul's question in v. 15a is an intentionally provocative one (in the sense of goading a person into actually thinking about something), and this is because it was preceded by Paul's having pointed out that the Galatians had *just as much* received him as God's messenger as they had come to accept Jesus as the Christ. So, if both of those assertions are true, then what has happened in the meantime? Where indeed is their blessing? And, by asking the Galatians *where* their blessing is, Paul is in effect asking them *what* is their blessing.

The Greek word translated as "blessing" is *makarismos*. We have already encountered this idea of blessing in connection with God's promise to Abraham in 3:13-14: "The Christ has bought us back from the curse of the law, having become himself a curse on our behalf, because it stands written, "Cursed is every one who hangs on a tree," so that, in the person of the Christ who is Jesus, the *blessing* of Abraham might come upon all the nations, so that we might receive the promise of the Spirit by means of faith." In that passage the word translated as "blessing" is *eulogia*, so is there any possible difference between these two Greek words—*eulogia* and *makarismos*—when they are rendered by the same English word? How great a role does context play here?

Recall that the Greek word *eulogia* has been used in the Septuagint to refer to God's blessing of all mankind through his promise to Abraham (Genesis 12:1-3): "I will *bless* you…and you shall be a *blessing*. I will *bless* those who *bless* you....and in you shall all the tribes of the earth be *blessed*." Here the verb is *eulogeō*, which means "to speak positively about someone or something," and here it must be kept in mind that the supreme blessing would be one that God himself bestows (the "good word" about his obedient slave), and the content of this blessing would presupposes obedience to the master and the corresponding favor it would involve. There is a point where the purely verbal dimension of blessing shades off into what we would reckon as being grace and ultimately the benefits of salvation: God *blesses* by announcing the content of salvation, and the manifestation of that salvation is the *blessing* proper. In 3:13-14 Paul declares that the death of Jesus *as the Christ* is what ensures that the "blessing of Abraham" (*eulogia tou Abraam*) will come upon all the peoples of the earth, and that "we might receive the promise of the Spirit by means of faith."

Given this, the word *makarismos* stands closely related to *eulogia*, but the additional connotation of *makarismos* concerns the calling or considering of someone to be blessed, and the presumption here is that the means of blessedness is already clearly known, and, most importantly, there is a direct manifestation of that blessing. By this point the Galatians could probably remember how by means of Paul's exhortation and guidance they were made aware of what made for the Holy Spirit's presence and workings among them, but now Paul is asking them to go one step further: not only to remember how since the gospel's beginning it had been with the Holy Spirit, but also to remember what changes the Holy Spirit had authored among them. If the gospel had announced to the Galatians their induction into God's blessing of the nations through the Christ, then just how did that blessing manifest itself? What, or, more precisely, *who* was the source of their being able to call themselves blessed— their *makarismos*? In other words, since the coming of the gospel to them, *in whom* could the Galatians originally and consistently consider themselves to be blessed? When Paul asks, "So where is your blessing?", he is in effect demanding to know from the

XI. The Current Danger (4:8-20)

Galatians if they are going to consider themselves blessed by means of the Holy Spirit or by means of the law.

The question is crucial because of what Paul wishes them to grasp once more—that it was he who brought the gospel to them, that it was he who witnessed their reconstitution in the Christ, and that it was he who also experienced how the Holy Spirit became manifest in their lives and in their actions. Paul himself recalls in v. 15b what a blessed sharing it was as these gifts became evident among the Galatians and how they in turn responded to him with faithful affection and what must have been a heartfelt concern: "For I declare to you that, if possible, you would have plucked out your own eyes and given them to me."

But what has happened to this warm relationship founded as it must have been on a fellowship of the Spirit? In v. 16 Paul makes the painful contrast between what was and what now is: "Have I then become your enemy by telling you the truth?" This verse must be linked back to Paul's earlier use of the word "truth" (*alētheia*). When Paul speaks of his trip to Jerusalem in 2:1-10, he explicitly mentions his determination not to submit to the admonishments of the "false brothers" when it came to placing the law above the gospel's requirements: "not for a moment did we submit to them in obedience all in order that the *truth* of the gospel (*alētheia tou euangeliou*) might be preserved for you" (2:5). When Paul confronts Kephas and the others in Antioch about their inconsistency regarding the practice of table fellowship, he is able to say, "But when I saw that they were not consistent about the *truth* of the gospel (*alētheia tou euangeliou*), before them all I said to Kephas, "If you who were born as Jew are now living like a pagan and not like a Jew, how can you compel the pagans to live like Jews?"(2:14) Last of all, when Paul openly confronts the Galatians in 3:1 about their own situation, he is at his most emphatic: "O foolish Galatians! Who has bewitched you that you should not obey the *truth* (*alētheia*), before whose eyes Jesus the Christ was clearly portrayed as crucified?"

In these three instances of the word "truth" one can detect a progression in the way the word is used. The full phrase "the truth of the gospel" is employed in the first two, but in 3:1 Paul speaks only of "the truth" because by this point the identification is clear enough—the "truth" and the "gospel" are interchangeable terms, and keep in mind the stipulation that the "gospel" is always the gospel *as it was preached* to the Galatians by Paul. In 4:16 Paul continues this progression because, instead of using the noun "truth," he now uses a participial construction based on the verb "to utter the truth" (*alētheuō*). Another way of rendering v. 16 would be, "having told you all the truth, why should I now have become your enemy?" The indignation apparent in 4:16 is a function of the contrast with the preceding verse: there Paul had praised the Galatians for what had been their exemplary dedication to him, and now, having done no more than proclaim the truth to them, he wants to know why they have made an enemy of him by turning away from that very truth he had preached to them and which they had so wholeheartedly received.

Up until now Paul has not explicitly identified his opponents. Earlier in the letter he referred to "the ones who are confusing you and who even want to alter the gospel of the Christ" (1:7), and later in 2:12 he speaks of the advocates of circumcision as being the cause of Kephas' inconsistent behavior in Antioch, and even now in v. 17 he continues to refer to them obliquely: "Their zealous concern for you is to no good purpose, rather, they only want to exclude you so that you might show zealous concern for them." One can very well imagine adherents of that group which Paul had labeled as the advocates of circumcision (*hoi ek peritomēs*) coming in the wake of his first (or even second) mission in the Galatian region and there making a passionately focused argument for the necessity of observing the Mosaic law. Thus Paul can speak of their "zealous concern," of their

XI. The Current Danger (4:8-20)

determined advocacy on behalf of the law as being a fully necessary thing, but here he is warning the Galatians of the secret harm contained in their purpose.

Note too that the last time Paul used any language about "zeal" (verb *zēloō*) was in connection with his description of his own "former life in Judaism" (1:13-14):

> *For you have heard of my former life in Judaism,*
> *how I was persecuting the church (*ekklēsia*) beyond measure*
> *and that I was destroying her,*
> *because I had advanced in Judaism beyond many of those among my own people*
> *on account of the fact that I was so exceedingly jealous (*zēlōtēs*) for the*
> *traditions of my fathers.*

The word for "church" (*ekklēsia*) occurs only three times in the entire letter (1:2, 13, 22), and in each instance it is the term that refers to the early messianic community. I suspect that Paul is making an intentional play on words in 4:17 when he frames the verse with the verb for "zealous concern" (*zēloō*) in order to highlight what he insists will amount to the exclusion of the Galatians from the Christian *ekklēsia* if they submit to the designs of his opponents:

> *Their zealous concern (*zēlousin*) for you is to no good purpose,*
> *rather they only want to exclude you (*ekkleisai*)*
> *so that you might show zealous concern (*zēloute*) for them;*

The word for "excluding you" in v. 17 is the verb *ekkleiō* (literally, "to be locked out of something"), and here it appears in its aorist infinitive form, *ekkleisai*, and has a homonymic resemblance to *ekklēsia*. If the foundation of the Christian *ekklēsia* is the new gospel-based identity that transcends the exclusionary categories of Jewish ethnicism or pagan practice, then any move by the Galatians to follow the advocates of circumcision and their agenda amounts to an exclusionary repudiation of the new Christian inclusiveness of the *ekklēsia* (cf. 2:11-14). Paul is thus rhetorically linking his own destructive pre-gospel "zeal" with the program offered by the circumcision advocates: each operates as a repudiation of the gospel that Paul now preaches.

What these advocates of circumcision said—their Judaizing version of the gospel—while it might have had a *prima facie* semblance of pious legitimacy and been powerfully persuasive, was at the same time a dangerous diversion from the "truth of the gospel" as Paul had proclaimed it. He is cautioning the Galatians that whatever might have appeared to them as a "good purpose" was but an illusion because their embrace of the law and its requirements would be on their part a self-exclusionary act vis-à-vis the gospel, and, as Paul intimates, whatever sense they might have been given about the gospel's fulfillment would be a deceptively false assurance. In language that prefigures the last two chapters of the letter, Paul warns the Galatians that his opponents "only want to exclude you [i.e. through the law they want to *separate* you from the ones who receive and hold the true gospel] so that you might show zealous concern for them [i.e. that the Galatians' dedication to the law becomes in effect their compliant exaltation of the circumcision advocates]."

But Paul still remains carefully respectful here when it comes to the relationship between the gospel and the law. He is concerned that the Galatians see the difference between, on the one hand, that which is truly and thus unsurpassably good (the gospel), and, on the other hand, *only by reason of a strict comparison with it*, that which is a lesser order of good (the law). It is in this way that he can assume the comparative superiority of the gospel vis-à-vis the law and at the same time not discount the law vis-à-vis the gospel. He proceeds in v. 18: "yet it is a good thing to have zeal always for what is good and not only when I am present with you." The Galatians are not to be dismissive or even scornful of the law, but rather they must be under no illusions about either it or the gospel. In so many ways the gospel presupposes the law, but it is not ultimately dependent upon it nor does the gospel derive its final validity from it.

XI. The Current Danger (4:8-20)

There is an undeniable poignancy in what Paul next writes. Up until this point Paul has addressed the Galatians as "brothers and sisters" (*adelphoi*), but now he appeals to them as "my children" (*tekna mou*). The shift in wording is apt because he is likening his love and concern for them to that of a woman who is giving birth to a child: "My children, you for whom I am once more laboring in birth until the Christ himself might be formed (*morphōthē*) among you." Just as any mother's foremost concern is for the safety and the well-being of her child, a level of affectionate wishing that most concretely begins with the agonies of childbirth, so too Paul is now like such a mother undergoing both the physical ordeal of birth-giving and all the emotional anxiety that accompanies the raising of any child. His ardent wish for the Galatians is that the Christ he had preached to them—as the passive subjunctive form of the Greek verb *morphoō* denotes—would take shape in their midst. He wants the word of God to take root in their hearts "on the basis of a hearing with faith" (3:2), and, like a fetus that develops and grows in the womb, it would be "by means of the faith whose content is the Christ Jesus" (3:26) that the Christ himself might "undergo gestation" within them and become manifest in the fruit of obedience.

Just prior to this, in v. 18, when Paul had commended always having zeal for a good thing, he had added, "and not only when I am present with you." The natural conclusion to draw from such a statement would be that it represents Paul's simple wish that (1) the Galatians remain faithful to the original gospel message (the supremely good thing), and (2) that they should view the law (the lesser good thing) respectfully in relation to it. But the phrase "when I am present with you" (*pareinai me pros hymās*) occurs again in v. 20: "I have wanted to be present with you now and to change my tone because I have been having my doubts about you." If the first instance connotes a mood of trust, the second is the expression of Paul's continuing concern for his Galatian children.

Recall that, as preached by Paul, the gospel message is about what will now form—in no less strict covenantal terms—the basis for God declaring any man righteous. The gospel is the declaration of Jesus as the Christ, and how faith in him as the Christ is the basis for the new righteousness, and here righteousness is understood solely in terms of obedience to the revealed covenant purposes of God (1:11-12). Previously righteousness had been based on adherence to the law, but, as Paul writes in 3:21-22, "For if a law capable of giving life had been given, then in fact righteousness would have been on the basis of the law; rather, scripture has consigned all things under sin in order that the promise that is based on the faith of Jesus the Christ might be given to the ones who believe." So far Paul has argued not so much for the insufficiency of the law vis-à-vis the gospel as he has contended for the unalloyed primacy of the gospel. Indeed, if "scripture has consigned all things under sin," and if the law by itself was incapable of "giving life" (understood here as not relieving man's unshakably exilic state of disobedience), that was because—in accordance with the Pauline gospel—that same scripture's true meaning was contained in God's pre-Sinai promise to Abraham that "through you shall all the nations be blessed" (3:8).

XII. What Does Scripture Say? (4:21-5:6)

Having heard about the emergence of a new set of priorities in the Galatian churches that he had founded, one that favored the doing of the law at the expense of maintaining the faith-based attitude central to his gospel, Paul has made the case once again for faith's position of supremacy. It is in this continuing state of concern for the Galatians that Paul has "had his doubts about them," and so Paul concludes the long argument in the third and fourth chapters of his letter with a scriptural example in order to let scripture itself have the final word. There is a discernible rhetorical ploy in what Paul presents because it is as if he is now saying to those Galatians who are so taken with the law, "If you will not listen to me and all of what I have said about such matters, then for one last time listen to what the law itself has to say!" In vv. 21-22 he writes:

^{21} λέγετέ μοι, οἱ ὑπὸ νόμον θέλοντες εἶναι,
τὸν νόμον οὐκ ἀκούετε;
^{22} γέγραπται γὰρ ὅτι Ἀβραὰμ δύο υἱοὺς ἔσχεν,
ἕνα ἐκ τῆς παιδίσκης καὶ
ἕνα ἐκ τῆς ἐλευθέρας.

^{21} *Tell me, you who wish to be under the law,*
do you not hear what the law says?
^{22} *For it stands written that Abraham had two sons,*
one from a slave woman and
one from a free woman.

Having begun with Abraham back in 3:6, Paul would naturally wish to conclude with him. The eleven verses that make up the final section of chapter four (4:21-31) have been interpreted in various ways, but for some readers the passage comes off as something of a digression, a momentary lapse of apostolic focus or even of purpose. Just what is Paul doing here? Why does he resort to what some English translations dub as an "allegorical" reading of scripture? Given that he has so far built such an inspiring argument about faith's primacy, why would he now fall back on the more formalized exegetical technique that we might associate more readily with the Judaism he wished to transcend? I think that the simple answer to any of these questions is that *Paul never stopped thinking scripturally.*

The great Abraham narrative that makes up Genesis 12-22 is the weaving together of many important themes—election, blessing, covenant, inheritance, and the twin dynamic of promise/faith—but, as the narrative itself makes clear, the one element that binds all these themes together for Abraham is the possession of a living son, and not just any son, but one born from his own person. When God called Abraham from Mesopotamia and directed him to go to Canaan, he was already married to Sarah. It is this husband-wife relationship between Abraham and Sarah that determines the relative status of all the other characters in the narrative. Hagar would never be *any more* than the Egyptian maid-servant of Abraham's wife Sarah, and it was the latter who asks her husband to take Hagar "as a wife"; and Ishmael, the son that Abraham begets through Hagar at Sarah's behest, is never more than a son born through a maid-servant. There is a primeval logic at work here: the son of a slave always remains a slave.

The circumstances of Ishmael's birth are telling. Because she remains childless, Sarah's decision to offer Hagar to Abraham is motivated by her own wish to have children:

> Now Sarai, Abram's wife, bore him no children. She had an Egyptian maid whose name was Hagar; and Sarai said to Abram, "Behold now, the LORD has prevented me from bearing children; go in to my maid; *it may be that I shall obtain children by her.*" So, after Abram had dwelt ten years in the land of Canaan, Sarai, Abram's wife, took Hagar the Egyptian, her maid, and gave her to Abram her husband as a wife. And he went in to Hagar, and she conceived…And Hagar bore Abram a son; and Abram called the

XII. What Does Scripture Say? (4:21-5:6)

name of his son, whom Hagar bore, Ishmael." (Genesis 16:1-4, 15, RSV) (italics added)

The name *Ishmael* means "God hears" in Hebrew, a reference to the pregnant Hagar's wilderness ordeal when she fled there in order to escape from Sarah's harsh treatment. While the Sarah-Hagar relationship is a puzzling one for our current sensibilities, what needs to be understood is that Sarah's plan to "obtain children by her [Hagar]" ends up being an anxious half-step in the face of the promises already made by God to Abraham. Her move is predicated on an unwillingness to heed that promise and to live in faithfulness to it. But it should be noted too that Abraham's acquiescence before Sarah's request signifies a complicit degree of uncertainty on his own part. In this respect both Abraham and Sarah are cooperative in the first son's siring "according to the flesh" (*kata sarka*), a circumstance contrasted with the second son's origin "by means of a promise" (*di' epangelias*). This duality between the "fleshly" arena of human desires and what will be the Spirit-directed realm of divine power will govern much of chapters 5 and 6. Seen as a whole, the Abraham narrative in Genesis is a gradual unfolding of promise, circumstance, reaction, and progress:

12:3 "...*and by you all the families of the earth shall bless themselves.*"

12:7 "*To your descendants I will give this land.*"

14:16 "*I will make your descendants as the dust of the earth...*"

15:4,6 *And behold, the word of the LORD came to him, "This man shall not be your heir; your own son shall be your heir"....And he believed the LORD; and he reckoned it to him as righteousness.*

17:19 *And God said to Abraham, "I will establish my covenant with Isaac, whom Sarah shall bear to you at this season next year."*

21:2 *And Sarah conceived, and bore Abraham a son in his old age at the time of which God had spoken to him.*

21:12 "...through Isaac shall your descendants be named."[1]

It culminates in the birth of two sons—Ishmael in chapter 16 and Isaac in chapter 21—but the text makes it clear that God is only directly involved in the birth of Isaac. He is conspicuously absent from the Ishmael narrative and does not appear at all until Hagar's wilderness ordeal, but yet he stipulates what shall be the fate of each son. In vv. 23-25 Paul continues with this characterization of Abraham's two sons, and specifically with what the first son and her mother signify:

²³ ἀλλ᾽ ὁ μὲν ἐκ παιδίσκης κατὰ σάρκα γεγέννηται,
ὁ δὲ ἐκ τῆς ἐλευθέρας δι᾽ ἐπαγγελίας.
²⁴ ἅτινά ἐστιν ἀλληγορούμενα·
αὗται γάρ εἰσιν δύο διαθῆκαι,
μία μὲν ἀπὸ ὄρους Σινᾶ εἰς δουλείαν γεννῶσα,
ἥτις ἐστὶν Ἁγάρ.
²⁵ τὸ δὲ Ἁγὰρ Σινᾶ ὄρος ἐστὶν ἐν τῇ Ἀραβίᾳ·
συστοιχεῖ δὲ τῇ νῦν Ἰερουσαλήμ,
δουλεύει γὰρ μετὰ τῶν τέκνων αὐτῆς.

²³ *But the son from the slave woman was born according to the flesh,*
and the son from the free woman by means of a promise.
²⁴ *These things have another meaning*
because the women are two covenants:
one is from Mount Sinai and gives birth to slavery,
the one which is Hagar.
²⁵ *Now Hagar is Mount Sinai in Arabia;*
and she corresponds to the current Jerusalem
because she along with her children serve as slaves.

---

[1] Niels Peter Lemche summarizes the whole of the Abraham narrative in this perceptive way: "Abraham was just, not because he was perfect—he was far from that, never really understanding what God demanded from him—but because he always trusted Yahweh...It was not a crime to be stupid, and Abraham's stupidity is proverbial. After all, Abraham is only human. It is a crime to disobey God. In the historical narrative in the Old Testament, the patriarchs serve as paragons for later Israel, not because they were something special but because their faith in God, unlike the faith of later Israel, never wavered." *The Old Testament between Theology and History* (Louisville, Kentucky: Westminster John Knox Press, 2008), 190-191.

XII. What Does Scripture Say? (4:21-5:6)

Paul wishes that we remind ourselves of the differing circumstances accompanying the births of Ishmael and Isaac, and specifically of how Ishmael's birth was tied to the anxious desperation displayed by both Sarah and Abraham: "the son from the slave woman was born according to the flesh." The difference here is a key one—even though Abraham has already received from God the promise that "your own son shall be your heir" (Genesis 15:4), Sarah has not received any such promise, and by chapter 16 she has grown impatient with her circumstances. She decides to do things in the only immediate course left to a woman in her position: she offers her maidservant Hagar to Abraham with her calculating hope that "I shall obtain children by her." This particular practice was a common and acceptable one in the ancient Near East, and so we must set aside its questionable aspects and focus instead on how it functions in relation to the dynamic at work among God, Abraham, and Sarah.

First, there is God's promise to Abraham in Genesis 15. In the wake of the defeat of the four kings in chapter 14 Abraham is apprehensive about his lack of an heir. In 15:3 Abraham laments, "And Abram said, "Behold, thou hast given me no offspring; and a slave born in my house will be my heir." But in 15:4-6 (RSV) God's response to Abraham's complaint sets the stage for the events in the following five chapters:

> And behold, the word of the LORD came to him, "This man [Eliezer of Damascus] shall not be your heir; *your own son shall be your heir.*" And he brought him outside and said, "Look toward heaven and number the stars, if you are able to number them." Then he said to him, "So shall your descendants be." And he believed the LORD; and he reckoned it to him as righteousness.

Second, given the immediate problem of no male heir, there is Sarah's decision to take matters into her own hands, and the result is that Ishmael is born as the "son of the slave woman," and, as Paul wishes to make abundantly clear, he is thus born "according to the flesh," that is, not on the basis of God's promise, which, after Ishmael's birth in chapter 16, is repeated and made even more explicit in chapters 17 and 18:

> And God said to Abraham, "As for Sarai your wife, you shall not call her name Sarai, but Sarah shall be her name. I will bless her, and moreover I will give you a son by her; I will bless her, she shall be a mother of nations, kings of peoples shall come from her." Then Abraham fell on his face and laughed, and said to himself, "Shall a child be born to a man who is a hundred years old? Shall Sarah, who is ninety years old, bear a child?" And Abraham said to God, "O that Ishmael might live in thy sight!" God said, "No, but Sarah your wife shall bear you a son, and you shall call his name Isaac. *I will establish my covenant with him as an everlasting covenant for his descendants after him.* As for Ishmael, I have heard you; behold, I will bless him and make him fruitful and multiply him exceedingly; he shall be the father of twelve princes, and I will make him a great nation. *But I will establish my covenant with Isaac, whom Sarah shall bear to you at this season next year."* (17:15-21, RSV)

> They said to him [Abraham], "Where is Sarah your wife?" And he said, "She is in the tent." The LORD said, "I will surely return to you in the spring, and Sarah your wife shall have a son." And Sarah was listening at the tent door behind him. Now Abraham and Sarah were old, advanced in age; it had ceased to be with Sarah after the manner of women. So Sarah laughed to herself, saying, "After I have grown old, and my husband is old, shall I have pleasure?" The LORD said to Abraham, "Why did Sarah laugh, and say, 'Shall I indeed bear a child, now that I am old?' *Is anything too hard for the LORD? At the appointed time I will return to you, in the spring, and Sarah shall have a son."* (18:9-14, RSV)

Third, when all of this comes to pass *as promised by God*, when Sarah gives birth to a son who is named Isaac in Genesis 21:1-3, then what Paul says about Sarah in v. 23b is realized: "and the son from the free woman [was born] by means of a promise." The final prepositional phrase "by means of a promise" is rendered in the Greek as *di' epangelias*, and Paul has deliberately and instructively contrasted the scriptural circumstances surrounding the births of Ishmael and Isaac in order to make a

XII. What Does Scripture Say? (4:21-5:6)

basic point about God's saving relationship with Israel. Ishmael was born "according to the flesh," that is, his birth had more to do with human calculation in response to mortal anxiety than it did with the larger story conveyed by scripture about God's persistent purpose in the salvation of Israel. If Ishmael is born as a result of willful human action, then Isaac's birth is depicted as being entirely a matter of the divine will as it has been expressed "by means of a promise."[2] The willingness of both Sarah and Abraham to seek an heir through Hagar stands as human action in bondage to the perception that some things are "too hard for the LORD" (Genesis 18:14).

This brings us to the expansive boldness of what Paul is claiming in 4:21-31, and how, contrary to many assumptions that the passage stands apart from or is but an appendix to his impassioned argument about faith's primacy which he has mounted in chapters 3 and 4, there is every reason to view the end of chapter 4 as the scriptural crowning—and thus the supreme summarizing—of Paul's plea to the Galatians. I said earlier that while Paul does many things, the one thing he never does is refrain from thinking scripturally. When you peel apart these last verses in chapter 4, what you find is a magnificent invocation and weaving together of multiple biblical themes, ideas, and events done for the sake of driving home the simple point at the heart of his appeal to the Galatians: Whose children are you? Paul's exposition in these verses is marvelously concise, but is it an incidental piece of allegorization on his part? First a few words concerning problems associated with allegorization, and what Paul is actually doing here.

---

[2] In 3:18 Paul first mentions the idea of inheritance (*klēronomia*), and henceforth it functions synonymously in the letter with the notion of promise (*epangelia*). Abraham inherits nothing unless it is through the son with whom God blesses him. If Isaac is the divinely promised seed (*sperma*) that only comes "by means of a promise," then Abraham's faith in that promise is the scriptural *typos* (paradigm) for the Christian believer "in order that the promise that is the faith of Jesus the Christ might be given to the ones who believe" (3:22).

When we sample modern English translations of 4:24a, we find it rendered typically in either of two general ways:

"Which things are an allegory..." (KJV)

"Now this is an allegory..." (RSV)

"This is allegorically speaking..." (NASB)

"Now this may be interpreted allegorically..." (ESV)

"This can be regarded as an allegory..." (JB)

"These things may be taken figuratively..." (NIV)

"Which things are symbolic..." (NKJV)

Either there is the designation of Paul's reference to Abraham's two sons and the interpretation that he is attaching as being an instance of "allegory" (KJV, RSV, ESV, NASB, JB), or, alternatively, in the NIV and the NKJV respectively, a figurative or a symbolic significance is attached to them. I find that none of the above seven renderings conveys the bold simplicity of the interpretation Paul is offering. After all, he is not dealing here with matters of a historical nature as these are popularly understood, i.e. whether or not they actually happened and thus possess an attributable historical reality. To the contrary, the traditional Christian notions of "allegory" (colored as these now are by modernist historicism) have zero relevance to what Paul seeks here. When he writes in 4:24a that "these things have another meaning" (*hatina estin allēgoroumena*), he is in effect declaring, "If you know what the law says, then what does the prophet Isaiah have to say about it?" The attitude of "naïve realism" that has plagued centuries of Christian exegesis and the critical scholarship that has either aided or challenged it has no

XII. What Does Scripture Say? (4:21-5:6)

place in the exegetical landscape where Paul now walks at the end of the fourth chapter.[3]

It is due to these considerations that I have chosen to render 4:24a as "These things have another meaning." My choice was tied to the following considerations. First, the traditional polarity between literalizing and allegorical understandings of scripture cannot maintain itself consistently. Scripture by its very nature is bound by a *de facto* literalism, by the very fact that we must be willing to deal with a text *as a text*, and therefore not to go racing beyond its immediate content. We must learn to respect a text and deal with its details in ways always immediate to the text and its place within a body of canonical literature. Second, this does not mean that we are to restrict ourselves to a narrowly historicizing appropriation of the text and thus construing it in the naively-realistic approach to scripture that has become so thoroughly characteristic of modern thinking. The more ancient, original orientation of scriptural understanding was that the text told a story that was *parabolic* in nature from start to finish. If we visualize any parabolic curvature, what we soon discover is that anything we wish to say about this parabolic figure and any of the linear truths it contains is a function of what the figure's curving space encompasses. In other words, the parabolic truth of scripture is only ever a matter of the way the points and lines stand in relation to each other. Thus, when Paul begins to speak about the two mothers of Abrahams's sons, what he can say about them is dictated by the way they correlate with things relevant found in the scriptural canon: if there is indeed another meaning for one thing, it is there to be found in the adjoining spaces of the scripture.

---

[3] See, for example, the peremptory but necessary way in which Thomas L. Thompson adjudicates this matter, *op. cit.*, pp. 4, 73, 139, 230, 396-7. In addition, see the very relevant comments on the subject of "biblical pedagogy" in the first chapter of Marc Philip Boulos, *Torah to the Gentiles: St. Paul's Letter to the Galatians* (St. Paul, Minnesota: OCABS Press, 2014), 15-33.

This, I think, is the clue to the way in which Paul intends *allēgoroumena* in 4:24b to be understood. In his commentary on Galatians, Paul Nadim Tarazi notes how the Greek verb *allēgoreuō* ("to allegorize") is a compound form derived from the combination of the adjective *allo* ("other") and the verb *agoreuō* ("to declare something in the open public space [agora] of the city").[4] The "other" thing being stated here presupposes not novelty but rather things common to all the city's citizens, i.e. the scriptural world they inhabit. Put most baldly: the things we encounter in scripture—the persons, places, events, and, above all, their connecting ideas—these things do possess at any given moment more than one meaning, not in the sense that we are free to interpret them in accordance with any innovative and/or fanciful way we see fit, but rather in the sense that any scriptural passage potentially points to other passages or scripturally-grounded ideas, that any single passage can be related meaningfully to others, and that this interpretation is all done under the informing guidance of the textual tradition in which it is occurring. The more one studies the Bible, the more he should be able to see that it consists of multiple strands that form a single vast interconnected story. What Paul offers in these verses does not rank as a traditional allegorical reading because his approach here is a straightforward example of typological correspondence. Typological interpretation is the most natural method for interpreting biblical texts in that it relies on the available internal evidence rather than external, imported ideas.[5]

---

[4] Paul Nadim Tarazi, *Galatians: A Commentary* (Crestwood, New York: St. Vladimir's Seminary Press, 1994), 242ff.

[5] Roger Scruton (*The Soul of the World*, Princeton, New Jersey, Princeton University Press, 2014, p. 38) writes about how there is an *acoustic plurality* found in music when two or more notes (each acoustically singular) resonate together to form that single musical sound we know as a chord. The latter, though a musically singular moment, consists of an acoustic plurality. The listener hears musical chords as a single though composite cluster of sounds and not as a string of discrete ones. In a way parallel to this understanding of acoustic plurality, there are what amount to moments of *scriptural plurality* in the Bible, i.e. when biblical figures, events, and terminology mingle and merge when cited in other subsequent contexts, and, because of their juxtaposition, we are able to hear the meanings produced by their simultaneously mutual resonations.

XII. What Does Scripture Say? (4:21-5:6)

Recall that Paul is once more challenging the Galatians to reconsider what the law actually says. Recall too that the law—the Jewish Torah—was the "parabolic" account of how salvation was rooted in Israel's relationship with the God who had chosen her to be his obedient covenant-partner. Paul has already relied inferentially upon much material from Genesis concerning Abraham, Sarah, and the birth of Isaac, but now he would have the Galatians look at it once more in order to see what for him were its critical implications. I repeat 4:21-24 for the sake of continuity:

> *²¹ Tell me, you who wish to be under the law,*
> *do you not hear what the law says?*
> *²² For it stands written that Abraham had two sons,*
> *one from a slave woman and*
> *one from a free woman.*
> *²³ But the son from the slave woman was born according to the flesh,*
> *and the son from the free woman was born by means of a promise.*
> *²⁴ These things have another meaning*
> *because the women are two covenants:*
> *one is from Mount Sinai and gives birth to slavery,*
> *the one which is Hagar.*

The scriptural account of God's promise to Abraham, that he would grant to Abraham a son by his wife Sarah, and that this son Isaac would be the true heir of all that God intended for Israel's salvation, is contained in Genesis 15-22, and the traditional understanding of that narrative sees a direct line of promise and inheritance proceeding from Abraham through Isaac to Jacob and his sons. The descendants of the latter under Moses' leadership would receive the law on Mount Sinai, but with the explicit understanding that it was to the law-obeying nation of Israel that the substance of the God's original promise would be extended. This is the traditional understanding of the Torah's narrative, that the law—and obedience to it—was the one thing guaranteeing the salvation of the Jews. Paul's Jewish

---

Paul relies on this phenomenon, I think, when offering his "allegorical" reading of Abraham, his two sons, and their respective mothers.

contemporaries saw the law as synonymous with the rites and practices of the temple-complex in Jerusalem. The progression could be depicted schematically in this way:

Abraham/promise → law → earthly Jerusalem/temple

But now Paul is offering a radical re-interpretation of this traditional schema, one that must be seen in connection with the one he began earlier in the letter. Recall that in 3:6-8 Abraham is commended for his faithful response to God's promise: ("Just as Abraham believed God, and it was reckoned to him as righteousness"...Through you [Abraham] shall all the nations be blessed"), but Paul wastes no time in declaring the law's insufficiency vis-à-vis faith in 3:10-12:

> *10 For as many as there are who live on the basis of the works of the law,*
> *they are living under a curse;*
> *for it stands written,*
> *"Cursed is every one who does not abide by all the things written in the book of the law,*
> *and do them."*
> *11 And as it is evident that by the law no one is declared righteous before God,*
> *because "he who is righteous shall live on the basis of faith,"*
> *12 for the law is not on the basis of faith,*
> *rather "he who does these things, by them shall he live."*

Central to Paul's reordering of things is his focus on the respective circumstances surrounding the births of Ishmael and Isaac: Ishmael was "born according to the flesh" and Isaac was "by means of a promise." Once again the prepositions are relevant to the thrust of his argument.

The Greek phrase for "according to the flesh" is *kata sarka*, and the preposition *kata* means "in accordance with something." The implication is that whatever comes about *kata*-something has come about because it is simply following the parameters already laid out for that particular thing. Therefore, Ishmael's being born *kata sarka* means that his was a strictly human conception and birth and nothing beyond what that in itself

XII. What Does Scripture Say? (4:21-5:6)

might mean. Contrasted to this is Isaac's birth "by means of a promise," in Greek *di' epangelias*,[6] and the preposition *dia* serves to highlight the directly effecting role of God's promise in Isaac's conception and his being born.

And now, having made the contrast in this manner, Paul wants to make it clear that, within the interpretive parameters set by scripture itself, "these things have another meaning," that these are persons and events which point beyond their original scriptural contexts, and stand in relation not only to other biblical texts but also correlate with the situation of the Galatian churches. Hence, when he invokes Abraham, his two sons, and their respective mothers, we arrive at the meaning Paul intends for the *allēgoroumena* (quite literally, "the other things to be said"), i.e. that their meaning will now consist of more than what the original Genesis text contains. Genesis 15-22 is already full of language about blessing, promise, covenant, and inheritance, and so we might very well ask at this point, "What more can we read into this account as it stands?" It is right after his declaration in 4:24a that "these things have another meaning" that Paul sets to work by asserting in 4:24b "because the women are two covenants." This sets the stage for the way Paul declares a radical reordering of the traditional Jewish view of that people's covenantal relationship with God.

First, as I said above, the traditional view consisted of a sequence in which God's promise to Abraham was foundational to the covenant only to the extent that it formed a patriarchal prelude to the Exodus-Sinai-Entry into Canaan sequence of events, which was in turn viewed as culminating in the establishment of the Jerusalem temple. According to this view, the son born to Sarah continued the patriarchal lineage that in turn received the law at Mt. Sinai and would ultimately erect the

---

[6] Paul has already employed the phrase "by means of a promise" in 3:18, a verse expressing the same promissory action on God's part: "For if the inheritance is on the basis of the law, it is no longer on the basis of a promise; but God had given it to Abraham *by means of a promise*."

temple in Jerusalem as the cultic center of the Israelite people. Thus was Sarah's role fixed within this traditional sequence: she had mothered a people to whom God had given the law and who in alleged obedience to it built the Jerusalem temple. But now, second, Paul asserts that Sarah does not occupy the place traditionally assigned to her because, in his interpretation, what Jewish tradition had assigned to Sarah was now characteristic of Hagar. He begins laying it out in this fashion in vv. 24-25:

> *24These things have another meaning*
> *because the women are two covenants:*
> *one is from Mount Sinai and gives birth to slavery,*
> *the one which is Hagar.*
> *25 Now Hagar is Mount Sinai in Arabia;*
> *and she corresponds to the current Jerusalem*
> *because she along with her children serve as slaves.*

By identifying Hagar with Mount Sinai, and, by extension, with the whole of the Jewish tradition of the law, Paul is recasting the old understanding of covenant based on law with an understanding of covenant based on faith. He has not mentioned the gospel yet (and any mention of it or of the Christ is absent in vv. 21-31), but where Paul is going with this should not be any surprise. If the traditional view of the law included Sarah, then her traditional role must be given to another: therefore, where Jewish tradition had seen the free woman Sarah, Paul now only sees the slave woman Hagar because it is "her children" who make up "the current Jerusalem" (i.e. the contemporary temple establishment) and who "serve as slaves" through their adherence to the insufficiency of the law.[7]

---

[7] Paul's clustering of Mount Sinai, Hagar, Arabia, and "the current Jerusalem" in 4:24-25 is the one textual clue we might have to what he meant in 1:15-17 when describing his apocalyptic commissioning to preach the gospel, and how "I did not go up to Jerusalem to the ones who were apostles before me, *rather I went away into Arabia* and again I returned to Damascus." My contention is that "Arabia" serves as a short-hand way for Paul to designate the time he spent re-examining the Torah tradition in the light of God's revelation, and how "Damascus" functions textually as the designation for his obedient response to that revelation.

XII. What Does Scripture Say? (4:21-5:6)

The key idea here is not the law *per se*, nor even how the law stands in relation to the gospel, but rather it is the image of the city of Jerusalem and what that—in addition to its concrete reality—scripturally symbolizes. When Paul speaks here of "the current Jerusalem," he uses the Greek phrase *hē nyn Ierousalēm*, which literally means "the now Jerusalem." He explicitly identifies Hagar with that image, and it should be noted that when he writes "she corresponds to the current Jerusalem," the Greek text is *systoichei de tē vyn Ierousalēm*. The verb rendered here as "corresponds" is *systoicheō* (quite literally meaning "to stand in the same line), and the related noun form (*stoicheia*) has already figured in 4:3 and 4:9 in contexts dealing with what makes for our pre-gospel state of bondage. If the "elemental things of this world" (*stoicheia tou kosmou*, 4:3) are emblematic of what makes for our state of servitude prior to the coming of the gospel, then, as Paul contends here, "the current Jerusalem" now stands symbolically ("in the same line") for the enslaved condition of "not being known by God" (4:9). Paul has already expressly identified the law with slavery (the entire section of 3:23-4:11 is based on this understanding), and now all of what he has claimed about the customary Jewish practice of the law vis-à-vis the faith characteristic of the gospel is distilled into his contrast between what he holds to be two visions of Jerusalem. He continues in vv. 26-27:

²⁶ ἡ δὲ ἄνω Ἰερουσαλὴμ ἐλευθέρα ἐστίν,
ἥτις ἐστὶν μήτηρ ἡμῶν·
²⁷ γέγραπται γάρ·
εὐφράνθητι, στεῖρα ἡ οὐ τίκτουσα,
ῥῆξον καὶ βόησον, ἡ οὐκ ὠδίνουσα·
ὅτι πολλὰ τὰ τέκνα τῆς ἐρήμου
μᾶλλον ἢ τῆς ἐχούσης τὸν ἄνδρα.

²⁶ *But the Jerusalem above is free,*
the one who is our mother;
²⁷ *for it stands written,*
"Rejoice, O barren one, you who do not give birth!
Break forth and shout, you who are not in birth pains!

*For the desolate one has many more children
than she who has a husband."*

Paul speaks of "the Jerusalem above" (*hē anō Ierousalēm*) as being a higher and more directly God-based reality, one that is "free" (*eleuthera*) because, just as "the current Jerusalem" represents those children who "serve as slaves" (i.e. who never achieve the maturity/majority status of faith, cf. 4:1-2), "the Jerusalem above" also reflects its true pedigree ("the son of the free woman [Sarah]…born by means of a promise" as opposed to being "the son of the slave woman [Hagar]…born according to the flesh"). Paul is declaring that if the earthly Jerusalem, the historical city and its long-standing practices, serves as both the symbolic image and the practical reality of obedience to the law, then "the Jerusalem above" is the no less scripturally-resonant domain of faith in the gospel, of what will constitute the true basis for Israel's adherence to the Abrahamic promise, and its realization through faith, repentance, baptism, and the gift of the Holy Spirit. It is "the Jerusalem above" which gives birth to the believer because only she who is free can be the mother of those who are now free in the gospel.

It is at this point that Paul quotes Isaiah 54:1, a verse which will require some explanation, but, once done, one can see exactly why Paul chose to include it at this point in his letter. First, it is a useful rule that, whenever Paul refers to the Old Testament, one should check the entire passage from which the quotation is taken and take careful note of what is going on in it. Read at least the entire chapter where it occurs, if not the adjacent chapters as well. Second, the overall context of the passage must then be related to what Paul is saying and then the connections (often multiple ones) can be discerned.

At this point in the text many readers fail to see Paul's rationale for quoting Isaiah 54:1. It seems to have little direct bearing on the "other things" he is saying here, but, if Paul is quoting Isaiah, then the reason for it lies in what the prophet says. The apostle has been speaking of the relative child-bearing

XII. What Does Scripture Say? (4:21-5:6)

circumstances of two women, Hagar and Sarah, and, at one immediate level, the prophet's language is applicable to them. On the one hand, the "barren one" is told to rejoice: "you who do not give birth...you who are not in birth pains" should "break forth and shout," words that can be associated with Sarah and her long-time barrenness. In Genesis 11:30 (RSV) she is introduced and initially described in such terms before Abraham makes the journey from "Ur of the Chaldaeans" and eventually to Canaan: "Now Sarai was barren (*steira*); she had no child." It was Sarah's growing frustration with her barrenness that eventually resulted in Abraham's fathering of Ishmael through the Egyptian slave woman Hagar. But God's promise to Abraham was vindicated when that same "barren one (*steira*)" gave birth to Isaac, a circumstance that allows the reader to see the two women in the context of God's promise coming to pass: "For the desolate one (*hē erēmos*) has many more children than she who has a husband." In the Genesis narrative Hagar "has a husband" by virtue of her physical union with Abraham, but her "children" are limited by the fact that God has decreed that Israel's inheritance shall come through Isaac. It is thus that Isaiah's admonition to rejoice should be directed at Sarah, for it will ultimately be through Isaac that God will bless the nations of the world:

> And the angel of the LORD called to Abraham a second time from heaven, and said, "By myself I have sworn, says the LORD, because you have done this, and have not withheld your son, your only son, I will indeed bless you, and I will multiply your descendants as the stars of the heaven and as the sand which is on the seashore. And your descendants shall possess the gates of their enemies, and by your descendants shall all the nations of the earth bless themselves, because you have obeyed my voice." (Genesis 22:15-18, RSV).

On this point the scripture is clear: while God promises to make Ishmael's descendants numerous enough (17:20), their relative numbers will not compare to the blessings which God will bestow upon the world through Isaac.

But, on the other hand, is this exactly what Isaiah had in mind in 54:1? How specific of a subject can we assign to the verse from its context? Was the prophet talking directly about Sarah's giving birth to Isaac or how that even played a part in God's plan for the redemption of "all the nations of the earth"? In order to understand Paul's rationale for quoting Isaiah 54:1, we need to take a closer look at chapters 52-54 of that book.

The book of Isaiah can be divided into two parts. The first part, chapters 1-39, contains prophetic oracles directed at Judah when the latter is facing threats from the northern kingdom of Israel, Damascus, and the Assyrians. The second part, chapters 40-66, presupposes a people already exiled in Babylon and centers on the themes of consolation, restoration, and redemption. Peculiar to the second part are four sections that have come to be known as the "suffering servant songs" (42:1-4, 49:1-6, 50:4-9, 52:13-53:12). These are texts that tell of a "servant" (*pais*) who is subjected to shameful, torturous treatments for what would appear to be the redemptive sake of Israel and for the manifestation of God's glorious purposes. The texts became the subject of intense Christian interest because the figure of the "servant" was related to the redemptive suffering of Christ as this was understood in the Church's earliest preaching. It is the last of these four texts, Isaiah 52:13-53:12, which has received the most attention both because of its length and its suggestive detail. This fourth suffering servant song plays a key role in chapters 52-54 of Isaiah because of where it occurs in relation to 54:1, the verse Paul quotes.

The principal feature of these three chapters is the repeated declaration that God will have mercy upon his people and that he will redeem them. Indeed, when this bloc of text speaks of God's "people," that is exactly the language it invariably uses: instead of God addressing his people, for example, as Israel (or any of its variations), the text either refers to them as "my people" or it speaks of "Jerusalem" (or, alternatively, "Zion" or the "daughter of Zion"). It is these overlapping designations that

XII. What Does Scripture Say? (4:21-5:6)

made Paul focus on this section of Isaiah because sandwiched within the prophet's themes of consolation and redemption is the final, and the most powerful, of the suffering servant songs. In my opinion, everything turns on this juxtaposition, on the fact that Isaiah weaves within the fabric of his utterances about God redeeming his people/Jerusalem the enigmatic figure of the suffering servant. The latter's appearance in the progression of these three chapters is the only indication of how any of this might come to pass (beyond any of the traditional language about the might and the will of the Lord being revealed). In what follows I will rely on my own translation of the Septuagint version of the Isaiah text.

Isaiah 52:1-3 sets the stage by using language that is simultaneously characteristic but yet suggestive of things unseen and unexpected:

> *¹ Awake, awake, O Zion,*
> *put on your strength, O Zion,*
> *and you, O Jerusalem, the holy city, put on your glory;*
> *there shall no more pass through you the uncircumcised and the unclean.*
> *² Shake off the dust and arise,*
> *seat yourself, O Jerusalem,*
> *take off the band from your neck, O captive daughter of Zion.*
> *³ For the LORD says these things:*
> *"You have not been sold as a slave for nothing,*
> *and not with silver will you be redeemed."*

Important in this passage is God's declaration in 52:3 that, "You have not been sold as a slave for nothing, and not with silver will you be redeemed." The Lord is here issuing a summons to Jerusalem/Zion, for her to step up out of the dust that signifies her captivity, the enduring state of her slavery, and once more to take her rightful seat of glory. There is the more immediate prophetic sense of the passage as applying to the end of the Jewish captivity in Babylon and to the re-establishment of Jerusalem and her temple, events that had all come to pass long before the first century A.D., but even so, there was before

Jesus' time a lingering conviction that the Jews were still in a state of captivity, an exilic condition that encompassed more than the grim practicalities that characterized the Roman occupation of Palestine. Even though the temple was there in Jerusalem more extravagantly equipped than ever before in Israel's history, even though it functioned now with an outward grandeur and institutional intricacy previously unknown, it was still arguably the case that the glory of Jerusalem's temple was not fully realized, that the people's redemption was incomplete. And, perhaps most critically, this was a general perception linked to the belief in a messiah-to-come, a set of expectations rooted in an interpretative tradition concerning the prophets, one which gradually arose and developed in those five centuries before Jesus. The expectations concerned a messianic king of Israel who would appear in connection with the end of days, an eschatological time when Jerusalem would at last achieve her fully redeemed and glorified state. Isaiah was speaking directly to this when he assured the people/Jerusalem (the prophetic tradition often conflated the two) that such an eventual glorification was to be the ultimate outcome of God's promise, that "not with silver will you be redeemed."

If Jerusalem was not going to be redeemed with silver, if she was not to be bought back with marketplace coin, then what was going to be offered as the price of Israel's redemption? I would argue that our only reliable textual clue comes in Isaiah 52:13-53:12, the passage known as the fourth suffering servant song. The passage itself is prefaced by 52:11-12, two verses that are telling in part because of the way they explicitly invoke the Exodus:

> *11 Depart, depart, go out from there,*
> *and do not touch any unclean thing,*
> *go out from the midst of it,*
> *let the ones who bear the vessels of the LORD be separated;*
> *12 for you shall not go out tumultuously,*
> *nor shall you go out in flight;*
> *for the LORD shall go out in advance of you,*

XII. What Does Scripture Say? (4:21-5:6)

and the God of Israel is he who shall gather you together.

In Exodus 13:21-22 (RSV) we read that when Moses and the Israelites were beginning their departure from Egypt, God was there to lead them on the trek: "And the LORD went before them by day in a pillar of cloud to lead them along the way, and by night in a pillar of fire to give them light, that they might travel by day and by night; the pillar of cloud by day and the pillar of fire by night did not depart from before the people." Isaiah is thus prophesying that a new Exodus will take place, and that, just as God began the constitution of his people Israel by going before them out of Egypt, so too will he again "go out in advance of you": "And the LORD will reveal his holy arm before all the nations, and all the ends of the earth will see the salvation that comes from our God." (52:10)

Isaiah 52:13-53:12 contains much language and imagery that can be related to the crucifixion of Jesus, but I will deal here only with its final two verses because 53:11-12 in many ways summarize the connection we can make between this *christos* of prophecy and the figure of the crucified Jesus as it is contained in the passion narratives of the gospels:

> ¹¹ *And the LORD wishes to take away the pain of his soul,*
> *to show him light,*
> *to form him by means of understanding,*
> *to declare righteous the righteous one* (dikaios) *who serves the many so well,*
> *and he himself will bear their sins.*
> ¹² *For this reason he will inherit many men,*
> *and he will divide up the spoils of the mighty ones;*
> *in exchange for these things his soul was handed over to death,*
> *and he was reckoned among the lawless ones,*
> *and he bore the sins of many,*
> *and on account of their iniquity he was handed over.*

Of particular interest here is the progression of clauses in 53:11. If this scriptural servant truly is God's most exemplary servant, then he will want "to take away the pain of his soul," that is, God will see to it that the servant fully realizes his "servanthood." He will also "show light" to the servant by allowing him to see and to understand what the fulfilling of his exemplary servant status will entail. Finally, when the servant through his sacrificial death has "served the many so well" by taking "their sins" upon himself, God will declare to be righteous him who was, in a sense, already fully righteous (*dikaios*) by virtue of the actions indicated in 53:12.

It is at this point that all of the biblical themes and threads which Paul has been handling and stitching together converge and are given expression in a single declaration, and, in the case of his quotation of Isaiah 54:1, what serves as a culminating prophetic utterance. All along he has argued not only for the *content* of God's promise to Abraham, but for its *structure* as well: in the most simple terms, that the acceptance of Paul's gospel is predicated on Israel and the nations being as faithful to the *promise* of God's blessing/salvation as they would have to be to its *manifestation* in time (i.e. Paul's preaching of it). In 4:21-26 Paul has framed his argument in terms of the figures and the types contained in the Genesis story of Abraham, but the particular details of that patriarchal account had to be blended with the whole of Israel's history and, not least of all, with the prophetic tradition which itself culminates in the vision of Jerusalem's redemption and restoration.

In the interpretive synthesis demanded by the gospel that Paul has preached to the Galatians, each of the two women—Hagar and Sarah—is linked to the two Jerusalem's that now stand as scriptural and historical symbols of Israel's religious destiny. Even though Genesis 21:8-21 relates how Abraham allowed Sarah in the wake of Isaac's birth to banish Hagar and Ishmael, it turns out that in Paul's interpretive re-presentation of these events a bit of Hagar must have remained even after the pair "departed and wandered in the wilderness of Beersheba" (21:14). Paul presents Hagar as having given birth to slaves, associated here with Mt. Sinai and the law, those who are now the inhabitants of "the current Jerusalem." The identification here

XII. What Does Scripture Say? (4:21-5:6)

could not be more clear: Paul equates any adherence to the law which views itself as more important than the crucified Christ of his gospel as being "slavery." Standing in contrast to this condition is the image of "the Jerusalem above," which Paul describes as being "free" and "the one who is our mother." It is this interpretive sequence—the materials from which it is shaped and the way Paul has shaped them—that sets the stage for Paul's employment of Isaiah 54:1.

If "the current Jerusalem" is the scriptural image of a city inhabited by the hitherto plentiful children of Hagar who "serve as slaves," the latter (who are the law-clinging Jews and thus nominal descendants of Abraham) are to be distinguished from the relatively lesser number of "free" children to whom "the Jerusalem above" has given birth, namely, those who have become the true descendants of Abraham by means of faith in the gospel (3:29, 4:6-7). Keep in mind that, while Paul's linking of Hagar with the main body of Abraham's descendants is, strictly speaking, a departure from the general narrative of scripture, it is an identification demanded by (1) a greater set of facts—namely, the gospel of the Christ Jesus —and (2) Paul's determination to make sense of the language in Genesis concerning God's salvific promise to Israel in a way that would meld the two streams nourishing him: scripture and revelation. It is thus that Paul can write in 4:26-27:

> [26] *But the Jerusalem above is free,*
> *the one who is our mother;*
> [27] *for it stands written,*
> *"Rejoice, O barren one, you who do not give birth!*
> *Break forth and shout, you who are not in birth pains!*
> *For the desolate one has many more children*
> *than she who has a husband."*

There is a polyphony of persons, sacred history, and eschatological directions involved in the way Paul has chosen to employ Isaiah 54:1. First, Sarah is the one being identified scripturally as the "barren one" who only gave birth to Isaac when aged ("you who do not give birth" eventually would have a preeminent reason to rejoice). Second, the next line can be interpreted as also applying to Sarah, but now we can sense some of the semantic shifting in meaning already underway because, in the light of the gospel and its apostolic dissemination, "you who are not in birth pains" can refer to the relative childlessness that characterized "the Jerusalem above" prior to the coming of the gospel (that is, now that the gospel is being preached, it is vocally producing its own children).

And third, the final line, "For the desolate one (*hē erēmos*) has many more children than she who has a husband," once again invokes Sarah's situation before Isaac's birth, before the fact that she gave birth to the son through whom the promise of God's blessing would be carried forward through the physical generations. Chapters 51 and 52 of Isaiah contain references to God restoring the "desolate places" (*ta erēmata*) of Jerusalem to life and causing them to "break out in joy" (51:3, 52:9)[8], and here we can see that there is a genuine significance to the fact that the fourth suffering servant song immediately precedes Isaiah 54:1. If Jerusalem/Israel is to be restored to life, she will become in effect a new city, a new reality, a heavenly realm united with the parts of this earth ready to receive such a new life, but what makes it possible is the appearance and the declaration of him who "was wounded on account of our sins, and he was stricken on account of our lawlessness; he was our lesson in peace, by his bruising we have been healed." (53:5) So, if we respect the textual continuity represented by Isaiah 52-54, and if we do not pause at the end of chapter 53 (itself an artificial division) even if we have not inadvertently come to view 52:13-53:12 as being something on the order of an interpolation, then the entirety of

---

[8] The only reference to Sarah outside of Genesis occurs in Isaiah 51:2, and the verse is especially relevant because of the way Sarah is described: "Look to Abraham your father and to Sarah *who is in birth pains over you* (*tēn ōdinousan hymas*): for he was one, and I called him, and I blessed him, and I loved him, and I multiplied him." Compare this to Paul's own statement of apostolic concern in 4:19: "My children, *you for whom I am once more laboring in birth* (*hous palin ōdinō*) until the Christ himself might be formed among you."

XII. What Does Scripture Say? (4:21-5:6)

chapter 54 can be more properly seen as the vivid continuation of what we have read about the tormented, sacrificial figure we know as the "suffering servant."

When that is taken into account, the "desolate one" can be read simultaneously as (1) Sarah, who is the "birth-less" scriptural progenitor of the messiah's line, and who figures as the "barren" one who will eventually give birth most abundantly; and (2) the "Jerusalem above," she who, after our acknowledging of Sarah's role on one level, becomes our true mother on a more significant level *by virtue of the gospel*; and (3) the "suffering servant" himself, that most unlikely (i.e. "desolate") of messianic figures who is now understood as the prophetic foreknowledge of Jesus, whom Paul declares to be the Christ of God. In order to round out the "allegorical" contrast at work in this passage, she who is "the current Jerusalem" (Hagar) can be said to "have a husband" (the Jewish temple), and together they have produced children. Hence the contrast of Hagar with her who has stood silently through these many childless years awaiting the "fullness of time" (4:4), that is, Sarah now seen as symbolically representing the generative force that is the gospel proclamation. What brings about the blending of all these images, persons, and themes into a single picture is the prophetic vision of God's will realized in the form of a man "made to suffer pain for us":

> [4] *This man bears our sins,*
> *and is made to suffer pain for us,*
> *and we reckoned him to be in pain, in suffering, and in affliction.*
> [5] *He was wounded on account of our sins,*
> *and he was stricken on account of our lawlessness;*
> *he was our lesson in peace,*
> *by his bruising we have been healed. (Isaiah 53:4-5)*

The gospel image of Jesus as the dying messiah (rooted as it is in the preaching of Paul),[9] when seen in conjunction with the portraits the prophet Isaiah offers of a "suffering servant," is

---

[9] Paul Nadim Tarazi, *The New Testament: An Introduction, Volume I: Paul and Mark* (Crestwood, New York: St. Vladimir's Seminary Press, 1999).

thus not reducible to the story of two historically unrelated but historically relatable vignettes, but rather it serves as an example of the budding process inherent in the growth of scripture. By quoting Isaiah 54:1 at this point in his letter, Paul is inviting the listener to hear the progressing connection between what the Isaiah scroll contains and what he writes. The prophet's "suffering servant" has no clear identity because scripturally he figures as promise, but the crucified messiah of Paul's gospel has a name and is preached as the fulfillment of promise. It is in this way that 4:21-31 is not so much a matter of either historical causality or opportunistic proof-texting as it is of ears ready to receive the resonance.[10]

The rest of Isaiah 54 is in many ways a commentary on the declaration made in the initial verse of that chapter. It is a description of what will happen when God re-establishes Jerusalem in glory. Isaiah 54:17 culminates in the assertion that "inheritance (*klēronomia*) is for the ones who serve the LORD; and you are to be righteous (*dikaios*) before me, says the LORD." The fact that in these three chapters of Isaiah the image of Jerusalem is repeatedly and quite evocatively used in conjunction with references to God's "people"—that just as God promises to restore Jerusalem, he will also restore his people, reconstituting them in what will be a renewed glory—this allows us to understand why Paul should quote Isaiah 54:1. The prophetic vision of Jerusalem's glorification was, scripturally speaking, an integral part of Paul's own eschatological vision, one in which the not unrelated threads of divine promise, faith, and obedience to that promise converge and re-emerge in the gospel declaration of Jesus as the Christ. When viewed from the traditional Jewish understanding of salvation as framed by scripture, it is an understanding that is as revolutionary as it is reactionary. On the one hand, Paul's gospel affirms everything about the Israelite tradition by appealing to its founding

---

[10] Paul Nadim Tarazi, *The Chrysostom Bible—Isaiah: A Commentary* (St. Paul, Minnesota: OCABS Press, 2013), 190-193.

XII. What Does Scripture Say? (4:21-5:6)

circumstances (in his scheme, promise precedes the law); but, on the other hand, it does so in a way that simultaneously subverts and completes that same tradition.[11]

If Jerusalem is to be restored, if God's people are going to be reassembled for the sake of righteousness and inheritance in the Lord, and, if in Israel's scriptural foundation these two things amount to the same thing, then let it all happen through the fulfillment of God's original promise and his calling forth of those who are to be reckoned as Abraham's true children, namely, the children who stand to inherit the content of that very foundational promise. This must be related to what Paul writes next in 4:28-31, the concluding verses of chapter 4:

²⁸ ὑμεῖς δέ, ἀδελφοί, κατὰ Ἰσαὰκ ἐπαγγελίας τέκνα ἐστέ.
²⁹ ἀλλ' ὥσπερ τότε ὁ κατὰ σάρκα γεννηθεὶς
ἐδίωκεν τὸν κατὰ πνεῦμα,
οὕτως καὶ νῦν.
30 ἀλλὰ τί λέγει ἡ γραφή
ἔκβαλε τὴν παιδίσκην καὶ τὸν υἱὸν αὐτῆς·
οὐ γὰρ μὴ κληρονομήσει ὁ υἱὸς τῆς παιδίσκης μετὰ τοῦ υἱοῦ τῆς ἐλευθέρας.
³¹ διό, ἀδελφοί, οὐκ ἐσμὲν παιδίσκης τέκνα ἀλλὰ τῆς ἐλευθέρας.

²⁸ *And we, brothers and sisters, are children of promise just as Isaac was.*
²⁹ *But just as it was then when he who had been born according to the flesh was persecuting him who was born according to the Spirit,*
so too it is now.
³⁰ But what does scripture say?
"Cast out the slave woman and her son;
for the son of the slave woman shall not inherit along with the son of the free woman."
³¹ Therefore, brothers and sisters, we are not children of the slave woman

---

[11] Niels Peter Lemche (*op.cit.*, p. 392) neatly summarizes this process in the following terms: "The New Testament represents an independent description of the experience of the early Christians as belonging to a Jewish, messianic sect. The Old Testament—or rather, the literature that was to be included in the Old Testament—provides the mental framework for this sect, which would not have survived without it. In this way the group managed to survive the death of its messiah by interpreting it in the light of the last of the Servant Songs in Isaiah."

but of the free woman.

In a deference to scripture that Paul would find entirely sensible, he has relied on Isaiah to make the final and, precisely because it is scriptural, the decisive connection: the "barren one" is now giving birth *by means of the gospel* since every believer in the Christ is one of Sarah's offspring. The only other place where Sarah is mentioned in the Old Testament outside of Genesis occurs in Isaiah 51:2. This verse belongs to the trio of verses that opens Isaiah 51 (Septuagint translation my own):

> *¹ Hear me, you who pursue what is righteous (*dikaion*) and who are seeking the Lord:*
> *look to the solid rock which you have hewn*
> *and to the hole of the cistern (*lakkos*) that you dug.*[12]
> *² Look to Abraham your father and to Sarah who is in birth pains over you:*
> *for he was one, and I called him, and I blessed him,*
> *and I loved him, and I multiplied him.*
> *³ And I am calling out to you now, O Zion,*
> *as I called out to all her desolate places (*ta erēmata*),*
> *and I will make her desolate places (*ta erēmata*) like a garden,*
> *and her western places like a garden of the Lord;*
> *in her they will find gladness and rejoicing,*
> *thanksgiving and the voice of praise.*

She who for so long was "not in birth pains," let her truly shout aloud at the number of true children whom she is now bringing forth for the world to see! In Paul's eyes the gospel becomes the only possible framework for our understanding both the origin and the outcome of the divine-purpose-unto-the-salvation-of-all-the-world. In other words, how God initiated the redemption of the world through a covenantal promise to Abraham and how he is now bringing it to completion by means of the proclamation concerning his own Son.

---

[12] Note the occurrence of the Greek word *lakkos* for "cistern" in 51:1 and in Jeremiah 2:13. The latter is quoted in Section II above in connection with the "broken cisterns" hewn by the disobedient inhabitants of Judah and Jerusalem.

XII. What Does Scripture Say? (4:21-5:6)

It is thus that those who believe in the gospel are every bit as much "children of promise just as Isaac was," but, that having been said, Paul also wishes that the Galatians might see how their situation extends beyond the kind of interpretive parallelism described above and is being played out in the current controversy afflicting their community. In order to make his case, he points out to them just how relentless the parallelism actually is: "just as it was then when he who had been born according to the flesh was persecuting him who was born according to the Spirit, so too it is now." The allusion here is to Genesis 21:8-13 (RSV), which recounts how Sarah came to insist upon the expulsion of Hagar and Ishmael after the weaning of Isaac takes place:

> And the child [Isaac] grew, and was weaned; and Abraham made a great feast on the day that Isaac was weaned. But Sarah saw the son of Hagar the Egyptian, whom she had borne to Abraham, playing with her son Isaac. So she said to Abraham, "Cast out this slave woman with her son; for the son of this slave woman shall not be heir with my son Isaac." And the thing was very displeasing to Abraham on account of his son. But God said to Abraham, "Be not displeased because of the lad and because of your slave woman; whatever Sarah says to you, do as she tells you, for through Isaac shall your descendants be named."

But how can Paul meaningfully speak of persecution here and draw any kind of parallel between Genesis 21 and the reports he has received about the Galatian churches? Recall that Paul had first preached the gospel of Jesus as the Christ to the Galatians, but, with the arrival of those advocating circumcision, a new set of priorities was now being promulgated. Just as he had initially indicated in the first chapter of his letter, it is precisely the issue of *which gospel* was true and authoritative that Paul is addressing. The circumcision party's position with respect to the law was creating division within what had been presumably the original Christian unity in the Galatian churches created by Paul's preaching. We can safely assume that at the time of Paul's writing this division was characterized by some degree of persecution, that is, it involved a consistently organized and maintained effort by the circumcision party to advocate its position and to supplant Paul's original faith-centered gospel message.

It would be in this apparent friction between the two points of view that we can locate the persecution of which Paul speaks. Keep in mind too what has already been said about how, in Paul's hands, the law-centered Israelite tradition is identified with Hagar and Ishmael, not in any objectively new let alone absolute sense, but solely regarding the way in which that tradition now stands in relation to the Christ-centered gospel of Paul. In Genesis 21:8-13 we read that the potential conflict between Ishmael and Isaac only became open when Isaac reached the age of weaning. The Genesis account is a spare one, but the main outlines tell us enough. When Sarah sees the elder Ishmael "playing with her son Isaac," the juxtaposition of an older but with respect to the promise/covenant of God *illegitimate* son playing with the younger but with respect to the promise/covenant of God *legitimate* son becomes the dramatic setting for Sarah's declaration that Ishmael's apparent superiority would be overturned and reversed because it was counter to God's own covenant-promise. It is only in this sense that we can speak of Ishmael ("he who had been born according to the flesh") persecuting Isaac ("him who was born according to the Spirit"), that is, in the fact that he was playing with the younger Isaac as the older and therefore principal heir while possessing only an apparent primacy in relation to him. It is exactly this *relational primacy with regard to inheritance* that forms the textual basis for the language in 4:28-29 about persecution. Thus, as presented by Paul, the older and law-associated figure of Ishmael represents what is the false version of the covenant's definitive mode of inheritance, that is, the way his opponents insisted that it can be only on the basis of the law (*ek nomou*). In contrast to Ishmael, Paul presents the younger promise-/gospel-associated figure of Isaac as symbolizing the one true inheritance that comes to us only on the basis of God's encrypted-Christ

XII. What Does Scripture Say? (4:21-5:6)

promise to Abraham, and, most immediately, by means of our faith that Jesus is the Christ. In 3:18 he had argued that the prospect of inheritance had never been on the basis of the law because, if it had been, it never would have been on the basis of a promise (*ex epangelias*). What counts, according to his gospel, is that "God had given it to Abraham by means of a promise" (*di' epangelias*).

Paul is trying to show the Galatians why it is wrong to place an unjustifiable and unnecessary emphasis on the law over what he would no doubt see as the unambiguous requirements of the gospel. But what in his eyes had formed the traditional basis of inheritance, namely, that it would be through obedience to the law (call it the Ishmael Thesis), could no longer be maintained in light of the gospel. Paul contends that, just as scripture shows us how Isaac was a "child of promise" strictly by means of the covenant-promise and not by means of the law, so too in what is his no less scripturalized gospel "we are children of promise" (call it the Isaac Thesis). Paul's rhetorical appeal to scripture in 4:30 ("But what does scripture say?") also serves to make the outcome of the current controversy among the Galatians over the law's relevance and application clear and understandable. He quotes the words of the insistent Sarah in Genesis 21:10 to indicate that for them the only viable thesis shall be the Isaac Thesis: that the Galatians are to "cast out the slave woman and her son" (i.e. reject what is ultimately the law-based scheme of the circumcision advocates) because what these two figures represent "shall not inherit along with the son of the free woman." If, scripturally speaking, inheritance is absolutely predicated on our being declared righteous in the eyes of God, then, as Paul has argued from the beginning, our being declared righteous is a function of our being obedient to what God is now declaring through the gospel. It is at this point that we can profitably recall Isaiah 54:17 (quoted above) and its language concerning inheritance and righteousness: "inheritance is for the ones who serve the LORD; and you are to be righteous before me, the LORD." According to Paul's gospel, righteousness in the eyes of God is no longer measured in terms of obedience to the law, but rather it is a reflection of *our faith in the faith of him who is the Christ*, and how that secures the inheritance that is properly God's gift to the entire world.

But if this kind of righteousness counts as the terms of our salvation in the Christ, how does any of it happen? The apostle makes it clear that our salvation in the Christ occurs when (1) precisely this messiah comes to us solely by means of the written and in turn proclaimed word about him, and (2) whether or not we will trust in that word. This is our scriptural ancestry as Paul has presented it to us. This is what constitutes the Christian *toledot*, that is, the scriptural account of the believer's progenitors seen as the human means arranged by God to keep the believer in obedient relation with him.[13] It is thus that the fourth chapter of Paul's letter ends with a simple admonition to the Galatians: "Therefore, brothers and sisters, we are not children of the slave woman but of the free woman" (4:31), a declaration which we should not simply regard as being a summary statement of the exquisitely crafted argument he has been building up to this point. It is far more than that. Having presented a scripture-based appeal in chapters 3 and 4 in order to argue for the primacy of the Christ over the law, Paul was working to lay the foundation for the Christian *sense of identity* that his gospel both presupposes and ultimately demands of the believer.

Paul Nadim Tarazi provides an outline of the scriptural logic at work here.[14] In the ancient world any tribe was identified by the name of its forefather. Any tribe's history was therefore understood as being an account of its founder's personal history that continues in various ways to mark the fate of his offspring. This is very much what Paul has done in chapters 3 and 4 of his

---

[13] Paul Nadim Tarazi, *The Chrysostom Bible—Genesis: A Commentary* (St. Paul, Minnesota, OCABS Press, 2009). The point of the scriptural *toledot* (genealogies) is to tell us not just from whom we are descended, but, more importantly, where we are supposed to be headed. Will God be present in our destiny?

[14] Paul Nadim Tarazi, *The Old Testament: Introduction, Volume 3: Psalms and Wisdom* (Crestwood, New York: St. Vladimir's Seminary Press, 1996), 1-15.

XII. What Does Scripture Say? (4:21-5:6)

letter: he has detailed what God has said to the ancestor (Abraham) and what he has done to direct that ancestor's destiny. In other words, whatever God has done with the ancestor applies just as much to his descendants. There is thus a determinative "oneness" associated with the ancestor (cf. Isaiah 51:2), with the result that whatever happens in his name will come to be known by his name. This helps us to understand at a deeper level the great summarizing declarations Paul makes in these two chapters:

> Therefore know that the ones who live on the basis of faith are the sons of Abraham. (3:7)

> So that in the person of the Christ who is Jesus the blessing of Abraham might come upon all nations, so that we might receive the promise of the Spirit by means of faith. (3:14)

> And if you are the Christ's, then you are the seed of Abraham: you are the heirs in accordance with the promise. (3:29)

> All so that you are no longer a slave, but rather a son; and if you are a son, then it is through God that you have been made an heir. (4:7)

> Therefore, brothers and sisters, we are not children of the slave woman but of the free woman (4:31)

XIII. What Does the Gospel Say? (5:1-6)

We should read the end of chapter 4 and the beginning of chapter 5 with no break or sense of division between 4:31 and 5:1, no awareness at all that Paul has concluded one part and its now launching a new train of thought. There is full continuity of argument at this point, and the first six verses of chapter 5 really serve to crown what Paul has carefully argued since 2:11. The real clue here is that he signals this continuity with the marker "therefore, brothers and sisters" (*dio, adelphoi*) in 4:31. Many might view this language simply as Paul concluding the section of 4:21-30, but yet there is complete continuity of thought and argumentation at this point with what follows in chapter 5. Here is 5:1 with 4:31 included to illustrate the rhetorical flow of things:

*³¹ διό, ἀδελφοί, οὐκ ἐσμὲν παιδίσκης τέκνα
ἀλλὰ τῆς ἐλευθέρας.
¹ τῇ ἐλευθερίᾳ ἡμᾶς Χριστὸς ἠλευθέρωσεν·
στήκετε οὖν καὶ μὴ πάλιν ζυγῷ δουλείας ἐνέχεσθε.*

*³¹ Therefore, brothers and sisters, we are not children of the slave woman
but of the free woman.
¹ It is for freedom that the Christ has set us free:
therefore stand fast and
do not place yourselves again in a yoke of slavery.*

The word "free" has already occurred in the letter. It first appears in 2:3-5 when Paul is describing his journey up to Jerusalem with Barnabas and Titus, and how their companion, the uncircumcised Titus, was not "compelled to be circumcised." But 2:4-5 is worth reviewing in the light of what chapters 3 and 4 contain: "I say this on account of false brothers in the faith who had come in secretly, the ones who came in to spy out our freedom that we have in the Christ Jesus so that they might bring us back into slavery; not for a moment did we submit to them in obedience all in order that the truth of the gospel might be preserved for you." The Greek word for "freedom" is *eleutheria*. It denotes the status of being *eleutheros* (literally, "a free man"), a term whose semantic punch depends on the contrast it forms with its opposite, namely, any man who is not free because he is a slave (*doulos*).

What follows in chapter 5 is Paul putting the finishing touches on what is indisputably the key aspect of his gospel. We need to understand precisely why the idea of freedom vis-à-vis the law should not be construed as being in any way an absolute ideal because all of Paul's notions of what constitutes our *relative* freedom in the Christ are wholly determined by our being in faithful relation to the Christ. In short, if we are in any sense free with regard to the law, then it is only by virtue of our belonging to the Christ, of the new identity that we now have in him through the gospel.

It was in the last part of chapter 4 that Paul had described "the Jerusalem above" (4:26) as being "free" (*eleuthera*)[1] because she is "the one who is our mother." The religious connection there was a prophetic one: the scriptural image of Jerusalem as being redeemed by God and restored to glory provides Paul with a way to make sense of Israel's redemption by means of the crucified Christ. Paul sees Jesus as the messianic savior of Israel, as being the agent of God's long-promised salvation, and thus it is the gospel proclamation of the Christ's death and resurrection that is the catalyst for the transformation of "the current Jerusalem" into "the Jerusalem above" in conjunction with Isaiah's messianic language (52:2-3) about Jerusalem's glorification as an integral part of Israel's redemption:

*² Shake off the dust and arise,
seat yourself, O Jerusalem,*

---

[1] *Eleuthera* represents the declined feminine form of the masculine-nominative-singular dictionary form of the noun/adjective *eleutheros*. Both "Jerusalem" and "mother" are feminine nouns.

XIII. What Does the Gospel Say? (5:1-6)

> *take off the band from your neck, O captive daughter of Zion.*
> *³ For the LORD says these things:*
> *"You have not been sold as a slave for nothing,*
> *and not with silver will you be redeemed."*

Just as Saul the Pharisee had viewed Israel's redemption as being predicated on her obedience to the law, so now Paul the Apostle sees Israel's redemption as being entirely based on her belief in Jesus as the Christ. In the schematic I presented above, there is the traditional Jewish view of salvation with its defining emphasis on the law and the cultic centrality of the Jerusalem temple-complex:

> Abraham/promise → law → earthly Jerusalem/temple

It is important to understand that Paul's gospel is a re-interpretation of this traditional view and not a rejection of it. By itself, the traditional view (and all of our assumptions concerning its apparent workings) gives the appearance that it is a self-contained whole, a plain enough example of how a sacred tradition arose and developed historically. But, however much the traditional view might strike us as being fixed and contained in character, there was always room in Jewish religious awareness (as abundantly witnessed in the Old Testament) for God to act "out of the blue," for him to intervene in history in entirely unexpected ways. Indeed, Israel's own prophetic tradition is a testament as much to the fact that God had acted like this as it is to the fact that he will continue to act like that. It is thus, for example, that the prophet Isaiah could speak of Israel's fate in the not always specific terms of Jerusalem's restoration and glorification (with the fourth suffering servant song being the sole indication of how it might all come to pass). On the one hand, Isaiah's language might have seemed congruent enough to the Jews down through the centuries given their scriptural narrative dealing with the rebuilding of Jerusalem and the temple's re-establishment; but, on the other hand, not all of the developments of second-temple Judaism satisfied the messianic hopes of the Jewish people, and in particular the string of foreign occupations (Persian, Seleucid, Macedonian Successor, Roman) only witnessed to the non-fulfillment of those hopes.

It is one thing to speak of what constitutes Israel's continuing condition of slavery in the worldly sense, of the people's state of political subjugation at the hands of pagan powers, but to speak of the law itself as being a slave-state in its own right, that is, where the Christ and our redemption in him are concerned, that is a startling logic whose only source is the gospel. Paul's preaching to the Galatians was a re-drawing of the above schematic for the way in which the Jews were to understand the salvation being proclaimed in the name of "God the Father and the Lord Jesus who is the Christ" (1:3) Instead of the older progression (Abraham→law→temple), he who hears the gospel must reckon henceforth with a new progression:

Abraham/promise → the Christ → heavenly Jerusalem/temple-less kingdom of heaven

Paul's critique of the law really came down to a single point—that the law failed to make any man righteous precisely because no man could perfectly obey the law. We are fully entitled to leave open the possibility that the law *could* make a man righteous if he could but live in perfect obedience to it and realize it in every detail and nuance. But that is precisely Paul's contention, namely, that no man can pull it off because his own unshakeable tendency toward disobedience prevents him from ever achieving it. *This* is what constitutes man's enslavement under the law: that no matter how much he consciously tries to live in accordance with the law, he will always fall short of the law's inherently absolute requirement (3:8-12). In other words, since his otherwise commendable life spent in an imperfect obedience to the law can never result in his being declared righteous, what makes for any man being declared righteous must come ultimately, absolutely, and irreducibly from a source other than his own strivings. The law was there to teach man about sin, but sin's final defeat, indeed, its overthrow could not be through the law. Sin—and ultimately death and its author, the devil—can

XIII. What Does the Gospel Say? (5:1-6)

only be remedied through a perfect righteousness, through the actual obedience of a single man, he who is a suffering sacrifice for the sake of all (3:13-14).

This is the true core of the gospel. Paul's preaching is an undeniable re-definition of some long-standing things, but one based every bit as much on the ancient Hebrew conviction that God will operate when, where, and how he pleases. God's promise to Abraham about what would constitute *blessing*, about how *inheritance* would come to pass, about how *redemption* would be achieved, all of that was now realized in the Christ, and Paul's gospel testifies to the advent not so much of a new reality as it is of a familiar old reality now fully and finally revealed. The apostle tells us that it was the Christ whom God had promised to Abraham (3:15-18), and now all of what had characterized the law—its noble requirements, its uncompromising ethic, its sacrificial system of worship—that must be understood in relation to the Christ and to the righteousness that he embodied by his faithfulness (*pistis*). He is a reality whose embodiment could not be located in an earthly temple nor could his essence be enumerated by holy prescriptions. He is a living reality, a master to whom one belongs, a lord who furnishes our lineage. If the law stands for slavery, then the kind of faith that Jesus represented, that is, what made for the freest possible relationship to the law which he manifested, that is what will be the defining characteristic of the law's opposite, the freedom of which Paul now speaks.

When Paul writes in 4:31 that "we are not children of the slave woman, but of the free woman," he has in mind not a formal summary statement about what has gone before (although all of it is certainly presupposed and included in what is to come), but what are to be the new conditions of our freedom. If scripture is there to instruct us in the nature of the un-freedom that was the law, then the gospel will complete the lesson by telling us of what freedom will consist. In 5:1 Paul continues by saying, "It is for freedom that the Christ has set us free; therefore stand fast and do not place yourselves again in a yoke of slavery," and here we must say a few things about how we are to approach Paul's use of the word "freedom" in this context.

First, freedom here is no abstraction, nor is it an absolute principle whose validity derives from the fact that it stands supremely on its own. As we shall see, it will be as concrete a thing as the doing of the law. Second, Paul's treatment of these two positions—slavery and freedom—brings both down to earth because he sees each one in the light of the cross and its not uncertain demands. The problem here is that our modern tendency is to over-intellectualize them, to conceive of slavery and freedom as absolute principles, and thus to sacrifice any sense of the concrete urgency contained in Paul's words. It is better to keep both positions steadily in front of us, to see them in their perpetual relative tension, and to see how each one fares in the light of the gospel.

Some indication of what is involved in this can be sensed in the way one chooses to translate the first half of 5:1. I have rendered it as "It is for freedom that the Christ has set us free," casting the dative prepositional phrase at the beginning (*tē eleutheria*) as the express goal of the verbal action. The verb is *eleuthereō*, and it simply means to set someone free, literally, to make an unfree man into a free man (*eleutheros*), an act which keeps its most basic meaning when its alternative (i.e. yoking a man into slavery) is kept in mind. So far, so good, because if the Christ's saving death has redeemed us from the curse of the law, then he has freed us from the latter's slave-condition in order that we might now *faithfully* enjoy the status of free men. This translation emphasizes the status of our faith-freedom as being the direct corollary of a more fundamental faith in Jesus as the Christ and the meaning of the redemption promised to us in him.

But an equally plausible way to understand the dative phrase *tē eleutheria* would be to interpret it as an instrumental dative, and thus 5:1a would read as "It is *through freedom* that the Christ has

XIII. What Does the Gospel Say? (5:1-6)

set us free." Rendering it in this fashion shifts the emphasis to the faith of the Christ himself, to his superlatively obedient righteousness before God that makes possible our own faith-freedom. If we are going to enjoy a relative state of freedom in the Christ, and if our faith is the manifest expression of that freedom, then any believer's faith will only have become possible because of Jesus' initial display of righteousness. It also makes more explicit the reason why we should more properly view the Galatian letter as being, not about a strictly formal law/works vs. faith dichotomy, but about the proper way to understand the law in relation to the Christ. This is reflected in the two schematics I presented above: in the first one representing the traditional Jewish view, the middle element is the law; while in the second Pauline one, the middle element is (Jesus as) the Christ. The parallelism between the law and Christ is crucial, and it provides us with, I think, a more direct way to understand both the actual content of Paul's gospel to the Galatians and the case that he is now making for its authority.

I would contend that, even though these two translations involve slightly different wording and possible emphases, each one still allows us to arrive at the same place, namely, that the believer's condition of faith is one characterized by the relative freedom that he has only by virtue of the fact it is a faith in Jesus as the Christ, and that such a faith, even though the law in its slave-condition foretold the Christ, does not need the law in order to manifest itself. At no point would Paul argue that we believe in the Christ *because* of the law, and it was precisely Jesus' "once and for all" obedience to the law that simultaneously fulfilled it and transcended it. This is the *relative freedom* of the faith to which the gospel calls us: that, by virtue of the need for its perpetual proclamation, it was both originally on the basis of a faithfulness (*ek pisteōs*) and no less so practically by means of a faithfulness (*dia pisteōs*) that we shall live, both temporally and in the promised kingdom to come, and here living is to be equated with our being declared righteous (*dikaios*) in the eyes of God. We are free in faith because, where life/righteousness itself was concerned, the law was a dead-end (what 2:15-18 emphasizes). This is what permits Paul to write in 2:19-20: "because by means of the law (*dia nomou*) I have died to the law in order that I might live to God. I have been crucified along with the Christ; and so it is no longer I who live, but it is the Christ who lives in me, and what I am now living in the flesh I am living as a result of my believing in the Son of God, who loved me and gave himself on my behalf." When it comes to this point, never forget the slave-market logic: the law was our old master, and our belonging to him was the condition of our slavery, but the gospel proclamation of Jesus as the Christ is the shattering of that old lordship, our redemptive purchase from what constituted our former state of slavery and which now makes up our relative freedom from that slavery, namely, our identity as belonging to God now *by means of* (*dia*) our trust in the faithfulness of his Christ and not *by means of* (*dia*) the law (2:21).

This is the basis for Paul's radically uncompromising insistence to the Galatians in 5:1 that they must "stand fast and do not place yourselves again in a yoke of slavery." Given what Paul has managed to say so far about the law-Christ relationship, he is now even more adamant about its implications in 5:2-4:

² ἴδε ἐγὼ Παῦλος λέγω ὑμῖν
ὅτι ἐὰν περιτέμνησθε,
Χριστὸς ὑμᾶς οὐδὲν ὠφελήσει.
³ μαρτύρομαι δὲ πάλιν παντὶ ἀνθρώπῳ περιτεμνομένῳ
ὅτι ὀφειλέτης ἐστὶν ὅλον τὸν νόμον ποιῆσαι.
⁴ κατηργήθητε ἀπὸ Χριστοῦ,
οἵτινες ἐν νόμῳ δικαιοῦσθε,
τῆς χάριτος ἐξεπέσατε.

² You see, I, Paul, am saying to you that,
if you should let yourselves be circumcised,
then the Christ will be of no value to you.
3 For I am declaring to every man who lets himself be circumcised
that he is obligated to do the whole of the law.
4 You have been cut off from the Christ,
whoever you are who are being declared righteous by the law—

XIII. What Does the Gospel Say? (5:1-6)

you have fallen away from grace.

Here Paul is declaring how the Galatians—in terms that really could not be more to the point—were to grasp with a renewed clarity the meaning of salvation contained in his gospel. The current distracting debate among the Galatians had caused them to lose sight of what he had originally preached to them: "O foolish Galatians! Who has bewitched you that you should not obey the truth, before whose eyes Jesus the Christ was clearly portrayed as crucified?" (3:1). In other words, his subject is now nothing less than the actual means by which salvation is effected, and what will be the sole conditions under which we are declared righteous before God and not before men. This is Paul's reminder that his gospel's exclusive vantage point renders any *extra-gospel* human preference, inclination, or convention to be of no account. What Paul says about the source of our salvation is very terse and to the point, and, even though it reflects the severe slave-market logic mentioned above, it is still the language of a glorious conviction.

Did Jesus die on the cross so that the believer could renew his covenant-consciousness with a revitalized attitude toward circumcision? Was the Christ's resurrection from the dead the signal for the people of God to rededicate themselves to the observance of the law? In other words, was Paul's gospel about our rediscovering what it means to be subservient to the law, or was it about discovering what the crucified Christ means? Which of the two was going to make it possible for us to be declared righteous before God?

This is a classic either-or appeal. Paul is not interested in convenient arguments aiming at a both/and arrangement because he himself has argued at length for the law's self-contained character, that the observance of its statutes and obligations is an autonomous, self-referential system of being declared righteous ("you who are being declared righteous by the law"), and so, in accordance with slave-market logic, submitting to the one master is by definition the rejection of the other.

Furthermore, the death of the Christ was a saving death, a redeeming purchase that transfers us slaves from our old master to the *noblesse oblige* of our new one who has acquired us for his own purposes. This, I think, is the import of the sometimes chilling effect that 5:4 has on the reader: "You have been cut off from the Christ, whoever you are who are being declared righteous by the law—you have fallen away from grace." The slave must ultimately demonstrate his loyalty and continually make it clear *which master* he does serve. Therefore, if any slave who has been "bought back from the law" subsequently continues serving his old master, then that slave is repudiating his new master's lordship and placing himself outside of the latter's grace (*charis*), i.e. his beneficent care and protection. Paul is stating that the Galatian Christian who has now decided, under pressure, to let himself be circumcised cannot suppose that he is thereby growing in his faith or deepening his identity in the Christ. To the contrary, by letting himself be circumcised, he is actually rejecting Jesus and declaring the identity of his true master. If he acts in a way that shows the law to be his master, then whatever grace that comes with belonging to the Christ is lost to him ("the Christ will be of no value to you").

How do the Galatians belong to the Christ? What will make for their identity in him? The possibility of belonging to the Christ (*tou Christou*) was only ever "on the basis of a hearing of faith," of faith in the gospel that declared the possibility in the first place! Identity always has a content, and the way in which that content is understood, indeed, what frames it and in turn is trusted and obeyed, is what constitutes the identity. The pagan Galatians in their pre-gospel condition enjoyed another identity, one that, by definition, was not framed by Paul's gospel. But now Paul is summoning the Galatians back to what was the sole basis for their gospel-identity and the telltale "proof" of it. Paul has already highlighted the witness-bearing activity of the Holy Spirit in 3:2-3: "Only this one thing do I wish to learn from you: Did you receive the Spirit on the basis of the works of the law or was it on the basis of a hearing with faith? Are you in this way

XIII. What Does the Gospel Say? (5:1-6)

so foolish, that, having begun with the Spirit, you are now completing yourselves in the flesh?" For Paul there is no surer proof of faith, of our fundamental belonging to the Christ, of our identity in and through him, than the manifestation of the Holy Spirit. It is thus that he continues in 5:5-6 by invoking this decisive activity and presence of the Holy Spirit:

⁵ ὑμεῖς γὰρ πνεύματι ἐκ πίστεως ἐλπίδα δικαιοσύνης ἀπεκδεχόμεθα.
⁶ ἐν γὰρ Χριστῷ Ἰησοῦ οὔτε περιτομή τι ἰσχύει
οὔτε ἀκροβυστία
ἀλλὰ πίστις δι' ἀγάπης ἐνεργουμένη.

⁵ For it is by the Spirit that we are eagerly hoping for the righteousness that is on the basis of faith,
⁶ because it is in the Christ Jesus that neither circumcision
nor uncircumcision amounts to anything,
but rather what does matter is faith activated by means of love.

If Paul has warned the Galatians that letting themselves be circumcised amounts to a repudiation of the Christ he has preached to them, that the result of their submitting to a ritual cutting of the flesh is a falling away from his grace, now he presses the issue of what the Holy Spirit has to do with circumcision. He ends 5:4 by confronting the freshly circumcised Galatian believer with the charge that his act only means that "you have fallen away from grace," and so now it is important that we keep 5:4 and 5:5 closely linked in our minds because the latter provides the explanation for Paul's startling assertion in 5:4.

There is a great deal going on in the grammatical compactness which makes up 5:5, and it is worth unpacking in detail what it contains in order to see the seamless steadiness of Paul's argument.

- First, there is the explicative conjunction *gar* which comes after the initial pronoun "we" (*hēmeis*), a part of speech which indicates that, when placed in a following statement, what is now set off by the *gar* conjunction serves as an explanation or contextual addition to what has already been stated (and for this reason it is often translated as "because" or "for"). Thus what we read in 5:4, "You have been cut off from the Christ, whoever you are who are being made righteous by the law—you have fallen away from grace," is explained by what follows in 5:5.

- The main verb comes at the end of the verse, *apekdechometha*, and it has the general meaning of "we ourselves are awaiting/expecting (something)." Paul uses it in the present tense, and so what it indicates is something ongoing in relation to the past aorist-tense actions of 5:4, 'You *have been cut off* from the Christ, whoever you are who *are being declared righteous* by the law— you *have fallen away* from grace. For it is by the Spirit that we *are eagerly hoping for* the righteousness which is on the basis of faith." But even more interesting is the fact that the one present-tense verb found in 5:4 belongs to the clause "whoever you are who are being declared righteous by the law" (*hoitines en nomō dikaiousthe*), and so there is a simultaneously parallel but divergent verbal action that should not be missed. The hope of some Galatians for a righteousness deriving from their circumcision must be seen in opposition to the gospel-based hope for righteousness that Paul advocates.

- What Paul says "we are eagerly hoping for" is "the righteousness which is on the basis of faith," and in this phrase stands the direct object of the verb: *ek pisteōs elpida dikaiosynēs apekdechometha*. The true direct object in the

XIII. What Does the Gospel Say? (5:1-6)

phrase, however, is the word "hope" (*elpis*), and so the *elpis dikaiosynēs* would simply be the "hope of righteousness," but, given that the phrase "on the basis of faith" comes before the direct object, I have expanded this crowded Greek arrangement into the more manageable English rendering of "we are eagerly hoping for the righteousness that is on the basis of faith," a translation which I think does justice to all of the implications contained in the Greek text's dense syntax.

- Finally, at the head of the above direct-object phrase is the even more compact expression, *pneumati*, which I understand as an instrumental dative and here it simply means "by the Spirit." Its placement at the head of the main phrase "we are eagerly hoping for the righteousness which is on the basis of faith" tells us how it is made possible and solely realized. It is only "by the Spirit" that the Galatians are able to hope *in this way*—by virtue of their having chosen faith over the law—for such a thing. In 5:4 Paul portrays the hope for righteousness as having been based on circumcision, but now, by stressing the total state of opposition, Paul links righteousness and any potential hope for it to the gospel-borne presence of the Holy Spirit. The contrast is a most deliberate one on Paul's part: the implication is that any righteousness based on circumcision represents a self-sufficient work in which the Holy Spirit plays no necessary part.

It is now that we can see the full import of 5:5 in relation to 5:4. According to Paul, those Galatians who have let themselves be circumcised are letting their righteousness be based on a particular requirement contained in the law, and, because of this, they are no longer basing their righteousness on what the gospel contains. They have cut themselves off from the Christ because theirs is a hope for righteousness rooted in a cultic requirement, one having to do literally with the flesh. As Paul argues, this stands in total opposition to the "hope for the righteousness" that is born in the gifted presence of God's Spirit. If the Galatian believer has obedient trust in the declaration of Jesus as the Christ, then that suffices where his being declared righteous is concerned. What was prophetically foretold (e.g. Isaiah 54-55, Jeremiah, 31, Ezekiel 37) is told once more in the gospel-word of Paul.

In 5:6a Paul continues both the momentum and the direction of his argument by the employment of an additional *gar* phrase. If it is only by virtue of the Holy Spirit's enabling presence ("For it is by the Spirit...") that the Galatians are able to continue hoping for the kind of righteousness by the content of the faith they hold in their hearts, then that is "*because* it is in the Christ Jesus that neither circumcision nor uncircumcision amounts to anything." The explanatory phrase "because it is in the Christ Jesus that..." is the Greek *en gar Christō Iēsou*, and so now Paul is saying that because we are "in the Christ Jesus," that is, when we are *in him*, when we belong to him by virtue of our trusting in him as the Christ, when we thus reckon our identity in terms of him being our new master to whom we owe a totalizing obedience, it is only then are we able to see and know that "neither circumcision nor uncircumcision amounts to anything." The clear implication here is that, if the Galatians are obedient to Paul's gospel, then they are "in the Christ" and not "in the law" (*en nomō*), and because they are in the Christ and not in the law, then they have the Christ as their sole vantage point.

Recall the Greek preposition *en* and the highly flexible ways in which it is used. The most basic meaning of this preposition is to denote—with a literal locativeness—being "in something," but it can also be used to mean "by," "with," or "among." Paul has already employed it in different contexts in order to make use of

XIII. What Does the Gospel Say? (5:1-6)

these variable senses and semantic settings, [2] but the way in which 5:6a utilizes it ("because it is in (*en*) the Christ Jesus that...") is worth noting here because of what the context is highlighting. One of the recurrent ways in which scripture employs this preposition is to indicate the place, point, or locus where a particular kind of life is to be found. When used in this figuratively locative way, the preposition *en* is communicating to us that the something in question is happening only by virtue of the causative thing being present, and that the subservient thing is under its aegis and thus compliant with its authority. In other words, it tells us—within each prepositional context—who or what is the master.

It is in this way that the relative power-settings contained in 5:4 ("you who are being made righteous by the law") and 5:6 ("because it is in the Christ Jesus that...") are specified and fully contrasted. Paul's point is clear: if the Galatians are obedient to his gospel, then there is no debate about who is master. When they are able to comprehend all things from that perspective, then, as the Greek text revealingly indicates, their being circumcised or uncircumcised has no inherent validity. Related to this is therefore the meaning of the Greek verb *ischyō*, which I translate in this context as "amounts to anything," but its basic meaning has to do with any person or object having a genuine strength, power, effectiveness, etc.

But if neither circumcision nor uncircumcision is what matters, then what does matter? Certainly what does matter is the crucial ingredient of *faith* in the gospel as Paul has preached it to the Galatians, of their being in the Christ by virtue of said faith, but that same faith Paul now qualifies in 5:6b when, given his declaration that circumcision is of no consequence, he writes "but what does matter is faith activated by means of love." Even though the Greek text of 5:6b does not explicitly contain the same verb as 5:6a (*ischyō*), the Greek syntax presupposes it: if

---

[2] 1:16, 24; 2:17, 20; 3:5, 11, 12, 14, 19, 26, 28; 4:14, 18, 20, 25, 5:4, 6.

"neither circumcision nor uncircumcision amounts to anything" when the Galatians are in the Christ Jesus, then Paul stipulates that what does amount to something is "faith activated by means of love."

Up until this point Paul has spoken about faith only in relation to the way in which the Galatians received the gospel and continue to stand fast and remain obedient to it, but now he is qualifying that faith in a most remarkable way. If faith is the only proper reaction to the gospel's content, if that same faith involves seeing the crucified Christ in relation to the promises and purposes of the Old Testament God, are we then talking about faith as an intellectual appropriation of the gospel? Are we adding it all up in our minds, finding it to be conceptually pleasing in ways that also touch upon our inner emotional disposition or needs? In other words, what accompanies the believer's attitude of faith beyond the plain fact of his faithful acceptance? We must be careful here, not so much because of Paul's language, but, more directly, because of our own contemporary prejudices about the psychology of believing and the ways in which these can lead us unthinkingly in the wrong direction when we seek to understand just what Paul meant by a "faith activated by means of love."

There is a widespread assumption in our popular culture that what we call "love" is something that exists by itself. That love is a self-sufficient, independently operating aspect of our human essence, and that it can most freely and honestly manifest itself only when it is not being culturally or socially conditioned. This is the presupposition which fuels our age's all-you-need-is-love ideology, namely, that innocently facile belief that the phenomenon which we call "love" somehow exists prior to and in an unconditional state of autonomy apart from any single human manifestation of it. I raise this consideration now because, in many ways, the rest of Paul's letter is an exposition of just what he does mean by a "faith activated by means of love." In what follows I wish to indicate how Paul is telling us

XIII. What Does the Gospel Say? (5:1-6)

that the love of which he speaks is not the open-ended, celebratory emotionalism of our day, but rather an aspect of our being which is *concurrent*, both literally and figuratively, with the faith whose *only* source is the gospel.

To our modern eyes the Greek text of 5:6b suggests a kind of causality. The phrase "faith activated by means of love" (*pistis di' agapēs energoumenē*) leads us in the direction of assuming that (1) "faith" is only ever activated (in the Greek, literally, "energized") by love, and that (2) without "love" faith by itself would be a stillborn attitude. The Greek grammar would seem to support these assumptions, but a closer look reveals a more fundamental perspective. This is not to argue that either of the two assumptions above is false (each, in its own conditional way, is true). What is truly necessary, however, is our seeing these two elements—faith and love—not in causal relation to each other, but rather in relation to belonging to the Christ.

First, there is the faith that is the fundamental attitude or conditional response to the gospel. In 3:2 and 3:5 Paul twice asks the question about faith's relative standing to the law (1) where the gospel is concerned, and (2) where it is connected with the Holy Spirit as the proof not only of the gospel itself but of the Galatians' faith in it:

> ² *Only this one thing do I wish to learn from you:*
> *Did you receive the Spirit on the basis of the works of the law*
> *or was it on the basis of a hearing with faith?*
>
> ⁵ *Therefore he who supplies the Spirit to you*
> *and who works mighty acts among you,*
> *does he do that on the basis of the works of the law*
> *or on the basis of a hearing with faith?'*

Paul has preached the gospel to the Galatians. They heard it, and the Holy Spirit was manifest among them because they received the message with an attitude of faith. But in every respect faith itself is a gift from God. It is not a resourceful response we make on our own, but a *concurrent* outcome of the Holy Spirit and the human heart coming together for the sake of the common "hearing-work" (*akoē-ergon*) we label as faith. It is in this sense that faith is a literally con-current phenomenon, that is, it represents two currents of activity—one divine, one human—coinciding interactively in order to be the locus of illumination in the believer's life. But in order to understand how faith "works," one must take into account love.

Second, what kind of love? Not the free-ranging emotional autonomy we so often understand love as being, but, instead of regarding love as the great metaphysical emotion-force in its own right, we need to see it as what happens to us when—in and through the gospel—we encounter the living Christ. This means that the love we discover is one that directly exhibits his nature, his teaching, his healing, his sacrifice, his resurrection, and his sovereign power. It is not our love. It will never be *our* love. It will only ever be the way we manifest the love of the Christ. This is an important point because all of us suffer from the tendency to substitute our sundry personalized ways of understanding love, how we think we are demonstrating it, and often the ways we betray it, for the very love of the Christ.

Thus, when Paul speaks of love (*agapē*) as being the force that energizes faith (*pistis*), he means that in the process of hearing the gospel and receiving it by means of faith, we will have learned something about the nature of love and its ineffable relationship with faith. It is not that our faithful response to the gospel will have caused any kind of pre-existing verity of love to be cast now in a Christian flavor, but, more accurately, it is as if we never knew anything at all about the nature of love in the first place, and only now, in the context of our faithful hearing of the gospel, are we finally learning what love really is. Perhaps most importantly of all, faith is the name we give to what will be our continual instruction in the nature not of what can never be any more than a *specifically* Christian love but rather of love itself. This is what I think Paul means when he says that the only thing that "amounts to something" when we are in the Christ, that is,

XIII. What Does the Gospel Say? (5:1-6)

when we belong to him and are abiding in him, is a "faith activated by means of love." If faith is God's purest gift to us, if it is he who makes it possible for us to hear with faith and to obey, then it is God too who sees to love's role in our salvation.

Paul himself has hinted at this in 3:5 when he asks, "Therefore he who supplies the Spirit to you and who works mighty acts among you..." The Greek text for the phrase "[he] who works mighty acts among you" reads as *energōn dynameis en hymin*, and the same verb *energeō* is used in 5:6b. If God possesses one "mighty act" (*dynamis*) *par excellence*, it is that of his love. Not love in the sense of one-size-fits-all (predicated as that would be on human adjudication), but love as being, first and foremost, his love and therefore strictly a matter of God's adjudication. The love we are learning is his love. The love we are learning is oriented by faith. The love we are learning and what we in turn are to manifest must correspond to what we believe.

Thus, there is nothing in the strictly modern sense that is ecumenical about the Christian gospel: it is a proclamation that only ever truly reveals itself in its *specificity*. The gospel, by virtue of the fact it is a message not lacking in specificity, requires not only that we keep faith and love closely bound together, but that we understand at every step of the way that it is the Christ who binds them together. This is the key to the *universalism* of the Christian message, its more ancient and therefore more genuine ecumenicity. In addition, some people are tempted to suppose that Christian faith is no more than a quality super-added to what is an already existing personal disposition of love, and, in this way, when Paul speaks in this context of "faith activated by means of love," there is the unfortunately distorting interpretive assumption that the gospel is an imperative message about coming to embrace a faithful inclination toward Christian belief, and that this represents an attitude that is only ever actualized by the addition of one's own loving outlook on life. This is a mentally convenient reversal of what Paul is actually telling the Galatians, namely, that it is only by means of specifically

Christian faith, that is, one that entirely originates in the gospel declaration of Jesus as the Christ and thus has no other point of reference, that we will come to know and to understand the nature, not of love as a universal force existing on its own, but of the divine love itself. When a Christian employs the word "love," he must carefully keep in mind that the love in question is only ever God's love, the kind that we come to know through Jesus who is the Christ and in the Holy Spirit.

XIV. A Matter of Persuasion (5:7-12)

Paul has already indicated to the Galatians that it was not their observance of the law which made the Holy Spirit manifest among them. To the contrary, it was strictly "on the basis of a hearing with faith" (3:2, 3:5) that the Galatians could count themselves, when viewed against the backdrop of God's salvation for all of mankind in the Christ, as "children of promise just as Isaac was...[he] who [was born] according to the Spirit" (4:28-29). It was this message that he had delivered to them originally, and it was by means of this message that he had entrusted them to God, but in the interim the advocates of circumcision had in effect demolished the sensitive balance between faith and the Spirit that Paul through his gospel message had so laboriously erected in the Galatian churches. In 5:7-10 he continues his interrogation:

⁷ ἐτρέχετε καλῶς·
τίς ὑμᾶς ἐνέκοψεν τῇ ἀληθείᾳ μὴ πείθεσθαι;
⁸ ἡ πεισμονὴ οὐκ ἐκ τοῦ καλοῦντος ὑμᾶς.
⁹ μικρὰ ζύμη ὅλον τὸ φύραμα ζυμοῖ.
¹⁰ ἐγὼ πέποιθα εἰς ὑμᾶς ἐν κυρίῳ ὅτι οὐδὲν ἄλλο φρονήσετε·
ὁ ταράσσων ὑμᾶς βαστάσει τὸ κρίμα, ὅστις ἐὰν ᾖ.

⁷ *You had been running so well.*
Who hindered you then from being persuaded by the truth?
⁸ *Your persuasion now does not come from him who calls you.*
⁹ *A little leaven leavens the whole lump.*
¹⁰ *I am persuaded that, being in the Lord, you will not think otherwise;*
and he who is confusing you will bear his judgment, whoever he is.

What is interesting about these verses is that they, in a way that I don't think is incidental, are a glance back over the whole letter. Their vocabulary is retrospective in that it invokes the general outlines of what has gone before. Compressed in them is the whole of Paul's appeal to the Galatians, and the basis on which he is pleading with them to re-establish themselves in what he had delivered to them.

First, in 5:7a there is the verb *trechō*, which means "to run (a race)." Paul has already employed it in 2:2 when he is describing his second trip to Jerusalem: "and I went up by revelation; and I laid before them the gospel that I am preaching among the nations, but privately to those who were of reputation, lest in any way I should be running (*trechō*) or had run in vain." The implication here is that, since his gospel mission was recognized by those reputable apostles in Jerusalem, it was the same gospel that he had preached to the Galatians and in which he had established them. Paul "ran" in this gospel and in no other one: it was not a running in vain, and he had bequeathed this to the Galatians, a fact that allowed them to "run so well." The main point here is the validity of Paul's gospel, attested to by the Jerusalem notables (even though Paul quietly but confidently discounts their seal of approval in 2:6), and how that validity cannot be seen apart from the fact that he founded the Galatian communities by means of this same word. So, if the Galatians were "running so well" in the Holy Spirit, then it was because Paul had taught them how to run so well *in that very truth*.

Second, 5:7b amounts to a restatement of the immediate occasion for Paul's letter. If the Galatians had been running so well as a result of the gospel Paul had preached to them, and if their acceptance of that gospel was because they had been *persuaded* by its truth, then what reason should they now give for their embracing any alternative to that truth? Recall that up until now Paul has used the word "truth" (*alētheia*) as a virtual synonym for his gospel (2:5, 14; 3:1, 4:16). 5:7b contains the Greek verb *peithō*, which means "to persuade," and this word figures prominently in 5:7-10. Forms of this verb occur in 5:7b, 5:8, and 5:10, and in my English translation I have attempted to preserve what must be Paul's completely intentional repetition of the verb *peithō* in this portion of his plea to the Galatians.

If the Galatians had been "running so well," it was because they had been "persuaded by the truth" of Paul's gospel, so now, given that the Galatians were turning toward circumcision, he

XIV. A Matter of Persuasion (5:7-12)

asks, "Who hindered you then from being persuaded (*peithesthai*) by the truth?" In other words, if the Galatians had at one time been persuaded by the truth (i.e. if they had accepted Paul's gospel), then why are they no longer persuaded by its truth and are therefore accepting something else in its place? Paul had posed this same question earlier in 3:1 with the same passive infinitive form of *peithō*: "O foolish Galatians! Who has bewitched you that you should not obey (*peithesthai*) the truth, before whose eyes Jesus the Christ was clearly portrayed as crucified?"

This same appeal also occurs much earlier in the letter. In 1:9-10 Paul is declaring the primacy of his gospel over against anything other than it: "As we have said before, so now I am saying again: if any one is preaching to you a gospel other than that which you received from us, let him be accursed! For am I now winning over (*peithō*) men or God? Or am I seeking to please men? If I were still pleasing men, I would not be a slave of the Christ." The rhetorical punch in this passage consists of the fact that Paul is arguing in effect that part of the validity of his gospel (its *persuasive* power) is that it neither derives from nor does it appeal to any human comfort zone of customary practice or human tradition. Paul confirms this very point in the following verses (1:11-12): "For I want you to know, brothers and sisters, that the gospel preached by me, it is not according to man; for neither have I received it from man nor was I taught it; rather it came by means of a revealing of Jesus the Christ himself." Paul had founded and formed the Galatian churches by means of his gospel, but the incursions of the circumcision party and the introduction of their "other gospel" (1:6) are the reason why he is making his interrogative appeal to them.

He continues this line of questioning in 5:8 by stating that "Your persuasion (*peismonē*) now does not come from him who calls you." If the issue is one of relative persuasion, then Paul is writing because the current persuasion of the Galatians is in the direction of circumcision and away from the gospel as he had preached it to them. Even though there is a standing interpretive ambiguity in the phrase "him who calls you" (just like in 1:6, it could be explicated as referring either to God or to Paul), I am inclined to view it as an sideways reference to Paul himself but with the understanding that, in accordance with Paul's own argumentation, through the gospel message God is speaking now through him. In this connection I think that 3:1 provides the best clue: if the Galatians initially had obeyed the truth, then it was only because Paul had "clearly portrayed [Jesus the Christ] as crucified" to them.

5:9 has a proverbial ring to it, and scripturally it can be linked to Matthew 16:5-12, when Jesus warns his disciples, "Take heed and beware of the leaven of the Pharisees and Sadducees." (16:6, RSV) This passage comes after Jesus has fed the four thousand at the end of chapter 15, and his warning is immediately preceded by the Pharisees and the Sadducees demanding a sign from him. Jesus' refusal to grant such a "sign" (*sēmeion*) upon their request culminates in his declaration that "an evil and adulterous generation seeks for a sign, but no sign shall be given to it except the sign of Jonah." (16:4, RSV) What does Jesus mean when he refers to the "sign of Jonah" in a context like this?

Jonah, that most reluctant of the prophets, is the simultaneous symbol of human frailty and arrogance in the face of divine power. The book of prophecy bearing his name tells of what happens when humans either choose to rebel against the manifestation of that power or decide to cooperate wholeheartedly with its possibility. When God calls upon Jonah to preach repentance to the Ninevites, the man boards a ship to flee in the opposite direction. A storm threatens to sink the ship, and when the crew learns of Jonah's flight from God, they toss him overboard with the hope that their "sacrificing" of him will propitiate his god and thus save themselves. At God's command, Jonah is swallowed by a "great fish," and he spends three days and three nights in the creature's belly. The psalm-like "prayer of

XIV. A Matter of Persuasion (5:7-12)

Jonah" (2:3-10) is the great prophetic nexus of the work, being, on the one hand, the desperate outcry of a man facing death under what can only be described as the most fantastic circumstances imaginable, and, on the other hand, it is his proclamation of steadfast faith in "the LORD of deliverance" (Septuagint: *Kyrios sōtēriou*). Despite Jonah's delivery from what was the certainty of death, the remainder of the book is the story of his ongoing exasperation with God's power. First, there is the prophet's annoyance with God that he would extend his mercy to the pagan Ninevites who in this instance would actually repent and escape destruction. Second, Jonah is thoroughly peeved with this astonishing manifestation of the divine mercy. The prophet ends up "being grieved" (*elypēthē*) with God because he is not acting like the God this irascible prophet wishes him to be.

Thus, when Jesus speaks of the "sign of Jonah," he is asking the Pharisees to put two and two together, to relate scripture to their current situation, and to see what they value the most (the law) in relation to what is going on around them (God's eschatological power). When the Pharisees first asked Jesus for a sign in Matthew 12:38, they ironically asked for "a sign *from you*," but when both the Pharisees and the Sadducees gather to make this request again in 16:1, it becomes an appeal tinged with even greater and now *official* doubt: "And the Pharisees and the Sadducees came, and to test him they asked him to show them a sign *from heaven*." Jesus upbraids them for their inability to interpret "the signs of the times" (*ta sēmeia tōn kairōn*) even though they easily enough "interpret the appearance of the sky." We can find the direct contextual meaning for what Jesus meant when he declared the sufficiency of the "sign of Jonah" as it was described in connection with the earlier episode in Matthew 12:40-41(RSV): "For as Jonah was three days and three nights in the belly of the whale, so will the Son of man be three days and three nights in the heart of the earth. The men of Nineveh will arise at the judgment with this generation and condemn it; for they repented at the preaching of Jonah, and behold, something greater than Jonah is here."

Jesus is saying two important things here. First, that Jonah's experience "in the belly of the whale" will become a scriptural prefiguration of his own coming death and resurrection. This would be the greater and more telling fact, but at that time it was an intimation lost not only on the religious officials but really on anyone else listening to Jesus: they simply would have had no idea of what he was talking about. Second, that what happened with the "men of Nineveh" is also a prefiguration of what will happen "with this generation," namely, that a pagan nation which repented will judge and serve to condemn an Israel that has not repented. And why should Israel repent? What is happening in the midst of "this generation" that would necessitate Jesus making such a declaration? Matthew 14 and 15 record an amazing series of events relevant to what Jesus will say in chapter 16. First there is the death of John the Baptist, followed by the feeding of the five thousand. Then Jesus walks upon stormy waters in the middle of the night in order to teach his disciples something about the nature of faith. He contends with the Pharisees and the scribes over what makes a man holy and what is defiling. He shows mercy to a Canaanite woman's daughter. He feeds the four thousand, and all the while he is healing the multitudes: "And great crowds came to him, bringing with them the lame, the maimed, the blind, the dumb, and many others, and they put them at his feet, and he healed them, so that the throng wondered, when they saw the dumb speaking, the maimed whole, the lame walking, and the blind seeing; and they glorified the God of Israel." (15:30-31, RSV)

It is against such a backdrop that Jesus says what he does to the Pharisees and the Sadducees in 16:2-4, in effect saying to them, "If you have forgotten what the scriptures say, then look around you and take note of what the God of Israel is doing!" When Jesus is alone with his disciples, it is then that he warns them about the "leaven of the Pharisees and the Sadducees."

XIV. A Matter of Persuasion (5:7-12)

(16:6) At first the disciples think in terms of regular bread and their lack of it at that particular moment, but Jesus redirects their concern to the real bread of God's miraculous power which they had themselves experienced but now had distractedly forgotten. Not only had Jesus healed the multitudes of their diseases and crippled conditions, but he had fed them with the most miraculous, the most powerful bread of all. *This* is the bread that counts. This is the bread that is real, that is life-giving, the bread that is *from heaven*, from what is symbolized by "the Jerusalem above."

This helps to explain Jesus' continued exasperation with the religious leaders: that even in the presence of such a bread being made real and available to them they would still ask for a validating sign *from heaven* (Jesus had acknowledged their relative blindness in 15:14). Similarly, when Jesus warns his disciples about the Pharisaic "leaven," he must redirect their attention to what they too had experienced: not just one feeding, but two! His language about "leaven" here goes to the heart of what constitutes any bread, namely, the simple understanding that only God's leaven will produce God's bread, and, in the case of a Pharisaic leaven, it will produce only Pharisaic bread. When Jesus says in 16:11 (RSV), "How is it that you fail to perceive that I did not speak about bread? Beware of the leaven of the Pharisees and the Sadducees," he is asking them to think in terms of any bread's source, what it is that enables the mixture to rise, to become real bread, and to offer genuine nourishment. The point here is that if there is a real difference between God's bread and Pharisaic bread, then one must look to the leaven used in each case in order to understand what makes them different from each other. Recall that it is between the two feedings (15:1-20) that Jesus contends with the Pharisees over what constitutes righteousness, a passage that by itself could serve as a discourse on the nature of godly leaven. It is in 16:12 (RSV) that this point comes home to the disciples: "Then they understood that he did not tell them to beware of the leaven of bread, but the teaching of the Pharisees and the Sadducees."

It is in accordance with this same figurative sense that Paul resorts to the imagery of leaven in Galatians 5:9. Just as it is the Christ crucified whom Paul preached to the Galatians, and just as it is the same Christ who cautioned his disciples about the false leaven of the Pharisees, so too Paul now appeals to what must be the true leaven contained in his gospel. When he declares that "a little leaven leavens the whole lump," he is referring to how much this relatively small material ingredient makes the decisive difference in the baked result: that such a tiny amount of leaven placed in a lump ends up determining the nature of the loaf that will be produced. The same imagery is also employed in Matthew 13:33 (RSV): "He told them another parable. "The kingdom of heaven is like leaven which a woman took and hid in three measures of flour, till it was all leavened."

Paul's contention is that a Pharisaic loaf (a circumcision-loaf) has been introduced among the Galatians and is substituting itself for the original bread (a grace-loaf) which he had offered to them. He is pointing out this difference to the Galatians in the light of his assertion in 5:6 that "in the Christ Jesus neither circumcision nor uncircumcision amounts to anything, but rather what does matter is faith activated by means of love." What must have been their current enthusiasm for circumcision has forced Paul to ask them of which bread they will now partake. Will it be the bread of his gospel, or will it be a bread which has no relation to his gospel? Since it is the leaven which makes the loaf, which "little [amount of] leaven" will they choose, one reflecting a Pharisaic zeal or one proffered directly by God? Paul's point is simply that the choice makes all the difference in the world.

But Paul only wishes to encourage the Galatians in the direction of what they surely already know, of what the Holy Spirit has revealed to them and allowed them to see realized since the first day of his preaching among them. Being certain himself that "a little leaven leavens the whole lump," in 5:10 he

XIV. A Matter of Persuasion (5:7-12)

expresses his confidence in what he hopes will be their faithful discernment of the situation:

> [10] I am persuaded that, being in the Lord, you will not think otherwise;
> and he who is confusing you will bear his judgment, whoever he is.

The Greek verb for persuasion (*peithō*), which has already appeared in 5:7-8, occurs again in 5:10, a feature which serves to bracket this passage having to do with the convictions that must accompany a Christian faith. It would be useful as this point to look at 5:7-10 again with its "persuasion" terminology highlighted:

> [7] *You had been running so well.*
> *Who hindered you then from being persuaded* (peithesthai) *by the truth?*
> [8] *Your persuasion* (peismonē) *now does not come from him who calls you.*
> [9] *A little leaven leavens the whole lump.*
> [10] *I am persuaded* (pepoitha) *that, being in the Lord, you will not think otherwise;*
> *and he who is confusing you will bear his judgment, whoever he is.*

I think that the key phrase in this passage comes in v. 10 when Paul writes, "I am persuaded that, *being in the Lord*, you will not think otherwise." What I have rendered here as "being in the Lord" (*en kyriō*) preserves what I regard to be an essential ambiguity in the original Greek text. The ambiguity concerns the subject of the phrase "being in the Lord"—does it refer just to Paul, to the Galatians, or to both at the same time?

I shall argue that the context demands that we consider "being in the Lord" as applying both to Paul and to the Galatians. The overall context is Paul's exhortation to the Galatians to remain true to the gospel that he had preached to them, and in which he had formed them as a community. The whole basis for Paul's appeal to them is his contention that he is speaking on behalf of the Lord God. The clear implication here is that since Paul has spoken "in the Lord," then all of what has happened is due to the gospel unleashing the Holy Spirit's presence and power among the Galatians who heard his message and who responded to it in faith, a set of circumstances that serves as the most direct evidence of the Galatians "being in the Lord."

In 5:10 Paul is declaring his unwavering confidence that what God has initiated among the Galatians will not alter in any way. The evidence for his certainty comes in the form of the inclusion of the personal pronoun with the verb. New Testament Greek (unlike English) does not typically include the pronoun with the verb, and, when it does appear, this is a textual feature so rare that it invariably signals an intentional emphasis on the subject's part. The Greek text begins with *egō pepoitha* ("I am persuaded that..."), a grammatically highlighted indication that Paul wishes to emphasize his complete conviction that the Galatians "being in the Lord, will not think otherwise," namely, that because they were constituted by his preaching "in the Lord," they will in a likewise manner remain faithful to the truth.

Paul's language in the second half of 5:10 refers directly back to what he had written in 1:6-7. In what was his first remonstrance with the Galatians, Paul wrote:

⁶ I am astonished that
in this manner you are so quickly turning away from him
who called you in the grace of the Christ,
*and that you are turning to a different (*heteron*) gospel—*
*⁷ which is not another (*allo*) one—*
*but now there are the ones who are confusing (*tarassontes*) you*
and who even want to alter the gospel of the Christ.

In that passage Paul first confronts the Galatians about what he perceives to be their new situation—that in his absence they are now subscribing to a gospel different (*heteron*) from what he first proclaimed to them, and that they are doing so at the behest of "the ones who are confusing (*tarassontes*) you and who even want to alter the gospel of the Christ." In 5:10 Paul emphatically expresses his confidence that the Galatians "will not think otherwise," that is, if they remain "in the Lord," then they will not think in terms of anything other than (*allo*) what Paul has

XIV. A Matter of Persuasion (5:7-12)

transmitted to them. Just as Paul had declared initially in 1:6, whether the circumcision party's recasting of his gospel amounts to something *heteron* or *allo*, it will not make any difference because what they are promoting is *anathema* in Paul's eyes (1:8-9): it is "other than (*par' hou*) what we preached to you."

This is the meaning of the rhetorical appeal contained in the Greek phrase "you will not think otherwise" (*ouden allo phronēsete*): that Paul is adjuring the Galatians not to embrace the "otherwise" (*allo*) more recently advocated among them by the circumcision party, namely, the pursuit of (and therefore the unnecessary reliance upon) a ritual marking of the flesh. Note too how Paul's statement in 5:8, "Your persuasion now does not come from him who calls you" is an echo of what he first asserted in 1:6a, "I am astonished that in this manner you are so quickly turning away from him who called you in the grace of the Christ." In 5:10b Paul states quite baldly that "he who is confusing (*tarassōn*) you will bear his judgment, whoever he is"— that is, he is declaring that the members of the circumcision party behind these changes will be answerable to God for their actions, for their determination to "alter the gospel of the Christ" (1:7, 5:10b), which, by Paul's definition, only serves to reveal them as working *against* God by their insertion of ritual observation as an intermediate requirement between the believer and God.

Paul's position here is a positively uncompromising one, and his strident insistence on the absolute sufficiency of his gospel might strike our modern ears as being perhaps too drastic of a position to hold, but we should remind ourselves that Paul always speaks not on his own behalf but in the name of the God who sent him. With regard to many things we are prone to think in terms of compromise and/or accommodation as being necessary ways to deal with differences of opinion especially in connection with weighty matters, but the ultimate basis for Paul's condemnation of the circumcision party must be seen in the light of his own understanding of the gospel message *as he had received it*: "For I want you to know, brothers and sisters, that the gospel preached by me, it is not according to man; for neither have I received it from man not was I taught it; rather it came by means of a revealing of Jesus the Christ himself." (1:11-12) Paul's position might be easier to understand if we frame it in terms more readily understood and accepted by us, namely, via our customary distinction between the essential and the non-essential. Paul sees the ritual requirements of the circumcision party as being wholly non-essential when viewed strictly *and* necessarily in the light of the grace that the believer has through his faith in the Christ. By contrast, that which is truly essential—the very grace of God in our lives—is facilitated entirely by the gospel, and by nothing else. How shall we belong to the Christ? On which basis? By what means does it occur? Paul will insist that it is solely by means of his gospel and the grace that it allows, and not at all by means of super-added cultic acts.

Those who argue for the necessity of such acts, for what they would have others understand as playing an essential role in the plan of salvation contained in the proclamation that Jesus is the Christ, Paul consigns to the judgment of God. What needs to be noticed here is that Paul is arguing two things: (1) that what he has preached to the Galatians, the content of his gospel, that *this most singular message* is what God wishes to tell us, and, as such, it requires no emendation or qualifying addition; and (2) that those who would amend it by introducing additional ritual requirements are not speaking in accordance with what God is now making clear to all who are hearing the unadulterated gospel. The meaning could not be more clear: because the circumcision party is advocating what God no longer requires of those who would belong to him, they are out of step with God's will and purposes, and, regardless of how well intentioned such efforts might be, they run contrary to the will of heaven where our salvation is concerned.

While Paul's language in 5:10 may seem harsh, there is the simple apostolic imperative of his own experience behind it. If

XIV. A Matter of Persuasion (5:7-12)

God has commissioned Paul to preach what can only be a faith-based gospel to the nations, then what God is now seeking to accomplish through the preaching of such a gospel should not be compromised by a shifting away from faith's centrality in order to favor more ancient Jewish prescriptions for the marking of ethnic identity. What had served to distinguish Israel from the nations cannot be opportunistically reinterpreted now as a way to mark the nations' eschatological identity in God. For the circumcision party to insist on the old markers is, under these radically new circumstances, to work counter to God's purposes and thus to invite his judgment upon them. Scripturally speaking, judgment is always a matter of how things will shake out in the end based on the obedience that is now, and Paul is wholly and most urgently in the mean time counting on the Galatians being able to see why circumcision—if they reject the "otherwise" and abide by the gospel in which they were founded—is not so much worthless as it is eschatologically unnecessary. The important thing to see here is that Paul is speaking entirely from personal conviction: his point is simply that if his gospel is true in God's eyes, then those who would "alter" it will have to face the judgment their actions will have earned them. There is nothing of the speculative thinker in Paul, and it is a false step even to begin treating him as such. It is as if he knows only what he knows, and that he can only do what he has been called to do—all that lies beyond what God has called him to do is entirely in God's hands.

And what has God called Paul to do? Was it to preach circumcision? Was it to declare the necessity of the pagan world adopting the law of Israel? Was the gospel to be a matter more of circumcision rather than of the cross? It is against the backdrop of what must have been the ongoing criticism of him mounted by his opponents in the Galatian churches that Paul in 5:11-12 continues to insist on the nature of the message that guides his conviction:

¹¹ ἐγὼ δέ, ἀδελφοί,
εἰ περιτομὴν ἔτι κηρύσσω,
τί ἔτι διώκομαι;
ἆρα κατήργηται τὸ σκάνδαλον τοῦ σταυροῦ.
¹² ὄφελον καὶ ἀποκόψονται οἱ ἀναστατοῦντες ὑμᾶς.

¹¹ And I, brothers and sisters,
if I am still preaching circumcision,
why am I still being persecuted?
If so, the scandal of the cross has been taken away.
¹² I wish that the ones who are troubling you would cut themselves off!

In order to make the point about just what his most fundamental convictions are, Paul resorts to some delicious irony. Paul of course never preached the necessity of circumcision, so here he asks—knowing the exact contrary to be the truth in this situation—why he is still the subject of persecution if he was simply preaching circumcision all along. It would have been obvious to the Galatians that he had *never* preached circumcision, a fact underscored by what must have been their full awareness that Paul was continuing to be persecuted *for precisely that point*! Since Paul is being persecuted, he continues floating his hypothetical irony even further in order to underscore just why he is being persecuted. If Paul had been preaching circumcision all along, then there would have been no scandal of the cross, but, since the Galatians have eyes and ears, there was most surely the scandal of the cross at the very center of Paul's preaching.

Since the core of his gospel message is an obvious one not only to the Galatians but to us, then let there be no apologies about its importance, no debate about its unassailable centrality, and ultimately no waffling about where its life-giving role is concerned. Paul preached no more and no less than the crucified Christ (3:1), and, when seen against that most essential foundation, any unnecessary addition, all secondary requirements, all agitation rooted in the superfluous, all of these things come off as the most pointless diversions where God's power and authority are concerned. Is it any wonder then that Paul, when confronted with the petty ritualism being

XIV. A Matter of Persuasion (5:7-12)

promulgated by the circumcision party and their persecution of him based on that, should express himself in truthful indignation? Paul's wish is that, if the ritual cutting of the flesh for the sake of identity is so important to his persecutors that they would place it before the Christ himself, then perhaps it would be best if such folk should suffer the ultimate results of what their misplaced zeal demands. That is, if the members of the circumcision party are so concerned about the necessity of their ritual, if they are so willing to place it before the eschatological might of God and the mystery of his power as revealed to the world in the form of a Christ crucified and now resurrected from the dead, then let us by all means commend them for their utterly determined zeal, and hope that—in keeping unrestrainedly with this brand of zeal—they don't spare themselves when it comes to an imperative marking of the flesh.

Paul's phrasing in 5:12 operates at a number of levels. First, there is the prospect of simple self-inflicted mutilation. If his critics are so insistent upon circumcision, then Paul is vividly suggesting here that it might be best if they went all the way and did not stop at the foreskin! Second, the Greek verb used here (*apokoptō*) refers to the cutting off of something from a main body, suggesting that an emphasis on circumcision at the expense of faith and grace through the Christ only serves to remove those who embrace such an emphasis from the main body of God's people: "You have been cut off from the Christ, whoever you are who are being made righteous by the law—you have fallen away from grace." (5:4) Finally, the verb is suggestive of pruning in general. The trimming of excess or less than vital branches from a tree or bush is sometimes necessary in order to ensure the health of the plant and to stimulate its further growth. Paul must have been hinting as well that the removal of Pharisaic "dead wood" (rather than its re-grafting) would have been both necessary and helpful, a case of self-pruning for the growth of God's saving word in the world.

I have already referred to John 15:1-17 in connection with the way that Paul in 3:28 describes the nature of the gospel-based unity undergirding the messianic community that is "one in the Christ Jesus." The same passage from John's gospel is relevant to the whole of Galatians 5. In particular John 15:3-6 (RSV) corresponds thematically to Paul's appeal up to this point:

> You are already made clean by the word which I have spoken to you. Abide in me, and I in you. As the branch cannot bear fruit by itself, unless it abides in the vine, neither can you, unless you abide in me. I am the vine, you are the branches. He who abides in me, and I in him, he it is that bears much fruit, for apart from me you can do nothing. If a man does not abide in me, he is cast forth as a branch and withers; and the branches are gathered, thrown into the fire and burned.

Just as Jesus is addressing his not entirely persuaded disciples on the eve of the Passover feast, Paul is writing to his own wavering disciples and imploring them to abide in the same word that he first preached to them. If it was Jesus' wish was that his disciples might grasp how the cross would become the inextinguishable sign of God's love for mankind (15:13), it was due to the way that Paul voices here his deadly earnest concern that the Galatians could be summoned back to the crucified Christ "formed" in them by their hearing of his gospel (4:19).

XV. Walking Bodily In The Spirit (5:13-24)

Yet, even though Paul is obviously exasperated by this point in his letter, it should be emphasized that his contemptuous dismissal of the circumcision party in these terms must be seen in connection with what now follows. It is clear that Paul has no patience with admonitions for circumcision when there are far greater and more profound issues at stake. If salvation in the Christ as preached by Paul hinges on the terms by which the Galatians are declared righteous in the eyes of God, will it be a matter of Mosaic observations, or will it result from the gospel word and the validating effects of God's Holy Spirit among those who hear it and heed it? Paul's peremptory wish in 5:12 is immediately followed by one of his supremely inaugural declarations in 5:13, a verse which in many ways introduces the visionary exhortation that is the rest of his letter to the Galatians:

¹³ ὑμεῖς γὰρ ἐπ' ἐλευθερίᾳ ἐκλήθητε, ἀδελφοί·
μόνον μὴ τὴν ἐλευθερίαν εἰς ἀφορμὴν τῇ σαρκί,
ἀλλὰ διὰ τῆς ἀγάπης δουλεύετε ἀλλήλοις.

¹³ For you have been called to freedom, brothers and sisters,
only do not use this freedom as an opportunity for the flesh,
rather, by means of love be servants of one another.

This announcement is another instance of the Greek explicative conjunction *gar*. It means that what Paul says in 5:12 is the basis for why 5:13 is so necessary and true. In the light of his gospel, Paul consigns the pointless admonitions of the circumcision party to a frenzied self-mutilation that has nothing at all to do with what God now wishes to reveal to mankind, namely, that *on the basis of* faith and *by means of* our faith in the faith of Jesus the Christ *(pistis Christou)*, we are entering into what is the new age of an eschatological freedom. When Paul writes that, "you have been called to freedom, brothers and sisters," he is referring not to an ultimate condition of freedom, but rather to the relative state of freedom that constitutes the believer's faith-based identity in the Christ. It is strictly on the basis of faith that the believer is able to experience the grace of God, to enjoy the generous workings of the Holy Spirit (John 15:11), and to participate in the new reality of belonging to the Christ. Thus, in relation to the law, the new state of God's grace is a radical new condition of freedom (*eleutheria*), a liberated state in the sense that an older master (the law) is exchanged for the good graces of a newer, greater master (the gospel image of the crucified Christ). Seen in this way, "the ones who are troubling you" are guilty of serving up distractions, and, because their exhortations can never be any more than distractions, they work against the new state of relative freedom entailed by the gospel. Recall 5:1 and its clarion import: "It is for freedom (*eleutheria*) that the Christ has set us free; therefore stand fast and do not place yourselves again in a yoke of slavery."

And what kind of freedom does Paul mean? Is he speaking of freedom solely as it relates to the law, to what some might suppose is the believer's release from any standing obligation to observe the minutiae of the law? If by means of the gospel we are called to freedom, how shall we characterize this freedom in relation to the law? On the one hand, when addressing what he means here by freedom, Paul will in part touch upon the concepts and standards relevant to the current crisis in the Galatian churches: the whole question of the law's relevance vis-à-vis the role of faith as stipulated by his gospel. But, on the other hand, he will also approach the issue of Christian freedom in terms that do not entail a wholesale abrogation of the law, but rather seek to raise the concept of the law to that new level foretold by the prophet Jeremiah in 31:31-34 (RSV):

> "Behold, the days are coming, says the LORD, when I will make a new covenant with the house of Israel and the house of Judah, not like the covenant which I made with their fathers when I took them by the hand to bring them out of the land of Egypt, my covenant which they broke, though I was their husband, says the LORD. But this is the covenant which I will make with the house

XV. Walking Bodily In The Spirit (5:13-24)

of Israel after those days, says the LORD: I will put my law within them, and I will write it upon their hearts; and I will be their God and they shall be my people. And no longer shall each man teach his neighbor and each his brother, saying, 'Know the LORD,' for they shall all know me, from the least of them to the greatest, says the LORD; for I will forgive their iniquity, and I will remember their sin no more."

In short, Paul will claim that the gospel and the law of love that undergirds it are the perfection of the Mosaic law precisely because they are the latter's true content.

5:13 marks the beginning of a crucial passage in Paul's letter because so far his arguments against the circumcision party have sought to defend the primacy of faith against any attempt to reassert the necessity of circumcision or the observation of Torah. If faith's part is what he claims it to be, if it truly plays the role his gospel assigns to it, and if the gift of the Holy Spirit is its manifestation, then he must say something about that faith and why he equates it with freedom. Keep in mind Paul's appeal to scripture in 4:21-31, and the way that he re-interpreted the traditional Jewish equation of freedom with obedience to the law. The latter conception had viewed Abraham's true children as free, i.e. as true members of the covenant-family of Israel, to the extent that they were observant of the law.[1] Paul's opponents argued that belonging to the messianic community built around the Christ Jesus was still predicated on being circumcised and following the law's commandments.[2] It was only in this way that the Galatians could reckon themselves as free sons of Abraham and thus full recipients of God's original promise to the patriarch. Paul's re-interpretation stood both the traditional Jewish understanding and the derivative stance of his opponents on their heads by equating freedom with faith's unconditional trusting in the sacrificial death of Jesus on the cross.

---

[1] A point of view still evident in James 1:22-25.
[2] Paul Nadim Tarazi, *The New Testament: An Introduction, Volume I: Paul and Mark* (Crestwood, New York: St. Vladimir's Seminary Press, 1999), 32-33.

When Paul tells the Galatians that they "have been called to freedom," it is as much a summons as a cautionary warning. In effect he is telling them, "Just because I have told you not to regard the law as being what determines your relationship to God and to his anointed one, Jesus of Nazareth, do not take that as an open invitation to practice your own version of moral nonchalance, or to assume that one is free to make it up as he goes along with plenty of personal leeway." To the contrary! Even though they have been called to freedom, it does not equal an absolute state of freedom vis-à-vis the law. Rather, by insisting on the necessity of a faithful trusting in the crucified Christ as preached by him, Paul reveals the way in which he retains the law for the sake of what God now wishes us to know about it. He has already made it abundantly clear to the Galatians in 5:5-6 that this does not translate to behaving in an openly *unlawful* manner:

> *5 For it is by the Spirit that we are eagerly hoping for the righteousness on the basis of faith,*
> *6 because it is in the Christ Jesus that neither circumcision nor uncircumcision amounts to anything,*
> *but rather what does matter is faith activated by means of love.*

What makes for the relative condition of this freedom, what establishes its true context, is the more fundamental condition of "faith activated by means of love." But our faith in Jesus as the Christ means that our relationship to God is not directly founded on the premise of obedience to the law. The gospel declares faith to be the new covenant terms between God and man, but yet, at the same time, it is virtually impossible for there to be a gospel without the law, and, perhaps, most revealingly of all, it is equally impossible for there to be the law without the gospel. This is why Paul declares in 5:6 that, if "neither circumcision nor uncircumcision amounts to anything," then "what does matter is faith activated by means of love." If what flatly "does not matter" is the relative condition of circumcision or uncircumcision, then what is more important, more necessary, and more decisive than any physical mark in the flesh is the

XV. Walking Bodily In The Spirit (5:13-24)

believer's condition of faith. Here the understanding is that faith-as-love, when viewed in Paul's explicitly genealogical perspective, is rooted in what scripture declares about the nature of God's covenantal love. This is the Hebrew *hesed* (most often translated as *eleos* in Greek), what is rendered regularly in the RSV as "steadfast love." The implication is that God is always steadfast in pursuit of the love that must form the core of the covenantal relationship between him and the human family, the covenant that will constitute the "people" mentioned in Jeremiah 31:33. The ultimate expression of this love and the community-founding power it unleashes is found in the crucifixion of the Christ. The idea is that if God loves his people self-sacrificially, and has demonstrated it by the cross, then they are to love him comparably in return. Paul has already stated this dynamic in 2:19c-20: "I have been crucified along with the Christ; and so it is no longer I who live, but it is the Christ who is living through me, and what I am now living in the flesh I am living as a result of believing in the Son of God, who loved me and who gave himself on my behalf." In other words, if the law is about anything, Paul is asserting that it is about this.

The classic summary of this relationship is Deuteronomy 6:4-9, a passage that should be read in close conjunction with Jeremiah 31:31-34 and its vision of what will make for the "new covenant with the house of Israel and the house of Judah":

> "Hear, O Israel: The LORD our God is one LORD; and you shall love the LORD your God with all your heart, and with all your soul, and with all your might. And these words which I command you this day shall be upon your heart; and you shall teach them diligently to your children, and shall talk of them when you sit in your house, and when you walk by the way, and when you lie down, and when you rise. And you shall bind them as a sign upon your hand, and they shall be as frontlets between your eyes. And you shall write them on the doorposts of your house and on your gates."

The Deuteronomy quotation figures in the Synoptic gospel narratives about what shall be reckoned as the "great commandment." Of the three versions, Luke's gospel contains the most concise and for that reason hard-hitting account of God's expectation:

> And behold, a lawyer stood up to put him to the test, saying, "Teacher, what shall I do to inherit eternal life?" He said to him, "What is written in the law? How do you read?" And he answered, "You shall love the Lord your God with all your heart, and with all your soul, and with all your strength, and with all your mind; and your neighbor as yourself." And said to him, "You have answered right; do this, and you will live."

But what makes this an effective setting is the way it becomes a segue for presenting the parable of the Good Samaritan (Luke 10:30-37). What prompts the parable is the lawyer's (*nomikos*) query, "And who is my neighbor?" The lawyer's motive for asking is especially relevant here because we are told that he was "desiring to justify himself" (*thelōn dikaiōsai heauton*), literally, "wishing to declare himself righteous." In Luke 10:37, after the lawyer has ascertained which the three figures mentioned in the parable "proved neighbor to the man who fell among the robbers," Jesus tells the man, "Go and do likewise."

This is the scriptural didactic for Christian love. But love without the underpinning of the law, without a positive, interactive relationship with the law, is always in danger of becoming a maelstrom of prejudicial inclinations. In short, in the absence of divine indication in one direction of another, men tend to justify and to follow what they think they need and then correspondingly seek to justify that in their own minds. Under such circumstances, men freely imagine what is not so much the good as the desirable. When Paul tells the Galatians in 5:13 that they have been "called to freedom," in the same breath he warns them not to "use this freedom as an opportunity for the flesh, rather, by means of love be servants of one another." What exactly does Paul mean here by the term "flesh"? At first glance

XV. Walking Bodily In The Spirit (5:13-24)

it would appear that he is setting "freedom" in opposition to the "flesh," and that the "flesh" must be aided by the introduction of love's governing power. In addition, there is the popular American tendency to view the pursuit of strictly fleshly matters as being what more reliably defines freedom. Thus we need to be extremely careful because this word down through the centuries it has acquired a range of connotations and associations that have not always been useful or even relevant in relation to what Paul is arguing here. The Greek word for "flesh" is *sarx*, and we must first establish what Paul means by the term, and this will require some digression on the subject of biblical anthropology.

People always make assumptions about who they are and why they are who they are. This means that we are guided by certain presuppositions about our origins, about the shape of human nature, about why we think, behave, believe, or feel the ways we do. Our own age is no different in this respect, and there remain plenty of competing models of human behavior, different philosophical schools and ideologies that range across the entire spectrum of available assumptions about what makes us human and why. Of the distinctively modern ideas, these have in common a reliance on both the philosophical worldview and the corresponding findings of modern empirical psychology. What these philosophical-psychological models have in common is a strict mind-body dualism: this means that each person consists of two separable components—a rational, discursive mind that operates as part of his inner mental (and thus non-material) half; and a physical body which is a wholly materialistic, organic entity operating in a more or less machine-like manner. The standing problem associated with this dualism is specifying the exact nature of the relationship between the two parts: how separate is the immaterially conceived mind from our material body, or are they more closely related and interdependent than some may have supposed? This is the classic mind-body dualism of our time (a view not unknown in ancient times), and it dominates all of our modern assumptions about human nature.

This sort of mind-body dualism may not seem that far removed from what makes up traditional biblical anthropology. The latter is based on its own brand of dualism, with each human person consisting of two distinguishable parts. On the one hand, there is the created material human body (*sōma*), and, on the other hand, there is the God-breathed, intangible life-force (*psychē*) that animates it. Christian tradition, however, has placed great emphasis on the seamlessness of the human person, on what is held to be the indivisibility of our created being, that even though we formally distinguish body from life-force, these two elements together form what constitutes a single psychosomatic unity. In a word, our created integrity should precede any divisions we introduce. Comparatively speaking, this is perhaps a more unified view of human nature than what passes in many modern quarters, but yet what are we to make of this arguably more integrated duality found in the Bible? Is it not only more sensible, but also more defensible, than the stubborn dichotomy characterizing the modern point of view? Setting aside for the moment the issue of the relative cohesiveness of our human nature, we are still left with establishing just what Paul meant when he refers to the *sarx*.

Part of the problem with any consideration of biblical anthropology is that the scriptural terminology is not always used either consistently or even with uniform meanings. For example, the *sōma/psychē* unity is the classic biblical understanding of human personhood, but this becomes more problematic especially in the New Testament writings where certain passages have been interpreted to suggest a tripartite human nature consisting of body (*sōma*), life-force (*psychē*), and spirit (*pneuma*). The latter conception has gained a more recent currency in our popular culture, and, even though this is a description taken up and developed in some patristic writings, it does not represent the more basic scriptural picture of human nature. I will have more to say about the way we are to understand scriptural references to the "spirit" below.

XV. Walking Bodily In The Spirit (5:13-24)

In addition to these kinds of problems, there is also some standing confusion over the word *sarx* when it is conventionally translated as "flesh." Many would view it as being more or less synonymous with the word *sōma* (conventionally translated as "body"), but with the understanding that *sōma* pertains to the concrete fullness of our material body (in a way that more or less corresponds to our modern notion of the physical body), while *sarx* amounts to what the "flesh" *does by inclination* over and above its mere physical existence. At the popular level we have come to view the English word "flesh" as a collective name for our unbridled, appetitive nature, i.e. that curious bundle (fallen or otherwise) of impulses, instincts, inclinations, and drives that traditional ethical thought holds to be the raw materials of our human nature. If Paul explicitly refers to *sarx* instead of *sōma*, later Christian interpreters have clouded things by viewing *sarx* in unhelpfully figurative or fanciful ways. These amount to the positing of a supra-somatic tendency of the human body—when left to its own presumably fallen devices—to indulge itself at the expense of the person's allegedly higher faculties ("soul" and/or "spirit") by following its own lower inclinations.

This kind of *de facto* dualism—while characteristic of much Christian exposition and preaching down through the centuries—is not at all what Paul has in mind when he writes that, having been called to freedom, the Galatians should "not use this freedom as an opportunity for the flesh." In order to understand the import of 5:13, we should keep in mind the following considerations.

First, the freedom of which he speaks here is the conditional freedom of their now belonging to the Christ, of their status *tou Christou*, that is, of their new *identity* as belonging to the Christ just as the newly purchased/redeemed slave now belongs to the master who has acquired him. This identity is entirely a function of the Galatians hearing and accepting the gospel message. In short, God had everything to do with it while they brought nothing to the table except faith in hearing and obedience of heart.

Second, the acceptance of the gospel by the Galatians involved their entire person. It cannot be stressed too highly that Paul's point is not that each believer's *psychē* may have embraced the gospel message while his unruly *sarx* was perpetually at odds with anything that would diminish its own carnal autonomy. The whole point of the traditional biblical division between *sōma* and *psychē* was not that there were two component elements that we should matter of factly distinguish from each other, but rather, as far as the ancient was concerned, the human person was still very much a single integral being, a whole man before he was anything else, and that this was a modality of being that was incompatible with the schematic modernist image of the human being as an autonomous mind functioning as the "ghost in a machine." Man consisting more or less of *sōma* was the prevailing ancient understanding, and, given the wholesale integrity of being that it presupposed, it is the case that Paul's use of *sōma* was a way to refer to the *embodied* entirety of our person and not just to the purely material component of our nature. In other words, while it is true that there is a discernible life-force (*psychē*) animating each of us, it is also the case that any individual human being was more basically (if not concretely) regarded as not only having *soma*, but also being—quite literally—*sōma*. If the most immediate reality of any human being is understandable in terms of an overall *somatic* nature (we do, after all, have unambiguous physical boundaries), then such a scheme raises the question of how each "somatic unit" relates to God.

This is the consideration that allows us to see the Pauline differentiation of *sarx* from *sōma*: *sarx* is what designates *sōma* when the latter lives solely concerned with itself. Thus, when Paul uses the word *sarx* in chapter 5, he will be using it in shorthand fashion to designate the condition of any human person who exists isolated in his individual somatic being with

XV. Walking Bodily In The Spirit (5:13-24)

no reference to God. Recall how Paul has already employed the word *sarx* in exactly this fashion when in 2:15-16 he writes, "But we, who by nature are Jews and not pagan sinners, knowing that a man is not declared righteous on the basis of the works of the law but by means of the faithfulness of Jesus as the Christ, even we believed in Jesus who is the Christ, so that we might be declared righteous on the basis of the faithfulness of the Christ Jesus and not on the basis of the works of the law, because no man (*pāsa sarx*, literally "every flesh") is declared righteous on the basis of the works of the law." In general the ancient regarded our human nature in terms of it possessing a distinctive, indivisible wholeness, and this was because he had no compelling reason, theoretical or otherwise, to dissect our human being into component elements and to assign to each of them characteristic strengths and relative weaknesses.

Third, when Paul tells the Galatians that their newly found "freedom" of belonging to the Christ was not to be "an opportunity (*aphormē*) for the flesh," he is still speaking of the wholeness of our person in relation to the Christ, that all of our being—regardless of whether we wish to make the mistake of emphasizing body over the soul, or vice versa—was entirely a matter of our learning what it means to become "servants of one another…by means of love" (5:13).[3] Paul's language here is full of radical implication. The Greek for "be servants of one another" is *douleuete allēlois*, an imperative verb phrase that literally means "serve one another as slaves"—and the sole basis for our slave-service to each other is going to be a self-sacrificial love (2:20, 5:6). In the next verse he quotes Leviticus 19:18 in order to make it clear that the kind of love required of us shall

---

[3] The Greek word for "opportunity" in 5:13 is *aphormē*, a distinct lexical item in its own right, but given the way Paul wields it here, it functions as the metathesized opposite of the positive verb he used in 4:19 to express his concern for the Galatians that "the Christ might be formed (*morphōthē*) among you." Thus, Paul's warning in 5:13 serves to underscore linguistically the antithetical nature of what stems respectively from the flesh and the Spirit.

not be a conveniently blank slate on which we will be free to sketch love's visage as we please:

¹⁴ ὁ γὰρ πᾶς νόμος ἐν ἑνὶ λόγῳ πεπλήρωται,
ἐν τῷ· ἀγαπήσεις τὸν πλησίον σου ὡς σεαυτόν.

*¹⁴ For the entire law is fulfilled in one word,
in this very scripture, "You shall love your neighbor as yourself."*

To the contrary, the kind of love God expects us to exhibit will not be one of our own crafting, one that is reflective of transitory tastes or even shaped by strongly emotional prejudice; nor will it be the occasion for continuously evolving definitions of self-love. If we wish to know something about the nature of this love, then the best place to begin is by looking at the nature of the divine love as it is first made known in the Old Testament.

Paul is deliberate in his quotation of Leviticus 19:18 because the use of this scripture serves simultaneously an expansive and a restrictive purpose. If some find that Paul is vague or suggestive at this point, it is because he has something quite specific in mind while at the same time something fluid and open to the prompting that is God's own grace. First, there is the more expansive sense in which the Christian understanding of love will be one that goes beyond the mere letter of the Mosaic law; and second, there is at the same time the sober appreciation that one will not be free to make it up as he goes along, that it will not be automatically permissible for him to define Christian love in terms directly dictated by his time or culture and any of its reigning prejudices. In short, there is an astonishing circularity at work in Paul's dynamic understanding of Christian love. On the one hand, it is rooted ever so firmly in the traditional Hebrew notions of moral uprightness and communal affection, but, on the other hand, it sets off in new directions because it establishes a new basis for communal relationships, that is, one which is based on each member of the

XV. Walking Bodily In The Spirit (5:13-24)

messianic community belonging equally—and obediently—to the Christ.

We can assume that the original Christian communities that Paul founded in the Galatian region had most likely experienced some amount of controversy, division, and discord as a result of the incursions made by the circumcision party, and it is with such disputes as a backdrop that we can understand why he writes as he does in the following verse:

*¹⁵ εἰ δὲ ἀλλήλους δάκνετε καὶ κατεσθίετε,
βλέπετε μὴ ὑπ᾽ ἀλλήλων ἀναλωθῆτε.*

¹⁵ But if you would rather bite and devour one another, take care that you are not consumed by each other!

Verse 15 allows us to see how 5:13-15 forms its own thematic unit. Verse 14 is the natural center because it deals with what is most important in the "whole law" (*pas nomos*), namely, that "You shall love your neighbor as yourself." When 5:13 warns the Galatians about not "using this freedom as an opportunity for the flesh," he admonishes them to avoid the latter by "being servants of one another." This is counter-balanced in 5:15 where Paul describes what happens when the Galatians choose not to heed his gospel nor the scripture on which it rests. The two verses contrast what they will do to "one another." Each verse employs the third-person reflexive pronoun *allēlōn* ("each other"),[4] a detail that helps to depict in vividly contrasting ways the prospect of what one "flesh" will do to another "flesh" in two entirely different situations. What anchors the two scenarios is the scriptural rule found in 5:14. Verse 13 is thus what happens when the "whole law" is fulfilled, while verse 15 describes what happens when there is no obedience and, by implication, opportunity is made for the flesh.

---

[4] 5:14 uses the second-person singular reflexive pronoun *seauton* ("yourself") in the quotation from Leviticus 19:8.

Paul's point in 5:15 is that the recent squabbles are an affront not just to the presence and the peace of the Holy Spirit (the latter, he insists, is the validation of his preaching), but to what is the fulfillment of the same scriptural law on which the circumcision party had based its particular claims. Paul's proclamation of the gospel among the Galatians had established the peace of their shared faith, it had made possible the manifestation of the Holy Spirit's power in their common baptismal life, and, as he has argued, these things had nothing at all to do with circumcision's perceived necessity. Since the Galatians had presumably given themselves over to arguing among themselves precisely about that necessity, Paul is telling them that such bickering and the "consuming of each other's flesh" that it produces are nothing less than the negation of his gospel!

But what does matter? The gospel, of course! And if it is the gospel that matters, then the Holy Spirit should be the only legitimate focus for the Galatians. Any of their contending about circumcision and any other formal requirements of the law will have sabotaged both the extent and the depth of the peace that is the one indubitable sign of the Spirit, the eschatological here-and-now of God's presence. It is to the shared reality of faith's Spirit-based freedom that Paul now appeals in 5:16-18 when he expands on what he meant when in 5:13 when he spoke of his gospel as being the occasion for freedom:

^{16} λέγω δέ, πνεύματι περιπατεῖτε
καὶ ἐπιθυμίαν σαρκὸς οὐ μὴ τελέσητε.
17 ἡ γὰρ σὰρξ ἐπιθυμεῖ κατὰ τοῦ πνεύματος,
τὸ δὲ πνεῦμα κατὰ τῆς σαρκός,
ταῦτα γὰρ ἀλλήλους ἀντίκειται,
ἵνα μὴ ἃ ἐὰν θέλητε ταῦτα ποιῆτε.
18 εἰ δὲ πνεύματι ἄγεσθε,
οὐκ ἐστὲ ὑπὸ νόμον.

^{16} *And I am saying to you, that if you are walking in the Spirit, you shall not accomplish the wishes of the flesh.*
^{17} *For the flesh is arrayed against the Spirit,*

XV. Walking Bodily In The Spirit (5:13-24)

and the Spirit likewise against the flesh;
and since these things are set against each other,
you will end up not doing the things you intended.
¹⁸ But if you led by the Spirit,
then you are not under the law.

The crucial thing to note about this passage is the exact meaning of the opposition between the Spirit and the flesh. Recall that when Paul speaks of the "flesh" (*sarx*), he has in mind the entirety of our fallen human being. This means that the "flesh" encompasses the whole of our person, body and life-force, when it chooses to stand alone and without God. The point here is that, as fallen beings, our condition is a fundamentally rebellious one. We still remain creatures fashioned in the image and likeness of God, but, because our fallenness consists of our wishing to live without God, it is for this reason that Paul employs the term "flesh" to denote what makes up that circumstance. If the "flesh" designates the fullness of our living without God, then the "Spirit" serves to indicate the fullness of our living with God. Pay very close attention to what Paul says about the relationship between the flesh and the Spirit.

First, Paul stipulates that walking in the Spirit is a path different from our carrying out "the wishes of the flesh," and here some explication is required because this simple point is crucial to the whole of his letter. The verb used in 5:16a is *peripateō*, and it literally means to "walk about." Paul employs this verb repeatedly in his letters to describe the nature of our relationship with God, it being a verbal usage that goes back to the description of God's communion with Adam and Eve in the garden. In the Septuagint translation of Genesis 3:9-11 we read about how God "walked about" in the garden for what was a very specific purpose:

> And they [Adam and Eve] heard the voice of the LORD God as he walked about (*peripatountos*) in the garden in the afternoon; and they concealed themselves, both Adam and his wife, from the face of the LORD God there among the trees of the garden. And the

LORD God called Adam, and he said to him, "Adam, where are you?" And he said to him, "I heard your voice as you were walking about (*peripatountos*) in the garden, and I was afraid because I am naked, and I hid myself." *(translation my own)*

The purpose of this walking about was God's daily communion with his human pair, but the passage relates how, in the wake of the serpent's temptation and the pair's succumbing to sin, the nature of that relationship has changed. Instead of *freely* walking in the presence of God, Adam and Eve now *choose* to flee from that presence and to conceal themselves. The point here is that, scripturally speaking, this verb is henceforth used in connection with what characterizes the kind of "walking" relationship we have with God.

Second, on what will it be based? What will be the nature of the stride we take in relation to God? Will it be on his terms and thus reflect our obedience to his will, or will it reflect the narrowness of our fallen condition? This brings us to the second consideration contained in 5:16a, namely, how shall the Galatians walk with God? The answer is that they are to continue doing what they have been doing ever since Paul first proclaimed the gospel to them: they must keep walking "in the Spirit" (*pneumati*). This is another instance in the text of the instrumental dative, a common grammatical device in the Greek New Testament to indicate not only the mode or means by which something is done but also what makes the action/event possible. In this case, if the Galatians are going to walk with God, then it will be in accordance with the guidance of the Holy Spirit. It will not be according to the "wishes of the flesh" (*epithymia sarkos*) because, as we have seen, the "flesh" and all that it "wishes" is incapable of autonomously serving God in love and obedience. In other words, it is only by virtue of the Holy Spirit that fallen man is at all able to enjoy communion with God. Given the simple fact of our fallen condition, it will have nothing to do with any innate capacity or inward spiritual prowess on our part because Paul's understanding of this issue is uncompromising in its directness and simplicity. Communion

XV. Walking Bodily In The Spirit (5:13-24)

with God consists of our being able to call upon God *as Father*, that is, that only by faith, repentance, and baptismal dedication can we now enjoy the same relationship that Jesus has with God the Father. If Jesus is the Christ, if he is the crucified, resurrected, and glorified Son of God, then we too by virtue of the gift of the Holy Spirit will be able to participate in the faithful hoping for this same relationship: "And as proof that you are sons [on the basis of a similarly Abrahamic faith in God's promise fulfilled in his Christ], God has sent forth the Spirit of his Son into our hearts where the Spirit cries out, "Abba, Father!"—all so that you are no longer a slave, but rather a son; and if you are a son, then it is through God that you have been made an heir." (4:6-7)

It is the disposition of our fallen humanity to be arrayed against the will of God, and, as a result of its rebellious orientation, it will pursue only those things which its sense of self-sufficiency dictates and which it actively promotes in order to keep each of us in a state of captive attention. It is thus that Paul writes in 5:17 about the Spirit-less preoccupations of our fallen human nature: "For the flesh is arrayed against the Spirit, and the Spirit likewise against the flesh; and since these things are set against each other, you will end up not doing the things you intended." The point here is not that the flesh and the Spirit exist in a state of absolute and perpetual opposition, but simply that each is set against the other because each pursues things in accordance with its own fundamental orientation. Remember that the flesh was created to be *holy* flesh. Its original dedication was to have been the worship of God and thanksgiving. Its orientation was supposed to be toward God and fellowship in his kingdom. Toward that end, the Bible instructs us that we must submit to the Holy Spirit in order that we might learn how to walk in the freedom of the afternoon garden.

When Paul writes in 5:18, "But if you are led by the Spirit, then you are not under the law," he is telling the Galatians about a crucial aspect of the nature of the freedom already mentioned

(5:1,13) and which is theirs only as a result of belonging to the Christ. By contrast, the law, though holy and given by God, functioned as an external set of commands, and, as such, it was an outward discipline of the whole person. The only "proof" of faith is the Holy Spirit (what Paul argues from the beginning of chapter 3 until the letter's end), and thus, in the wake of the gospel's proclamation, everything turns on the conditional as it is stated here by Paul: "*if* you are led by the Spirit" (*ei de pneumati agesthe*), then you are subject to the new discipline whose purpose is to *create* the correct orientation of our person in the eschatological moment of the kingdom. So if, in accordance with the gospel's dynamic of freedom, "you are not under the law" (*ouk este hypo nomon*), then it is because the law—though not discarded or even rejected—is being laid aside in favor of God's direct action in our lives.

But if that is true, what has happened to the law's authority? Does it still apply to the Galatian believers in the way Paul's opponents argue, or is there some other basis for them to be declared righteous in the eyes of God? In 3:21-24 Paul outlines the transition from a law-centered basis (*ek nomou*) to one based on faith (*ek pisteōs*). He contends that the law does not give life because, if it did, then "righteousness would be on the basis of the law (*ek nomou*)" (3:21). What is important is the promise of God that "through [Abraham] shall all the nations be blessed," and his gospel argues that "the promise based on the faith (*ek pisteōs*) of Jesus the Christ" will "be given to the ones who believe" (3:22). The law was there to tutor the people until "we then might be declared righteous on the basis of faith (*ek pisteōs*)" (3:24), but no one is "declared righteous on the basis of faith" until Paul first preaches the gospel and it is trustingly received "on the basis of a hearing with faith" (*ex akoēs pisteōs*). Thus the freedom of which Paul speaks is not a freedom from the law *per se*, but rather it is what marks the believer's standing awareness that he is "free" with regard to the law's direct lordship in his life, indeed, that what henceforth defines how he exists is his "free" knowledge about who is the true lord of his life.

XV. Walking Bodily In The Spirit (5:13-24)

This is a delicately balanced moment in Paul's argument. One must be on guard not to fall into the trap of emphasizing one element (either the law or faith/freedom) at the expense of the other, or of mistakenly seeing the law as coming to an irretrievable end and being replaced by a self-styling attitude of unconditional spontaneity. There is certainly room in Paul's thinking for gaiety and inspirational latitude (the Holy Spirit, after all, is superior to what we ourselves devise in the name of spontaneity), but behind any expression of it there is always his sober concern that God be served in all things and that we should not resort to mistaking our personal inclinations and promptings for the express will of God. One of the reasons why the Christian Bible retains the Old Testament is that the law contained in it is relevant to the formation of our Christian consciousness. Obviously the ritualistic portions of the law will not function in precisely the same way as they did prior to the Christ, but now that we have heard the gospel, now that we have responded to it in faith, now that we live knowing that we belong to the Christ, it is only now that we can finally begin to understand what Jesus meant when in Matthew 5:17-18 (RSV) he declares to his disciples: "Think not that I have come to abolish the law and the prophets; I have come not to abolish them but to fulfill them. For truly, I say to you, till heaven and earth pass away, not an iota, not a dot, will pass from the law until it is accomplished." Collectively as the church and individually as believers, we are charged with discerning on the basis of scripture what is the guidance of the Holy Spirit, and with putting into practice what is the truly life-giving expression of God's love for his creatures. So where does this leave us in relation to the law? Are we to conclude that "being led by the Spirit" entails jettisoning the law's moral vision, in effect wiping the slate clean, so that we might prepare ourselves to follow the Spirit in what will be a continually evolving social and ethical praxis? Does this mean careening into some variety of antinomian laxity? Does it require a disdainful revisionism where traditional morality is concerned? No, it does not necessarily mean any of those things, and, if we are truly "led by the Spirit" (the Greek verb here is in the passive voice!), then let none of these outcomes be our fate as we seek to avoid ministering to each other in arrogance, complacency, or presumption.

Does Paul in any sense correlate the law with the flesh? Is there any way in which there is something like a direct connection between the two? I would answer in the positive by saying that perhaps only in the sense that the law consists of the practical provisions for dealing with the reality of sin. When Paul speaks of the "wishes of the flesh" in 5:16, he is referring to those appetites that do not have God's blessing and which originate in the God-less flexing of the self. It was the purpose of the law to instruct us, not just about sin and its nature, but about how God would one day bless all the peoples of the world: "the law had become our tutor (*paidagōgos*) concerning the Christ in order that we might then be declared righteous on the basis of faith. But the coming of faith we are no longer under a tutor: because all of you are sons of God by means of the faith whose content is the Christ Jesus." (3:24-26) If the law did serve to teach us about the nature of sin, one of the premier lessons contained in that instruction was that, just as sin consists of actions, that is, individual bits and sequences of behavior and their accompanying levels of awareness, so too does faithful obedience to God consist of the "works of our hands." This point needs to be kept fully in mind when looking at what Paul next does in 5:19-23.

Recall that in 5:17 Paul makes it clear that, whether it is a matter of the flesh or of the Spirit, what matters is *what we do*, and here "what we do" comprises all that we think, feel, say, or do in relation to either force. Paul underlines this point when, in connection with the conflict between the flesh and the Spirit, he writes that "and since these things are set against each other, you will end up *not doing* the things you intended." This means that good and evil, virtue and sin, righteousness and wickedness, are actions just as much as they are impulses or inclinations. Given that our universal human condition is a fallen one, a state in

XV. Walking Bodily In The Spirit (5:13-24)

which we—by ourselves—are powerless over sin, this means that there will be a fundamental difference between the "the wishes of the flesh" and those of the Spirit, and the difference here is precisely one of *origin*.

This difference in origin will account for the language Paul uses in the two lists that constitute 5:19-23. If the flesh and the Spirit are the names Paul is using for the two different modalities of human behavior—with the flesh standing for human action with no reference to God, and the Spirit being the designation for genuinely God-directed behavior—then we will be able to recognize either modality based on which behaviors are exhibited. Here is the entire passage:

> [19] φανερὰ δέ ἐστιν τὰ ἔργα τοῦ σαρκός,
> ἅτινά ἐστιν μοιχεία, πορνεία, ἀκαθαρσία, ἀσέλγεια,
> [20] εἰδωλολατρία, φαρμακεία, ἔχθραι, ἔρις, ζῆλος,
> θυμοί, ἐριθεῖαι, διχοστασίαι,
> αἱρέσεις,
> [21] φθόνοι, φόνοι, μέθαι, κῶμοι,
> καὶ τὰ ὅμοια τούτοις,
> ἃ προλέγω ὑμῖν, καθὼς προεῖπον
> ὅτι οἱ τὰ τοιαῦτα πράσσοντες βασιλείαν θεοῦ οὐ κληρονομήσουσιν.
> [22] ὁ δὲ καρπὸς τοῦ πνεύματός ἐστιν ἀγάπη, χαρά, εἰρήνη,
> μακροθυμία, χρηστότης, ἀγαθωσύνη, πίστις,
> [23] πραΰτης, ἐγκράτεια·
> κατὰ τῶν τοιούτων οὐκ ἔστιν νόμος.

> *[19] Now the doings of the flesh are evident ones,*
> *they being adultery, fornication, uncleanness, lewdness,*
> *[20] idolatry, sorcery, hatred, contentions, jealousies,*
> *outbursts of wrath, selfish ambitions, dissensions,*
> *heresies,*
> *[21] envy, murders, drunkenness, revelries,*
> *and the things that are like them;*
> *concerning them I am warning you just as I warned you before—*
> *that the ones who practice such things will not inherit the kingdom of God.*
> *[22] But the fruit of the Spirit is love, joy, peace,*
> *patience, kindness, goodness, faith,*

²³ *gentleness, self-control;*
and the law has nothing against them.

The first thing to notice is the different way Paul introduces each list. Initially there are the "doings of the flesh," followed by the "fruit of the Spirit." The description in each case is deliberate and telling. The first list in 5:19-21, the longer of the two, is a veritable table of contents for what the flesh does when it is left to its own devices. Remember that the flesh *by itself* is neither evil nor depraved, but the flesh *by itself* is doomed to wander in the direction of selfish desire and potentially destructive conduct. Each of the things Paul places in this list is a result of what happens when the individual person is the only available horizon, when there is nothing which might stand higher than the self, when there is no sense of being accountable in any way either for what one wants or what one does. These constitute the "doings of the flesh," literally, its "works" (*erga*), and it is clear from the text that Paul has spoken to the Galatians before about such matters and what they mean. In 5:21 he makes the crucial declaration that "the ones who practice such things will not inherit the kingdom of God." Notice here that Paul speaks of "the ones who practice such things" (*hoi ta toiauta prassontes*), and the choice of verb is significant. The verb *prassō* connotes habitual action, what one chooses to do on a regular basis (our English word "practice" derives from it), and this must be distinguished from *poieō*, the more regular Greek verb for action. What Paul wishes to stress here is that the Galatians cannot abide in such behaviors, and, if they do, then they are putting themselves at the greatest possible risk where their belonging to the Christ is concerned, and here *the loss of one's identity in Christ is described in terms of not inheriting the kingdom of God*. 5:21 is the only place in his letter where Paul employs the phrase "kingdom of God" (*basileia theou*), and here it serves as a parallel way to describe the convert's identity in the Christ. 4:6-7 is once again relevant to Paul's argument: "And as proof that you are sons, God has sent forth the Spirit of his Son into our hearts where the Spirit cries out, "Abba, Father!"—all so that you are no

XV. Walking Bodily In The Spirit (5:13-24)

longer a slave, but rather a son; and if you are a son, then it is through God that you have been made an heir." This means that, if you belong to the Christ, if you are *tou Christou*, then you are charged with being obedient to his will and conducting yourself in accordance with the things that typify the behavior of a subject who belongs to and is representative of the kingdom of God. The man whose identity consists of belonging to the Christ will be recognizable on the basis of *what he does*, but what he does will not be a matter of his own doing, rather it will be reflective of the continually unfolding grace that is the interplay of faith, obedience, and perseverance. Thus the kingdom of God is not a club, but rather a consistency of conduct.

This is the reason why Paul declares the second list to be the "fruit of the Spirit" (*karpos tou pneumatos*). Each is, if you will permit me the redundancy of expression, a charismatic gift. Each item in the list is the direct manifestation of God's indwelling presence and power in the believer's life. As such, none of what Paul lists in 5:22-23 is a "work" *per se*, but rather, each is the quiet miracle of God's presence, a case of the Spirit bearing action-based fruit in our persons despite our inclinations, and a reminder of what conduct must be evident in any person who truly belongs to the Christ. Why else would Paul assert in 5:23 that, when it comes to such things, "the law has nothing against them"? If the law is all about righteousness understood as obedience to the will of God, then whatever true fruit the Holy Spirit bears in those who believe is even more directly a matter of God's own righteousness manifesting itself.

We are now standing at what may very well be the point of the most radical implication in Paul's gospel. Up until now it has been easy to think in the conventional terms of faith as being something we believe because we assent to it, and that our mental subscription to the gospel, considered factually, is sufficient to establish our Christian identity. Part of the problem here is that what moves inwardly within us we all too readily consign to the working of our mind, and thus what God accomplishes in us through his word is all too often conceptualized and abstractly framed rather than being seen as a moment of God's subjectivity. In other words, if the Holy Spirit moves within us, we waste no time corralling this action and domesticating it, making it subject to some of the other forces which command us at the more selfish levels of our being. There is an unmistakable inner urgency that characterizes the Pauline gospel, indeed, one could say that this urgency is what is most essential about it. But without this urgency and all that it entails—the shock, the confrontation, the challenge, the surrender, the conversion, the transformation—indeed, if these things atrophy and no longer reoccur, then the crucified Christ avails us nothing.

Thus, when Paul speaks of the "fruit of the Spirit," he means just that: that these things are what the Holy Spirit himself accomplishes through us. They are what he makes possible for us to manifest by our actions, to make real in the moment-to-moment unfolding of what is an old time now made miraculously new, the eschatological advent and duration of a time when God is now king. There is an inescapable sense in which we must offer ourselves to the Christ every day, that we must take nothing—literally nothing—about our faith for granted because it is ultimately the only immediate measure of how much we belong to the Christ. If we belong to him, then the "fruit of the Spirit"—which, having originated initially in the Spirit, only secondarily becomes our "works"—these will be evident in our actions. But if we do not belong to him in any meaningful sense, then our actions (our immediately carnal, Spirit-less "works") will speak for themselves. Recall how Jesus, in a passage where he is addressing the gravity of "blasphemy against the Spirit" (Matthew 12:33, RSV), makes it clear that this is a decisive matter concerning either the presence or the absence of the Spirit: "Either make the tree good, and its fruit good; or make the tree bad, and its fruit bad; for the tree is known by its fruit." If a tree's fruit (*karpos*) is good, then it is not because the "tree" *has* the Holy Spirit. To the contrary, if a tree's

XV. Walking Bodily In The Spirit (5:13-24)

fruit is good, it is only because the tree has *done* what the Holy Spirit commands, and thus it is only in this sense that it *belongs* to him. The issue of who belongs to whom, and, by extension, of who possesses whom, is a critical one and it colors the rest of what Paul says in his letter.

What is necessary here is a real precision of understanding, a consistently maintained view of how grace operates. A Christian often falls into the habit of speaking about grace in terms of his having *received* it, but, more properly, if his experience is one involving the gift of grace, then that grace is available only because God has granted it. In short, *we do not have grace, God gives grace*. And if, by virtue of the gospel and our obedience to it, we belong to the Christ, then, as the proof of our new identity, we will come to experience the grace of the Holy Spirit in our lives and *only* it will transform us. In 5:24-25 Paul writes:

²⁴ οἱ δὲ τοῦ Χριστοῦ Ἰησοῦ τὴν σάρκα ἐσταύρωσαν
σὺν τοῖς παθήμασιν καὶ ταῖς ἐπιθυμίαις.
²⁵ εἰ ζῶμεν πνεύματι,
πνεύματι καὶ στοιχῶμεν.

²⁴ *And those who belong to the Christ Jesus have crucified the flesh along with its passions and desires.*
²⁵ *If we are going to live by the Spirit,*
let us also conform ourselves to the Spirit.

Here Paul's language could not be more explicit: he speaks of those "who belong to the Christ Jesus" (*hoi tou Christou Iēsou*), and, because they "belong to the Christ Jesus," then they "have crucified the flesh." What does it mean to crucify the flesh? It means that, because of the believer's new identity in the Christ, then he is in the process of putting to death that which had hitherto ruled over him, his old master, all the fallen energies and inclinations, the former delusions and casual conclusions that, because they aimed at anything other than God, constitute the raging autonomy of the self. It is a strict either/or proposition: either you belong to the Christ, and thus pursue self-control in accordance with the Christ as your new master; or you do not belong to him, and let all the old governing habits of carnality continue unabated.

But have we not heard this kind of language before? Indeed we have in 2:18-20, and that key passage is worth repeating in full in order that we might see how much the two texts bear on each other:

¹⁸ For if I am building up again those things [the law] that I have taken apart,
then I prove myself to be a transgressor
¹⁹ because by means of the law I have died to the law
in order that I might live to God.
²⁰ I have been crucified along with the Christ;
and so it is no longer I who live,
but it is the Christ who is living in me,
*and what I am now living in the flesh (*en sarki*)*
I am living as a result of my believing in the Son of God,
who loved me and gave himself on my behalf.

In both passages Paul is writing about identification. In which terms do we see our identity? What establishes it, or, more precisely, *who* establishes it? And if, in response to the gospel, we reckon the Christ as our new master, then we belong to him, and if we belong to him, then we will share in all that happens to him. If he walks in righteousness, then so shall we. If he is the light of the world, bringing light to those who walk in darkness, then so shall we. If he is crucified for the sake of God's righteousness because a lesser, man-made righteousness could not bear the sight of him, then so shall we. If he has been raised from the dead by God in power, then so shall we. And if he sits at the right hand of God in the glory of his kingdom, then so shall we. This is what Paul means in 2:20 when he writes, "I have been crucified along with the Christ; and so it is no longer I who live, but it is the Christ who is living through me," and here the implications are not so much mystical as they are an illuminating description of the raw, practical reality of the believer's new identity in the Christ. If you belong to the Christ, then, in any narrowing sense of the word, is it ever about you? What are we

XV. Walking Bodily In The Spirit (5:13-24)

really to expect in the most definite, concrete terms? If you belong to the Christ, then look to him for clues about what is in store for you.

In 2:19 Paul writes that "by means of the law I have died to the law," and this is because it is only in the light of the gospel that we can come face to face with how man's disobedience has generated the law's relative insufficiency, how it has a circumstantial inferiority dictated entirely by man's bondage to sin and death. The circumstance is a strictly relative one only because, if a man were actually able to fulfill the law, that is, to live in complete accordance with it, then, by definition, his life of obedient devotion to the law would enable him to be declared righteous. But, as Paul points out in 3:10-12 when he quotes Deuteronomy 27:26 to highlight Israel's failure to obey the whole of the law, the law was not to accomplish what God had already reserved for faith to achieve:

10 For as many as there are who live on the basis of the works of the law,
they are all living under a curse;
for it stands written,
"Cursed is every one who does not abide by all the things written in the book of the law, and do them."
11 And as it is evident that by the law no one is declared righteous before God, because "he who is righteous shall live on the basis of faith,"
12 for the law is not on the basis of faith,
rather, "he who does these things, by them shall he live."

The Christian believer must reckon with the sacrificial death of Jesus—the core of the gospel message—as being the single moment in human history when these standing tensions and impossibilities were confronted and overcome. When Paul states in 2:20 that "I have been crucified along with the Christ," he is speaking about how, by means of faith and the baptismal grace of the Holy Spirit, he too suffers an ongoing crucifixion. What must die in the believer is the "flesh," his carnal person who, because he lives at the beck and call of sin, is condemned to death because by himself he is unable to muster life. Recall that

Jesus was crucified because his was a perfect righteousness, because he was the true Israel, because he was able to do what Israel had been unable to do, and his righteousness reached its zenith when he was hanging dead on the cross. When Jesus was crucified, he was carrying out the perfection of human flesh (*sarx*) through the crucifixion of its fallen attributes. What we know as "its passions and its desires" (*pathēmata* and *epithymiai*, respectively) denote the superficial, heteronomic manifestations of what are the underlying natural aspects and habits of our created being—these are what must be confronted and put to death in our own persons. To the extent that any of us belongs to the Christ, we must be engaged in a constant effort to "crucify the flesh" because, as the word of Paul's gospel makes clear to us, it is only by a dying that death can be overcome. Man dies apart from God because he sins apart from God, and man sins because he submits to the devil. It is the garden scene (Genesis 3) repeating itself countless times in every human life. But if we have given ourselves over to the Christ, then we no longer must fight on our own. Indeed, it is by the "energizing" grace of God (3:5) that we humans are able to pull off anything in the name of his Son. The strength we have, the hope we harbor, the obedience we manage, none of these things we accomplish on our own. This is because each is a moment-to-moment intrusion of grace that is heaven's victory over the rebellious self: it is the Holy Spirit who crucifies the flesh! Thus, when Paul writes in 2:20, "and so it is no longer I who live, but it is the Christ who is living in me, and what I am now living in the flesh I am living as a result of my believing in the Son of God," he is speaking of how the miracle of God's grace is also the concomitant miracle of the obedient faith to which he commends the Galatians.

XVI. Measuring Up to the Law of the Christ (5:25-6:10)

This whole dynamic, this continuous process of the disobedient self's dissolution and its restoration to an originally intended condition of obedient communion with God, all of this is effected by the Holy Spirit in what forms the believer's eschatological newness of life. The old has been put to death in what will be a continuous process of crucifixion: each defiant piece of us must die if we are going to belong to the Christ Jesus. No amount of human will accomplishes it, nor does any formal membership guarantee it. It only ever happens against our autonomy-craving will, that is, when we are led by the Spirit of God and not driven by our own inclinations (5:18). Let this therefore be stated with no hesitation: the guidance of the Spirit occurs when we hear, read, study, and conform ourselves to the written word of God. This concerns most directly the writings of the Old Testament, with which we can presume the Galatians had some familiarity, but what transmits this written word to them and cements it in a new scriptural edifice is the preached word of the Pauline gospel. The Apostle has contended all along that the irruption of the Holy Spirit among the Galatians has been entirely due to what he proclaimed to them (3:1-5, 4:6-7). It had nothing directly to do *per se* with carrying out the precepts of the law, and if they were now resorting to circumcision *ex post facto*, how were the Galatians to account for the fact that the Spirit had preceded the painful procedure? On this point Paul had challenged them most directly when in 3:5 he asks, "Therefore he who supplies the Spirit to you and who works might acts among you, does he do that on the basis of the works of the law or on the basis of a hearing with faith?" Thus, all that matters is the Spirit, and the Spirit comes but by one way. But does the Spirit effect all things with the believer on hand as a passive spectator? The gospel answers in the negative.

Paul indicates as much in 5:25 when he declares with a lapidary simplicity: "If we are going to live by the Spirit, then let us also conform ourselves to the Spirit." The Greek verb which I have rendered as "to conform oneself to something" is *stoicheō*, a word which connotes things being done in a natural and unforced manner. It is etymologically related to the "weak and impoverished elemental things (*stoicheia*)" mentioned in 4:9, but here the implication is clearly one of returning to our created being's original vocation, of our conforming at last to what we were supposed to have conformed all along. Do we do this on our own? Not at all! If we are able to "conform ourselves to the Spirit," it will have occurred solely on account of the divine gift of grace in our lives, i.e. when we surrender to the externality of God's will, and it is only in this way—in what is the way of the disciple—that we begin to discern our God-intended personhood. Nor is it as if there is a clean causality at work in 5:25 because the two clauses—"If we are going to live by the Spirit" and "then let us also conform ourselves to the Spirit"— describe two scenarios that continually interact and mutually reinforce each other. Their common purpose corresponds to the miracle of God's grace in the believer's life. They tell us about what forms the sole foundation for Christian discipleship and service (*diakonia*) to each other.

In John 12:23-26 (RSV) Jesus refers to this process of surrender, service, and the intertwining death that is our co-crucifixion with the Christ. Just as Jesus dies, to the law and to the world, to the whole span of fallen reality that is man's habitual domain, so too must the believer follow in the same footsteps, being the fruit as much as he is called to bring forth the fruit of the Spirit:

> And Jesus answered them [Andrew and Philip], "The hour has come for the Son of man to be glorified. Truly, truly, I say to you, unless a grain of wheat falls into the earth and dies, it remains alone; but if it dies, it hears much fruit (*karpos*). He who loves his life loses it, and he who hates his life in this world will keep it for eternal life. If any one serves me, he must follow me; and where I

XVI. Measuring Up to the Law of the Christ (5:25-6:10)   321

am, there shall my servant (*diakonos*) be also; if any one serves (*diakonē*) me, the Father will honor him.

To serve means to follow, both literally and figuratively, to be led by the figure of the shepherd/Spirit, just as Paul has already indicated in 5:18 when he writes about the necessity of our being "led by the Spirit." This means that ours must forever be a new behavior having the scriptural God as its sole point of reference. It is what Paul has in mind when, by way of the prefacing statement contained in 5:25, he begins to flesh out this new behavior—"If we are going to live by the Spirit, then let us also conform ourselves to the Spirit"—and he begins describing what these expectations are for the Galatians in 5:26-6:2, a passage whose importance is not always fully appreciated. Consider it with 5:25 introducing it:

²⁵ εἰ ζῶμεν πνεύματι,
πνεύματι καὶ στοιχῶμεν.
²⁶ μὴ γινώμεθα κενόδοξοι,
ἀλλήλους προκαλούμενοι,
ἀλλήλους φθονοῦντες.
¹ ἀδελφοί,
ἐὰν καὶ προλημφθῇ ἄνθρωπος ἔν τινι παραπτώματι,
ὑμεῖς οἱ πνευματικοὶ καταρτίζετε τὸν τοιοῦτον
ἐν πνεύματι πραΰτητος,
σκοπῶν σεαυτὸν μὴ καὶ σὺ πειρασθῇς.
² ἀλλήλων τὰ βάρη βαστάζετε
καὶ οὕτως ἀναπληρώσετε τὸν νόμον τοῦ Χριστοῦ.

²⁵ *If we are going to live by the Spirit,*
let us also conform ourselves to the Spirit.
²⁶ *Let us not take up vain kinds of glory,*
by challenging one another
or by envying each other.
¹ *Brothers and sisters,*
if a man is caught up in a certain transgression,
let you who are walking in the Spirit restore such a man
in a spirit of gentleness
while keeping a close eye on yourselves lest you be tempted.
² *Bear one another's burdens*

and in this manner you shall measure up to the law of the Christ.

First, Paul singles out what I have rendered in 5:26 as "vain kinds of glory" (*kenodoxoi*), and he exhorts the Galatians not to pursue those things that do not belong to living obediently to the Spirit. Second, he adds some specificity to his plea by attaching two participial phrases "by challenging one another or by envying each other." The term *kenodoxoi* is a revealing one because of (1) what it literally denotes, and (2) how it relates to the way Paul will treat the issue of boasting. It is a compound word consisting of the Greek words *kenos*, which means "vain" or "empty,"[1] and *doxa*, which means "glory" or "right belief."[2] Thus, a *kenodoxos* is a man who entertains an empty, conceited opinion about a matter. What he believes to be true might be admirably real in his own mind, but, in relation to what is actually true, it will never be anything more than a vain pretending. In this verse Paul is cautioning the Galatians not to "become" (literally) those who would be guilty of embracing "vain kinds of glory" (*mē ginōmetha kenodoxoi*). The implication is that his warning concerns not only what the circumcision party is advocating among them, namely, those ritual obligations which have done so much to divide the members of the Galatian churches and to sow profitless dissatisfaction among the believers, but that it also pertains to the overall depth and quality of their own life in the Spirit.

If one is tempted to embark upon a "challenging" mode and to seek out things in a way that unnecessarily provokes his neighbor (*allēlous prokaloumenoi*), then he is in effect putting to death the Holy Spirit. Why pursue circumcision and rancorously

---

[1] Paul also employs *kenos* in 2:2, where it more directly underscores the term's association with what is contrary to the will of God: " and I laid before them the gospel that I am preaching among the nations, but privately to those who were of reputation, lest in any way I should be running or had run in vain (*eis kenon*)." Here the larger context clearly supports the idea that whatever is at variance with the "truth of the gospel" (2:5) is an empty, vain supposition.

[2] The "vain kinds of glory" (*kenodoxoi*) pursued by men stand in permanent contrast to the true "glory" (*doxa*) that men owe exclusively to God (1:5, 1:24).

XVI. Measuring Up to the Law of the Christ (5:25-6:10)   323

insist upon it when the "fruit of the Spirit" is more immediately needful and truly life giving? In addition, how is the Spirit to be served and allowed to bear fruit in the community if its members are motivated by a spirit of envious and divisive regard for each other (*allēlous phthonountes*), that is, if circumcision is presented as being commendable in itself, and controversy over this question divides the church? Circumcision aside, what good does it do the believer if he imagines that the Holy Spirit distributes himself differentially? Paul's point is that, with or without the circumcision party and its agenda, the Galatians are not to pursue what originates in human vanity and stems from an egocentric sense of self-importance.

The mounting seriousness of Paul's exhortation in this passage should not be passed over lightly. In 5:25 he has baldly asserted, "If we are going to live by the Spirit, let us also conform ourselves to the Spirit," and thus he means that the only legitimate criterion for Christian conduct is what identifiably originates in and belongs to God's own Spirit. Paul's standard for encountering the Spirit is a double-track affair: (1) the believer only receives the Spirit via the scriptural and/or preached word about God's will, and (2) the believer conforms himself to the Spirit when he obeys the content of that word. Strictly speaking, anything that falls outside of such a boundary is illegitimate, and, as he has indicated, it will end up being no more than a vain form of self-pride. In 6:1 Paul gives some indication of the standing danger involved in the delicate dynamic of "conforming oneself to the Spirit":

> [1] *Brothers and sisters,*
> *if a man is caught up in a certain transgression,*
> *let you who are walking in the Spirit restore such a man*
> *in a spirit of gentleness*
> *while keeping a close eye on yourselves lest you be tempted.*

The key portion of this verse is the phrase I have translated as "you who are walking in the Spirit." The RSV is typical among English translations when it renders the text as "'you who are spiritual,"³ and here the Greek text *hymeis hoi pneumatikoi*, when literally translated, would support such a wording, but there is a crucially important point to be made here in connection with some of the mistaken assumptions underlying the ways in which we have come to employ the word "spiritual" and the erroneous conclusions that continue to result from it. This will require revisiting the subject of biblical anthropology.

Recall that basic biblical anthropology understands man as a whole being, consisting of a body (*sōma*) together with its animating life-force (*psychē*). While wholeness has been the consistent emphasis of the biblical vision of man, contrast must be made here with how classical Christian theology came to view mortal death. The latter elaborated an understanding of death as a cosmically unnecessary tragedy because it represented the sin-induced undoing of the uncomposite unity of man's original created being. Thus mortal death was dramatically pictured as our body and soul being ripped in two, a rupturing event that violated the seamlessly wrought perfection that man's created nature was supposed to represent. But the original scriptural view of death is not that—on some metaphysical level—death was not part of creation's design, but simply that men do die and that what matters is how men die *in relation to God*. What further complicates this picture for us is that, as noted earlier, to this basic polarity of body and "soul" is sometimes added a third element, "spirit" (*pneuma*), resulting in a tripartite view of man's nature: instead of body and soul, there is now a trio of body, soul, and spirit. The latter scheme has great currency in our popular culture which is now replete with references to man as a restless, creative, and retail consumption-oriented being consisting of those eagerly participating elements: body, soul, and spirit. But the elevating of *pneuma* (understood here strictly as lower-case "spirit") to the status of an integral element of our being is a corruption of the scriptural view of man's nature as

---

[3] The same rendering appears in the KJV ("ye which are spiritual"), NKJV, NIV, ESV, and NASB translations.

XVI. Measuring Up to the Law of the Christ (5:25-6:10)

consisting solely of the meager unity of his body and its animating force. When *pneuma* is added as a third constituent element in human nature, it is accorded a status that, biblically speaking, it neither possesses nor merits. Since we have already mentioned that the Bible's own usage of these terms can be occasionally misleading or hard to understand, just what are its references to *pneuma* supposed to mean? And, perhaps more directly, what are we as Christians really saying and implying when we employ our now encrusted terminology concerning the "spiritual"?

Contributing to this confusion is the fact that the term "spiritual" has taken on a referential life of its own apart from what can be justified either scripturally or even with reference to our own indulgent Orthodox Christian theological tradition. In its most widespread application, the word "spiritual" has come to denote things that are of a religious nature, and these are dualistically opposed to the non-spiritual realms of the worldly and/or the strictly material. The poverty of this usage is that what we in this fashion describe as the "spiritual" only receives the full measure of its meaning when it is contrasted (explicitly or otherwise) with its dichotomous other, those *non-spiritual* things that lie outside the domain of the religious proper. Further complicating this picture is the role played by Western civilization's own legacy of classical culture and humanism, how the latter have been rich sources for our now omnipresent references to the power and durability of the "human spirit." Thus modern man speaks freely of this *human spirit* as being an integral part of his nature, and he has no difficulty regarding it as a constituent element within each of us. Regardless of whether we are praising its essential durability or its potential elasticity, its predictability or its adaptability, if we are emphasizing it as what we have in common or as what sets us individually apart, we fully assume that each of us is in possession of this indomitable, surging spirit to which our culture readily refers. Yet, even though it might make—strictly in other contexts—for a wonderfully poetic and inspiring image, *there is, biblically speaking, no such thing as the human spirit.*

Instead of a putative human spirit, there is only the simple wholeness of our created being and its inevitable orientation—whether positive or negative—with respect to God. The biblical language about what would appear to be a human *pneuma* is not a reference to a true structural element within our created being. Rather, its scriptural usage has more to do with the *mode* in which we choose to live, in this case, either in communion with God or not. To be in communion with God means to live in a *spiritual* mode, and the clue here is Paul's use of the adjective *pneumatikos*, a term which lets us see that it is the Holy Spirit who is the only operative element here. If we are oriented toward God and seek to do his will, then how we behave (and whether we actually do his will or not) will be strictly a matter of the Holy Spirit operating within us, of our behaving Spirit-ually because he is the sole source of our "walking" behavior. Being *pneumatikos* is not what we are, but entirely a matter of *what we do*.

Thus, when Paul writes in 6:1 of the *hoi pneumatikoi* (literally, "the spiritual ones"), he is referring to those "who are walking in the Spirit" by virtue of their faith and a demonstrable obedience to the proclaimed word of God. Therefore, when it is assumed that there is an inherent "spiritual" element within our human nature, one that exists with its own structural autonomy apart from God, one that does not necessarily depend upon God to receive the gift of his Holy Spirit in order to manifest "spiritual" qualities, then the stage is set for all manner of potential delusion and pretension. Simply put, if our actions manifest the truth and the power of God, then we are walkers in his Holy Spirit, and in no biblically justifiable sense of the word are we ever "spiritual" persons as if that in any way meant that we personally possess some special status and/or a definable skill on our part, one that is in any way separate from the Spirit. All of what the Holy Spirit accomplishes in us and through us is a gift, and never an accomplishment. It is for the same reason that the word

XVI. Measuring Up to the Law of the Christ (5:25-6:10)

"spirituality" should be avoided at all costs: it shifts attention away from God and refocuses it on our person and the context it freely constructs for itself.

Paul writes as he does in 6:1 because he clearly has something other than self-regard in mind. "If a man is caught up in a certain transgression," that is, if a man is overwhelmed by sin and lacks any apparent means to resist it, then "let you who are walking in the Spirit restore such a man in a spirit of gentleness." Such an intervention is only possible because the Holy Spirit is his own motivator and grants clarity, compassion, and consideration to him who believes and submits to cooperate with God's work. How shall such work proceed? It will be "in a spirit of gentleness" (*en pneumati prautētos*) that God's own Spirit will manifest himself and that will unmistakably characterize the work of restoring each other from sin (keep in mind that "gentleness" ranks as one of the Spirit's "fruits" in 5:23). The Greek word translated here as "gentleness" is *prautēs*, and it denotes not only gentleness, but also those closely related qualities of humility and modesty. When all things are done in love, in a gentle spirit of humility, then the believer, when he endures the full weight of this modesty, will be able to administer the peaceful appeal to the sinner's situation. But, even though the believer conducts himself in a "spirit of gentleness," he is no pushover because his behavior, when rooted in the Spirit, will be as much a matter of boldness as it is of humility, as much a state of relaxation before God's power as it is a state of alertness to what is unfolding. It is this keen awareness of the divine dynamism which lies behind what Paul is writing here to the Galatians because, when the sinner's restoration is carried out in such a "spirit of gentleness," that is, when grace truly is a grace-*full* event, then it will have been because all compassion, all shared healing, indeed, all boldness in the face of sin and evil will have taken place "while keeping a close eye on yourselves lest you be tempted." How will he who "walks in the Spirit" be tempted?

There is for any believer a standing temptation not to give God the glory. When God's power makes it possible for him to accomplish something, the believer may very likely experience a not so fleeting inclination to regard it as being in some way his achievement, a deed made possible, not through God's grace or providential mercy, but by virtue of the believer's own charismatic power and his personal "spiritual" skills being brought into play. This combination of over-estimation and self-elevation is temptation's "fruit." When pride and personal delusion join forces to produce in our heart an inflated sense of ability and importance, this is no less than the devil's easily acceptable coaxing that whatever we touch turns into a "spiritual" gold and will result in some well-deserved glory being brought to our names. This dangerously mistaken assumption—the too often self-referential language of "spiritual" gifts—belongs to the category of the *kenodoxa* (literally, the "empty glory" corresponding perfectly to our own English word "vainglory") to which Paul refers in 5:26. The stipulated "spirit of gentleness" (characterized by discernible amounts of modesty and humility) directly concerns the relative inward balance and awareness of the believer as much as it does a compassionate focus on the needs of the brother suffering in sin. In 6:2-5 Paul expands on our awesome responsibility before the Holy Spirit:

²ἀλλήλων τὰ βάρη βαστάζετε
καὶ οὕτως ἀναπληρώσετε τὸν νόμον τοῦ Χριστοῦ.
³εἰ γὰρ δοκεῖ τις εἶναί τι
μηδὲν ὤν,
φρεναπατᾷ ἑαυτόν.
⁴τὸ δὲ ἔργον ἑαυτοῦ δοκιμαζέτω ἕκαστος,
καὶ τότε εἰς ἑαυτὸν μόνον τὸ καύχημα ἕξει
καὶ οὐκ εἰς τὸν ἕτερον·
⁵ἕκαστος γὰρ τὸ ἴδιον φορτίον βαστάσει.

² Bear one another's burdens
and in this manner you shall measure up to the law of the Christ.
³ For if anyone thinks himself to be something
when he is nothing,
he is deluding himself;

XVI. Measuring Up to the Law of the Christ (5:25-6:10)

⁴ but let each one test the mettle of his own work,
and only then will he have cause to boast in himself
and not in another.
⁵ For each man will have to bear his own load.

In 6:2 Paul provides the direct context for Christian charity. First, that we should be concerned with the welfare of others, not just for their material circumstances, but for their relative healthiness before God, their overall fitness in the faith. The kind of solicitude that this entails is one that, if genuinely founded in the Spirit, transcends the gossipy preoccupation with the affairs of others and shall have no trace of condescension about it. It will be compassionate love in a pure form, the sympathetic willingness of the believer to expend himself for the sake of his brother and solely for the latter's benefit. This is the Christian *agapē*, the believer's inner orientation of "faith activated by means of love" (5:6), which is put to service for answering the needs of others and working for peaceful correction. The "activation" to which Paul refers is the both the work and the result of the Holy Spirit: "For by the Spirit (*pneumati*) we are eagerly hoping for righteousness on the basis of faith, because in the Christ Jesus neither circumcision nor uncircumcision amounts to anything, but rather what does matter is faith activated by means of love" (5:5-6). Here, in a nutshell, is the simple progression of salvation through the gospel: Spirit—faith—hope—love. The Holy Spirit presides over our faith in the gospel message, and, as the proper fruit of our obedient hope in the word of God, he instructs us in compassionate love, in the simple scriptural law of loving our neighbor as ourselves (5:14).

Second, it is thus that Paul can write of our mustering love for the sake of others as being that which will enable us to "measure up to the law of the Christ." Recall that love is the first "fruit of the Spirit" listed in 5:22, and that, together with the other elements included there, "the law has nothing against them" (5:23), a point which should make it easier for us to comprehend just what he has in mind when referring to the "law of the

Christ." By the old law's reckoning circumcision was a vital matter, but now neither it nor uncircumcision "amounts to anything" because a new law is incumbent upon us, the one that Jesus reiterates throughout the gospels: "A new commandment I give to you, that you love one another; even as I have loved you, that you also love one another. For by this all men will know that you are my disciples, if you have love for one another." (John 13:34-35, RSV) Paul has explicitly declared this in 5:14 when he quotes Leviticus 19:18: "For the entire law is fulfilled in one word, in this scripture, "You shall love your neighbor as yourself." If we are moved to concern for others by the Spirit's prompting and to do something for them under his guidance, then we are living in compliance with the "law of the Christ." Here the emphasis will be on doing what makes for this law's content, what will work to make manifest the lawful content of the "new commandment I give to you." Yet critical too is the believer's focused awareness of just what is happening and how.

When Paul writes of our being "tempted" while ministering to others "in a spirit of gentleness," he means that *as human beings*, even in the midst of God's very work, we are continually susceptible to imagining that we have played a far greater role in any of it than the more simple truth would warrant. This is why in 6:3-4 Paul sounds what is by now a familiar cautionary note: "For if anyone thinks himself to be something when he is nothing, he is deluding himself; but let each one test the mettle of his own work, and only then will he have cause to boast in himself and not in another." The familiarity consists of the way 5:25-6:5 echoes what Paul has already written in 2:1-10. The key item here is the Greek verb *dokeō* ("to suppose something subjectively about oneself or others"), and it links the two passages.

First, in both cases Paul is addressing the issue of authority in the church vis-à-vis his gospel. In chapter 2 he writes of going to Jerusalem to "[lay] before them the gospel that I am preaching among the nations, but privately before those who were of

XVI. Measuring Up to the Law of the Christ (5:25-6:10)

reputation (*tois dokousin*), lest in any way I should be running or had run in vain." These men of reputation were "James and Kephas and John, the ones who were reputed to be pillars (*oi dokountes styloi einai*)" (2:9). In 2:6 Paul further emphasizes what can only be their relative authority in relation to his gospel: "And from the ones who were reputed to be something (*tōn dokountōn einai ti*), and what they were is of no consequence to me—God does not go by appearances—these men who were of repute (*oi dokountes*) added nothing to me." Paul repeats this idea of the insufficiency of any strictly human authority in 6:3 when he writes, "For if anyone thinks himself to be something (*dokei tis einai*) when he is nothing, he is deluding himself." In other words, the only genuine (and therefore authoritative) nexus for God's power and the working of the Holy Spirit is the preached word concerning it. Attributing it to anything other than that runs the risk of chalking up one more "vain kind of glory" (*kenodoxa*, 5:26). The phrase "to be something" (*tis/ti einai*) appears in both 2:6 and 6:3, and in each case the clear implication is the pitfall posed by any inflationary sense of importance.

Second, this relative "nothingness" of human supposition appears in both 2:6 and 6:3 in the form of the Greek negative pronoun form *ouden* (or its equally negative variant *mēden*). In 2:6 it appears twice: "And from the ones who were reputed to be something, and what they were is of no consequence (*ouden*) to me—God does not go by appearances—these men who were of repute added nothing (*ouden*) to me." In 6:3 it appears in the variant form *mēden*: "And if anyone thinks himself to be something when he is nothing (*mēden ōn*), he is deluding himself."

This is a standing danger for any believer because the opportunities for this kind of delusion are limitless. Sometimes we are quick to take credit for what God alone accomplishes among us. We forget that, first and foremost, we are never more than the instruments for the execution of his will in the world. When we lose sight of that basic fact, then we turn ourselves into candidates for what can only ever be a harmful self-delusion, that of "thinking ourselves to be something when we are nothing." The point here is not that there is an inherent worthlessness about our person vis-à-vis the workings of the kingdom of God. To the contrary, if the Holy Spirit is actively guiding our actions, then it will be due in part to that cooperative role we have to play in the unfolding of God's grace. This is the standing charismatic wonder of God's power.

It will be charismatic because grace is forever a gift and never a possession. It is a wonder because, when it does occur, it is always immediate in its implication. If we, as believers, lay exclusive claim to any of that either before or after the fact—whether to elevate ourselves in our own eyes or in the eyes of others—not only will we have been tempted, but we will have accepted the devil's invitation to "think ourselves to be something" when, comparatively speaking, "we are nothing." For the believer to realize this fully, for him to live in awareness of its implications, this requires his remaining soberly focused and living with ready mind and disciplined heart for what God needs from him at any given moment. It is not that he ranks as a dispensable element in the building up of God's kingdom here on earth. Rather, entirely to the contrary, his participation is absolutely crucial where Christian community is concerned. Paul is indeed concerned about the individual awareness that should accompany this personal participation, that essential degree to which the believer is ready to evaluate himself in any given situation.

In 6:4 he writes that "but let each one test the mettle of his own work, and only then will he have cause to boast in himself and not in another." This is a most serious point. It is the requirement for there to be an accompanying transparency in the believer's life—for truth of conviction, for depth of sincerity, for a determination to take nothing for granted where the working of God's will is concerned. Of what does "testing the mettle of one's own work" consist? If we have surrendered ourselves but

XVI. Measuring Up to the Law of the Christ (5:25-6:10)

have still fought, if we have believed without wavering, if we have contended with no thought of our own gain, then we will "have cause to boast in ourselves and not in another." But isn't this precisely what Paul would not have us do—for us to find a reason according to which we might credit ourselves for something that God has done? Not exactly. Paul's point is that if we have allied ourselves with the Holy Spirit, if we have served as his soldiers, if we have acted in selfless obedience to him, then, under those circumstances, a person can freely "boast in himself and not in another" because *only in that sense* will he have accomplished the good and helped to create the wonder. Thus the "boasting" of which Paul speaks is not a directly selfish boasting in oneself, rather it will be what underlies the believer's unruffled awareness that he has cooperated with a good infinitely greater than his person. This is why Paul adds in 6:5 that, "For each man will have to bear his own load." If each of us is directly responsible to God, if each of us is determined to conduct himself in accordance with a no-nonsense reckoning of God's actions and a personal awareness of them and compliance with them, then each of us will be doing all that is possibly required for the "bearing of one's own load."

But does the language in 6:5 about the bearing one's own load contradict what 6:2 says about the necessity of "bearing one another's burdens"? Not really, because when each of us is bearing his own burden, he is doing what is necessary to help keep the Spirit/self dynamic represented by his life alive and operating. If a man's outlook and behavior result from the Holy Spirit's guidance in his life, and when this bears fruit corresponding to that guidance, then the other people around him cannot help being affected by it. Paul is writing, in effect, about how "walking in the Spirit" amounts to an interlocking network of responsibilities and actions: first, if in the Holy Spirit we are obligated to each other, then that is only because, second, we are equally in the Holy Spirit directly responsible for ourselves. This is the gist of what Paul writes in 6:6-10, a passage in which he summarizes the awesome prospect of our joint responsibility before God and to each other:

> ⁶ κοινωνείτω δὲ ὁ κατηχούμενος τὸν λογον
> τῷ κατηχοῦντι ἐν πᾶσιν ἀγαθοῖς.
> ⁷ μὴ πλανᾶσθε,
> θεὸς οὐ μυκτηρίζεται.
> ὃ γὰρ ἐὰν σπείρῃ ἄνθρωπος,
> τοῦτο καὶ θερίσει·
> ⁸ ὅτι ὁ σπείρων εἰς τὴν σάρκα ἑαυτοῦ
> ἐκ τῆς σαρκὸς θερίσει φθοράν,
> ὁ δὲ σπείρων εἰς τὸ πνεῦμα
> ἐκ τοῦ πνεύματος θερίσει ζωὴν αἰώνιον.
> ⁹ τὸ δὲ καλὸν ποιοῦντες μὴ ἐγκακῶμεν,
> καιρῷ γὰρ ἰδίῳ θερίσομεν μὴ ἐκλυόμενοι.
> ¹⁰ ἄρα οὖν ὡς καιρὸν ἔχομεν,
> ἐργαζώμεθα τὸ ἀγαθὸν πρὸς πάντας,
> μάλιστα δὲ πρὸς τοὺς οἰκείους τῆς πίστεως.

> ⁶ *Let him who is instructed in the word*
> *share in all good things with him who instructs.*
> ⁷ *Do not deceive yourselves—*
> *for God is not to be mocked—*
> *it being true that whatever a man sows,*
> *this too he will reap.*
> ⁸ *For he who sows for the sake of his own flesh*
> *will on the basis of the flesh reap what corrupts;*
> *but he who sows for the sake of the Spirit,*
> *he will on the basis of the Spirit reap what lives.*
> ⁹ *And let us not grow weary when doing good,*
> *for in due season we shall reap if we do not lose heart.*
> ¹⁰ *So then, as we do have the opportunity,*
> *let us do good to all men,*
> *especially to those who are of the household of faith.*

I think that, even in Paul's own estimation, 6:6 could serve as a general description of what is incumbent upon the members of the Galatian churches. In the wake of his preaching the gospel among them, they became in effect a vast catechetical community divided, at any given time, into those who teach the

XVI. Measuring Up to the Law of the Christ (5:25-6:10)

word and those who are taught the word. This, however, did not necessarily refer to a strict division of labor, with clearly defined groups of catechizing teachers instructing equally distinct groups of catechumen-students. The distinction here is of a more general nature, and, given its mention in this context, it is Paul's way of referring to the *communal* reality of the Galatian churches. Thus, he "who is instructed in the word" could be *any* believer, any person who has heard the word of God and accepted it, and he should "share (*koinōneitō*) in all good things with him who instructs." Of course, he who is instructed in the faith by another will naturally stand in a dependent relationship with the instructor, but the "good things" which they are called upon to share go beyond materiality and involve what should be the mutualizing gifts and graces which comprise the "fruit of the Spirit" (5:22-23). 6:6 is about the sense of reciprocal obligation that should be the basis of any Christian community, namely, the awareness that none of us ever stops being a catechumen where either the content or the direction of our Christian faith is concerned. The real clue here is Paul's use of the verb *koinōneō* to indicate that this kind of "sharing" is what will be directly expressive of the call to Christian fellowship (*koinōnia*) contained in his gospel.

And about this undeniable circumstance—which is ultimately about the primacy of the Holy Spirit, indeed, what it is that corresponds to the very reality of the kingdom of God—none of us should be under any illusion. Paul underscores this point himself in 6:7-8 when he employs some highly pointed and by no means figurative language about the nature of this shared life in the Spirit:

> [7] *Do not deceive yourselves—*
> *for God is not to be mocked—*
> *it being true that whatever a man sows,*
> *this too he will reap.*
> [8] *For he who sows for the sake of his own flesh*
> *will on the basis of the flesh reap what corrupts;*
> *but he who sows for the sake of the Spirit,*

he will on the basis of the Spirit reap what lives.

Put most simply, we *are* what we *do*. If we live totally preoccupied with ourselves and driven by the shape of our immediate needs, if we live with the aim of satisfying those needs with the least amount of concern for others, and if we pursue life with no higher standard than what belongs to the moment or its accompanying impulses, then we cannot legitimately imagine that our conduct will have any trace of God in it. The deception here is entirely self-administered.[4] Paul's warning is about what limits this self-deception: it being the case that God "is not to be mocked," that is, we are not to imagine that we are free to calculate the extent of things in his absence, that we can apply our own yardstick, fashion our own rules, or abide by them simply because we feel like it. Quite the contrary! The rules are not our own, and what we do as individual persons never represents a uniquely exploratory moment in the search for "what feels right or good." This is why the last portion of 6:7, "it being true that whatever a man sows, this too he will reap," serves as an explanatory background for (1) the standing possibility that man will deceive himself about what is good and why, and (2) that the fullest possible accounting of God must be taken in our consideration of what belongs to the flesh and what belongs to the Spirit.

Man is a sower (*speirōn*). This means that, in his life and with his life, he spreads seed: actions, whether mental or physical, take place and these result in a crop, a harvest of behaviors. But there is nothing at all *neutral* about what a man sows, and Paul's emphasis is on what any man *actually* sows—not before men but in the eyes of God—that is, on how the origin, the content, and the product of the sower's seed are all closely tied together. In

---

[4] The verb used in 6:7a is the prohibitive one consisting of the negative particle *mē* plus the present middle/passive voice imperative form of *planaō* ("to deceive"). The middle and passive voice forms of the verb are identical, but I prefer a middle-voice reading of it because it places the emphasis on self-deception. A passive-voice reading is equally applicable given the machinations of the circumcision advocates among the Galatian churches.

XVI. Measuring Up to the Law of the Christ (5:25-6:10)

6:8 Paul once again lays out a not unfamiliar dichotomy: "For he who sows (*ho speirōn*) for the sake of his own flesh (*sarx*) will on the basis of the flesh reap corruption." When the rudderless needs of the flesh are given free rein, when God is deleted from the picture, and there is no longing for the Holy Spirit's nurturing wisdom, then any man, even though he might happen to enjoy himself in the process, will have done no more than sown "for the sake of his own flesh" (*eis tēn sarka heautou*). As we have already seen, when man tries walking alone, what starts in the flesh will end in the flesh, in the blank finality of physical death, when the wholeness of our being is given over to corruption. The body dies, but the scripture tells of the "soul" that lives on in disconnected separation from God, and that is the unremedied torment of Sheol, of that soul crying out to him who is able to rescue it from the endless distance that is death:

> *For in death there is no remembrance of thee;*
> *in Sheol who can give thee pleasure?   (Psalm 6:5, RSV)*

> *What man can live and never see death?*
> *Who can deliver his soul from the power of Sheol?   (Psalm 89:48, RSV)*

> *Like sheep they are appointed for Sheol;*
> *Death shall be their shepherd;*
> *straight to the grave they descend,*
> *and their form shall waste away;*
> *Sheol shall be their home.*
> *But God will ransom my soul from the power of Sheol,*
> *for he will receive me.   (Psalm 49:14-15, RSV)*

This is the simple reality of sin. It is the severing of man's relationship with God, and its characteristic mark, the way it is done, as Paul writes, is "on the basis of the flesh" (*ek tēs sarkos*), that same prepositional construction which he uses to indicate the underlying instrumentality of something's occurrence. In this case, when the flesh is proceeding on its own, then it will only produce what unaccompanied flesh is able to produce in the end, namely, it "will…reap what corrupts" (*therisei phthoran*). Paul uses the word for "corruption" (*phthora*) to characterize the mortal death of any man who has lived paying no heed to God.

According to Paul's gospel, there is nothing neutral about the flesh. There are only two ways to view it: the flesh either exists in covenantal agreement with God or else it autonomously goes about pursuing its own inclinations. By definition, a covenantal relationship with God is one in which the believer commits himself to the realization of the divine will through faith, obedience, and grace. The entire point of the gospel is that God's will for the salvation of mankind has been realized in Jesus of Nazareth, who is his suffering servant, the crucified Christ, whose saving death was foretold by the prophets, and whom we thus confess as the Son of God. What characterized the gospel's reception and acceptance was the visible gift of the Spirit among the Galatian believers, and thus Paul's preaching of the gospel was the proverbial line of demarcation for them. Everything prior to it would be a matter of the flesh if only because it was not totally and explicitly oriented toward the realization of God's covenantal will as presented in the gospel-image of the slain messiah. The gospel concerned these new and now overt circumstances of that realization, and Paul appealed to the Holy Spirit's manifest presence as the proof of God's power, as the validation of Paul having proclaimed God's truth, and as the confirmation of the Galatians' having accepted his message to them. He who stands apart from the realization of God's covenantal purpose in history—which is no less than the salvation of all men in the great eschatological moment represented by Jesus the Christ—will not become a participant in the endless life of the heavenly kingdom. His fate will be no more than the reaping of corruption, death literally being the final word. But whoever submits to the gospel's intervening word, with joyful thanksgiving and expansive praise, is by his acceptance of the gospel and participation in it sowing such things "for the sake of the Spirit" (*eis to pneuma*), and his actions will be strictly "on the basis of the Spirit" (*ek tou pneumatos*), adding up to a commitment, a participation, and an identification which together make it charismatically possible for the believer to "reap what lives" (*therisei zōēn aiōnion*).[5]

Where God's covenantal plan is concerned, there can be no second-guessing. There can be no hesitation, no elevation of the self over what God the Father reveals to us who have been "instructed in the word" (6:6). We are not to "deceive ourselves," thinking that somehow it might be other than what Paul has preached, that we might be able to apprehend the gospel in figurative terms of our own choosing or by having it conform to our own inclinations. None of this is possible, "for God is not to be mocked." What a man *does* in relation to the gospel is measured entirely in accordance with the standard set by the gospel: "whatever a man sows, this too he will reap." (6:7) And what is that standard?

Paul has already indicated what that standard shall be when he enumerates the "fruit of the Spirit" in 5:22-23. These are the activities and the effects of the Holy Spirit, and, by comparison, the qualities, virtues, gifts, and blessings contained in that list make circumcision seem to be little more than a technical trifle, a second-order level of cultic concern. What matters a ceremonial cutting of the flesh when that which is dearer, more immediate to God is at stake? But, perhaps most importantly of all, is 5:22-23 not in effect a rewriting of the traditional Jewish codes dealing with holiness and ritual exclusion, indeed, their transposition to a key more resonant in God's ear? Recall how Paul concludes his listing of the Spirit's "fruits" with the plain assertion that "the law has nothing against them" (5:23b). If the transitional eschatology contained in Paul's gospel message has a distinctive melody, it would be the silence of the Spirit working

---

[5] I have chosen to render the Greek *zoē aiōnios* in 6:8 as "what lives" rather than the customary translation of "eternal life." Classical Christian theology elaborated *aiōnios* as what characterized the metaphysical timelessness of the believer's post-resurrectional existence. Paul had more immediate things in mind: the kind of life that is *aiōnios* is what properly pertains to the *aiōn*, and what makes for the shifting from "this encompassing evil age" (1:4) to the Spirit-guided age. This is Pauline eschatology straight and simple.

in the hearts of men and producing an alternative music, one that is the articulation of man's submissive relationship to God made possible by the prophesied gift of the Holy Spirit (Joel 2:28-29). This is what constitutes the "what lives" to which Paul refers in 6:7b, how the destiny of each man—considered here simply as the covenant-life of the eschatological *aiōn*—will depend on what he "sows," that is, what he does in this life in obedience to the gospel he has heard with faith.

Here there is nothing nuanced let alone obscure about what Paul is saying. We are commanded to do the good, to live out our lives in such a way that they unmistakably reflect the Spirit's impact and his bounty. Paul continues in 6:9-10 with words expressive of the simple imperative each believer now faces:

> *⁹ And let us not grow weary when doing good,*
> *for in due season we shall reap if we do not lose heart.*
> *¹⁰ So then, as we do have the opportunity,*
> *let us do good to all men,*
> *and especially to those who are the householders of faith.*

And this "good" (*to kalon*) of which Paul speaks is no less than the collective "fruit of the Spirit," and the instrumental process of the cited "in due season" (*kairō idiō*) is no less than God's righteousness being made manifest in our lives (cf. 5:5-6), the time appointed (*kairos*) for a potential harvest granted to us as reapers in the field "if we do not lose heart." It is our abiding in the faith that will make all the difference here, and it will be an inner endurance that we owe entirely to God: "what does matter is faith activated by means of love." (5:6)

And in 6:10 Paul rounds out this state of hopeful expectation for the Galatians when he writes, "So then, as we do have the opportunity, let us do good to all men, and especially to those who are the householders of faith." The phrase "as we do have the opportunity" (*hōs kairon echomen*) is Paul's way of saying that the "due season" (*kairos*) is here and now, that we are already standing waist deep in a field ready for harvest, and that the

XVI. Measuring Up to the Law of the Christ (5:25-6:10)

work of the Holy Spirit is openly incumbent upon all who hear and believe. The good that we are called to do is, first of all, for "all men" (*pros pantas*), and second, "especially to those who are the householders of faith." Now to our ears it might seem as if the presence of the adverb "especially" (*malista*) in the last clause of 6:10 privileges the fellow believer over the non-believer, but I would argue that in Paul's logic of the Holy Spirit precisely the opposite is intended. If the gift of the Holy Spirit is ever genuine and sustained in our lives, then by necessity the resulting goodness will truly go out "to all men." Yet, by the same token, if our faith-activated love has gone out "to all men," then by definition it will be something that we can muster equally for "those who are the householders of faith." In other words, the only genuine proof of Christian love is when it is openly demonstrated for all, and, if it truly is for all, then it will naturally and most assuredly be just as readily available for our brothers and sisters in the faith.

XVII. A New Creation (6:11-18)

I do not think it is any accident that Paul mentions "the householders of faith" (*oikeioi tēs pisteōs*) at this point in his letter. Everything that he has written so far has concerned these "householders," who are, quite literally the members of a single unified "household" (*oikos*). It has been his preaching of the gospel to the Galatians, their faithful acceptance of it, and their resulting experience of the Holy Spirit that has bound them together as a community—and now in 6:11 he is emphasizing his founding role in this scenario by making a telling declaration:

¹¹ ἴδετε πηλίκοις ὑμῖν γράμμασιν ἔγραψα τῇ ἐμῇ χειρί.

¹¹ See with what large letters I have written to you with my own hand.

This eight-word utterance in the original Greek contains far more than its literal content. First, there is its plain meaning, namely, that Paul has written the original copy of the letter with his own hand (rather than dictating it to a scribe, as was the widespread custom of the day), and this fact alone is enough to imbue it with personal significance and a seriousness of intended meaning. It would have been Paul's way of signaling to the Galatians that this was his most earnest communication to them about what were clearly matters of the deepest concern to him. Second, there is a reiteration of the "founding effect" contained in what he is now writing. Just as Paul's preaching to the Galatians constituted them as a community, so too he is speaking to them once more in a constitutive vein by reiterating his original message and remonstrating with them concerning the ritual diversions introduced by the circumcision party, pleading that they return to the original unity which they had in the Holy Spirit as a result of his preaching. Finally, there is in such language and situation biblical echoes of the giving of the law at Mount Sinai. Specifically, just as the Exodus narrative was an account of God having formed the Israelites as his people, that is, as his *ekklēsia*, and just as that scripture recounted what were the foundational events in that history, so too Paul's letter to the Galatians—at *this* time, under *these* circumstances—becomes a comparable kind of document.

What this means is that in his preaching and now in his letter-writing Paul is telling about how God is once more constituting his people in history through the gospel which is the proclamation of his Christ to the world. Paul's letter to the Galatians must be understood therefore as the writing—in a way that is strictly parallel to the Old Testament—that tells how God is now presenting the fullness of salvation to the world. First, in the form of God's promise to Israel, and second, how Jesus who is the Christ is the fulfillment of that promise. The result is a new giving of the law, the inauguration of a new scripture, a new telling of how salvation, which Jesus himself in the encounter with the Samaritan woman declared to be "from the Jews" (John 4:22, RSV), has now become a salvation for all mankind through the gospel of Paul. Recall too this language from Exodus about things being divinely written:

> And he [the LORD] gave to Moses, when he had made an end of speaking with him upon Mount Sinai, the two tables of the testimony, tables of stone, written with the finger of God. (Exodus 31:18, RSV)

> And Moses turned, and went down from the mountain with the two tables of the testimony in his hands, tables that were written on both sides; on the one side and on the other were they written. And the tables were the work of God, and the writing was the writing of God, graven upon the tables...And as soon as he came near the camp and saw the calf and the dancing, Moses' anger burned hot, and he threw the tables out of his hands and broke them at the foot of the mountain. (Exodus 32:15-16, 19, RSV)

> The LORD said to Moses, "Cut two tables of stone like the first; and I will write upon the tables the words that were on the first tables, which you broke"...and he [the LORD] wrote upon the tables the words of the covenant, the ten commandments. (Exodus 34:1, 28c, RSV)

XVII. A New Creation (6:11-18)

Thus, when Paul writes about the "large letters I have written to you *with my own hand (tē mē cheiri)*," he is invoking this prior scriptural image of the divine law being transcribed and/or communicated by an intermediary. In 3:19 he has already stipulated this heraldic role: "Why then the law? It was added because of our transgressions until such time as the seed would come to whom the promise had been made, it having been ordained by angels *at the hand of an intermediary (en cheiri mesitou).*" The imagery is simple and direct: what God wills is written down, it is "scripted," and throughout the history of Israel God's law is written down, preserved, and *shared.* The recording of the law in written form (understood as the transmission of God's original authorship) becomes the Old Testament basis for the nation's institutional continuity because, when the people assembled, the law was read aloud and proclaimed in their presence. Even though we may not presume that Paul wrote this letter with any conscious expectation that it would one day be counted as scripture, that it would eventually be incorporated into an official canon of writings, yet it is still reasonable to conclude that Paul's letters to the churches he founded were "scriptural" in intent. First, they were authoritative in content, and second, they were intended, as a rule, to be read before the people, constituting them in exactly the same way that the ancient law did for the people of Israel.

Paul wants the Galatians to know that he has written this letter himself, that it is his personal word to them about these deeply important matters. But what are these matters? Namely, that there is a heart to the gospel, a center and a core around which all other things move and have varying significance in relation to it. The heart of Paul's gospel is that "Jesus the Christ was clearly portrayed as crucified" (3:1), and this constitutes the *factum* of the believer's salvation in the Christ because he is called to a trusting faith in the sacrificial nature of Jesus' death on the cross. All of those other things—including the arguments of the circumcision party—are of lesser significance because they stand in an undeniable relation to the one thing that is the most important. In 6:12-13 Paul addresses once more what he sees as being the true motives of the circumcision party, and why their elevation of things unimportant is unjustifiable in the light of what is truly important:

*¹² ὅσοι θέλουσιν εὐπροσωπῆσαι ἐν σαρκί,
οὗτοι ἀναγκάζουσιν ὑμᾶς περιτέμνεσθαι,
μόνον ἵνα τῷ σταυρῷ τοῦ Χριστοῦ μὴ διώκωνται.
¹³ οὐδὲ γὰρ οἱ περιτεμνόμενοι αὐτοὶ νόμον φυλάσσουσιν
ἀλλὰ θέλουσιν ὑμᾶς περιτέμνεσθαι,
ἵνα ἐν τῇ ὑμετέρᾳ σαρκὶ καυχήσωνται.*

*¹² However many there are who want to put forward a good face in the flesh,
these are the same men who would compel you to be circumcised,
but only in order that they might not be persecuted due to the cross of the Christ.
¹³ For even the ones who have been circumcised do not themselves keep the law,
yet they wish that you should be circumcised
in order that they might boast in your flesh.*

What frames these two verses are the phrases that occur in the first line and in the last line: "…who want to put forward a good face in the flesh," and "…in order that they might boast in your flesh." Paul describes the circumcision party as those "who want to put forward a good face in the flesh" (*thelousin euprosōpēsai en sarki*), and the literalism of the Greek text fortunately carries over into the English. He is declaring the circumcision party's concerns to be nothing more than an interest in the making of a superficial impression, of "putting forward a good face" as opposed to presenting a truthful face, one that in this context is actually reflective of God's will for our salvation. Paul's position is that any insistence on circumcision amounts to a betrayal of that gospel whose enduring heart is the "cross of the Christ." It is precisely "due to the cross of the Christ" that the believer will be persecuted (more on this below) since the pagans regarded circumcision as being little more than a ritual curiosity and hardly worth any measure of outrage. Paul has already made it clear (5:2-4) that circumcision, though part of Israel's most ancient and venerable religious tradition, places the believer at odds with God if the former still seeks to see it as what

XVII. A New Creation (6:11-18)

guarantees his being declared righteous. In 5:2 Paul wrote, "You have been cut off from the Christ, whoever you are who are being made righteous by the law—you have fallen away from grace," a scenario that he explicitly contrasts with being "persecuted due to the cross of the Christ." Instead of heeding what God is now revealing, the circumcision party's position represents an intentional movement in the opposite direction. All focus must be instead on the "cross of the Christ" since that is the true basis for the believer's salvation and not the comparatively risk-free submitting of oneself to circumcision.

There is no serious or outright persecution which attaches itself to the latter act, and Paul has already hinted that the Galatians have paid something of a price for that in which they have chosen to believe as a result of his preaching (3:2-4). Since the focus of his preaching to them always had been the cross and never concerned circumcision, he charges his opponents with deceitfully urging circumcision upon the Galatians "so that they might boast in your flesh" (*hina en tē hymetera sarki kauchēsōntai*). The implication here is a clear one: in the light of Paul's gospel, just as any reliance on circumcision can never be anything more than a misguided pretense, so too in the light of that same gospel does submitting to circumcision's physical mark become a false basis for boasting. The assumption here is that, if this is a mistaken basis for boasting, then there must be a basis for boasting that is legitimate.

Paul has protested with the Galatians (and, by implication, he has argued with his opponents) about the relative value of circumcision, about why it is at best a secondary thing and never, as these others have been urging them to suppose, that it is central. As he pointed out in 5:11, if in fact it had been circumcision which had made it possible for them to be declared righteous in the sight of God and thus worthy of salvation on his day of judgment, then he would have come to them simply preaching about circumcision and other details of the Mosaic law. But he didn't, and hence his persecution. Instead he came to them proclaiming the crucified Christ, and, just as the law had been their "teacher," instructing God's people in the way of their Lord, so now it is the Christ crucified who will act as their teacher. If in ages past Israel had boasted on the basis of the law, on which basis should Israel now boast? What will he who has heard the gospel have learned about what a true boasting requires? Before what shall any man marvel, and why? In 6:14 Paul answers these questions:

*14 ἐμοὶ δὲ μὴ γένοιτο καυχᾶσθαι
εἰ μὴ ἐν τῷ σταυρῷ τοῦ κυρίου ἡμῶν Ἰησοῦ Χριστοῦ,
δι' οὗ ἐμοὶ κόσμος ἐσταύρωται
κἀγὼ κόσμῳ.*

*14 But by no means let it be for me to boast in anything
except in the cross of our Lord Jesus the Christ,
by means of whom the world has been crucified to me
and I to the world.*

Jesus has come to teach us one thing: be prepared for the cross, and for all of what it will entail. Be prepared for a world that will not understand you, one that will ridicule you and persecute you, one that will hate the God whom you proclaim and serve because you belong to him. The Christ has come to instruct us in the glory of the cross because our identity will now be in him by virtue of the gospel. Not only must we prepare ourselves for the cross, we must take it up and boldly appreciate it as something to be taken up. Let us not imagine that the cross is on the order of a formal requirement, that it is somehow an incidental sign or a metaphorical image for something much deeper, perhaps more personal, and about which we might boastfully glorify ourselves. It is no such thing, and that is because the cross must be understood *as a destiny*, the only way to our fulfillment *in the Christ* by means of a Christ-like purification of our persons. In 6:4 Paul has already declared the necessity of this process when he writes, "but let each one test (*dokimazetō*) the mettle of his own work, and only then will he have cause to boast in himself and not in another." The verb

XVII. A New Creation (6:11-18)

dokimazō is regularly used in the prophetic passages of the Septuagint where God speaks of proving and thus purifying ("testing") the metal of his rebellious people by burning away whatever impurities it contains. Jeremiah 9:7 (translation my own) exemplifies this usage: "For this reason the LORD says, 'I will try them by fire, and I will prove (*dokimō*) them; thus I shall do because of the evil I find in the face of the daughter of my people." The point of both Jeremiah 9:7 and Galatians 6 is that it is only ever God who conducts the test. In each case it is strictly a matter of who is obedient to his word, and now that word is exclusively about the cross of his Christ.

Even if the cross is in a very profound way the Christian destiny, few of us go straight to the cross. Rather, other things happen first. As it stands written in Mark's gospel, Jesus says, "If any man would come after me, let him deny himself, and take up his cross and follow me. For whoever would save his life will lose it; and whoever loses his life for my sake and the gospel's will save it." (8:34-35, RSV). No man seeks out the cross deliberately. No man's plan includes the cross and its imposition, but Jesus only wishes us to comprehend that if we are going to follow after him, if we are going to be the sheep who hear his voice and thus belong to his fold, then we must be willing to take up the cross, and then—and only then—will we be able to walk in his wake.

For this the world will hate us. For this the world will make fun of us, openly scorning us and heaping no small amount of ridicule upon our heads. Their laughter will be loud and sharp because of our willingness to do what no man who knows but the world's horizons would want to do. Is this what Paul means when he writes about the world having been "crucified to me, and I to the world"? Does he have in mind some kind of mutual rupture, a reciprocal and irrevocable parting of the ways? On the one hand, yes, but, on the other hand, not entirely because here something greater than any sense of our having declared war on the world is involved. First, if any man is going to be crucified, then there must be a cross in his life, a form of suffering—whether material or mental, whether it should involve the outer contours of what he calls life or the inner regions of his heart—these are the structures upon which he will be bound and left to die. But second, when Paul writes that it is *by means of* the cross of the Christ that "the world has been crucified to me, and I to the world," we must be clear about what he means.

It means that from this point onward—that is, from our hearing of the gospel—things cannot be the same, that the world which was so real, so commanding, so all encompassing, indeed, so finally enveloping, that it no longer holds us in its power. Yes, it may have killed us, whether literally or figuratively, but, for those of us who have heard the gospel and have received it with faith, we will not have the same kind of relationship to this same world as we had before. We will no longer stand either directly or incomprehensibly in its power, because we know someone more powerful than it. We will be subject no more to its seeming finality, to the peremptory workings of its ways, because we belong to—and are thus saved by—him who opposes every limit set by the world. The basis for our salvation in the Christ is neither through circumcision nor through uncircumcision *per se* (cf. 5:6), but rather it will be what is revealed to us "in the cross of our Lord Jesus the Christ" (*en tō staurō tou kyriou hēmōn Iēsou Christou*). It is by his gospel that Paul has declared the cross to be the most immediate and thus the only trustworthy sign of God's action in the world. The circumcising hand must give way to the hand of God as revealed to us in the cross.

There is salvation in the cross of the Christ because—in Paul's preaching—it becomes the supremely concrete and therefore the non-negotiable expression of God's will to save the world. It is in the following verse that Paul expands upon his language about our being crucified to the world and the world to us when he relates these things to what shall be the purpose of our identity "in the Christ Jesus":

XVII. A New Creation (6:11-18)

¹⁵ οὔτε ἐν γὰρ Χριστῷ Ἰησοῦ περιτομή τί ἐστιν
οὔτε ἀκροβυστία
ἀλλὰ καινὴ κτίσις.

¹⁵ This is because when we are in the Christ Jesus¹ neither circumcision nor uncircumcision is anything at all, but rather what does matter is a new creation;

The important thing to notice here is the prepositional-phrase parallelism between 6:14 and 6:15. Just as Paul writes in 6:14 that the basis for his boasting shall be strictly *"in the cross (en tō staurō) of our Lord Jesus the Christ,"* so too does he stipulate in 6:15 that it is only when we are "in the Christ Jesus" (*en Christō Iēsou*) that we are a "new creation." It is by virtue of our being "in the Christ Jesus," by our belonging to him and having our identity formed by means of the word about him, that we will undergo crucifixion and become dead to the world when we see that the world does not hold the final card, that there is a clear limit to the world's lordship. The most important thing to emphasize here is that each believer dies to the world in order that he might be born anew, so that he might become the "new creation" (*kainē ktisis*) of which Paul writes, and much of the glory, expressed here in terms of a rightful "boasting," will consist of the fact that *only by dying to the world can we truly, finally, and fully live in it.*

This does not mean that we can or should turn our backs on the world, nor does it necessarily mean that we must set out to practice or perfect a metaphysical abandonment of the world, trying to maintain either an ethical or even a spiritual distancing of ourselves from all that we might naively and even rudely

---

[1] I have opted to include the phrase "in the Christ Jesus" in 6:15 even though many English translations omit it because it does not appear in one of the earliest manuscript copies of the Pauline letters (P⁴⁶), c. 200 A.D. The phrase is well attested in later major manuscript copies from the fourth and fifth centuries (e.g. Sinaiticus, Alexandrinus, Ephraemi). Even if the phrase is a later emendation to the original text, it is an entirely understandable addition given that the context demands it. Whether a man is circumcised or uncircumcised would mean something only in the context of the law, but if he is in the Christ Jesus, then either state is rendered meaningless.

consider to be "worldly things." No, it is only by embracing the world, by living in it a life of Christ-like expression that we can ever understand what Paul had to say about any of this. It was in his *Letters and Papers from Prison* that Dietrich Bonhoeffer wrote:

> I discovered later, and I'm still discovering right up to this moment, that it is only by living completely in this world that one learns to have faith. One must completely abandon any attempt to make something of oneself, whether it be a saint, or a converted sinner, or a churchman (a so-called priestly type!), a righteous man or an unrighteous one, a sick man or a healthy one. By this-worldliness I mean living unreservedly in life's duties, problems, successes and failures. In so doing we throw ourselves completely into the arms of God, taking seriously, not our own sufferings, but those of God in the world—watching with Christ in Gethsemane. That, I think, is faith; that is *metanoia*; and that is how one becomes a man and a Christian (cf. Jer. 45!). How can success make us arrogant, or a failure lead us astray, when we share in God's sufferings through a life of this kind?[2]

This means that, no matter how much we may have died in our souls to the world, no matter how much we might have shared in Christ's sufferings, no matter how much we will have given of ourselves for the sake of others, if these things are not done in the world and connected to it, that is, not in the arid perfectionism of our imaginations but in the most immediate grip of the world in all of its createdness, then *nothing* will have happened—there will not have been a new creation. Salvation in the Christ Jesus must in some sense be the offering of the self to the world done too for the sake of the world because he to whom we now belong did the same.

---

[2] Dietrich Bonhoeffer, *Letters & Papers From Prison* (New York City, New York: Touchstone Books, 1997), 369-370. The reference to Jeremiah 45 could not be more relevant: "Thus says the LORD; Behold, what I have built I am breaking down, and what I have planted I am plucking up—that is, the whole land. And do you seek great things for yourself? Seek them not; for, behold, I am bringing evil upon all flesh, says the LORD; but I will give you your life as a prize of war in all places to which you may go." (45:4-5)

XVII. A New Creation (6:11-18)

It is by virtue of a single point in time and space, the setting for one man being crucified outside the walls of an ancient Semitic capital, that every other conceivable setting for us will be determined, the unfolding of the possible itself. It is a strange thing indeed to think in terms of all of what is potentially human as being *connected* in this way: that we could reduce all things to this single point, and see them solely in connection to it and to nothing else. It is a most demanding undertaking—a no less significant crucifixion in itself—but on its necessity Paul is adamant. It is no theoretical exercise, no means to expand either mind or consciousness; rather it is the urgency to let things simultaneously contract and dilate, to see all things in relation to the cross and the cross in relation to all things. We, as Christians, are never finished with what this requires of us.

Let us also remind ourselves that creation never stopped being God's prerogative. In scripture we encounter creation again and again—first of all in the creation itself, but also in the fall, the flood, the scattering of the nations at Babel, the raising up of Israel as a people, and then throughout all the vagaries of her covenantal relationship with God. Covenant stands as the goal of divine creation, and the enduring image of its realization is the commensality of the kingdom. The entire length of the Bible makes it clear that God seeks one thing from his people— the fullness of covenantal life and all of what that demands of us. Paul encapsulates all of what is demanded of us when, in 2:11-14, he recounts how he confronted Peter at Antioch over the issue of table fellowship with the pagan converts. There the point was simply that in the "new creation" required by the terms of his gospel, there was no room left for reckoning in the old way of who was circumcised and who was not. As Paul stipulates, none of that is of any consequence because "in the Christ Jesus" it has been set aside for the sake of what God wished all along, i.e. the true terms of covenant. It is in the person of Jesus who is the Christ that the biblical concept of covenant is stretched to its limit, shattered, and then re-established in a proclamation the likes of which the world still too often regards as impossible. This is the inimitable boldness of the gospel message, namely, that in this one man, of whom the world in its habitual preoccupation would take little notice, we have the announcement of God acting in our historical stream of moments and calling us to him by means of a message whose table-turning radicality remains an eternal test.

The relevant Greek word here is *peirasmos*, which means "temptation," "test," or "trial." It denotes something done for the sake of seeing how a person responds. I do not think it is any accident that Paul employs this term when he reminds the Galatians of when he first preached his gospel to them (4:12-13):

> *12 Brothers and sisters, I am beseeching you, become as I am, for I too have become as you are.*
> *You have done me no wrong;*
> *13 and you know that it was on account of my bodily weakness that I preached the gospel to you the first time;*
> *14 and that trial* (peirasmos) *which came upon you by way of my body you neither despised nor rejected,*
> *rather, you received me as a messenger of God just as you received the Christ Jesus.*

There is an unmistakable sense in which the entire Christian *kerygma* consists of a single question: *Given what you now know about Jesus of Nazareth, do you belong to him or not?* And if you do belong to him, if it is in him that you have your identity, then how do you belong to him? Do you belong to him on the basis of faith, or by virtue of details like circumcision? Shall your identity in him consist of obedience to the Jewish law, or experiencing the Holy Spirit? Is the gospel message about how the realities of Jesus' life and death instruct us about our own circumstances, or is it about keeping them as far away as possible?

Paul never preached that it was on account of his circumcision that Jesus, a Jew, is the redeemer of mankind. If circumcision was once the visible sign of belonging to Israel, that identity has now been given a new shape in the preaching of Paul. The cross

XVII. A New Creation (6:11-18)

is now the emblem of possession and the sign of our purchased identity in the Christ—in effect the new circumcision not of men's bodies but of their hearts, demanded prophetically but now made real and immediate by the gift of the Holy Spirit. Scripturally, the Spirit's arrival was the signal of creation:

> In the beginning God created the heavens and the earth. The earth was without form and void, and darkness was upon the face of the deep; and the Spirit of God (*pneuma theou*) was moving over the face of the waters. (Genesis 1:1-2, RSV)

> But God remembered Noah and all the beasts and all the cattle that were with him in the ark. And God made a wind (*pneuma*) blow over the earth, and the waters subsided. (Genesis 8:1, RSV)

> These [thy creatures] all look to thee, to give them their food in due season. When thou givest to them, they gather it up; when thou openest thy hand, they are filled with good things. When thou hidest thy face, they are dismayed; when thou takest away their breath (*pneuma*), they die and return to their dust. When thou sendest forth thy Spirit (*pneuma*), they are created (*ktisthēsontai*); and thou renewest the face of the ground. (Psalm 104:27-30, RSV)

> When the day of Pentecost had come, they were all together in one place. And suddenly a sound came from heaven like the rush of a mighty wind, and it filled all the house where they were sitting. And there appeared to them tongues as of fire, distributed and resting on each one of them. And they were all filled with the Holy Spirit (*pneumatos hagiou*) and began to speak in other tongues, as the Spirit (*pneuma*) gave them utterance. (Acts 2:1-4, RSV)

Thus the sending of God's own Spirit was the sign (*sēmeion*) of the "new creation" that is the individual life "in the Christ Jesus," of God once more designating the order of his kingdom. Look at 6:15 in conjunction with 6:16 to see the continuity of what Paul is arguing:

¹⁵ οὔτε ἐν γὰρ Χριστῷ Ἰησοῦ περιτομή τί ἐστιν
οὔτε ἀκροβυστία
ἀλλὰ καινὴ κτίσις.

¹⁶ καὶ ὅσοι τῷ κανόνι τούτῳ στοιχήσουσιν,
εἰρήνη ἐπ' αὐτοὺς καὶ
ἔλεος καὶ ἐπὶ τὸν Ἰσραὴλ τοῦ θεοῦ.

*¹⁵ This is because when we are in the Christ Jesus neither circumcision nor uncircumcision is anything at all,
but rather what does matter is a new creation;
16 and for however many might conform themselves to this standard,
peace be upon them and
may there be mercy too upon the Israel of God.*

Paul highlights the Spirit's necessary role in the Galatians' eschatological status—their scripture-mediated identity in the Christ—by employing the same verb he used earlier in 5:24-25, a passage full of relevant content. There he wrote:

*²⁴ And those who belong to the Christ Jesus have crucified the flesh along with its passions and desires.
²⁵ If we are going to live by the Spirit,
let us also conform ourselves (*stoichōmen*) to the Spirit.*

These verses are based on the premise that there is a necessary correlation between (a) belonging to the Christ Jesus, and (b) conforming oneself to the Spirit, i.e. living in a way that is directly reflective of the Holy Spirit's inspiring guidance. In 6:15-16 Paul is reiterating this view of Christian identity by (a) asserting that our being "in the Christ Jesus" is to be the occasion for the kind of "new creation" that is bestowed only by the Holy Spirit, and (b) from this it follows that we are "conforming ourselves to this standard." Paul is saying that whoever belongs to the Christ Jesus, that is, whoever locates his identity in the scriptural word concerning the crucified messiah, that the manifestation of the Holy Spirit in the believer's life will be the only proof of that identity. There is thus a direct link link between what Paul stipulates in 5:25 and 6:15-16. The "fruit of the Spirit" catalogued in 5:22-23 is what constitutes "this standard" that he announces, a *kanōn* that is now a written one by virtue of his letter to the Galatians.

XVII. A New Creation (6:11-18)

The idea of the "new creation" can be linked to the passage in Matthew 19 recounting the meeting between Jesus with the rich man young man. It parallels Luke 10 when the lawyer also asks Jesus about what he needs to do to inherit eternal life (see my comments on 5:5-6). Paul used the same phrase "eternal life" (*zoē aiōnios*) in 6:8, and likewise understanding it in terms of the Spirit-guided life characteristic of the new *aiōn* is necessary for approaching for what Paul means when he speaks of the new creation. In Matthew 19:28-30 Jesus speaks to the exasperated disciples about what will happen to them when they have left everything and followed him, i.e. when they are guided by the Spirit and are thus conforming themselves to the "law of the Christ" (6:2):

> Jesus said to them, "Truly, I say to you, in the new world, when the Son of man shall sit on his glorious throne, you who have followed me will also sit on twelve thrones, judging the twelve tribes of Israel. And every one of you who has left houses or brothers or sisters or father or mother or children or lands for my name's sake, will receive a hundredfold, and inherit eternal life. But many that are first will be last, and the last first.

The Greek word translated by the RSV as "the new world" in this passage is *palingenesia*, a term with the literal meaning of "that which is created again." This parallels the idea of the new creation that is only possible with life in the scriptural Christ, and what relates the two passages is the requirement that any member of the messianic community will be subject to the same standard, and, by virtue of obedience to it, he will be in the eschatological position of sitting on thrones and judging the twelve tribes of Israel.[3] The notions of the new *aiōn* and the new creation are inextricably linked: without the latter the former is impossible, and vice versa.

The Greek text for "however many should proceed according to this standard" is *hosoi tō kanoni toutō stoichēsousin*, and the verb

---

[3] Paul Nadim Tarazi, *The New Testament: Introduction, Volume 4: Matthew and The Canon* (St. Paul, Minnesota, OCABS Press, 2009), 225-226.

used in 5:25 and 6:16, *stoicheō* denotes what makes for habitual patterns of behavior, i.e. a defining mode of conduct.[4] Paul is here declaring that, in the presence of such a Spirit-given grace, the twin blessings of peace (*eirēnē*) and mercy (*eleos*) are natural. First, that the indwelling of God's Spirit might result in the peaceful upbuilding of the kingdom in the messianic community, and second, that *should it happen*, it will indeed be the bestowal of God's mercy (the steadfast, covenant-aiming love of *hesed*) upon his people, an Israel expanded and now understood to include all mankind by virtue of a gospel based on faith—history's only truly universal appeal.

Paul's preaching is the replacement of the Israel of circumcision with the Israel of faith. Just as Israel's history was for so long dependent on the anchoring effect of the law, on a ritual obedience that must more properly be understood as *an obedience to a history*, so now with the declaration of Jesus as the Christ, that same history of Israel reaches a climax expressed by the cross. The scriptural history of Israel is the account of God's love for the world. In the gospel first preached to the Galatians that history is focused on the man Jesus, the enigmatic sufferer of whom the prophet Isaiah foretold. In this letter Paul has once more made the case for the non-negotiable content of his gospel, for why any emphasis on circumcision is at best a diversion given the gravity of the cross and the call that goes forth from it. Paul has relied on the raw truths of his own conversion: he has made his defense based solely on what he knows, and on what he has experienced and endured for the sake of the gospel. He stakes everything on what God has revealed to him (cf. 1:12, 15; 2:1) and what has been the ordeal of grace in his own life. It is thus that he is able to declare in 6:17 with an unassailable note of finality:

---

[4] Recall that the verb *stoicheō* is etymologically related to the *stoicheia* ("the elemental things") contained in 4:3 and 4:9. If those passages invoked what made for pagan lordship in the world's pre-gospel condition, Paul now writes of *stoichein* in terms of a liberating obedience to the gospel word.

XVII. A New Creation (6:11-18)

¹⁷ τοῦ λοιποῦ κόπους μοι μηδεὶς παρεχέτω·
ἐγὼ γὰρ τὰ στίγματα τοῦ Ἰησοῦ Χριστοῦ ἐν τῷ σώματί μου
βαστάζω.

*¹⁷ From this point forward let no one trouble me
because I bear the marks of Jesus on my own body.*

With these words Paul is saying to anyone who knows him and who would hear him, "If it is a sign in the flesh that you want, if it is a mark on the body that you seek and demand as proof of covenant with God, then let my scars serve as a truer kind of circumcision, one rooted directly in the cross and stemming from this faith of mine in Jesus as the Christ!" Here he has made his final—and arguably his most personal—point about the relative worth of circumcision vis-à-vis the new Christian attitude of faith, and these words in many ways serve as the culmination of all that he has so passionately argued and consistently maintained throughout his letter to the Galatians. What matters most is what God does, and God has done all things now through the cross. If the ground has shifted beneath their feet, if the old obedience is giving way before the new, then the single most important insight concerning any of this is that God himself—as declared in Paul's gospel—is the author of the new identity. It is for the sake of the latter's declaration that Paul has toiled so hard and expended himself to the point that his own body's evidence of injury becomes its own form of gospel utterance.

Why speak of circumcision when, as Paul argues, it is only the cross that makes the Christ real? Why search for any validation other than grace? What does a ritual cutting of the flesh matter when, in fulfillment of the prophetic word, God is pouring out his Spirit on all flesh? It is precisely on this note that Paul ends his letter by offering to the Galatians a parting blessing:

¹⁸ ἡ χάρις τοῦ κυρίου ἡμῶν Ἰησοῦ Χριστοῦ μετὰ τοῦ πνεύματος
ὑμῶν,
ἀδελφοί· ἀμήν.

¹⁸ May the grace of our Lord Jesus the Christ be with your spirit, brothers and sisters. Amen.

Once again, the grace (*charis*) of God is his actual presence among us—his movement in our hearts, his motivating trace in our actions, his sanctifying guidance of our behavior—and, as Paul has made clear, the Galatians have this only by virtue of the gospel he has proclaimed to them. Paul's sole wish for the Galatians is that God himself might be the impetus, the execution, and the purpose of all that they do given that they now belong to him in his Son Jesus the Christ. If the Galatians have been freed from the obligations of the Jewish ritual law, it is only because, ever since Paul's preaching among them, they have a new master in the Christ. The condition of their new servitude, which is simultaneously the freedom that must be the expression of their new word-based identity, is the Holy Spirit himself. But does the Spirit come on his own? Or does the Spirit in any way depend on the willful acts of men? In 3:2-3 Paul indicates these workings clearly enough: "Only this one thing do I wish to learn from you: Did you receive the Spirit on the basis of the works of the law or was it on the basis of a hearing with faith? Are you in this way so foolish, that, having begun with the Spirit, you are now completing yourselves in the flesh?"

Thus, in the final verse when Paul pronounces this blessing upon the Galatians, he is asking that the scriptural God truly be present and active in all things that they do: that the Spirit of God will be active among them not only by virtue of the preaching that communicated him to the Galatian churches in the first place, but also by their faithful obedience to it. Here it cannot be stressed enough that the Galatians have a "spirit" (*pneuma*) only to the extent that the Holy Spirit is active among them and they are conducting themselves in ways receptive to him and in modes reflective of him. When Paul declares his wish in 6:18 that "the grace (*charis*) of our Lord Jesus the Christ be *with your spirit (meta tou pneumatos hymōn),*" he is using *charis* as a reference to the activating, energizing, and directing presence of the Holy Spirit, and how the latter is only truly present among

XVII. A New Creation (6:11-18)

the Galatians in the form of their faithful conduct. The purpose of the Holy Spirit is not to create a *spiritual* reality crafted from some pre-existing *spiritual* materials (what the phrase "with your spirit" in 6:18 might suggest to certain eager ears), but rather, quite to the contrary, it is to create what is the fresh and tangible reality of the Spirit in the communal life of the believers. It was Paul who had first preached the gospel to the Galatians. From him they originally heard the word of salvation. He wants to know if anything has changed since that first and, by his argument, authoritative proclamation. Or is God now offering a revised message, a "different gospel" through those who advocate circumcision?

Let there be no mistake about how the Apostle would frame his message to the Galatians, and here I would conclude with those categories that constitute the Pauline anthropology. We who hear the gospel—who have heard the preached word about Jesus as the Christ, not just once but again and again—are but temporarily animated *sōma* (*psychē*-infused bodies) who must live obediently to that word and not in subjugation to the untethered inclinations of *sarx*. This is why Paul speaks as he does in 6:16 of the necessary "standard" (*kanōn*) of our conformity to the word concerning the "cross of our Lord Jesus the Christ" (6:14), and how seeing him "clearly portrayed as crucified" (3:1) is necessarily linked with the peaceful "fruit of the Spirit" (*karpos tou pneumatos*). In other words, the letter closes with the same wish later expressed, for example, in the ninth-century A.D. medieval hymn, *Veni Creator Spiritus*: that when we hear the word, the "creator Spirit" might come and make of us a creation who walks in the newness of obedience.

www.ingramcontent.com/pod-product-compliance
Lightning Source LLC
Chambersburg PA
CBHW022101150426
43195CB00008B/223